Big Sister, Little Sister, Red Sister

Also by Jung Chang

Empress Dowager Cixi: The Concubine Who Launched Modern China
Mao: The Unknown Story (with Jon Halliday)
Wild Swans: Three Daughters of China

Big Sister, Little Sister, Red Sister

Three Women at the Heart of Twentieth-Century China

JUNG CHANG

Alfred A. Knopf
New York
2019

THIS IS A BORZOI BOOK PUBLISHED BY ALFRED A. KNOPF

Copyright © 2019 by Globalflair Ltd.

All rights reserved. Published in the United States by Alfred A. Knopf, a division of Penguin Random House LLC, New York. Originally published in hardcover in Great Britain by Jonathan Cape, an imprint of Vintage, a division of Penguin Random House Ltd., London, in 2019.

www.aaknopf.com

Knopf, Borzoi Books, and the colophon are registered trademarks of Penguin Random House LLC.

Library of Congress Control Number: 2019943880

ISBN 9780451493507 (hardcover)   ISBN 9780451493514 (ebook)
ISBN 9780525657828 (open market)

Jacket images: (The Soong sisters) Historic Collection / Alamy; (fabric) Chakkrit Wannapong / Alamy
Jacket design by Chip Kidd

Manufactured in the United States of America
First United States Edition

To my mother

Contents

List of Illustrations

Third Section

Chiang's portrait on Tiananmen Gate (Academia Historica, Taipei)
May-ling returning to Chongqing from New York, 1945 (Academia
    Historica, Taipei)
The three sisters in Chongqing
Chiang Kai-shek's family, 1946 (Academia Historica, Taipei)
Chiang Kai-shek visiting his ancestral temple, 1949
Ei-ling at Chiang's birthday, 1956 (Academia Historica, Taipei)
Chiang meeting May-ling at Taipei airport, 1959 (Academia
    Historica, Taipei)
Red Sister visiting Moscow with Mao, 1957 (Alamy)
Ching-ling with Mao and Zhou En-lai on Tiananmen Gate, 1965 (Alamy)
Ching-ling at Mao's memorial service in Tiananmen Square, 1976
Ching-ling and Yolanda (Hong Kong University of Science and
    Technology Library)
Ching-kuo with the body of his father, 1975 (Academia Historica, Taipei)
Ching-kuo and his wife, Faina Vakhreva (Academia Historica, Taipei)

Fourth Section

Ei-ling (Gregory Kung)
Ching-ling (Gregory Kung)
May-ling (Gregory Kung)
Ching-ling in exile, 1927–8 (Alamy)
'May-ling Palace', the necklace made from a mountain (Alamy)
May-ling in America, c. 1943 (Getty)
Ei-ling with Debra Paget, 1969 (Gregory Kung)
May-ling leaving Taiwan in 1991 (Academia Historica, Taipei)
May-ling, aged around 100 (Gregory Kung)
Postcard of Li Yuan-hong, Sun Yat-sen and Huang Xing (private
    collection)
Statue park, Taipei (Jung Chang)

While every effort has been made to trace copyright holders, if
any have inadvertently been overlooked the publishers would be
happy to acknowledge them in future editions.

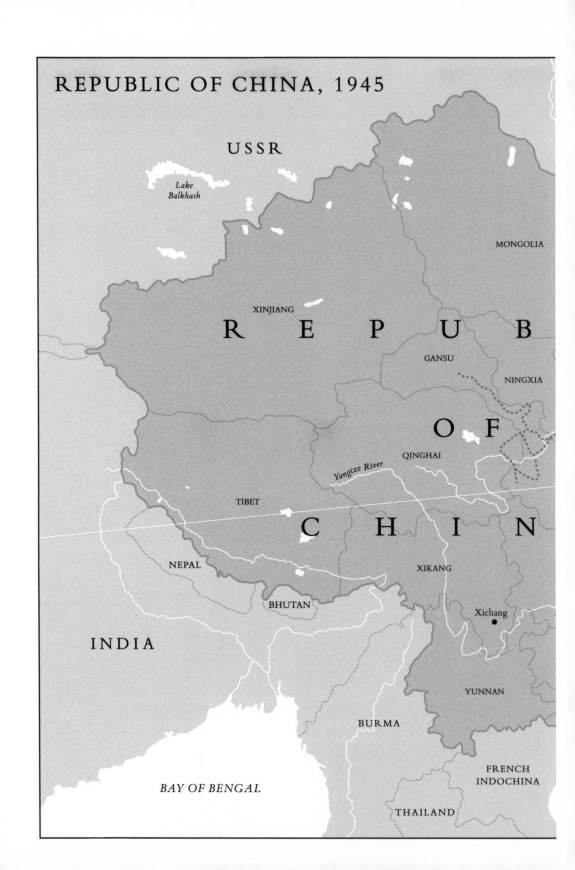

REPUBLIC OF CHINA, 1945

USSR

Lake
Balkhash

MONGOLIA

R E P U B

XINJIANG

GANSU

NINGXIA

O F

QINGHAI

Yangtze River

TIBET

C H I N

NEPAL

XIKANG

Xichang

BHUTAN

INDIA

YUNNAN

BURMA

FRENCH
INDOCHINA

BAY OF BENGAL

THAILAND

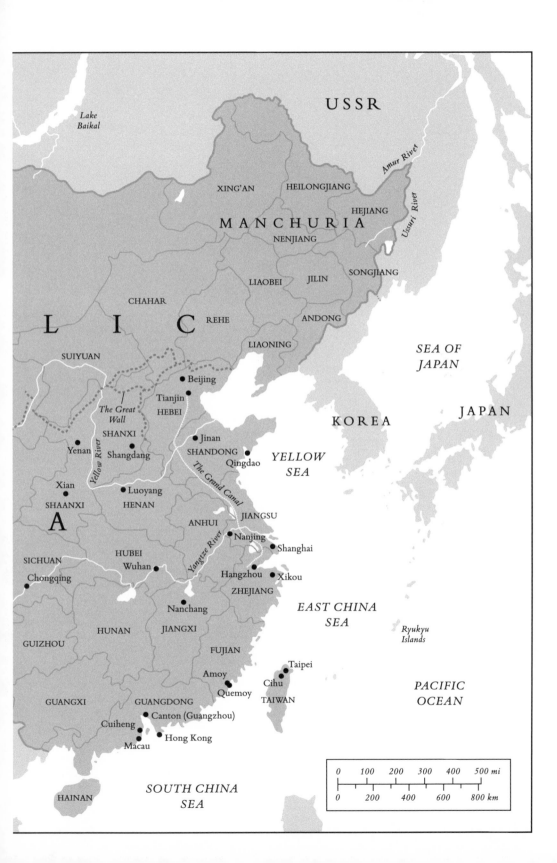

Introduction

The best-known modern Chinese 'fairy tale' is the story of three sisters from Shanghai, born in the last years of the nineteenth century. Their family, named Soong, was wealthy and prominent and among the city's elite. The Soong parents were devout Christians, the mother a member of China's most illustrious Christian clan (that of Xu, after whom a district of Shanghai is named), and the father the first Chinese to be converted in the American South by the Methodists, when he was in his teens. Their three daughters – Ei-ling ('Kind Age', born in 1889), Ching-ling ('Glorious Age', born in 1893), and May-ling ('Beautiful Age', born in 1898) – were sent as children to America to be educated, something extremely rare at the time; and the girls returned home years later speaking better English than Chinese. Petite and square-jawed, they were not great beauties by traditional standards, their faces not shaped like melon seeds, eyes not resembling almonds and eyebrows no arching willow shoots. But they had very fine skin, delicate features and graceful bearing, enhanced by fashionable clothes. The sisters had seen the world; they were intelligent, independent-minded and self-confident. They had 'class'.

What ultimately made them modern China's 'princesses', though, were their extraordinary marriages. One man who fell first for Ei-ling and then for Ching-ling was Sun Yat-sen, who pioneered the republican revolution that overthrew the monarchy in 1911. Known as the 'Father of (republican) China', Sun is revered throughout the Chinese-speaking world. Ching-ling married him.

Sun died in 1925; his successor, Chiang Kai-shek, courted and married May-ling, Little Sister. Chiang went on to form a Nationalist government in 1928, and ruled China until the Communists drove him to Taiwan in 1949. Little Sister was the first lady of the country for twenty-two years while he was in power. During the Second World War, as Chiang led the Chinese resistance against Japanese invasion, she became one of the most famous women of her time.

Her eldest sibling Ei-ling, Big Sister, married H.H. Kung who, thanks to his wife's connections, occupied the posts of prime minister and finance minister for many years. These jobs in turn helped Ei-ling as she succeeded in becoming one of the richest women in China.

The Soong family, which also had three sons, constituted the inner circle of Chiang Kai-shek's regime – except Ching-ling, Sun Yat-sen's widow, who joined the Communists. She was sometimes referred to as Red Sister. Thus two antagonistic political camps separated the siblings. During the civil war following the Second World War, Red Sister did her best to help the Communists beat Chiang, even though this meant the ruin of her family. After the collapse of Chiang's regime and the founding of Communist China under Mao Ze-dong, in 1949, Red Sister became Mao's vice chairman.

Clearly the sisters were exceptional beyond their influential marriages. In the Chinese-speaking world, people never tire of talking about them, including their private lives. I remember two particular stories from when I was growing up in Mao's China from the 1950s to the 1970s, when the country was under rigid totalitarian control and completely isolated from the outside world. One was that Mme Chiang – Little Sister – bathed every day in milk to keep her skin luminous. In those days, milk, highly nutritious and desirable, was scarce and unavailable to the average family. Using it as bath water was deemed an outrageous indulgence. Once a teacher attempted to redress this common myth and muttered to his pupils, 'Well, do you really think it would be pleasant to bathe in milk?' He soon entered the ranks of the condemned 'Rightists'.

The other story that left a deep impression on me was that Ching-ling, vice chairman of puritanical Red China, was living together with her chief bodyguard, who was less than half her age. It was said that they had developed a physical relationship as a result of the bodyguard carrying her on and off her bed, when she was old and wheelchair-bound. People endlessly speculated about whether they got married, and argued over whether the relationship was acceptable. The word was that the Party permitted the affair out of consideration for the fact that Ching-ling had been widowed for a long time and needed a man, and that the Party even allowed her to keep the prestigious name of Mme Sun. I remember this tale particularly well because it was so rare to hear gossip about the sex life of a leader of the country. No one dared wag their tongue about any other top officials.

After Mao died in 1976 and China opened up, I settled in Britain and learned much more about the sisters. I was even commissioned in the mid-1980s to write a short book about Red Sister, Ching-ling. But although I did some research and put together some 30,000 words, curiously I felt uninvolved with my subject. I did not even try to get to the bottom of the scandal involving the bodyguard.

In 1991, *Wild Swans: Three Daughters of China*, the book about the lives of my grandmother, my mother and myself, was published. I went on to write a biography of Mao with my husband, Jon Halliday. Mao and his shadow dominated the first twenty-six years of my life, and I was eager to find out more about him. Then, Empress Dowager Cixi, the last great monarch of China (uncrowned, as women were not allowed to be monarchs), caught my attention. Rising from a low-rank concubine to a stateswoman, Cixi ruled the empire from behind the throne for decades and brought the medieval country into the modern age. Both my subjects riveted me and absorbed twenty years of my life. Whom I should write about next was a difficult choice. The idea of the Soong sisters came up, but I ruled it out. After *Wild Swans*, I had been writing about programme-setters and history-changers, which the sisters were not.

As individuals, from the information available, they remained fairy-tale figures, summed up by the much-quoted description: 'In

China, there were three sisters. One loved money, one loved power, and one loved her country.' There seemed to be no mental conflicts, moral dilemmas, or agonising decisions – all the things that make human beings real and interesting.

Instead I thought of writing about Sun Yat-sen, the Father of republican China. Living from 1866 to 1925, and rising to prominence in the period from Cixi to Mao, Sun was a programme-setter like them, and was a sort of 'bridge' between them. Under Cixi, China had begun the journey towards parliamentary democracy, and was expecting greater freedom and openness. And yet, four decades after her death in 1908, Mao took power, isolated the country and plunged it into a totalitarian tyranny. What happened in those four decades, in which Sun Yat-sen played a key part? The question had been bugging me. Now, this was my chance to find out.

For the Chinese, and for those outside the Chinese-speaking world who have heard of him, Sun's image is that of a saint. But was he? What exactly did he do for China, and to China? And what was he like as a person? I wanted to discover the answers to these and many other questions.

It was as I was piecing together Sun's life – and that of people around him – that the depth of character of his wife and her sisters emerged and captured my imagination. Sun, I realised, was a consummate political animal who pursued his ambitions single-mindedly. That he was no saint was a relief (to a biographer). To follow his road to power, which was full of ups and downs, gangsters and gangster methods such as vendettas and assassinations, was like reading a thriller. And to uncover how this man made history was satisfying. But the women's lives, of which politics was only a part, gradually became richer and more appealing to me. I decided to make them the subjects of this book.

When I switched my focus to the sisters, my eyes were opened to just how extraordinary they were. Their lives spanned three centuries (May-ling died in 2003, aged 105) at the centre of action during a hundred years of wars, seismic revolutions and dramatic transformations. The backdrop moved from grand parties in

Shanghai to penthouses in New York, from exiles' quarters in Japan and Berlin to secret meeting rooms in Moscow, from the compounds of the Communist elite in Beijing to the corridors of power in democratising Taiwan. The sisters experienced hope, courage and passionate love, as well as despair, fear and heartbreak. They enjoyed immense luxury, privilege and glory, but also constantly risked their lives. In one narrow escape from death, Ching-ling suffered a miscarriage, and she was never able to have children. Her anguish would play a big role in her behaviour as Communist China's vice chairman.

May-ling also had a miscarriage that left her childless. Her husband Chiang Kai-shek, whose political career had taken off after he killed one of Sun's foes, was himself pursued by assassins, two of whom got close to her marital bed one night.

Ei-ling helped Little Sister fill the void left by childlessness, but she had to cope with her own lifelong disappointments, not the least of which was a universally bad reputation: she was seen as greedy and wicked Big Sister, while Red Sister was treated as a pure goddess and Little Sister as a glamorous international star. The relationship between the three women was highly charged emotionally, and not just because Ching-ling was actively working to destroy the lives of the other two. Chiang Kai-shek killed the man she loved after Sun's death – Deng Yan-da, a charismatic natural leader who had formed a Third Party as an alternative to the Communists and the Nationalists.

Modern Chinese history is intimately intertwined with the personal traumas of the Soong sisters. In writing about them – and China's colossi Sun Yat-sen and Chiang Kai-shek – I have been blessed with abundant materials. Copious correspondence, writings and memoirs, including many kept in China, have been published or made available. In Taiwan, now a democracy, archives have opened their doors. London, where Sun initiated his own 'kidnap' that launched his career, offers many insights. Above all, in America, to which the extended family was closely connected, institutions and libraries house numerous collections of documents that are simply treasure troves. A most valuable, fairly recent addition is

Chiang Kai-shek's diary, which he wrote every day for fifty-seven years, and which is unusually personal, with many revelations about his marriage with May-ling.

The story of the Soong sisters began as China embarked on its transition from monarchy to republic. The man who played the biggest part in this historic process was Sun Yat-sen. Sun and his republican revolution would shape the lives of the three sisters.

PART I

The Road to the Republic
(1866–1911)

I

The Rise of the Father of China

On 4 July 1894, Hawaii declared itself a republic after the reigning queen, Lili'uokalani, had been deposed the previous year. This event in the Pacific Ocean 6,000 miles from the Chinese coast had an impact that no one could have foreseen: it helped shape China today. A twenty-seven-year-old Chinese radical, Sun Yat-sen, landed on the archipelago, and stepped into a world where the word 'republic' was on everyone's lips. The royalists were plotting to restore Lili'uokalani while the republican troops were getting ready to crush them. The atmosphere was feverish. The young man, who was hatching a plot against the monarch of his own country, lit upon the idea that China, too, could become a republic.

This was a novel concept. Monarchy was the only political system the Chinese knew. At the time the country was ruled by the Manchu dynasty. The Manchus were not indigenous Chinese, but had conquered the land in the mid-seventeenth century. As they made up no more than one per cent of the population, they were considered minority foreign rulers and were never short of opposition from native Han rebels. Sun was one of them. The rebels usually called for the restoration of the pre-Manchu Han dynasty, the Ming (1368–1644). But this prospect was problematic. The Ming dynasty had become a rotten old tree that had been uprooted by a peasant uprising, before the Manchus took advantage of the chaos, invaded, and finished it off altogether. People were not keen to go back to the Ming. No one had a precise plan for the future. Thanks to events in Hawaii, Sun Yat-sen conceived a clear and forward-looking vision for China: a republic. That November, in sun-soaked Honolulu, he set up a political organisation called the Xing-zhong-hui ('Revive China Society'). The founding meeting was held at the home of a local Chinese bank manager, in a two-storey wooden house with large verandahs, shaded by latticed screens and tropical bushes. Each of the more than twenty members put his left hand on the Bible, in the Hawaiian style, and, raising his right hand, read out the oath written by Sun: 'Drive out the Manchus ... and form a republic.'

The combination of the two objectives proved to be a stroke of genius. It gave republicanism popular appeal. In less than two decades, in 1911 the Manchu dynasty was toppled and China became a republic of which Sun became known as 'the Father'.

The idea of a republic would have come to others sooner or later. Thanks to Hawaii, Sun Yat-sen latched on to it first. Sun's ambitious character, and the lengths he would go to in order to achieve his goals, were therefore critical in determining the course of republican China.

Sun Yat-sen, a dark-skinned, short man of well-proportioned and pleasant features, was born on China's south coast close to Hong Kong and Macau, the British and Portuguese colonies. The capital of the province was Canton, a hundred kilometres to the north, and Sun was Cantonese. His native seaside village, cradled by wooded low hills, had a picturesque name: Cuiheng ('Emerald Broadway'). But its soil was largely sandy clay unsuited to agriculture, and life was one of abject poverty. He was born on 12 November 1866, in a mud hut some ten metres by four, which he shared with his parents, Mr and Mrs Sun Da-cheng, his paternal grandmother, a twelve-year-old brother and a three-year-old sister. When he grew and took up more sleeping space, the older children had to spend the nights with relatives. The family ate sweet potatoes and rarely touched the more desirable rice. The men seldom wore shoes. Hoping that their newborn baby would have better luck in life, Mr and Mrs Sun named him Di-xiang, the Image of the North God, the celestial patron of the region.

At the age of four, the future iconoclast voiced his first objection to cherished traditions. His mother was in the process of binding the feet of his sister Miao-xi, then about seven. Foot-binding had been practised on Han Chinese women for a millennium. It involved breaking a baby girl's four smaller toes on each foot, and bending them under the sole to produce a foot shaped like a lily petal. A long piece of cloth was then used to wrap the feet tightly to stop the broken bones from healing and the feet from growing. Peasant girls tended to be subjected to this torture at an older age than upper-class toddlers, whose feet were usually bound when they were two or three so the crippled feet would remain tiny. Peasant women had to work, so the girls' feet were allowed to grow into a larger size. When Sun's mother, who herself had bound feet and was still suffering from the pain, started to mutilate her daughter, Sun saw his sister tossing about desperately grasping at something to alleviate the agony, and he pleaded with his mother to stop. Mrs Sun wept and told him that if his sister did not have a pair of lily-like feet when she grew up, she would be treated as an outcast and 'not a Chinese woman', and would 'reproach us'. Sun went on badgering his mother, and eventually she relented – only to take the girl to a specialist foot-binder in the village.

When he was five, his seventeen-year-old brother Ah Mi embarked on a journey of forty days to Hawaii to try to make a better living. The then independent kingdom under overwhelming American influence wanted to boost agriculture and welcomed Chinese farmers. Ah Mi worked hard, first as a farmhand, then starting his own businesses. He made good money, and sent much of it home. The family's lives improved drastically. A new house was built. Sun went to the village school at the age of nine. But he hated having to memorise Confucian classics almost as much as he loathed working in the fields. Later he told friends that ever since he could do such a thing as 'thinking', he was obsessed with the thought of escaping the life he was living. At last, in 1879 his brother sent for him, and Sun journeyed to Hawaii. From the moment he landed, the twelve-year-old fell in love with his new home. The harbour of Honolulu, with magnificent European-style buildings, struck him as 'a wonder-house'. The streets, clean and orderly, were heaven compared to his dirty and ramshackle village.

Ah Mi had intended for Sun to help him out in his businesses. But when Sun showed no interest in doing so, Ah Mi enrolled him in schools in Honolulu, firstly the Iolani College founded by missionaries of the Church of England for local and immigrant boys. Its curriculum was modelled on that of an English public school and its teachers were mostly Anglo-Saxons. Sun did well there and upon graduation three years later in 1882, he came second in the English grammar test. A proud Ah Mi gave a big party to celebrate. The prize from the school was a book on Chinese culture and history. The school did not want its pupils to forget their roots. Indeed it did not try to anglicise Sun; the child kept the distinctive hairstyle obligatory for Chinese men under the Manchus: a long queue on the back of the head. Sun adored the school: the uniform, the discipline and, in particular, the military drills – marching up and down thrilled him.

He went on to the highest educational institution on the archipelago, the American mission school Oahu College in Honolulu. (The most famous alumnus of the college, now known as Punahou School, is Barack Obama, who graduated almost a hundred years later in 1979.) Fees were high: one silver dollar a week, the price of a goat weighing over a hundred pounds. This was no small burden on Ah Mi, whose life was not easy. He had just bought land on the island of Maui, hoping to grow sugar cane. But his plantation was in the mountains, about 4,000 feet above sea level, brushed by the hem of the clouds; it was steep and rocky, with sparse clumps of weeds holding on tenaciously to the much eroded soil. Growing sugar cane was not possible, nor could cattle or sheep graze. Only goats would survive, and goats were Ah Mi's major assets. He made a sacrifice for his brother.

Down the mountains, Oahu was paradise for Sun. There were stone mansions to have lessons in, avenues of coconut trees to wander along, and well-tended lawns to play on. There was a fountain, overhung with ferns, where every day at lunchtime fellow female students would chatter and laugh while eating packed lunches. The girls were American, pretty, confident and vivacious. The teachers were mostly young women, including the headmistress and her deputy. The latter was rather publicly courted by a male teacher.

All this was a world apart from Sun's native Cantonese village and its women. The impact on the sixteen-year-old was immense. Throughout his life, Sun would desire women like the ones in his school, unlike many Chinese men who preferred their spouses to be the traditional type: obedient and self-effacing.

The company of these young women, who were all Christians (as were his male friends), may well have motivated Sun to join the church so that he could be in their community. But when he mentioned his desire to his brother, Ah Mi was upset. The North God was sacred for him. After heated rows, Ah Mi bought his headstrong brother a one-way ticket back to China, wasting the prepaid school fees.

An absence of four years made the homecoming only more unbearable. As soon as he arrived in summer 1883, Sun itched to leave. He quickly found a way. The most important place in the village was its temple, within which sat the North God, a heavily painted and gilded clay statue. The god clasped a sword, with his thumb pointing up to the sky, indicating divine power. On either side stood smaller secondary female figures, goddesses of the sea and fertility. Worshipping the North God was a way of life for people in this region.

One day, Sun drew a few friends aside and told them that he was going to the temple to 'wipe out some of this superstition by despoiling the very god'. Luke Chan, one of the boys, recalled that they were all shocked by Sun's idea, but also excited. They went in the middle of the day when the temple was empty; there was only a guard dozing against a wall. Leaving Luke and another boy to keep an eye on the guard, Sun entered the temple with a friend, Lu, an aspiring artist with wistful eyes and expressive full lips. Lu went only as far as scraping off some paint from the cheeks of one goddess; but Sun unhurriedly opened a pocketknife and cut off the thumb of the North God that pointed to heaven. When his other friends came in and saw the severed thumb, they were aghast. Luke later wrote that this was 'a tremendous step' for a peasant boy from a small village.

The temple guard woke up and the alarm was raised. While the other boys fled home, Sun nonchalantly let himself be seen and recognised as the ringleader. Incredulous consternation spread over Cuiheng. Furious elders berated Da-cheng for what his son had done and told him that Sun must be banished, otherwise the North God would not be appeased and could bring disaster to them all. With his bewildered father struggling to apologise, and reaching deep into his pocket to pay for the repair of the statue, Sun left home.

Luke noticed that Sun 'was perfectly cool and collected when he left the village in disgrace'. It struck him that Sun had probably 'planned and executed the move' in order to get away. Later, knowing Sun better, Luke came to the conclusion that Sun 'never did anything without first weighing both cause and effect against the final result'. From a young age, Sun had emerged as quite a strategist.

Having come home that summer, in the autumn Sun left for Hong Kong. The British colony, originally a cluster of small fishing villages at the foot of undulating hills, was now a spectacular metropolis. Its seafront reminded Sun of Honolulu, only grander. There the clever rebel made a beeline for the Diocesan Boys' School and Orphanage, run by the Anglican Church, where he knew he could find shelter – and he did, on the floor above the classrooms in a church house.

His parents, anxious for reconciliation, proposed that he marry the daughter of a friend from a neighbouring village. Like many, they thought that marriage and raising children would make their son settle down and behave responsibly. Sun agreed, and went home to marry his parents' choice the following year – after he had registered at the Central School in Hong Kong, which seems to have been his condition.

The seventeen-year-old bridegroom entered an arranged marriage that actually suited him well. His bride Mu-zhen, a year younger than him, was gentle and literate as well as beautiful. She was sweet-natured and not someone who would ever make a scene. After they were married, she stayed at home to look after his parents and the household, hobbling on a pair of bound feet, whereas Sun took off, only two weeks after the wedding. From now on, he would pop back occasionally, but otherwise led a separate life and acquired a string of mistresses.

Shortly after the marriage, in 1884 Sun had himself baptised in Hong Kong by Dr Charles R. Hager, an American missionary who lived on the floor above him. For his baptism, Sun changed his name from 'the Image of the North God' to Yat-sen, meaning 'a new man each day'. Sun did not genuinely believe in God, and friends observed that he rarely went to church. (Later he would ridicule the faith.) But Christian missions gave him a way out of his old life and offered him a valuable community. When Ah Mi, upset by the baptism, briefly stopped his school fees, the church came to his rescue and offered him a place in an Anglo-American missionary medical school in Canton, on the mainland across the sea and up the Pearl River.

Canton was a maze of unpaved narrow alleys where pedestrians jostled and sedan chairs swayed, sometimes preceded by road-clearers shouting at the tops of their voices. Competing for street space were also rows of vendors, some selling snakes and cats for food. Dirty, with sweaty and smelly crowds, Canton was not a place where Sun wanted to live. He soon made up with Ah Mi, returned to Hong Kong and enrolled in the newly opened Hong Kong College of Medicine for Chinese. Ah Mi was easily persuaded to fund him to pursue this most sensible career. A few months later, their father died; Ah Mi, in grief and feeling he must look after his kid brother, doubled the allowance. Sun was able to live five very comfortable years in a city he loved.

He graduated in summer 1892, but could not find a job. His diploma was not recognised in Hong Kong: the school's curriculum, in these initial years, did not fully comply with British standards. The neighbouring Portuguese colony Macau would not accept his diploma either. After sticking it out there for a year, he had to move to Canton, where the certificate was not an issue. But Sun still had no wish to live and practise in that city. It was now, with all hope, however half-hearted, of a medical career in his chosen cities extinguished, that Sun Yat-sen seriously took up the vocation of a revolutionary.

Sun's experience overseas had made him despise his own country, and he blamed all the problems on the Manchu rule. For a number of years, he and a few like-minded friends had talked about how much they loathed the Manchus, from the long queues trailing behind their heads, to the historical grievance of the Manchu conquest. Over tea and noodles, they dreamed about toppling the Manchu throne. Among his friends were Lu, his past co-despoiler of the village gods, and a new kindred spirit, Cheng, chief of the secret society the Triad in Canton. These two young men could not look more different: Lu had a gentle face, while Cheng very much looked the part of a gangster, with a dark gaze, heavily hooded eyes, and clenched teeth behind pulled-down lips. The friends might have seemed a bunch of unknowns, but their ambitions were big: they wanted nothing less than to end the Manchu dynasty and rule China themselves. They were undaunted by the fact that facing them was a giant state.

Their aspiration and daring were not unique. China had a long history of rebellions by ordinary men who made it to the throne. The Taiping Rebellion – the biggest peasant uprising in Chinese history – had originated in the region where Sun was born. The head of the rebellion, Hong Xiu-quan, hailed from a village not far from Sun's, and he had marched his army all the way to near Beijing, occupying large swathes of China and nearly overturning the Manchu throne. Hong had even established his own rival state. After his defeat, just before Sun's birth, his soldiers scattered, and one of them returned home to Sun's village. The old soldier used to sit under a giant ficus tree and tell stories about the battles he had fought. As a child, Sun was mesmerised. Now he expressed admiration for the Taiping leader and said he wished Hong had succeeded. When people jokingly told him he should be 'the Second Hong', he took the remark to heart and thought that he could indeed be just that.

Soon he spotted an opportunity. In 1894, Japan started a war against China and won spectacularly the following year. At the time, the Celestial Empire was run by the twenty-three-year-old Emperor Guangxu, who was a weakling and totally incapable of conducting the country's first modern war.* The mounting bad news brought a smile to Sun's face. 'We must not miss this opportunity of a lifetime,' he said to his friends. A plan was made. They would start a revolt in Canton and occupy the city; after this, which they termed the 'Canton Uprising', they would go on to seize other parts of China. Triad chief Cheng offered a suggestion that made the whole venture possible: they could use gangsters like his Triad 'brothers' as fighters. There were many large gangs in the country, and some members could be bought. Sun saw that he had a real chance.

This massive undertaking was extremely expensive. Huge sums were needed to pay for the gangsters as well as weapons. It was in order to raise funds that Sun travelled back to Hawaii in 1894 – and found the inspiration for the future after the Manchus: a republic.

The Hawaiian Chinese donated thousands of US dollars. Sun planned to go to America to raise more. At this juncture, a letter came from a friend in Shanghai. It urged him to return at once to start a revolution. China was suffering appalling defeats at the hands of the Japanese, and the Manchu regime was proving to be utterly incompetent and unpopular. Sun set sail straightaway.

The man who wrote the letter and helped trigger the republican revolution was Soong Charlie, a thirty-three-year-old former preacher for the American Southern Methodist Church and now a wealthy businessman in Shanghai. He had met Sun earlier that year when Sun briefly visited the city, and Lu, who after defacing the village gods had come to live in Shanghai, introduced them. The three of them talked politics deep into the night. Charlie shared Sun's anti-Manchu sentiments and admired Sun for being prepared to take action, unlike most people who just complained. Although

---

* The emperor had many phobias, one being the fear of thunder. When there was a thunderstorm, eunuchs would gather and shout as loudly as they could, in the vain hope of drowning out the sound of the thunder.

Sun was unknown at the time, he already gave off an understated and yet powerful sense of belief in himself, in what he was doing, and that he would succeed. This total self-confidence attracted quite a few followers like Charlie, who would help fund him generously.

Charlie was the father of the three Soong sisters. At this time, his eldest daughter, Ei-ling, was five, and the youngest May-ling was not yet born. The middle daughter Ching-ling, who would eventually marry Sun – in spite of Charlie's furious opposition – was a one-year-old baby.

As soon as they returned from Hawaii on Soong Charlie's advice at the beginning of 1895, Sun Yat-sen and his friends started preparation for their uprising. A Hong Kong bank manager called Yeung came on board with his organisation, a book club. Usually sporting a three-piece suit with a flamboyant pocket square, Yeung enjoyed good connections with the colony's business community. He brought with him potential support from local newspapers in both English and Chinese, and promised to recruit coolies, rather than gangsters. The book club had far more members than Sun's associates, and many of them were wary of Sun. One wrote in his diary on 5 May 1895: 'Sun Yat-sen appears to be a rash and reckless fellow. He would risk his life to make a name for "himself".' And on 23 June: 'Sun wishes everyone to listen to him. This is impossible.' Another remarked 'I will have nothing to do with Sun.'

So when the two groups came together to elect the 'president' for their new regime, Yeung won the vote. Sun was furious: the uprising was his idea – and he must be the president. Triad chief Cheng was angry too, and told Sun, 'Let me deal with Yeung. I am going to bump him off. I just have to kill him.' A listener cautioned, 'If you kill him, you create a murder case in Hong Kong, and we won't be able to go ahead with our revolt.' Sun agreed to let Yeung be called the president for the time being, until Canton was taken. Bloody power struggles were already in the offing before the republican revolution had even started. Equally striking was the clarity of Sun's ambition from the beginning – to be the president of China – for which he was willing to spill blood.

For now the comrades put their differences aside, and set the date of action for the ninth day of the ninth lunar month, traditionally the day for attending ancestral tombs. Many families had burial grounds in Canton and large numbers would converge there on the day. This would provide the rebels with cover to enter the city.

The government in Beijing had been warned about the plot, by its officials in the countries where Sun had been covertly raising funds and buying arms among overseas Chinese. It had alerted the Canton governor, who had also been warned by his own informants. He did not arrest Sun, but tightened security in general and had Sun watched quietly and closely.

Sun smelt danger. Then there was a last-minute complication: the coolies recruited by Yeung in Hong Kong could not arrive in time and Yeung asked that the action be postponed by two days. Sun decided to abort the whole plan. On the morning of the scheduled uprising, he called it off, and Cheng paid and dispersed the gangsters who had gathered. Cheng fled on the evening ferry to Hong Kong; Sun had a hunch that soldiers would be staking out the harbour and took a different route.

That evening, the local pastor who was a friend of Sun's gave a large banquet for his son's wedding. To pick a day traditionally reserved for tomb sweeping for a wedding was odd, as the Chinese would regard this as inauspicious. It is possible that the minister threw the banquet to provide concealment for Sun. Sun went to the banquet, where he lost himself in the crowd and slipped out to the Pearl River. A small boat was waiting. It took him downriver, travelling through tributaries unfamiliar even to the boatman. Sun directed the way: clearly he had studied the route. He first went to Macau, where he laid low for a couple of days before surfacing in Hong Kong. Sun did not wish to be known to be the first to bolt.

His friend Lu was not with him when he decided to abort the revolt, and did not flee in time. He was arrested and beheaded. Also executed when they and their recruits landed in Canton were several ringleaders from Hong Kong. Many coolies were arrested. Sun had long gone by this time. Hong Kong newspapers blasted him for abandoning his comrades to their fate. Possibly there was nothing he could do to help them without endangering himself. Still, his own well-planned flight showed a shrewd man exceptionally good at self-preservation.

Back in Hong Kong, Sun sought advice from Dr James Cantlie, his teacher at the medical college, with whom he had formed a bond. The doctor, who had kindly eyes and a typically Victorian bushy beard, was an energetic enthusiast who loved teaching and a frustrated radical with a keen adventurous spirit. He was deeply opposed to the Manchu rule in China and, in his own country, a fervent Scottish nationalist. A friend wrote of him: 'The most remarkable of all his uncommon qualities was his full-blooded nationalism.' While a medical student in London, he had taken to wearing a kilt in everyday life, which was exceptional at the time. Cantlie would save his ex-pupil's life and help to launch his political career.

Now, full of sympathy, Cantlie sent Sun to a lawyer who advised him to leave the island at once. Beijing was requesting the extradition of Sun and his co-conspirators. Sun (and Cheng) took the first steamer out of Hong Kong for Japan. There, Sun found that the Japanese government was considering extraditing him, and he had to get out. To disguise himself, Sun cut off his queue (which he disliked anyway), grew a moustache and wore a western suit. Looking like a modern Japanese man, he left for Hawaii.

A wanted list was circulated with Sun's name on top. The award for his capture was a thousand silver dollars. It was with this price on his head that Sun Yat-sen began his life as a political exile.

In Hawaii, Sun tried to raise enough money to have another go. This time, he was distinctly unsuccessful. People either abhorred the violence of his action, or were frightened of being associated with him. When he opened his mouth, they covered their ears and fled. But Sun was immune to embarrassment, just as he was unfazed by danger. He merely looked beyond Hawaii, and took off for the American continent in June 1896. Travelling from the west coast to the east, he sought out Chinese communities and preached revolution to them, before asking them to donate. Everywhere he went, however, whether San Francisco or New York, Chinatowns shunned him. As he would later say, his fellow countrymen treated him 'like a poisonous snake, or a venomous scorpion'; only a few Christians would talk to him. After a futile few months, he crossed the Atlantic to Britain.

Beijing monitored his movements. The Chinese Legation in London hired Slater's Detective Association to tail him. On 1 October, Henry Slater, the manager, filed the first report: 'In accordance with your instructions we despatched one of our representatives to Liverpool for the purpose of placing under observation a man named Sin Wun [a name of Sun's] who was a passenger on board the SS *Majestic* of the White Star Company and beg to report that a Chinaman answering the party's description was seen to disembark from the said ship at 12 o'clock noon – yesterday, at the Prince's Landing Stage, Liverpool.'

The detective agency then recorded in great detail Sun's trip to London: the train he intended to catch but missed, the train he took, how he collected his luggage from the parcels office at St Pancras Station and then 'proceeded in Cab No. 12616' to a hotel.

The next day Sun called on Dr Cantlie at his home, 46 Devonshire Street in central London. Cantlie had returned from Hong Kong in February that year. Before leaving, a friend of Sun's had come and 'told me that Sun wanted to see me, and that he was then at Honolulu', according to Cantlie's later testimony to the British authorities. Cantlie made a gigantic detour and travelled to Hawaii to see his former pupil. The doctor was indeed a kindred spirit.

Cantlie helped Sun get lodgings in Holborn. During his stay, Sun visited the Cantlies often; he had no other friends – and there was little else he liked to do. The detectives reported a typical day: he 'walked into Oxford Street looking in the shop windows ... and then entered the Express Dairy Co.'s establishment in Holborn where he had lunch after which he returned to No. 8 Gray's Inn Place, time being 1.45 p.m. At 6.45 p.m. he again came out and walked to a restaurant in Holborn where he remained three quarters of an hour subsequently returning to No. 8 Gray's Inn Place, time being 8.30 p.m. after which he was not again seen.'

The agency remarked after a week: 'Observation has been renewed each day but nothing of importance has transpired – the gentleman in question being only seen to take walks along the principal thoroughfares looking about him.' The Chinese Legation had asked the agency to pay specific attention to Sun's Chinese visitors. Slaters reported: 'he has not been seen to meet any of his countrymen'. After a few more days, the detectives all but stopped watching him.

Soon it was the anniversary of the aborted Canton Uprising. If he did not want his venture to fade into oblivion, he had to do something. An idea occurred to Sun. The Chinese Legation was at 49 Portland Place and, when he walked to Dr Cantlie's after getting off the bus at Oxford Circus, he passed in front of its door every time. It was a three-minute walk from the Legation to the doctor's home. Because of this extraordinary coincidence, one day Dr Cantlie said to him, 'Well, I suppose you are not going to the Chinese Legation.' Sun 'laughed', according to the doctor's testimony later, and said, 'I don't think so.' Mrs Cantlie said, 'You had better not go there; they will ship you off to China, and you will lose your head.'

Although they laughed about the idea, Sun's mind was ticking. He could go into the Legation, theoretically Chinese territory, and provoke an incident through, say, engaging the officials in an argument, even a fight, ending with him being kicked out into the London street. This would be the worst that could happen to him, he reckoned. But he could make a scene, which would draw attention. It might even be news. Of course it would be risky, but Sun was nothing if not audacious. His life consisted of taking calculated risks. He did some research, and came to the conclusion: 'This is England. The Chinese minister cannot charge me as a criminal. Even if they detain me, there is nothing they can do to me. The Chinese minister has no judicial right, and there is no extradition agreement between China and Britain.' That he might be smuggled from central London to China seemed improbable and Sun ruled it out. He also dismissed the thought that he might be murdered inside the Legation. It would have been far easier for the Chinese government to hire an assassin to bump him off in an unknown hotel room. The Legation was a town house opening onto a central London street, and most employees there were local British, including the housekeeper, the butler, the footman and the porter. They could hardly be expected to be party to his murder. What was more, it was a Scot, Sir Halliday Macartney, who was running the Legation at the time, as the Chinese minister, Gong, was sick. Sun found out about this from Dr Cantlie. The doctor knew Sir Halliday's role; he even knew where his fellow Scot lived.

That a British man was the boss inside the Legation building was reassuring when Sun contemplated his walk-in. A Brit would know British laws and could not possibly harm him fatally.

Sun sounded out Dr Patrick Manson, who was the first dean of his college in Hong Kong. A top-class scientist whose achievements would earn him the epithet 'the Father of Tropical Medicine', the doctor disapproved of Sun's action in Canton and told Sun to 'stop that sort of thing'. Manson later stated to the British authorities that Sun 'spoke about going to the Chinese Legation here, and I told him it was not advisable. He said he would take my advice and not go.'

But Sun went, on Saturday 10 October 1896, around the time of the first anniversary of his failed Canton Uprising. He entered the building and asked whether there were any fellow Cantonese there. A Cantonese interpreter, Tang, chatted to him. They agreed that Sun would return the next day, and that they would go together to the port to meet some Cantonese merchants. After Sun was gone, Tang thought about their conversation, and felt convinced that he had been talking to none other than Sun Yat-sen, the man most wanted by the Manchu authorities. Tang reported to Minister Gong.

Sun had not given much consideration to the minister. A bureaucrat, Gong was in fact deeply ambitious, though not very smart. Only thinking of the possible reward for capturing this enemy of the throne, he took over the case with alacrity and made all decisions personally, in spite of his feeble physical condition (he would die within months). He gave orders to detain Sun, while informing Beijing by cable that since Sun was a wanted criminal and the Legation was Chinese territory, 'naturally he should be detained'.

On Sunday morning, Sir Halliday directed the servants, including the English porter George Cole, to clear and clean a room on the third floor at the back of the house for Sun's detention. When Sun turned up, Tang pretended to show him round the house and led him to the room, where Sir Halliday ushered Sun inside. The Scot, with his imposing height, then announced to the 'diminutive' Sun (as he would be described by London journalists) that he knew Sun was a major criminal by Chinese law. 'Now that you are here, please stay for a day and a night, and wait till we get a reply' from Beijing. He then left the room and shut the door, telling Cole to 'see that that man does not escape'. Cole took turns with other servants to sit outside the room.

Sun had not anticipated this. He had wanted to be thrown out, not shut in. When he heard Tang ordering Cole to put another lock on the door, and then listened to the sound of the lock being fixed, his anxiety mounted. That night, he slept little.

Minister Gong cabled Beijing to report, in satisfaction, that he had captured Sun, and asked Beijing what to do next. He was used to simply following instructions. But Beijing did not know what to do. Britain had already refused to arrest and extradite Sun. The Chinese Foreign Office asked the minister to sort it out himself: 'How do you propose to ship him to Canton, in a way that England does not obstruct the move and that he will arrive? Please consult lawyers carefully and work out a scheme before making any move.' Beijing was clearly apprehensive at the turn of events, and even annoyed with Gong: 'We really hope you will exercise complete caution and cover all angles.'

Minister Gong had to ask Sir Halliday to find a solution. The Scot approached a friend who owned a shipping company, the Glen Line of Steamers, to sound out the possibility of chartering a ship to transport a 'lunatic' across the ocean. The company asked for £7,000 for a 2,000-ton cargo ship. Minister Gong cabled Beijing for authorisation, telling Beijing that if it rejected the option, he would have to release Sun. The Chinese Foreign Office did not reply. It clearly felt that to smuggle Sun from central London back to China was unworkable. But it did not want to reject the plan, since this would amount to giving orders to set Sun free. It did not want to bear the responsibility. There was silence from Beijing.

With no authorisation to pay the £7,000, Minister Gong could not pursue the Glen Line idea. Nor did he let Sun go. He did not want to bear the responsibility either. And so Sun was kept in his de facto prison.

Inside his cell, Sun took precautions against poisoning. His medical training now came in handy; he lived on bread and bottled milk and raw eggs. One day Tang the interpreter turned up and told him about the Glen Line plan, and this really scared him. He pleaded with Tang to 'beg' the minister, and through him, the throne, to spare his life, promising that he 'would never be involved in any rebellion again'.

His priority was to try and get a message to Dr Cantlie. He gave several notes to George Cole, beseeching him to take them to the doctor, and promising him a large reward. Cole handed the notes to Sir Halliday, who had told him that Sun was 'a madman'. Sensing that his notes had not arrived at their destination, Sun told Cole he wanted some fresh air, and Cole opened his window. There were bars on the window and Sun could not get through, but the gap between the bars was wide enough for him to put a hand out. He flung a note onto the roof of the neighbouring house, having wrapped coins in it to make it sufficiently heavy. A Chinese servant saw it, and Cole climbed over to pick up the note, which he again gave to Sir Halliday. The Scot told his servant to nail the window shut.

Eventually, Sun persuaded Cole that he was not a madman, but rather the equivalent of an opposition-party leader, 'and because I am the leader of that party, they have caught me here. They mean to bind and gag me, and they will get me on board a vessel and send me to China.' These words touched the porter, and he consulted the housekeeper, Mrs Howe, about whether he should help Sun. Howe replied, 'If I were you, George, I should.' Before Cole carried Sun's message to Dr Cantlie, this compassionate woman had acted herself. She wrote an anonymous letter and pushed it through the doctor's door. It read: 'There is a friend of yours imprisoned in the Chinese Legation here, since last Sunday.

They intend sending him out to China, where it is certain they will hang him. It is very sad for the poor man, and unless something is done at once he will be taken away ... I dare not sign my name, but this is the truth, so believe what I say.'

When Dr Cantlie heard the doorbell and found the letter, it was after 11 p.m. on Saturday 17 October. Sun had been locked up for a week. The doctor started a rescue campaign at once. He went straight to Sir Halliday's house, but there was nobody in. The doctor then took a hansom to Marylebone police station and then to Scotland Yard. He had difficulty getting anyone to believe his story. The inspector on duty at Scotland Yard thought he might be a drunk or a lunatic and told him to go home. Dr Cantlie spent the rest of the night in the street outside the Legation, in case there was any attempt to spirit Sun away.

Mrs Cantlie wrote in her diary that Sunday was 'a day of hopes and fears. Hamish [Dr Cantlie] went first thing to see Judge A ... then Mr H ... but got no satisfaction about doing something for Sun Yat Sen. Came home from church, and Hamish went to see Manson and see if he could find Sir Halliday MacCartney [sic]. Manson took our side and was wroth against the Legation. A man (Cole) who turned out to be Sun's warder arrived and brought two small cards beseeching us to rescue him.'

On the back of one card Sun had written 'I was kidnapped into the Chinese Legation on Sunday, and shall be smuggled out from England to China for death Pray rescue me quick!' These words had been written with a pencil first and then traced out with a pen. On the front, above his printed name, 'Dr Y. S. Sun', Sun had written Cantlie's name and address, and below added 'Please take care of the messenger for me at present, he is very poor and will lost [sic] his work by doing for me.'

On the second card was a more urgent plea, written only in pen: 'A ship is already charter [sic] by the C. L. for the service to take me to China and I shall be locked up all the way without communication to anybody. O! Woe to me!'

With these cards, and together with Dr Manson, Cantlie went to Scotland Yard for the second time, and after that, to the Foreign

Office. A member of the clerical staff at the Foreign Office immediately took up the matter and began to deal with it. The doctors went to the Legation to make it aware that the British authorities knew about the case. The Legation sensed that the game was up. Minister Gong urgently cabled Beijing, asking whether he should release Sun before trouble with the British government started. Again he received no reply. Still nobody wanted to be the one to say 'Release him.' Sun remained locked up in the Legation.

While the mandarins buried their heads in the sand, willing the trouble to go away, communications shuttled between the British Foreign Office, the Home Office and Scotland Yard – and Lord Salisbury, who was both the foreign secretary and prime minister. With his consent, policemen were posted outside the Legation, ready to spring on anyone who might try to smuggle Sun out of the building. Orders were given for all ships heading for China to be placed under surveillance. Meanwhile, Cole was interviewed. And the two highly respected doctors Cantlie and Manson swore affidavits. On the basis of this information, on Thursday 22 October, eleven days after Sun was detained, Lord Salisbury wrote to the Chinese Legation: 'The detention of this man against his will in the Chinese Legation was, in the opinion of HMG, an infraction of English law which is not covered by, and is an abuse of, the diplomatic privilege accorded to a foreign representative. I have, therefore, the honour to request that Sun Yat Sen may be at once released.'

Sir Halliday was summoned to the Foreign Office to hear Lord Salisbury's request. He complied, arranging for Sun to be delivered up at the Legation at 4:30 p.m. the next day. At that time on 23 October, Chief Inspector F. Jarvis and a Foreign Office official went to the Legation to collect Sun, accompanied by a joyous Dr Cantlie.*

---

* After Sun was released, the mandarins in Beijing sprang to life and sent a telegram to the Legation endorsing hiring a ship to transport him to China, adding details such as that Sun must be shackled and meticulously guarded. The telegram was backdated to when Sun was still in incarceration. Clearly, it was created for the sake of a paper trail for the eyes of the throne. Minister Gong, for his part, told Beijing he had already chartered a steamer and was about to ship Sun to China when the British government intervened.

When he was led downstairs to join Dr Cantlie, Sun was seen to be 'in good health and ... excellent spirits'. He was then delighted to find himself pursued by a large posse of reporters. Dr Cantlie had alerted the press. A big crowd had gathered outside the Legation, with photographers, sketchers and indignant onlookers, and they showered him with questions. In the days that followed, newspapers as far away as America and Australia, not to mention Japan, Hong Kong and Shanghai, were talking about him in elaborate details, with the eye-catching word 'kidnap' prominent in the headlines.

Sir Halliday wrote to *The Times* to explain that Sun had walked into the Legation of his own free will. But it made no difference. For the British, as Lord Salisbury pointed out, what mattered was that 'having come inside ... he was kept a close prisoner'. Sun adamantly denied that he had walked into the building freely, claiming that he had had no idea it was the Legation. He chose his words carefully, though, stating that he was 'accosted ... and compelled to enter'. At a later inquiry by the British government, Sun was even more careful and stressed that 'there was no real violence used; it was done in a friendly manner'. A violent kidnap would have necessitated a criminal investigation, in which case he would have to describe the process under oath, and the truth might have come out.

But he did not need to be so circumspect when it came to writing a book. With a great deal of help from Dr Cantlie, he rushed out a book with the snappy title *Kidnapped in London*. It was an instant bestseller and was translated into several languages. Sun was now well known, although his name generated ambivalent reactions. After their initial goodwill towards the victim, the British public cooled. They were averse to violent revolutions. Friends of the Cantlies would refer to Sun mockingly as 'that troublesome friend of yours'. The couple remained Sun's almost sole European supporters.

But what matterd to Sun was that his story reached Chinese radicals and that he became famous among them. They sought him out, and eagerly received him. When he at last left London in July 1897, heading for the Far East via Canada, the private detective who shadowed him noted that he had a busy schedule and that when he talked to Chinese audiences, 'they were very attentive to him and his conversation'. People opened their wallets as well. In Vancouver, Sun was able to swap his second-class ticket for a first-class cabin, paying the difference of a hundred Canadian dollars, and he 'was attired in a stylish sack suit which he has not been previously seen to wear'. From then on, as he told his childhood friend Luke Chan, laughing in obvious delight, 'I get what I want wherever I go.' Luke remarked, 'It was quite true ... he could travel from one end of the world to the other merely on his name. There was always transportation available, a house and food ready to his hand, funds when he asked for them ... and even motor cars and boats were obtainable if needed.' Walking into a kidnap in London established Sun as the only Chinese revolutionary with an international profile.

With this newly acquired fame, Sun Yat-sen looked for a base near China from which he could launch more revolts. Japan, which had once threatened to deport him, now let him stay, and provided him with living expenses and police protection.

In the year 1900, the xenophobic and anti-Christian society of peasants known as the Boxers were wreaking havoc in north China. Regarding the steps that the Manchu government took to suppress them as insufficient, an allied army of eight powers, including Japan, America and Britain, invaded Beijing. The court was driven out of the capital and fled into exile in Xian, an ancient capital in north-west China. For a moment, the Manchu throne looked wobbly. Sun proposed to the Japanese government that he would mobilise gangsters to seize some southern provinces and set up a 'republic' with its sponsorship. To start with, he suggested, he would organise a Triad revolt on the south-east coast across the sea from Taiwan, which had been under Japanese occupation since the 1894–5 war; Japan could use the 'disturbance' as an excuse to invade mainland China from Taiwan.

After much deliberation, Tokyo rejected the plan. Sun decided to create a fait accompli and told his friend Cheng, the Triad chief, to go ahead with the revolt on the coast, and he himself took off to

Taiwan, where the Japanese governor was itching to invade. In
early October, Cheng started the revolt on the south-east coast
with a few hundred men. They pushed on to Amoy, a big port.
But Tokyo issued a stiff order forbidding the governor of Taiwan
to do anything, and he had to refrain from sending over troops or
ammunition. The revolt collapsed. Taiwan expelled Sun. (Months
later, Cheng died suddenly in Hong Kong after a meal. The coro-
ner's verdict was a stroke. But suspicion of poisoning persisted.)

Sun went back to Japan, where he now felt unwelcome. He tried
to find another, friendlier base near China, but met repeated setbacks.
Thailand, British Hong Kong and French Vietnam all rejected him.
Foreign governments chose to work with Empress Dowager Cixi,
who was now in power. While Sun was agitating for violent revolution from outside, under her, China was undergoing a non-violent
revolution from within. A former imperial concubine, this extraordinary woman had seized power through a palace coup after her
husband's death in 1861, whereupon she had begun to bring the
medieval country into the modern age. Great achievements had been
made. In 1889 she had to retire when her adopted son, Emperor
Guangxu, came of age and took over; but after the catastrophic war
with Japan in 1895, she regained power, and restarted reforms in 1898.*
Although they were temporarily halted as the result of first an assassination plot against her involving Emperor Guangxu, and then the
Boxer mayhem, she pushed them to new heights once the maelstroms
were over. In the first decade of the twentieth century, she introduced
a series of fundamental changes. These included a brand-new educational system, a free press, and women's emancipation, beginning not
least with an edict against foot-binding in 1902. The country was to
become a constitutional monarchy with an elected parliament. This
enlightenment proceeded at the speed of 'a thousand *li* [i.e. 500 km]
a day', as Sun himself observed. Dr Charles Hager, who had baptised

---

* The reforms of 1898 are usually credited to Emperor Guangxu and other men,
with Empress Dowager Cixi cast as an anti-reform villain. This was not the case.
For the records that show the truth, see Jung Chang, *Empress Dowager Cixi: The
Concubine Who Launched Modern China*, Chapter 19.

Sun, bumped into him in Los Angeles in 1904, and argued with him that 'the reforms which he formerly advocated were being adopted' by the Manchu throne, and that China could renew itself under the monarchy. Sun simply said 'the Manchus must be ousted'.

In that decade, Sun's agenda – drive out the Manchus and form a republic – gained popularity among the Chinese. Thousands of students had by now come to study in Japan, and many espoused republicanism. When he landed in Yokohama after his travels in summer 1905, people flocked to him like pilgrims. He was escorted to Tokyo, where he was due to speak to a large packed hall. The crowd spilled into the streets, craning their necks to try to catch a glimpse of the visionary. When he arrived in a starched white suit, the applause was thunderous. Once he started speaking, the hall fell totally silent.

Sun was soon able to form an organisation in Tokyo, the Tong-meng-hui ('United League'). The Revive China Society, which he had founded in Hawaii, had petered out. The new organisation did not fare well either. Sun's colleagues accused him of appropriating donations for himself – and of being 'dictatorial'. Sun was not good at working with colleagues. His style was to make decisions himself, give orders, and expect to be obeyed.

On 15 November 1908, the empress dowager died. As the *New York Times* observed: 'As soon as she passed away, China at once felt the lack of a strong leader ... China has no leadership and is going to pieces fast.' The most powerful tidal wave was republicanism. The Manchus were foreigners and foreign rule was doomed. So, although Sun's organisation was not functioning, committed republicans continued to work by themselves, chipping away at the monarchy.

Three years after Cixi's death, on 11 October 1911 an anti-Manchu mutiny involving a couple of thousand soldiers broke out in Wuhan, a city on the Yangtze River in central China. This time, the rebels were no gangsters but government troops under the influence of republicanism. Sun was travelling in America at this time, and did not lead the mutiny. Army chief Li Yuan-hong, a stocky and unassuming man much loved by the soldiers and the local population (who called him 'the Buddha'), rose to the occasion and took leadership. He was the first man of high position and esteem to join the revolutionaries, and this made a huge difference to the republican cause.

Soon Li was joined by Huang Xing, the second-most influential man among the republicans. Heavy-built and rough-looking, Huang was a fearless fighter. That spring he had just led an impactful, albeit failed, revolt in Canton, in which he had lost two fingers. Now he led the resistance to the counter-attacks of the government army, and held the city for long enough to ignite republican uprisings and mutinies in other provinces.

Sun Yat-sen did not rush back. For well over two months he continued to travel in America and Europe, and then lingered in South East Asia. He needed to be sure that the republicans would win, so that he could return without the threat of execution. His travels were also a publicity tour. With the help of local Chinese students, he told the newspapers – or arranged for them to be informed – that the uprisings were under his orders, and that once a republic was founded, he would be its first president. He had a 'manifesto' issued in the name of 'President Sun'. Interviews with him were carried in newspapers in China, which further raised his profile there.

To explain his long absence to the revolutionaries, Sun cabled Huang that he was staying in the West to seek diplomatic support, which he said was the key to their success. He also claimed, through the press, that he was raising 'gigantic sums of money'. Several banks, he strongly hinted, promised to fund the republicans to the tune of tens of millions of dollars once he, Sun, was made president. Sun did try to see people who were in a position to give him endorsement or money, and while in London checked into the Savoy, one of the most expensive hotels, using its letterhead liberally. But he got nowhere. His world had been almost exclusively Chinatowns, and he had no access to the Western establishments.

On 18 December 1911, the Manchu court started peace talks with the republicans in the face of uprisings all over China. The revolutionaries were definitely winning. They set about forming an interim government to deal with the negotiations, and nominated Huang Xing to be the head. Huang accepted. As soon as he learned the news, Sun Yat-sen hastened for China and arrived in Shanghai on the 25th. He could delay no longer. He had to see in the birth of the republic, which had been his vision, and whose flame he had kept alight for nearly two decades. And he had to be there to stake his claim for what he saw as his rightful position: president of the Chinese republic.

2

Soong Charlie: A Methodist Preacher and a Secret Revolutionary

Charlie, father of the three Soong sisters, was one of Sun Yat-sen's earliest supporters. Born in 1861, he was Sun's contemporary and came from a similarly humble origin. A peasant lad from Hainan Island off China's southern coast, he, like Sun, left home to seek a better life overseas at the age of fourteen with his elder brother. His first stop was Java, where he could pass as a native, with dark skin, big and sunken eyes, and thick, out-turned (un-Chinese-looking) lips. An uncle adopted him and took him to America when he was seventeen. In Boston's cramped Chinatown, the uncle owned a tiny silk and tea store where the teenager was put to work as a dogsbody. Charlie had never learned to read and write; he wanted to go to school, but his uncle refused to let him. The adoption seemed to have been only a means to gain a free labourer. This was not the life Charlie had in mind and within months he ran away. One day in January 1879, he went down to the harbour and boarded the US Revenue cutter *Albert Gallatin*, asking for a job. Captain Gabrielson took a liking to him and made him a cabin boy. The captain, it seems, thought that Charlie was about fourteen year old: he was little more than five feet tall and looked several years younger than his real age. Charlie did not straighten out this little misunderstanding. Being thought of as a child made it much easier for people to show him kindness and affection.

Charlie had a knack of endearing himself to others. He was deferential, cheerful and easy-going. He worked diligently. Captain

Gabrielson treated him as a protégé and often invited him to stay in his home in Edgartown, Massachusetts. The captain's wife was the niece of the town's squire, Judge Pease, and they lived in a stately house. For the first time Charlie experienced comfort and luxury, as well as a carefree family life. The Gabrielsons were devout Methodists, and Charlie went to church with them on Sundays whenever he stayed. His religious conviction grew along with his attachment to the captain. When a year later the captain was transferred to another cutter – *Schuyler Colfax*, based in Wilmington, North Carolina – Charlie requested a discharge and joined him. In this city that took pride in its multitudes of churches, the captain introduced him to the Rev. Thomas Ricaud, who christened him in November 1880. Charlie was 'probably the first Celestial that has ever submitted to the ordinance of baptism in North Carolina', a local paper enthused, noticing that Charlie had 'elicited a very profound interest in the religious community'. People found him 'exceedingly impressive' as he went round shaking hands after the service, telling them how he had found the Saviour and how he longed to return to China and preach the gospel to his people.

Charlie's Christianity enhanced his appeal tremendously. At the time Protestant churches were rapidly expanding in China and the Methodists were among the most zealous 'Christian soldiers'. Charlie became famous in the tight-knit community of the Southern Methodists. Captain Gabrielson now faded out of his life, and Julian Carr, a tobacco magnate and philanthropist, assumed the role of his sponsor. Trinity College (Duke University today) in nearby Durham enrolled him in April 1881 as a special student to study the English language and the Bible. The president of the college, Braxton Craven, together with Mrs Craven, tutored him in English. After Trinity, Charlie went to Vanderbilt University in Nashville, Tennessee, the headquarters of the Southern Methodists, to train to be a missionary. Altogether, he was among the Methodists for seven years – an experience that would determine his future and that of his three daughters.

In his first – and only – letter to his father, written soon after he settled at Trinity, he expressed appreciation for his patrons, along with much religious fervour*:

Dear Father,
I will write this letter and let you know where I am. I left Brother in East India in 1878 and came to the United States and finely [finally] I had found Christ our Saviour ... now the Durham Sunday School and Trinity are helping me and I am [in] a great hurry to be educated so I can go back to China and tell you about the kindness of the friends in Durham and the grace of God ... I remember when I was a little boy you took me to a great temple to worshipped the wooden gods. ... but now I had found a Saviour he is comforted me where ever I go to ... I put my trust in God and hope to see you again in this earth by the will of God. Now we have vacation and I stay in Mr J. S. Carr house at Durham. Soon as you get my letter please answer me and I will be very glad to hear from you. Give my loves to mother Brother and Sisters please and also to yourself ... Mr and Mrs Carr they are good Christian family and they had been kind to me.

But Charlie's letter could not be delivered. He had sent it to Dr Young J. Allen, doyen of the Southern Methodist Mission in Shanghai, asking him to help forward it. But when Dr Allen wrote back and asked for Charlie's father's name and address in Chinese, Charlie could not provide them. He was completely illiterate in his mother tongue – because his family had been too poor to send him to school and because written Chinese was so difficult. He only copied out a few place names – Shanghai, Hong Kong and Hainan Island – from a map for missionaries and marked them on a simple sketch, indicating the approximate location of his village. His father's name was the transliteration of its sounds in the local dialect. As there were hundreds, if not thousands, of families in

---

* All errors in this and other letters by Charlie are reproduced uncorrected.

that region who had sons overseas, it was impossible for Dr Allen to proceed. Charlie had to abandon the attempt to contact his family.

He was lonely. One morning at Vanderbilt, he joined a group of boys for a meeting in a chapel where they sang and prayed and exchanged their religious experience. A classmate of his, the Rev. John C. Orr, recalled that Charlie 'got up and stood awhile before he said anything. Then his lips trembled and he said: "I feel so little. I get so lonesome. So far from my people. So long among strangers. I feel just like I was a little chip floating down the Mississippi River."' Orr wrote: 'The tears were running down his cheeks, and before he could say anything more a dozen of the boys were around him, with their arms about him, and assuring him that they loved him as a brother.'

Indeed wherever he went, Charlie was treated with kindness and decency. People regarded him 'with the greatest respect, and admired [him] for being ambitious and working his way through college'. Still, a fellow student at Trinity, Jerome Dowd, noticed that 'boys were disposed to tease him and play all sorts of pranks upon him'. At Vanderbilt the chancellor, Bishop McTyeire, was sometimes unpleasant. At the end of his studies, Charlie asked to receive further training in medicine. The bishop refused. As he wrote to Dr Allen, in a haughty tone, 'Soon[g] wished to stay a year or two longer to study medicine to be equipped for higher usefulness, etc. And his generous patron, Mr Julian Carr, was not unwilling to continue helping. But we thought better that the *Chinaman* that is in him should not all be worked out before he labours among the Chinese. Already he has "felt the easy chair" – and is not averse to the comforts of higher civilization. No fault of his ...'

Charlie was good at putting things in perspective and refused to take offence easily. Unfailingly he showed 'beautiful manners', and was 'very, very polite'. He remained 'full of life and fun', and when taunted was 'always ready to respond in a playful spirit', thus defusing the tension. People remembered his 'exceptional spright-liness' and 'a most genial and friendly nature'. He had a good sense of humour. When he was baptised, his surname was spelt as 'Soon', an approximation of the pronunciation of his name in his local dialect. One Vanderbilt classmate, James C. Fink, remembered that 'on introducing him to some of the boys, he smilingly remarked, "I'd radder be soon den too late."'

This appearance of geniality was partly the result of a determined and sometimes painful effort to suppress his emotions. Charlie loved women – as this letter to a schoolmate at Trinity in 1882 shows:

> [B]oth of Misses Field are here yet they will go home next friday morning. I tell you they are very pleasant young Ladies I like them ever so much ... Trinity is very pleasant now, but I don't know what it will be after the [girls] go off ... Miss Bidgood is here ... She looks as pretty as ever. I went to see her and Miss Cassie sometime since. She talk right lively ... I been had good times with the [girls] all day long. never looked at the books hardly ... Miss Mamie and two other [girls] gone to visiting last night we did had big time ... Fortisty and I went to called on Ella Carr and we had the best time you ever heard of.

But the young man could not develop any further relationship. Ella Carr, mentioned in this letter, was the niece of his benefactor Julian, and daughter of a professor at the college. Five decades later she told the local paper, the *Greenboro Daily News*, that Charlie had often come to her house to listen to her play the piano – until one day her mother 'told him to stop coming around the house so much'. He stayed away, saying goodbye with a photo of himself looking 'dapper and impeccably dressed'.

He was particularly close to a Miss Annie Southgate, daughter of an influential figure in Durham. In one letter to her in which he hinted at his feelings, he first apologised for losing someone's address and then wrote, 'Why don't and couldn't I make a mistake in reference to your address, I wonder?' 'There isn't any danger of my falling in love with one of Uncle R[ichard]'s daughters;

Miss Jennie is engaging to a young fellow, he is only seven feet and 9 inches in height, and Miss Ross is too young, for she is only 15 and has gone to her sister's to spend summer. So you see there's no chance for me to fall in love, if I want to.' (Later he would name one of his daughters, the future Mme Sun Yat-sen, Rosamonde, after Miss Ross.)

In words as explicit as possible, wistful, even poignant, Charlie expressed his love to Miss Annie: 'I suppose you are in some where, where ever you may be I hope you are having nice time. Miss Annie, I must confess that I love you better and more than any girls at Durham. Don't you believe I do?' This was as far as Charlie could go. He was falling in love, but held back from taking the plunge. There was no hope; he was a 'Chinaman'.

Charlie found controlling his emotions so necessary that he would later require his children to do so from a very young age. May-ling, the youngest of the three Soong sisters, remembered that when she was a child, her father often told his children 'not to show emotion, and to abhor sentimentality'. Once she 'sobbed and wailed' when her elder brother was leaving home for the first time to go to boarding school. She choked down her tears when she caught her father 'suddenly turning stern and seemingly unapproachable'. From then on, she rarely cried. 'I can count the times I have wept since I have grown up.'

In spite of the frustrations he experienced in America, Charlie adored the country. It later became his top priority to give his six children an American education. This motivated him to make money – and once he made it, his children's education would take a major portion of it. His three daughters all studied in America, with May-ling only nine when she went there and remained for a whole decade. Most extraordinarily, the girls lived there on their own, with no adult family members to look after them. Such was the total, unreserved trust and faith Charlie had developed for the Methodist community and the American society.

As he had always appeared 'very social, very talkative, and very playful', some of Charlie's fellow American students had thought him frivolous and found it hard to imagine 'that anything serious was going on in his mind'. But a most serious resolve had already formed: Charlie was determined to help make his native land more like America – *mei-guo* – the 'beautiful country'. At the end of 1885, he left his beloved America for Shanghai.

Shanghai was then already one of the most spectacular and cosmopolitan cities in the world. Situated near the place where the Yangtze, the longest river in China, flows into the sea, it had been marshland only a few decades previously, before the Manchu government allowed Westerners in to develop it. Now solid European-style buildings rubbed shoulders with fragile bamboo houses, paved broad streets meshed with wheelbarrow-trodden mud alleys, and parkland jutted into rice paddies. Outside the Bund, the waterfront, under the still gaze of the skyscrapers, numerous sampans rocked with the waves, offering a stirring sight of the city's vitality.

Dr Allen, head of the Southern Methodist Mission, made the city his home and devoted his life to introducing Western culture to China. It was he who pioneered modern education in the ancient empire. A solemn man with a long, bushy beard, Allen was a distinguished scholar in Chinese as well as Western culture and was greatly respected by intellectuals and the Manchu throne alike. He had just founded the trailblazing Anglo-Chinese College for men before Charlie's arrival, and Charlie had hoped to teach there.

Allen thought Charlie's ambition was presumptuous and even preposterous, because Charlie was illiterate in Chinese. Writing to Bishop McTyeire, Allen did not bother to conceal his contempt: 'The boys and young men in our Anglo-Chinese College are far his superiors in that they are – the advanced ones – both English and *Chinese* scholars . . . And Soon[g] never will become a Chinese scholar, at best will only be a *denationalized* Chinaman, discontented and unhappy unless he is located and paid far beyond his deserts – and the consequence is I find none of our brethren willing to take him.'

Allen waved Charlie out of Shanghai to a small town, Kunshan, and classified him as a 'native preacher', which meant Charlie was paid much less than foreign missionaries. This hurt Charlie deeply.

But he confined his anger to writing to Miss Annie and suppressed his urge to challenge Allen.

The mission head seemed bent on punishing Charlie in other ways. He refused to give him leave so he could go and see his family straightaway. Charlie was incensed and fought his corner this time. Still, he protested in such a way that it did not lead to an open conflict – as he assured Miss Annie. It was not until autumn 1896 that he returned to his home village. His parents had trouble recognising him. Once they realised this was the boy they thought they had lost forever, there were many happy tears. After the brief reunion, he was back in Kunshan, 1,700 kilometres away.

There were other problems confronting Charlie. China did not feel like home. He told Miss Annie, 'I am walking once more on the land that gave me birth, but it is far from a homelike place for me. I feel more homelike in America than I do in China.' He had to have a crash course to learn written Chinese, and then had to learn the Kunshan dialect. 'The language of this people is entirely different from that of my mother tongue; hence I am just as much a stranger to these natives as I have been in America or Europe.' The locals ridiculed him. Peasant boys would sneer and shout at him 'Little dwarf!' (At just over five feet tall, he was shorter than the average local man.)

Charlie gritted his teeth and struggled on. Eventually he was able to preach in the local dialect, somewhat haltingly. He confided the misery he endured to Miss Annie. Although his yearning for her was itself another source of agony, the tone of his letters was always measured and upbeat. When Miss Annie died in 1887, he was in 'great sorrow', as he wrote to her father.

Later that year, Charlie's life was changed: he married the eighteen-year-old Miss Ni Kwei-tseng. Miss Ni was a member of China's most illustrious Christian clan, Xu Guang-qi (after whom a district of Shanghai is named). Xu had been a high official in the Ming dynasty, and had been converted by the Jesuits at the beginning of the seventeenth century. He had collaborated with Matteo Ricci in introducing Western sciences into China. The Catholic lineage stopped when

Miss Ni's mother married a Protestant missionary and converted to Protestantism, which caused quite a stir.

Like her illustrious ancestors Miss Ni was a singularly devout Christian. Her daughter May-ling later recalled, 'I knew my mother lived very close to God ... one of my strongest childhood impressions is of Mother going to a room she kept for the purpose on the third floor to pray. She spent hours in prayer, often beginning before dawn. When we asked her advice about anything, she would say, "I must ask God first." And we could not hurry her. Asking God was not a matter of spending five minutes to ask Him to bless her child and grant the request. It meant waiting upon God until she felt His leading.'

Indeed, people commented that in her face, 'there was a strength of character and a spiritual serenity that added to her beauty of features'. She had a commanding presence. All her daughters and their husbands, however celebrated or powerful, sought her approval, which she did not grant easily.

She had begun her life as an unyieldingly independent child. When her mother tried to bind her feet, as she had done with her other daughters, Miss Ni reacted violently and developed frighteningly high fevers. Her parents had to abandon the effort and resigned themselves to the prospect that with her 'large feet', she might not find a husband.

Then Charlie the preacher entered her life. A relative of hers had introduced them. They were soulmates and were happy together. He sent a joyful and characteristically jokey notice to North Carolina about his wedding. It announced that he would be married 'at Shanghai, China on the 4th day of the Chinese 9th moon. Those who can figure out when that is are cordially invited to be present.'

Bill Burke, a friend from Charlie's Vanderbilt days, paid the newly-weds a visit in Kunshan. They lived in the mission parsonage, a small house down a narrow and winding alley from the ferry landing that doubled as a teahouse. Burke's abiding memory was the bride's natural feet: 'Her firm, full steps were graceful as any American woman's.' He could tell that Charlie was 'in love with his wife'. Charlie had at last found his life's companion, with whom he would discuss all his affairs and make all his decisions. They impressed people as 'a very congenial couple'.

Their first child, a daughter, Ei-ling, was born on 15 July 1889. Five more children would follow – two more daughters, Ching-ling and May-ling, and three sons: Tse-ven, Tse-liang, and Tse-an, born in 1894, 1899 and 1906. The boys were referred to by their initials: T.V., T.L. and T.A.

Expecting a big family and planning to give his children an American education, Charlie resigned his job as a preacher in 1892. Among the missionaries there was a rumour that he 'had gone back to the heathen custom of worshipping idols'. Charlie wrote an open letter to his friends in North Carolina: 'My reason for leaving the Mission was it did not give me sufficient to live upon. I could not support myself, wife and children, with about fifteen dollars of United States money per month.' He vowed to be 'an independent worker of our Methodist Mission', and was as good as his word.

Charlie went into business and, with his Americanised background and his outgoing character, not to mention industry and talent, success came quickly. He imported machinery for flour and cotton mills, and founded a publishing house to print the Bible – at a time when the American Bible Society, with which Charlie was affiliated, gave a Bible to everyone and anyone who wished to take one.

Quickly he entered the circle of Shanghai's upper class, and built his growing family a large house that was more European than Chinese in style. It was equipped with American comforts, with indoor heating. Charlie felt that he 'can never be Chinese enough to want to sit in a cold room with all my outdoor clothes on'. (He did not like Chinese food, either.) Also installed were American-style baths and beds. In his eldest daughter Ei-ling's description, the family had

bathrooms fitted with pretty Soochow tubs, with yellow dragons coiling around the outside and green glaze inside. Cold water was laid on; hot water prepared downstairs and carried up ... the heating was furnished by gas radiators, a refinement that many foreigners in Shanghai did without. The beds, instead of the hard, flat, wooden structures still used by most Chinese, were good, comfortable, mattressed American couches. The neighbors would come in just to peer at those beds, to feel them with critical jabbing fingers, and to agree with each other that they were most unhealthy and dangerous for the children.

By the standards of the rich in Shanghai, this large and comfortable modern house was not luxurious (it was certainly not ostentatious). It was also 'out in the wilderness' in the fields far from the city centre. People thought that the couple were eccentric; but Charlie had a practical reason: he was saving money in order to sponsor Sun Yat-sen's republican revolution.

Mrs Louise Roberts, an American missionary, rented a flat for her own small mission press in Charlie's compound, which housed his office as well as his home. Charlie often popped in for a chat and they became close. Through their friendship, she 'gained the impression that his chief interest, after his family, was to help his country to become the great land it should be'. Charlie had already dreamed of changing China when he left America, and in the decade since he had returned, the desire had grown more intense. In late spring 1894 he met Sun, and spent several sleepless nights talking with him (and their mutual friend Lu). He was impressed by the twenty-seven-year-old. After Sun left, he ruminated about their conversations. Towards the end of that year, after war with Japan had broken out and China had suffered catastrophic defeats, Charlie became totally disillusioned with the Manchu regime and convinced that the revolution proposed by Sun was the way to save the country. To him Sun was the right man; he had a Western education and liked Western ways. He was a devoted Christian – or so Charlie believed. (Sun knew Charlie's background and naturally played up his religious conviction.) So Charlie wrote to Sun, urging him to come home from Hawaii to take action. He helped fund the Canton Uprising; when that failed, with Lu executed and Sun in exile with a price on his head, Charlie never wavered and continued to support the fugitive, sending him money clandestinely over the years.

What he was doing was extremely risky. Had it been known, the Manchu government would have been after him, and Dr Allen, who was already ill disposed towards him, could have done him real damage among the religious community. Allen hated violent revolutions and in a journal he edited, in Chinese, he used the harshest language to condemn Sun Yat-sen, calling him a 'vile criminal'. Charlie had to hide his political persuasion, which he did well. No one suspected that this affable and wealthy businessman and pillar of Shanghai society was an underground revolutionary. And few imagined that underneath his sensible and congenial exterior, Charlie had a passionate, even impulsive, nature. On the basis of a few brief encounters, he committed himself to Sun's perilous and seemingly impossible venture. Hardly knowing the man, he became so smitten that he wrote to Sun: 'I know no man among the Chinese who is more noble, more kind and patriotic than yourself.'

Charlie sought nothing in return when the republican revolution succeeded. He asked for neither position nor fame, and did not present himself to Sun when Sun arrived in Shanghai and stayed there for a week at the end of 1911. He only revealed his secret, almost on impulse, to Mrs Roberts when the republicans took Shanghai in November. The morning after, he walked into her office with a spring in his step. Mrs Roberts started talking about the night before with obvious excitement. He beamed, and said, 'Now I can tell you all about it.' In an American radio interview years later, Mrs Roberts said, 'So he told me of his long friendship with Sun Yat-sen, and how he had helped Sun in every way possible, especially with money. "Not that I ever bothered to take a receipt for the amounts I sent him," he chuckled.' Charlie chuckled a lot and had 'always twinkling eyes', she observed. He asked her, 'Maybe you have wondered why we live so plainly here in this place?' The missionary replied, 'I haven't thought much about that, except that I felt you and Mrs Soong did not care for display, and I know you are very generous in your donations to church work. Also you are at a good deal of expense for the education of your children.'

'That is true,' Charlie said, 'but I have saved all that I could to help Sun's cause, because I felt that was the best way for me to help my country.' He chuckled again and started talking about something else: how to persuade his sister to come to Shanghai so she would be safe from the upheaval of the revolution.

PART II

The Sisters and Sun Yat-sen
(1912–1925)

3

Ei-ling: A 'Mighty Smart' Young Lady

When she was five years old, in 1894, Charlie and his wife sent Ei-ling, their first child, to McTyeire School, the Methodist boarding school founded by Dr Allen and named after Bishop McTyeire. The fact that the school's two founders had been either hostile or arrogant to Charlie made no difference. It was the best school for girls in Shanghai – and it was American. Ei-ling herself had asked to go there. She had noticed that its pupils were given a special place to sit at Sunday services. Even at this young age, Ei-ling showed the strong will and fascination with status that would shape her future. Her mother hesitated: the child was too young to board. Ei-ling persisted, and in the end they enrolled her for the autumn term. Grandma Ni protested tearfully. To the Chinese, one would not part with one's young children unless one was destitute, and sending their child away from home when they had a choice was downright 'cruel'. But Charlie and his wife encouraged their children to be independent, and they suppressed their feelings.

There was another indication of her later drive that would make Ei-ling one of the richest women in China: her reaction to the suitcase bought for her to take to school. For a week, as she informed her biographer Emily Hahn, she had been 'at a fever heat of excitement over the preparations, the clothes and The Trunk. It was her first private, individual trunk, a beautiful black, shiny one.' But, when she saw it with her new clothes inside, 'her disappointment was intense ... The Trunk was not filled to the brim.' She 'insisted upon bringing out all her winter clothes too and filling that space'.

The other thing that bothered the five-year-old was that she 'had lovely teas at home; would they at the school?' She set off only after her mother packed a basket of goodies she specified, 'one packet of Golland & Bowser's butterscotch and one of bitter black chocolate'.

Finally, she was on her way by her father's side, wearing a Scottish plaid jacket and green trousers and her hair bouncing in a pigtail. Her excitement faded when her father took leave of her; she clung to his neck sobbing and would not let go. She remembered this episode many decades later, but not how her father had broken free.

Her memories of school were chiefly of suffering. She was the only child of her age. The desks were too high and her feet could not touch the ground; her legs would go to sleep during the interminable lessons. She later confided that she 'suffered horribly from that, and nobody thought of it or of remedying the situation'. She had to find a way herself to get the blood circulating. Perhaps the worst memory was the fear at night. While the older pupils were working, she 'lay in bed alone in the great dormitory upstairs, quaking with terror'. The moment of comfort came when she heard the hymn 'Abide with Me', sung by the girls after they finished their evening work and were returning to the dormitory. It signalled the end of being alone. And at the sound of the singing she would fall asleep. For the rest of her life, whenever she heard the tune, a wave of relief would engulf her.

At the McTyeire school, Ei-ling developed an even stronger character and a dependence on religion. She never told her parents about her misery. Father and Mother did not encourage moaning. This school life meant that Ei-ling's childhood was largely a solitary one without playmates of her age. She grew introverted, even forbidding. All through her life, she made few real friends, so that when she was universally criticised, no one came to her defence.

The Soongs' second child, Ching-ling, was three years younger, born on 27 January 1893. A delicate baby, then 'a dreamy and pretty child', 'quiet and obedient', she was her mother's favourite. She was taught at home and not sent to McTyeire until she was eleven.

Perhaps Mrs Soong sensed Ei-ling's distress and took pity on her fragile second daughter. Ching-ling followed her mother round, quietly thinking her own thoughts. She reacted very differently from her sister to signs of privilege. She recalled, 'As a child I was taken to church on Sundays by my mother who was a devout Christian. When we arrived at church the pastor and his assistants used to drive away the poorly clad women in the front pew to give up their places to us!' This put her off missionaries, and planted the seeds for her conversion to Communism. Shy but friendly, she made a small number of friends and kept them.

The extrovert of the family was Little Sister May-ling. She went to McTyeire when she was five, because she wanted to emulate her eldest sister. Born on 12 February 1898, she was healthy, plump and spirited. In winter, her mother dressed her in a thick padded cotton jacket and trousers and she waddled about looking like a Halloween pumpkin, inviting teasing nicknames, which she did not mind a bit. Her cotton shoes, called 'tiger's heads', had colourful long whiskers, sticking-out ears and fearsomely bulging eyes. Her hair was plaited into two pigtails tied with red strings and then rolled into round loops. The style for young girls had an unflattering name: 'crab holes' which, again, did not bother her.

At McTyeire, May-ling had to walk down dark passages alone and catch up in difficult lessons. She insisted to her teachers that she found nothing difficult or intimidating. But one of them spotted her waking up in the middle of the night in fits of trembling, and saw her climbing out of bed and standing up straight beside it, reciting her lessons. The school soon sent her home. Little Sister retained her open and sunny disposition.

Family life was disciplined and religious. Because 'God wouldn't like it', no one was allowed to play cards – or to dance, which was deemed 'devil's doings'. There were the daily family prayers and the frequent visits to church. As a child, May-ling found the family prayer sessions boring and would slip out of the room with excuses. She dreaded the long sermons in church. Ching-ling did as her mother told her to do but kept her detachment, while Ei-ling slowly but surely turned into a devout woman.

The children seem genuinely not to have resented the strictness of their parents. Rather, it inspired devotion from all six children, who looked up to their parents and felt reassured by their constancy. They were not spoilt like many other rich children, but they had their own fun. Mrs Soong was a good pianist, and family evenings were often spent with her playing the piano and Charlie singing the songs he had picked up in America. Ei-ling would join in duets when she was home. The children were encouraged to run wild in the fields and climb trees. The siblings played among themselves. Whatever rivalry there might be between them, it was well under control. Their affectionate, close relationship extended long into their adult lives, and cemented the pillars and walls of the later famous 'Soong dynasty'.

Mr and Mrs Soong were determined to give their children an American education. Before Ei-ling turned thirteen, her father had called on his old Vanderbilt friend Bill Burke and arranged for him to take her to the US. The sweet-natured Irish giant of a man had come from Macon, Georgia, a centre for the Southern Methodists, where a ladies' college, Wesleyan, had the distinction of being the first in the world to grant degrees to women. Burke wrote to the president of the college, Colonel DuPont Guerry, who welcomed Ei-ling. When Burke took his young family back home for a short leave, he brought Ei-ling with them. At the time, America was tightening its Chinese exclusion laws to limit the number entering the country. To get round the problem, Charlie bought a Portuguese passport for Ei-ling, a practice that was not uncommon.

On a bright day in May 1904, Ei-ling, fourteen years old, stood poised and reserved at the jetty on the Bund in Shanghai, with a trunk full of new Western-style clothes. She was waiting to board a tender to take her and the Burke family to the large ocean vessel, the *Korea*, which would carry them to the other side of the globe. She would be the first Chinese woman to be educated in America. But there was no sign of excitement, no sadness at leaving her family, nor any fear for the journey to the unknown. She parted with her father, who had accompanied her to the ship, with a restrained verbal goodbye – and without tears, unlike their parting at McTyeire years before. The teenage girl had been moulded into a paragon of self-control. Still, when the ship set sail, she burst into sobs, albeit silently in a quiet corner. Burke spotted this, and later said that this was the first and only time he saw Ei-ling betray her feelings.

Ei-ling attracted much attention. One night there was a dancing party after dinner, and the ship's orchestra played a waltz on deck. Ei-ling passed by with the Burkes when one of the ship's officers approached her and asked her to dance. 'No, thank you, I cannot,' she shook her head sternly. The officer tried to coax her, 'Well, there's no better time to learn. Come, I'll teach you.' 'No, it's not right for me to dance,' the fourteen-year-old replied firmly. 'Why?' 'Because I am a Christian and Christians do not dance,' said the unsmiling face.

The Burkes travelled with her only as far as Yokohama in Japan. Mrs Burke was dying from the typhoid that she had contracted before the journey, and her family disembarked to stay with her. Burke arranged for a couple on board to look after Ei-ling. When she went to see them, they were not in, but the cabin door was open, so she sat down to wait. When they came down the passageway, the wife said loudly, 'I'm so tired of those dirty Chinamen … We won't see any more for a long time, I hope.' Ei-ling rose when they came in and made a hasty excuse for having called, saying that she now wanted to go back to her cabin. She later said that the remark had seared her heart forever. It was only partially soothed by the appearance of a middle-aged American missionary, Miss Anna Lanius, who knocked on her door, introduced herself and kept Ei-ling company during the voyage. (Among other passengers on board was Jack London, going home from Korea. The twenty-eight-year-old writer of *The Call of the Wild* had been covering the Russo-Japanese War, and had apparently sent out more dispatches on the war than any of his fellow American correspondents.)

A heavier blow than the unpleasant remark was awaiting Ei-ling when the steamer arrived outside the Golden Gate at San Francisco on 30 June 1904. The immigration officers refused to recognise her Portuguese passport and threatened to detain her. Ei-ling lost all her poise and flared up, saying: 'You cannot put me in a detention home. I am a cabin-class passenger, not from steerage.' She meant that she should not be treated the same as the coolies. In the end she was not detained, but was made to wait as a virtual prisoner on the *Korea*. When the ship sailed, she was moved to another vessel, and then to another.

She spent nearly three uncertain weeks on those ships. Miss Lanius stayed and moved with her, even though her own father was on his deathbed waiting for her return. Finally, through the help of the Methodist network, Ei-ling entered America. She remembered Miss Lanius warmly, but was angry about her treatment by the officials. For the remainder of the journey to Georgia, by train across the continent, she kept a gloomy silence. Burke, whose wife had died in Japan, joined Ei-ling for the trip. He was looking forward to pointing out the sights of America to her, hoping to lose some of his sorrow in her delight. He was sorely disappointed. Burke felt that he 'might as well have been trying to entertain a plaster mannequin'.

That she did not bother to be polite to the man who had helped get her an American education, and who had just lost his wife, shows Ei-ling to be a wilful young woman. She was still preoccupied with her bad experience more than a year later when an uncle of hers, Wen, came to Washington as a member of a Manchu government delegation. She persuaded him to let her go with them to the White House – in order to have it out with President Theodore Roosevelt. She made her complaint bluntly, and the president said he was sorry.

The train that carried the strong-willed girl pulled in at Macon on 2 August. For the next five years, Ei-ling led the life of a young American woman privileged enough to attend college at the beginning of the twentieth century. But her experience would not be like anyone else's. Macon was a religious town, with churches of different schools standing next to each other, their spires and domes vying for dominance. The town had not been universally enthusiastic about having her, the first female Chinese student in their midst. The *Macon Telegraph* felt the need to stress Ei-ling's Christian credentials: 'she was a product of our own missionary work', and Wesleyan would 'qualify her for Christian work among her own people in China'. President Guerry explained that 'she will not force herself or be forced upon any of the other young ladies as an associate', and issued a veiled appeal: 'I have no misgivings as to her kind and respectful treatment.'

So Ei-ling was greeted with an uncomfortable welcome, which could not have escaped her. Even when people were nice to her, there was something unnatural about it. Her reaction was to retreat into herself – so much so that in later years, when she became famous and her contemporaries were asked to recall what she had been like, no one could think of anything personal to say. They remembered her 'poise', 'her quiet dignity', and that she was 'a serious student, quiet and reserved'. That was it, other than the observation that she was 'never really made one of us'. Short, plain and somewhat stout, she easily evaded attention and lost herself in the corners of the campus among the big ash and beech trees and lush bushes, where she read, studied and thought. She wore American clothes, and swapped her pigtail for a high pompadour hair-do. On Sunday mornings, she joined fellow students to troop down the long hill to Mulberry Street Methodist Church. But she talked little with them and made no friends in those five years – unlike both her sisters and her father, who had all had friends in America, even intimate, lifelong friends.

Ei-ling grew to be fiercely self-sufficient and proud. One classmate saw that she looked 'insulted ... when one of the Wesleyan professors told her she had become a fine American citizen'. She once gave a recital of her own arrangement of *Madame Butterfly*, and stood on the stage not as a victim, but as a queen. She had asked her family to send her silk brocade to make her costume, and Charlie had sent her forty yards. The gorgeous colourful display mesmerised her fellow pupils, who enviously whispered to each other about her 'trunks of silks'.

The girls noticed that Ei-ling had an inclination for serious subjects, and that she was 'well informed on current history when the rest of us were not even interested'. Her last essay at the college shows a political maturity beyond her nineteen years. Entitled 'My Country and Its Appeal', she commented on China's cultural icon Confucius: 'His grossest mistake was the failure to regard woman-kind with due respect. We learn from observation that no nation can rise to distinction unless her women are educated and considered as man's equal morally, socially, and intellectually ... China's progress must come largely through her educated women.'

Ei-ling's description of China's modernisation was uncommonly spot-on, more so than most other contemporary or future narratives: 'We could mark the year 1861* as the beginning of her awakening.' Since then, 'China's great transformation, though gradual, has been apparent ... Since the Boxer trouble, which came as a blessing in disguise,' argued the teenager, 'China has experienced more rapid advancement than ever before.'

She kept herself informed about events in China and had her own considered opinions about them. These college years also reinforced her religious belief. 'China's plea is for more missionaries,' she wrote. The college authorities were impressed by her intelligence and pleased about her commitment to Christianity. They were convinced that the young woman 'will exert a strong Christian influence' in China. They were right: Ei-ling would later help convert China's ruler Chiang Kai-shek to Christianity, as well as turn the first lady, May-ling, into a profoundly religious person. These were events that made a big impact on Chinese history.

In 1908, during her last year at Wesleyan, Ei-ling's two sisters joined her. Ching-ling had won a government scholarship the year before when she was fourteen, and along with a group of other scholarship students she had been escorted to America by an official and his wife – Uncle and Aunt Wen. To their parents, it had made sense for May-ling to go too, even though she was

---

* The year Empress Dowager Cixi seized power, and initiated China's modernisation.

only nine. The most important consideration was that, with this group, she would have no problem entering America. Mr and Mrs Soong were so afraid of missing this chance for May-ling's education.

The two sisters arrived without a glitch. Ei-ling helped them settle in at Wesleyan, fussing over them and looking out for their needs. Her affectionate side, which had so far been bottled up, now had an outlet. It was here that she began to mother her two sisters, which she would continue to do even when they both became 'first ladies'. Ei-ling particularly mothered May-ling, who was nearly a decade younger. Once a student spotted Ei-ling 'scolding' May-ling for 'associating with some girl whom E[i]-ling thought was not a good influence. May-ling replied very impulsively, "But I <u>like</u> her – she <u>fascinates</u> me."' Little Sister was like a much-loved headstrong child winning over a doting parent. She had always looked up to Big Sister as a role model and at Wesleyan she became awestruck by Ei-ling's intelligence. She would say that Big Sister was 'undoubtedly the most brilliant mind in the family'. Later many people close to the sisters noticed how May-ling behaved like a daughter to Ei-ling, how she meekly did what Ei-ling told her to do, and how completely she was under Ei-ling's influence. At Wesleyan, they (unwittingly) demonstrated their relationship on stage in the college auditorium, in an operetta called *The Japanese Girl*. Big Sister played the Japanese emperor and Little Sister the emperor's attendant.

In 1909 Ei-ling graduated, and while her sisters got on with their studies at Wesleyan – and made friends quickly – she returned to Shanghai. She began her twenties aspiring to do big things in China. The republican revolution broke out in 1911, and her father revealed to her his relationship with Sun Yat-sen. His description of Sun conjured up a Christlike figure who had sacrificed himself for the salvation of his people. Ei-ling came to worship Sun. Even though she had never met him, she regarded him as a heroic uncle. While Charlie lobbied missionaries to support the republicans, she staged charity shows to raise money for them. Charlie had suggested in the past that she organise charity concerts and she had resisted the idea. Now, she was full of enthusiasm. She turned out to be a first-class organiser, with a systematic mind, full of ideas. A big theatre was hired for the events, with performances in English – something new even for Shanghai. Ei-ling longed to meet her hero and offer her service to his revolution.

Meanwhile, Sun was preoccupied with his battle to become the president of the forthcoming republic, which he considered his due. The fight started the moment he arrived in Shanghai on 25 December 1911. The fact that he had not participated in the uprisings and that he had delayed returning to China for well over two months earned him much scorn. Many revolutionaries regarded him as 'a coward'. *The Times* correspondent George Morrison reported that the republicans 'spoke with some contempt of a man who had been only a drummer of the revolution, who had taken no actual part, always keeping away in order to save his own skin'. Sun, they said, 'is always in the background whilst there is danger'. Because Sun had claimed to be staying abroad in order to raise funds for the revolution, newspapers asked him to confirm that he indeed brought back 'gigantic sums of money'. Sun had prepared his answer. He adroitly avoided telling an outright lie and, laughing as if this was a silly but amusing question, said: 'A revolution does not depend on money; it depends on passion. I have brought back not money, but the spirit.' One could construe that he did bring back money and just preferred not to talk about such a vulgar matter.

Sun tried to have himself made president. He needed to be voted in by the delegates from the seventeen (out of twenty-two) provinces in which uprisings had broken out. 'Election' was now the accepted route to office. Several dozen delegates had gathered in Nanjing to cast their vote for the 'interim president'.

Nanjing, an old royal capital, was cradled by the majestic Purple Gold Mountain and imbued with a rich cultural atmosphere. In bygone days, elegant barge houses on the canal in the city centre had been famed venues for poets, mandarins and quick-witted geisha to compose verse and music while downing dainty cups of fragrant liquor. After some satisfactory lines were created, they would give generously to the poor, dropping a handful of coins into little velvet bags dangling at the end of long bamboo poles extended from neighbouring houseboats. The canal looked most charming at dusk, when lanterns gleamed through the papered and latticed windows of the barges.

After the republican revolution, the city was virtually the territory of Chen Qi-mei, the 'Godfather' of Shanghai's main secret society, the Green Gang. A fragile-looking man with eyes that could instil terror, and thin lips that murmured lethal orders, he was a devotee of Sun. During the revolution he had taken control of Shanghai, and put himself in a position to call the shots in the nearby city of Nanjing, where the voting was to take place. The delegates were subject to his vetting. One from Fujian, called Lin Chang-min, belonged to a different political organisation and the Godfather dispatched a gunman to meet him at Nanjing railway station. Lin was shot at, but not killed. The warning was clear: stay away from the voting. Lin duly fled Nanjing.

To more stubborn opponents, the Godfather was not so gentle. An old comrade turned nemesis of Sun's, Tao Cheng-zhang, enjoyed a large following and had been attacking Sun in virulent language, accusing him of being 'a liar', 'a self-enricher' and having 'criminally harmed comrades'. Godfather Chen decided to silence him forever. He sent one of his henchmen, none other than the later Generalissimo Chiang Kai-shek, to carry out the task. Chiang found out that Tao was staying in a Catholic hospital in Shanghai. He walked into Tao's ward, respectably dressed in a suit, and shot Tao dead in the bed at point-blank range. Chiang proudly recorded this episode in his diary – assassins were lauded by the revolutionaries – musing that this may well have been the origin of Sun's favourable attention to him and the beginning of his political elevation.

Sun named the Godfather 'the first man of republican uprisings', even though Shanghai was not the first place to revolt. He was crucial to Sun's election.

There were only two other candidates: the leaders of the Wuhan Mutiny, army chief Li Yuan-hong, and republican number two,

Huang Xing. Luckily for Sun, neither entertained ambitions for the presidency. Huang, in particular, had no interest in being the policymaker and asked his supporters to vote for Sun.

A physical giant, Huang had a passion for the battleground, where he seemed to seek death. The bursting impatience with which he charged into a seemingly suicidal assault made people think he was 'crazy'. Victory in battle obsessed him. Despite holding on to Wuhan for a month and sparking off the republican revolution in many provinces, he felt dejected on account of having ultimately lost the city. On a steamer on the Yangtze River going from Wuhan to Shanghai, he brooded and told his friends that he had lost Wuhan because the Germans had given cannons to the government troops, and that he wanted to kill the six Germans he saw on the steamer. A Japanese friend dissuaded him, saying that the steamer was owned by a Japanese company and it was bound to conduct a thorough investigation and trace the killing to him, which would harm their cause. Huang conceded reluctantly, saying, 'Well then, let's throw the Chinese comprador into the sea and drown him. He helps the Germans do business and is most disgusting.' Huang also agreed that the killing should be delayed till they disembarked the next day. Once he gave the order to kill, Huang visibly brightened up, 'his energy restored', remarked the Japanese friend. With a smile, Huang told the group that the assassin he had chosen was an excellent hit man and 'extremely experienced'. Over lunch, the assassin fixed his gaze on the comprador in order to remember him, while the hapless man was cheerfully eating and drinking. It sent a chill down the spine of the Japanese comrade, even though he was no stranger to spilling blood. The comprador was gunned down at the foot of the gangway as he was leaving the steamer. The story did not end there. Soon afterwards, the same assassin was hired by somebody else to kill Huang, and he was forced to accept the job as his father was being held hostage. Huang got wind of this and confronted the assassin, who confessed. Huang comforted him and gave him money to leave China. Before long his body was washed up on a beach near Tokyo.

Huang regarded Sun as better suited to be leader. Still, Sun had to make major concessions before the voting. He told the delegates who came to Shanghai to see him that he wanted the word 'interim' taken out of the title 'interim president', but they said that they had no mandate to elect the president proper. That would have to be decided by a general election in due course. In fact, the delegates said, they were only electing someone 'to preside over the peace talks' between the republicans and the Manchu throne. Moreover, during the talks, because the republicans were far from certain that they would win, they had promised that if Yuan Shi-kai, the prime minister of the Manchu government, persuaded the throne to relinquish power (to avoid a bloody civil war), they would support Yuan to be the interim president. Sun was told that he had to honour this promise.

He conceded to the arrangement, and on 29 December, the delegates voted Sun the interim president. Sun went by a special train from Shanghai to Nanjing and was sworn in on 1 January 1912. On that occasion, he had to pledge publicly that he would step down in favour of Yuan if and when the throne surrendered power.

Sun made the pledge extremely reluctantly, and tried to prevent Yuan from taking over. Because Yuan could only assume office if the peace talks were successful, Sun tried to get the republicans to pull out of the talks and keep fighting. The delegates and most other republican leaders objected. One confronted him: 'Why do you not want peace talks? Is it because you don't want to give up the presidency?'

Secretly, Sun contacted the Japanese and asked for 15 million yuan so he could raise an army to continue fighting. In return, he promised to 'lease' Manchuria to Japan once he had toppled the Manchus. Sun knew that Japan craved this rich Chinese territory, larger than France and England combined, but Japan turned him down.

On 12 February the Manchu throne abdicated and handed power to the republicans. The following day, Sun was compelled to step down. He tried to impose a 'condition' demanding that Nanjing, where Godfather Chen held sway, be made the capital and Yuan take office there. His calculation was that with the Godfather in charge of the city, Yuan would never get to assume office. The delegates rejected his 'condition' and voted to keep the capital in Beijing. Sun flew into a violent temper, and 'ordered' another vote, threatening that he would send an army to 'escort' Yuan from Beijing to Nanjing. But the delegates declined to change their decision, and Sun had no army to send. There was nothing more Sun could do. In Beijing on 10 March, Yuan Shi-kai was sworn in as interim president of China. Sun had been in office for just over forty days.

Sun returned to Shanghai in April 1912 to try other ways to supplant Yuan. The chief attraction of Shanghai was its foreign Settlements, the areas that were governed by Western, and not Chinese, laws. As he prepared his battle, Sun wanted to be out of Yuan's reach. Westernised Shanghai was also much more to his taste. Now aged forty-five, for most of his life – since the age of twelve – Sun had hardly been on Chinese soil.

In Shanghai, the ex-interim president met Soong Charlie again, after nearly two decades. The man who had been so generous to him all those years ago now warmly welcomed him to stay. Charlie regarded Sun as the noblest man in China, and felt outraged that he had been pushed out in favour of Yuan Shi-kai, who had only left the Manchu camp at the last minute. To Charlie, Yuan was a cynical opportunist. Sun set up his headquarters in Charlie's house. At this time Ching-ling, nineteen, and May-ling, fourteen, were still in America; of his three daughters only the twenty-three-year-old Ei-ling was at home. She had been waiting eagerly to do something for her hero, and now volunteered to work as Sun's English-language assistant.

Being in the whirlwind of political events had drawn Ei-ling out of herself, and she had blossomed into an attractive and fetching young woman. Although still not exactly beautiful, she had shed much of her teenage weight and grown radiant and graceful. A certain deferential gentleness had been introduced to her efficient manner, perhaps because she was conscious that she was among important men who were doing great things. Visitors to the Soong house were impressed by her. John Cline, president of Soochow University which had also been founded by the Methodists, came to invite Sun to speak to his students, and was immediately struck. His description also provides a glimpse of Sun's life with the Soongs:

First I met Soon[g]'s private rickshaw coolie at the street door. He was the outer bodyguard. If he hadn't recognized me, I would have got no further. After him came another bodyguard, posted at the stairway. On the second floor, a secretary stopped me outside a private office, then he went in and came out with Eling [Ei-ling]. Eling was as far as I got. Soon[g] and Sun were having an important conference with party leaders inside. But Eling was as nice as she could be and after learning what I wanted, she said she would arrange it, and she did. A mighty smart and efficient young lady, that Eling. She's going to get somewhere in this world.

Her first conquest, it seems, was Sun Yat-sen. From his youthful days in Hawaii, Sun had been attracted to Westernised women. The Wesleyan-educated Ei-ling captivated him easily. William Donald, a ruddy, sandy-haired and bespectacled Australian newspaperman and Sun's adviser, observed (in his biographer's words) that when he and Sun were talking: 'Often [E]i-ling would take a chair near them, make notes as Donald talked and smiled encouragingly. Sun would transfer his quiet, expressionless gaze from Donald to her, and there he would keep it, not an eyelash flickering ... In Shanghai one day, he gazed intently across the desk at Donald after the sweetly timid [E]i-ling had passed through his office and whispered that he wanted to marry her. Donald advised him to sublimate his desire, since he was already married, but Sun said that he proposed to divorce his present wife.' Donald objected that Sun was like an uncle to the girl (he was twenty-three years older than her). 'I know it,' Sun replied, 'I know it. But I want to marry her just the same.' Tongues began to wag among fellow revolutionaries in Shanghai that Sun was living with

Ei-ling. This was only a rumour: the Soong parents would not have tolerated it and Ei-ling herself, religious like them, would certainly not have considered having an affair. She was undoubtedly aware of Sun's amorous intentions. The way Sun gazed at her would have made his feelings clear. But Ei-ling never reciprocated. Indeed, his unwanted attention may well have dampened her enthusiasm about him. He was not that noble after all. In fact, Ei-ling came to admire Mu-zhen, Sun's wife, who joined him with their children, and was always extremely deferential towards her. When they were going out together, she would take Mu-zhen's arm and support her as Mu-zhen's bound feet made it hard for her to walk. She made a point of calling Mu-zhen 'Mother', perhaps as a signal to Sun to stop his advances.

This was the first time Sun had been with his family since the Canton Uprising in 1895. For that dangerous undertaking, he had made no arrangements for his family – Mu-zhen, his mother, a four-year-old son Fo, a daughter Yan less than a year old. He had left them to fend for themselves when he fled Canton. His friend Luke Chan was back from Hawaii in the village for his own wedding and heard the news about the failed revolt. He took it upon himself to help the families of Sun and his brother Ah Mi to escape to Macau. Luke then escorted them to Hawaii – this time at Sun's request. When Sun arrived himself, he was only there to raise funds for another revolt and took little interest in the welfare of his family. After staying for six months – during which Mu-zhen became pregnant with their third child, a daughter Wan – he left again.

Sun was unmoved by the tears of the women in his family. Friends heard him say, 'Anyone who is engaged in the revolution must conquer tears.' This does not seem to have been too hard for him, as concubines and mistresses kept him company. A friend once asked him what his favourite pursuits were; he replied without hesitation: 'revolution' followed by 'women'. In Japan, for example, at least two Japanese women were known to be his consorts. One, Haru Asada, lived with Sun until her death in 1902, and was referred to in Japanese government files as his concubine. When she died, a gorgeous young girl in her mid-teens, Kaoru Otsuki, took her place. She is said to have had a daughter by Sun, who never set eyes on her father, as he left her mother one day and never returned or wrote.

Mu-zhen and Sun's mother were miserable. Old Mrs Sun, at a loss as to why her younger son chose to be an outlaw, was outraged at his total disregard for his family. Luke often heard her complaining 'bitterly at having to leave her village' and losing her home. 'Often when I visited them at [Ah] Mi's on Maui, the old mother would tell me her disappointment and grief at her son's actions. And poor [Mu-zhen] would weep at the mere mention of the Revolution.' Mu-zhen had already been hurt badly by the fact that she had married an absentee husband who gave her no support in raising a young family or in caring for his parents. On a pair of crushed and bound feet, the burden of life had been almost too much to bear. Then, on those same feet, she had to flee thousands of miles, carrying an infant and pulling along another child, supporting a mother-in-law who also had bound feet and could hardly walk, and carrying as many belongings as her exhausted body could. She had lived in fear and frenzy, first in hiding in Macau, and then in Hawaii on the other side of the globe.

What comforted the women was the unfailing generosity of Sun's brother Ah Mi and his wife. Mrs Ah Mi, a strong woman who had unbound her own feet, was in charge of the household, and she never treated the relatives as a burden. She was kind and fair, and there were seldom quarrels among the women. As time went by, Mu-zhen sought solace in religion and became a Christian, diligently studying the Bible every day. Ah Mi acquiesced. Mrs Ah Mi would go to church with her sister-in-law and celebrate Christmas with her at the pastor's. She did not become a Christian herself, out of respect for her husband's feelings. The extended family were thrown together in Hawaii, and became very close. Eventually Sun's mother gave up any hope for her younger son and resigned herself to a life without him. Although she never really stopped worrying about Sun, she felt that those years in Maui were the happiest in her life.

Misfortune struck after they lived in Hawaii for ten years: Ah Mi's businesses went bankrupt. The extended family had to decamp to Hong Kong, where Ah Mi rented a small tumbledown house. He could no longer afford the children's school fees. Old Mrs Sun went blind, but there was little money for her to consult doctors. She died in 1910 with neither of her sons by her side. Ah Mi was away from home and desperate to get back, but he could not raise the necessary fare. He was heartbroken – and angry with his brother, who took no responsibility at all for the family. One day when he and Sun were briefly together, he exploded at his brother, who hung his head and did not say a word.

After the republican victory, Sun fetched his family in 1912 and at last started to look after them. The eldest, his son Fo, was now twenty, and the daughters, Yan and Wan, eighteen and fifteen. They had rarely seen their father, and this was the first time they spent an extended period with him. Sun arranged for Fo to study in San Francisco, and tried to get scholarships for his daughters. But the family reunion was marred by Sun's lust for Ei-ling, which his daughter Yan noticed. When she became very ill the following year, just before she died she said bitterly that her father had 'behaved badly'.

Sun's behaviour also deeply hurt his concubine, Chen Cui-fen. She had met and fallen in love with Sun in the church circle in the early 1890s, when he was still a medical student. A beautiful nineteen-year-old with large eyes, high cheekbones and a strong jawline, she shared his life when he struggled to practise medicine, acting as his receptionist, nurse and all-purpose assistant, and when he then took up revolution as his vocation.

Coming from a poor family, Cui-fen was not bothered by hardship. The danger of a revolutionary's life did not daunt her either. During the preparation for the Canton Uprising, she helped smuggle arms into the city, hiding rifles in the coffin of a funeral procession and ammunitions and explosives under the seat in her sedan chair. Sun's friends were impressed by her manners. There was no shyness about her, or other conventional ways of femininity.

She maintained eye contact when talking to them, her long eyelashes not lowering as was required of women. Nor was she soft-spoken. At meals, she used men's chopsticks rather than the slender dainty ones deemed more suitable for women, and she would wolf down her food like a coolie. But she was a beauty. Cui-fen remained totally loyal to Sun when he was a fugitive for nearly two decades. She cooked, washed and cleaned for him and for any of his comrades staying with them uncomplainingly. Sun's friends told their long-suffering wives to model themselves on her.

But now she was an inconvenience to him in his newfound glory. The practice of keeping concubines went on as before under the new republic, but Sun was conscious that it was unacceptable to the Christian Soongs. Sun wrote to Ah Mi, asking him to offer Cui-fen to a friend as that man's concubine, promising to pay the man 10,000 yuan. Even by the standards of a society that condoned concubinage, this was an act of heartlessness, even treachery, by a newly successful man to a woman who had faithfully stuck by him. Ah Mi angrily rejected the proposal and instead invited Cui-fen to join his large household. Cui-fen did, and got on with everyone; she became like a sister to Mu-zhen.

However aggrieved Cui-fen felt about the way Sun treated her, she never publicly complained about him. Rather, she insisted that it was also her wish to leave Sun. She was a proud woman. And she was generous and forgiving. For the rest of her life, she would treasure the two gifts from Sun, a gold ring, and a watch that had been given to Sun by Dr Cantlie after Sun's release from his 'kidnapping' in London. Being an independent woman, she did not want to be a burden on Ah Mi, and went to Penang to try to start a business in rubber planting. The venture flopped. But there she adopted a daughter who became the joy of her life. The daughter grew up and married Ah Mi's grandson, adding another bond to the extended family. Years later, during the war against Japan in the early 1940s, Cui-fen's son-in-law voluntarily returned to China and joined the army, serving in the radio corps. Cui-fen and her daughter left neutral and safe Macau and travelled into the war-ravaged mainland with him. They accompanied him wherever he went, despite the constant Japanese bombing that pursued the radio corps. A loving family life was of paramount importance for Cui-fen. She died at the age of eighty-eight, surrounded by family.

Ah Mi himself had died, perhaps of a heart attack, long before her in 1915, aged sixty-one. His last years were marked by sadness. During Sun's brief tenure as interim president, friends had lobbied for Ah Mi to be made governor of his native province, Guangdong. Sun vetoed the nomination. 'My brother,' he said, 'is exceptionally straight, and if he gets into politics, he will come to grief for being always on the square.' When Ah Mi came to Nanjing to argue his case, Sun told him he was not cut out for politics and should stay away. Ah Mi had to accept the reality that for all he had given to his brother, and to the revolution, he could expect nothing in return. He was not even treated as a 'revolutionary' despite the fact that for some years he had been banished from Hong Kong and other British colonies for carrying out republican activities. Ah Mi went on bearing the responsibility of caring for the extended family until his death.

Sun's family roused great admiration in Ei-ling; she was full of sympathy for them, and was exceptionally warm and affectionate towards them, especially Mu-zhen. The smart young lady handled Sun's advances deftly, keeping him at arm's length while managing to work with him.

4

China Embarks on Democracy

Sun Yat-sen could not have failed to register Ei-ling's refusal. But his mind was focused elsewhere: he was totally absorbed in his fight to supplant Interim President Yuan Shi-kai.

Yuan was a fearsome rival. A short and burly man, he nevertheless exuded stature and inspired awe. Born in 1859, seven years Sun's senior, he came from a very different background. His birthplace was the landlocked northern plain of Henan, and his forebears were affluent landed gentry. He had a purely Chinese upbringing and was deeply rooted in tradition, rising through the ranks of the imperial army. He never travelled to the West, and his private life was an extreme version of the very rich Chinese male of the time. He had one wife and nine concubines – with seventeen sons and fifteen daughters between them. The women in his household were not allowed to go out, and they had bound feet. Three concubines were Korean – Yuan had been stationed there for more than a decade when it was a tributary state of China. The Korean women had to endure the agony of squeezing their unbound feet into small, pointed shoes for him.

Yuan's personal habits were conservative. After bathrooms were introduced into the presidential palace, he still eschewed the flush toilet, preferring his old wooden stool. The bathtub was used only once a year; the rest of the time, his concubines cleaned his body with hot towels. The route to a healthy life for him was the ancient Chinese recipe of drinking human milk; two wet nurses were employed to squeeze their milk into a bowl for him. He mistrusted

Western medicine and was reluctant to see Western doctors, which may have hastened his death from uraemia.

And yet he was an outstanding reformer. During the reign of Empress Dowager Cixi, he had proved to be an effective implementer of her radical reforms, including replacing the entire old educational system with Western-style schools. Westerners and Chinese alike were impressed by Yuan's performance. The Rev. Lord William Gascoyne-Cecil, who travelled the country, wrote in his 1910 book *Changing China*, 'In the provinces where H. E. Yuan Shi-Kai ruled the schools approached in some degree to the level of Western efficiency.' Among his many other achievements was to reshape the Chinese army on Western models. As he commanded the allegiance of the army, Yuan became the most formidable force in the land – which he demonstrated flamboyantly. At one time his guards, selected for their giant size, wore uniforms in leopard-skin patterns, and looked to astonished onlookers like 'tigers and bears'.

Yuan's power, together with his obvious ambition, made him a threat to Cixi's successors after her death, who lacked her authority, and they removed him from court. When the republican uprisings started, they were forced to reinstate him, in the hope that he could command the army to fight the republicans. Yuan was able to use this position to negotiate a deal for himself: he would 'persuade' the throne to abdicate, in exchange for the republicans endorsing him to head the republic. He got what he wanted. Sun Yat-sen considered that Yuan had 'stolen' the position from him. But Westerners welcomed the choice. Having had dealings with him, they respected him and regarded him as a reformist statesman. The Chinese public liked the idea too. Yuan provided some crucial continuity as China moved from age-old monarchy to republic.

Indeed, the country went through a remarkably peaceful transition. The fabric of society was undisturbed and ordinary life went on as before. The biggest sign of change turned out to be in men's hairstyle: the plaited queue trailing at the back of their heads, imposed by the Manchus in the seventeenth century, disappeared. Shear-wielding petty government employees prowled through the streets and marketplaces, slashing people's long hair. Another noticeable change was in clothing, as new Western-influenced styles became fashionable. Otherwise, there were few visible differences. The nation was shifting to a new era with extraordinary ease.

The smooth transition had much to do with the fact that the last years of the Manchu dynasty and the early years of the republic shared the same goal: to turn China into a parliamentary democracy. Before her death in November 1908, Empress Dowager Cixi had committed to transforming China into a constitutional monarchy with an elected parliament, and had authorised voting procedures. In early 1909, within months of her death, elections of provincial assemblies (*zi-yi-ju*) were held in twenty-one of the country's twenty-two provinces (except Xinjiang) – the first phase in forming a national parliament. Although no more than 1.7 million of the population of 410 million were registered to vote, the precedent was set. This was the very first election in China's long history. Amazingly, people did not seem to find the idea of an election alien. Fair competition as the route for high office was deeply ingrained in Chinese culture. Historically, China's political elite had been selected through competitive nationwide examinations open to all males. That system had been abolished in 1905 as a part of the modernisation process. To the frustrated elite, parliament offered an alternative route to power, and a large number of educated men competed for membership.

By the time the republican revolution took place, it was generally accepted that the 'parliament' was the future institution of authority. It had also been agreed that there must be a ruling constitution. The republican delegates who had voted for Sun to be the interim president called themselves members of an 'acting parliament', guided by a 'provisional constitution' which had been drafted. This 'parliament' opposed Sun when he tried to retain office, and voted decisively for Yuan Shi-kai to take over. Time and again, the delegates demonstrated that they would not take Sun's orders. Sun wanted to be obeyed – he had already been regarded as 'dictatorial' by his comrades. He came to the conclusion that parliamentary politics was not for him.

The country, on the other hand, was busy building a democracy. Following the election of provincial assemblies in 1909, a general election was held throughout the twenty-two provinces in 1913 to elect members of China's first ever parliament. Ten per cent of the total population – close to 43 million men – registered to vote. Observers from the American consulate found that in the two counties they observed, sixty to seventy per cent of registered voters cast votes. A French scholar concluded: 'these elections truly did constitute a national consultation ... There were 40 million registered electors ... The political debate was open and free and was recorded by the press. In many respects, this poll seems to have been more democratic and more meaningful than any that followed.' This first general election produced 870 members of parliament, an impressive constellation of highly educated specialists outstanding in different fields. They were scheduled to arrive in Beijing by the end of March for the opening of parliament.

Sun took no part in this historic venture, even though he was the nominal head of a political party that ran an energetic election campaign. The party, the Kuomintang ('Nationalists'), was founded by a thirty-year-old new star, Song Jiao-ren, a moustachioed Hunanese who was a thinker of rare calibre. A believer in democracy, he had devised a whole blueprint on how it could work in China, and played the leading role in drafting the provisional constitution. He had taken over the ramshackle and dysfunctional United League that had been Sun's organisation and merged it with four other political groups to form the new party. Launched in Beijing in August 1912, the Nationalist party voted Sun its honorary head, but its real leader was Song, a born organiser and a brilliant orator. People flocked to hear him. (Later some likened his personal charisma to that of US president John Kennedy.) Under him, the Nationalists carried out an effective campaign and became the majority party in parliament. Song looked set to become the first prime minister of the Chinese republic, while Yuan would be elected president. There was no place for Sun Yat-sen.

★

Sun declared that he was giving up politics to devote himself to building national railways. People rejoiced at such a benign ambition. Interim President Yuan invited him to Beijing. Literally meaning the Northern Capital, Beijing is situated on the edge of the Gobi Desert. Sandstorms periodically swept the city, and streets would turn into muddy streams after heavy rain. But the capital's magnificence could not be diminished. Here camels were the beasts of burden, and they walked with their loads in a stately manner in long caravan trains. The streets were arranged like a chessboard, with all the main thoroughfares leading to the Forbidden City, a vast compound of palaces closed off by majestic outer walls. The last emperor, Pu Yi, still resided inside, in accordance with the abdication agreement.

Towards the end of the Manchu dynasty, Beijing had undergone modernisation while carefully preserving its old-world essence. Some streets were paved and lit and kept clean. But camels, horses and colourful mule carts were still an everyday sight alongside bicycles and motor cars. The city's telephone service was relatively new, and on its way to bettering that of Shanghai.

In Beijing, Sun appeared gracious in public, shouting 'Long live Grand President Yuan!' Yuan laid out the red carpet. But it was clear to astute observers that their relationship was far from amicable; indeed it was cut-throat. Earlier that year Yuan had survived an assassination attempt by a group who dropped explosives onto his carriage from the upstairs window of a restaurant. Men and horses in his entourage had been killed. Yuan believed the assassins were acting at the behest of Sun. Sun was scared that Yuan might seek revenge. In addition to the tight security arranged by Godfather Chen, Sun kept William Donald, his Australian adviser, close to him on all occasions. Donald suspected that Sun calculated that any would-be assassin 'would catch sight of Donald, a foreigner, and pause to reflect on international complications'.

Sun made a big thing about his retirement from politics, telling Yuan that all he asked was to be given full authority to build railways. At the core of this request was that the Chinese government guarantee any foreign loans he might raise and, moreover, allow him to be the only man in charge of those vast sums. These demands roused Yuan's suspicion. Indeed, Sun's interest in building railways seemed to focus exclusively on collecting money. He showed no interest in any other aspects of the monumental project, not even equipping himself with elementary information. He talked about the length of the railways to be built, but the figures did not come from any study or consultation with experts, or discussion with anyone else. Donald described how Sun appeared to conjure up the mileage. One day he walked into a room where Sun stood on a large map of China with an ink brush. He was drawing black lines all over it.

'"Oh," said Dr Sun, looking up, his cheeks puffy as a cherub's, "I want you to help me with this railway map ... I propose to build two hundred thousand *li* [100,000 km] of railways in ten years," he declared. "I'm marking them on this map. You see the thick lines running from one provincial capital to another? Well, they will be trunk lines. The others are laterals and less important connections."'

Every now and then, Sun would 'take a piece of cotton, dip it in water, wipe out a crooked line and mark a straight one in its place ... The doctor with a deft stroke built a hundred miles of rails in one place, a thousand in another.'

Interim President Yuan was convinced that Sun was using railway building as a ruse to appropriate huge sums of money, with which Sun could build an army and stage a grab for power. He countered by declining to promise automatic government guarantee for any money Sun might raise and put Sun's railway company under the jurisdiction of the transport ministry – whilst authorising Sun to be in charge of railway building.

Outsmarted by Yuan, Sun went to Japan on 11 February 1913. He had suffered a setback but appeared in public in high spirits, laughing as he reminisced about his past surreptitious trips to Japan. Greeted by crowds of well-wishers and much publicity from the Japanese press, Sun told everybody he was there not for political purposes but to raise funds for China's railway network. He raised no money, but stayed in Japan for forty days.

*

Charlie and Ei-ling accompanied Sun to Japan. Charlie was still under Sun's spell and loyally followed him, neglecting his business and leaving his wife in Shanghai. Ei-ling continued to work as Sun's assistant.

In March 1913, Mu-zhen came to Japan with Wan, her daughter with Sun, perhaps to tell him about the grave illness of their other daughter, Yan (who would die in June). Sun was travelling round and met his wife in Osaka for half an hour. Ei-ling volunteered to accompany Mu-zhen to Tokyo. In Tokyo, their car hit a telegraph pole and they were badly injured. Friends cabled Sun at once, telling him that Mu-zhen's condition was particularly serious.

Charlie was beside himself with anxiety. As he was arranging the logistics for the trip, he rushed up to Sun and asked, 'What shall we do with the luggage?' He was assuming that Sun would want to change trains to go to Tokyo and visit his wife and daughter. A Japanese friend in Sun's entourage noted that Sun was chatting merrily with them when Charlie approached. His smile froze and, 'very coolly', he replied, 'What's the point of going to Tokyo as we are not doctors?' Then, it seems, he remembered he had actually been trained as a doctor and added, 'Even if we were, it would be too late by the time we got there. Besides, we have appointments in Fukuoka.' Even this samurai-like Japanese man found Sun's lack of concern astonishing.

Sun never got to Tokyo to see his wife and daughter – or Ei-ling. Days after the car accident came the news of the assassination of the Nationalist founder and leader, Song Jiao-ren. On the evening of 20 March, he had been leading the delegation of his party to travel from Shanghai to Beijing by train to attend the opening of parliament. At the ticket barrier at Shanghai railway station, he was shot and died later in hospital.

As soon as the news reached him, Sun issued a statement denouncing Yuan Shi-kai for being responsible. He raced to Shanghai the very next day to start a war with the express goal of toppling Yuan.

The assassin, a penniless man named Woo, was easily caught. He confessed immediately, but then suddenly and inexplicably died in detention. The identity of who was ultimately responsible is still being argued about today, over a hundred years later. Both Yuan and Sun are suspects. They both had motives: Yuan would be threatened if he had to share power with Song; Sun stood to lose any political role and be completely marginalised. The victim himself did not suspect Yuan. After he was taken to hospital, he addressed his last words to 'President Yuan', urging Yuan not to let his death cast a shadow on the budding parliamentary politics in China. He sent no message to Sun, the honorific head of his own party.

Most other Nationalist leaders did not jump to accuse Yuan. They asked Sun what evidence he had for his accusation. Sun said he had suspicions but no evidence: Yuan 'must have given the order for the assassination,' even if there was no proof.

Huang Xing, the de facto number two among the republicans, argued that the case should be solved through legal procedure, as there was a working justice system. He was against Sun's call for war, protesting that this would wreck the infant republic, and in any event they might not win. Huang had actually been standing next to Song at the ticket barrier when the shot was fired, and could have been the victim if the bullet had missed its target. His dispute with Sun over whether to start the war led to their split. Sun denounced him, privately, as a 'snake' and 'very bad man'. (Huang died three years later, in 1916.) Sun went ahead and ordered a series of riots against Yuan to try to force Yuan to resign in favour of him. This, the first war in the infant republic, unleashed decades of bloody internal strife. The 'Father of China' was the man who fired the first shot.

The war against Interim President Yuan had little public support and quickly collapsed. Sun was expelled from the foreign Settlements in Shanghai, where he had been based. He fled to Japan in August 1913 – this time as an exile, tolerated by the Japanese authorities only as a potential card to play. In October, Yuan was inaugurated in Beijing as president of China, and was recognised and congratulated throughout the world. In spite of repeated attempts, Sun had failed to make it to the top. But he did not give up trying.

The Marriages of Ei-ling and Ching-ling

Charlie was now forced to prolong his stay in Japan: it had become unsafe for him to go back to Shanghai as a result of his association with Sun. He missed Shanghai, his home and his friends dreadfully. One day he saw Mrs Roberts, his American missionary friend and neighbour, at Tokyo railway station. He was so excited that he put his arms around her and embraced her most affectionately (opposite sexes embracing in public was unusual in Japan then). When her train pulled out, she recalled, he stood waving 'with his eyes full of tears, and never have I hated more to leave anyone'.

Charlie spent much time at the local YMCA. There he met a young man he liked very much. H.H. Kung was a conscientious, good-natured and mild-mannered widower a few years older than Ei-ling. He came from Shanxi province in north-west China where his family was wealthy enough to afford a comfortable living. The large family house, in traditional Chinese style, had solid and elegant black roof tiles and latticed windows overlooking multiple courtyards. H.H. shared Ei-ling's educational background, having attended an American mission school and colleges in America. He was a graduate of Oberlin College and had a master's degree from Yale (both in chemistry). Above all, he was a devout Christian, baptised at the age of twelve after a mission doctor cured him of a tumour. In Tokyo, Oberlin paid him a salary to work at the YMCA.

Charlie invited H.H. for dinner, where he met Ei-ling and they soon fell for each other. In old age he said in his memoir, 'We often walked in the park. My wife loves poetry. She majored in English literature in college ... This was really love!'

Ei-ling had developed reservations about Sun's behaviour, not only personal but also political. She and H.H. shared a strong dislike for Sun's war against President Yuan. Because Sun used the murder of Song Jiao-ren as the pretext to start the war, H.H., who was an admirer of Song, challenged Sun to produce proof of Yuan's guilt. Sun admitted that he had no proof, only suspicion. H.H. was disgusted. In his memoir, he said that he felt what Sun did was in the interest of Japan rather than China: some 'Japanese groups wanted to help Dr Sun in order to create turmoil in China. The Young Officers Group wanted to grab hold of China. They tried to help Dr Sun in order to divide China ... I felt that the Japanese were trying to make use of Dr Sun.' He 'warned' Sun 'of the danger of being used by the Japanese', and gave Sun a piece of his mind: 'I thought that the only thing was for Yuan Shi-kai and Dr Sun to cooperate so that China could be united and not divided.' H.H. was also averse to Sun's dictatorial ways. After Sun returned to Japan from his failed war, he wanted to cast aside the Nationalist party as it was reluctant to support his war, and set about forming a new party, Zhonghua-geming-dang ('Chinese Revolution Party'). Sun demanded that members of the new party must swear absolute obedience to him personally. H.H. was appalled, and stayed away from Sun's circle. A friend wrote that H.H. 'never identified himself with the revolutionaries, though offers had been made to him'. In fact he 'despise[d]' them, and 'loyally supported the [Yuan] government ... at the sacrifice of personal popularity with some of the Chinese students'. Ei-ling agreed with H.H. and steered herself, tactfully but unambiguously, away from Sun.

The couple decided to get married and lead their own life. In September 1914, their wedding took place in Yokohama, in a small church on a hill, attended by relatives and close friends. Sun was not there. Ei-ling remembered well the details of the day: her wedding outfit, a jacket and skirt, was pale pink satin and embroidered in a design of deeper pink plum blossoms. Her hair was decorated with matching fresh flowers. After a wedding breakfast at the Soongs' house, the newly-weds drove off to begin their honeymoon, Ei-ling in an apple-green satin dress embroidered with little golden birds. The weather was changeable that day, but whenever they were outside the rain gave way to bright sunshine, and Ei-ling's outfit and hair were not spoiled. She and her bridegroom both thought the timely spells of sunshine were 'very happy omens'.

They returned to H.H.'s birthplace in Shanxi to set up home. H.H. worked as the headmaster of the local mission school and she taught there. Soon he went into business and with her help became very rich.

Sun made his displeasure about the marriage known, but he was far from heart-broken – a younger and prettier woman had appeared on the scene to replace Ei-ling: her sister Ching-ling, fresh from Wesleyan College, Macon, Georgia, who had arrived the year before at the end of August 1913. Unlike the circumspect Ei-ling, the younger sister was passionate and impulsive. And she was a beauty with porcelain skin. She took over as Sun's English-language assistant. It seems that Ei-ling kept quiet about Sun's attempts to court her. It was in her character to be reticent about such matters.

When Ching-ling was at Wesleyan between 1908 and 1913, her contemporaries remembered 'her special tailored coat-suit' and 'her room, which always had the odor of Oriental perfume'. She was 'more quiet, even, than her elder sister', and was 'so very timid and "reserved"'. But there was another side to her. A fellow student recalled: 'I remember the excitement with which [Ching]-ling received the news that China had become a republic. I was interested because of the animation she showed. She had always seemed quiet and reserved and I was surprised to see her show so much life.' Not only life, but political passion. In her room, she had hung up the national flag of China under the Manchu throne, the Yellow Dragon. Then, her room-mate saw her climb 'on a chair to pull down the Chinese dragon from the wall when her father sent her the new flag of the Republic', and heard Ching-ling's 'dramatic exclamation as she threw the old banner on the floor and stamped on it. "Down with the Dragon! Up with the flag of the Republic!"'

Sun Yat-sen was her hero. En route to meet him – and join her father – in Japan, she wrote to one of her teachers, 'I am taking a box of California fruits to Dr Sun from his admirers here, and I am also the proud bearer of a private letter to him.' Because of her family's association with Sun, the twenty-year-old was feted by Sun's admirers. Ching-ling, who had a penchant for mocking self-importance, wrote to a teacher, Margaret Hall, 'I ... went from dinners to theaters till I got used to high living ... I was an "honored guest" at the Chinese Students' Reception ... When I came on board I found my cabin decorated with flowers and deluged with papers, magazines and fruits. I felt very important indeed.'

Secretly the young woman modelled herself on Joan of Arc, and identified with heroines who fought for a 'cause' and embraced self-sacrifice. In a photograph taken around this time she has a defiant expression, as if fighting some immense injustice. When she met Sun, his political career was at its lowest ebb since the founding of the republic. His battle against Yuan had just failed, and he was living in a small bare room like a student's bedsit, subsisting on small donations from Japanese sponsors. All this, which might have put off other women, inspired a stronger love for him. To her, Sun's misfortune was injustice itself, and he was making sacrifices for the new republic. This thought moved her. 'He was made of stern stuff,' she said with tender-hearted awe. She longed to devote herself to him and share the burden of the trials in his life. Ching-ling fell in love.

Life with Sun was also glamorous and fun. Though an enemy of the president of China, Sun, as the former – and first – interim president, was much sought after socially. Ching-ling was invited to many functions and outings with him and had an exciting time. One of her letters to an American friend, Allie Sleep, described staying at a famous hot-spring resort – 'the most magnificent hotel in the world' – and mixing in glittering company: 'let me ... tell you about someone who I'm crazy for you to marry. He is the ambassador from Austria & the most good-looking bachelor in the world. All the embassy people were there.'

In another beauty spot, 'We saw a miniature fruit garden. It was great. There were all sorts of dwarf trees – apples, pears, pomegranates, persimmon trees. Life is so intensely interesting now. If you love pretty things, you must come and visit the East soon. I shall chaperone you and shut my eyes when you must pick the forbidden fruits.'

She found that she and Sun had much in common. Though baptised, Sun was never a genuine believer. Ching-ling had been sceptical about missionaries since childhood, and was inclined to view them with a mocking eye. Enthusing about a dancing party with a Hawaiian band on board the ship to Japan, she added: 'even the missionaries join in – oh! only as spectators of course'. She would share jokes with Sun about the church. 'When I told him how in school in America, where on Sundays we were all driven to churches, I used to hide myself in the closet behind the clothes, and come out to write letters home when the girls and matrons had all left, he laughed heartily and said, "So we will both go to hell."'

Sun felt blessed by this burgeoning relationship. He was smitten. Once, Ching-ling was away in Shanghai visiting her mother. Sun got an emissary to find a place to which he could send her love letters that her mother must not see. Waiting for replies from her, he lost appetite and sleep – his landlady easily diagnosed that he was lovesick. He confided in her: 'I just can't get Ching-ling out of my head. Since I met her, I feel I encountered love for the first time in my life. I now know the sweetness and bitterness of being in love.'

Perhaps the surest sign of Sun Yat-sen being in love was that the man who thought of himself as 'the saviour of China', 'the only great and noble leader' who 'must be obeyed unconditionally', started to feel insecure about the relationship and feared Ching-ling's rejection. The young woman could tell and enjoyed teasing him, announcing that she was departing for America imminently, when in fact she had no such plans. Leaving for Shanghai on one trip she claimed that she was going to get married there and that the next time he saw her she would be with a husband. When there was talk that President Yuan wanted to make himself emperor, Ching-ling told Sun that she planned to marry Yuan and 'be an empress', or an imperial concubine. This sent Sun into a frenzy and he wrote to her father, asking him to clarify whether it was true. Charlie was baffled and replied that 'I am inclined to think it is a joke rather than anything else', 'it is a baby talk of her', 'do not believe such novel talk of a young girl who likes to make fun of herself'. Charlie, it seems, failed to see that a girl would only make such a joke with the man who she knew was hopelessly in love with her. Then, he returned to Shanghai, after he was reassured that it was 'perfectly safe' for him to do so. Alone with Sun in Japan, Ching-ling's love for him blossomed.

In summer 1915, Ching-ling came to Shanghai to ask her parents for permission to marry Sun. They were shocked by the news and refused to give their consent. The arguments against were many, not least the obvious age gap. He was forty-eight; she was barely in her twenties. There were many good Christian young men for her to marry, they pointed out. A Yung and a Dan had been coming to the house often. Why not one of them, or someone else? Charlie could not have forgotten the car accident in Tokyo, and Sun's cold refusal to go and see his badly injured wife. The man might be an ardent revolutionary, but he would not make a good husband. The most emotional objection, though, was that Sun already had a wife and children. If he were to divorce his wife, this would show 'his faithlessness to the wife who had shared his trials, and whose children are older' than Ching-ling. If he would not divorce his wife, Ching-ling would be a concubine, which would not only bring shame to herself and her family but also violate Christian principles. In an earlier letter to Sun (as a result of Ching-ling teasing Sun and claiming she had plans to marry Yuan Shi-kai as a concubine), Charlie had stated that 'we are a Christian family and no daughter of ours will become anybody's concubine, be he a king, an emperor or a president of the greatest on earth'. Ching-ling herself 'detests even to talk with [a] concubine', her father had added. She would not speak to a 'No. 2' who was in their company. Big Sister Ei-ling

The three Soong sisters in Shanghai, c. 1917, after they had all returned
from studying in America.
From left: Red Sister, Ching-ling; Big Sister, Ei-ling; Little Sister, May-ling.

Left: Ei-ling in a photo studio in Beijing, 1912.
Centre: Ching-ling, in North Carolina in 1912, with her friend Allie Sleep,
with whom she would correspond for six decades.
Right: May-ling, aged ten, at Wesleyan College in Georgia. She spent a decade in America,
after her parents sent her there to study when she was nine.

Soong Charlie, father of the three sisters, early 1880s, North Carolina. He was the first Chinese person in the American South to convert to Methodism, and he later returned to China as a preacher.

Sun Yat-sen's detention in the Chinese Legation in London in 1896 created an international incident, raised his profile and helped make him the 'Father of China'. In this British newspaper sketch, Sun is shown (centre, with coat on his arm) being released with a police escort. He is taking the arm of Dr Cantlie, his former teacher who had rescued him.

Sun (front row, sixth from left) was the 'interim president' when the republic was declared on 1 January 1912; but he had to step down on 13 February, the day this photograph was taken. Huang Xing (front row, fourth from left) was the second most influential man among the republicans.

Sun with his family in 1912: his wife Mu-zhen (seated with him); daughters, Yan (standing, far left) and Wan (far right); and son, Fo. Sun had not been with them for well over a decade. At this time, he was pursuing Ei-ling (in dark robe), who was working as his English-language assistant.

Chen Qi-mei, 'Godfather' of Shanghai's Green Gang, played a major role in the rise of Sun.

Yuan Shi-kai, China's first president after the country's first-ever general election in 1913.

Song Jiao-ren, who founded the Nationalist party in 1912, was assassinated in 1913 when he led the delegation of his party to attend the opening of China's first parliament. Sun Yat-sen used his murder to start the first war in the infant republic.

Mrs Soong Charlie (seated) with her two elder daughters, Ei-ling (left) and Ching-ling (right), c. 1913–14.

Members of the Soong family on the occasion of Ei-ling's wedding to H.H. Kung, in Japan, September 1914. From left: T.L., Charlie, T.A., Ching-ling, Mrs Soong, H.H., Ei-ling.

The whole Soong family were together in Shanghai in 1917 for the first time in a decade. From left: seated on the floor: Ei-ling, T.V., T.A., Ching-ling; seated: Charlie and Mrs Soong; standing: T.L., May-ling.

Mikhail Borodin (left), Moscow's representative to Sun Yat-sen, was in Canton to help Sun overthrow the Beijing government. He designated Wang Jing-wei (right) Sun's successor.

Moscow set up the Whampoa military academy for Sun. Ching-ling (Mme Sun Yat-sen since 1915) was at its founding ceremony in June 1924. On stage, from left: Liao Zhong-kai, Sun's closest aide; Chiang Kai-shek, head of the academy (and later May-ling's husband); Sun; Ching-ling.

Ching-ling with her husband in
1924 – the year before he died.

Sun Yat-sen's catafalque moving
into his gigantic mausoleum in Nanjing
in June 1929.

Ching-ling (front row, centre) as a top-ranking leader of the Nationalist party when it was at its most Leninist in March 1927. To her right: Sun's son, Fo; to her left: her brother T.V. and Eugene Chen (next to T.V.). Mao Ze-dong, later supreme leader of Communist China, is in the middle row, third from right. Deng Yan-da is in the back row, third from right. The backdrop is a portrait of Sun Yat-sen, flanked by the flags of the Nationalist party and of Nationalist China.

The three sisters (from left: Ching-ling, Ei-ling, May-ling), c. 1927, before Chiang Kai-shek drove the Communists out of the Nationalist party. This is possibly the last picture of the sisters before they publicly espoused antagonistic political camps.

The wedding of May-ling and Chiang Kai-shek, December 1927. She became the first lady of China when Chiang established a Nationalist government in 1928.

also tried to talk her out of the idea, which infuriated Ching-ling. Amid one heated confrontation, Ching-ling fainted. She was carried upstairs to her bedroom, and the door was locked from the outside. During the following weeks, there were many exhausting scenes.

While Ching-ling was struggling against her family in Shanghai, Sun's wife arrived in Japan in September at his invitation to discuss a divorce. Mu-zhen was in grief as Sun's brother Ah Mi, who had been supporting her family all those years, had died earlier that year, aged sixty-one. She had lost the man who really cared for her and her children. Having just been dealt this blow, she accepted her faithless husband's announcement with indifference. She returned home to Macau, where she lived for another four decades. She and Sun never saw each other again.

There was no way, though, to seal their de facto divorce with a definitive document. They had been married in the traditional way, which did not provide for an honourable divorce for the woman. A divorce document was usually 'a letter to discard the wife' (xiu-shu). Sun did not wish to humiliate Mu-zhen in this manner.

He sent an envoy to Shanghai to bring Ching-ling to Japan, claiming that he was now divorced legally. In the early hours of one autumn night, the lovestruck young woman sneaked out of her family home and boarded a ship for Japan. According to the surveillance records of the Japanese government, Sun met her at Tokyo station on 25 October 1915, and they were married the next day. The ceremony was conducted by a Wada Mizu at his home, during which the couple signed three copies of a 'marriage contract' prepared by Wada in Japanese. Ching-ling, who spoke no Japanese, believed that Wada was a 'famous lawyer', and that the 'contract' had been registered with the Tokyo government and was legally binding. As a matter of fact, Wada Mizu was no lawyer – he was the owner of a small trading company – and the Tokyo government did not register marriages of foreigners. The 'marriage contract' was just a piece of paper Wada had produced and then signed as a 'witness', and it had no legal effect. The whole thing was a show for the benefit of the twenty-one-year-old, who was mission-school educated, and to whom a legal marriage was essential.

Sun invited none of his friends to the ceremony except one most faithful and dependable man, Liao Zhong-kai, who acted as the second 'witness'. Liao brought his eleven-year-old daughter Cynthia, who translated for the bride.

After the signing, Wada gave the newly-weds a quick supper. All three then left in the car that had brought Sun. It first dropped Wada at a geisha restaurant; Wada would enjoy his real dinner there. Then the car took the Suns home. It was no longer like a student's digs, but a 'little cozy house hidden among red maples', which Ching-ling loved. She said the wedding was 'the simplest possible', but 'we both hate ceremony and the like'.

The day after the wedding, her parents appeared on their doorstep. Ching-ling had left them a letter when she sneaked out of the house, and they had taken the next ship to Japan. Years later, Ching-ling wrote to her friend and biographer Israel Epstein (whom she called Eppy) about how they desperately 'tried to persuade me to leave my husband and return home ... My mother wept and my father who was ill with liver disease pleaded ... He even went to the Japanese government to appeal ... saying that I was under age and had been forced into marriage! Naturally, the Japan gov't couldn't intervene. Although full of pity for my parents – I cried bitterly also – I refused to leave my husband. Well, Eppy, altho' this transpired over half a century ago I still feel as if it happened a few months ago.'

The fact that Charlie went to the Japanese government to denounce Sun shows the extent of his distress. He had believed Sun to be 'noble' and someone who would never 'practice deception on ... friends'. Now his idol let him down badly. He confided to his old missionary friend Bill Burke, 'Bill, I was never so hurt in my life.' Charlie never forgave Sun. Ei-ling and her husband observed that his break with Sun 'has been complete ... and the old friendship has become an enmity'.

The news of the marriage went public. The missionaries regarded Ching-ling as having eloped and wanted Charlie to bring her back. Sun's comrades declined to recognise her as the leader's wife, calling her not 'Mrs Sun' but 'Miss Soong'.

Ching-ling disregarded all this and lived in the firm belief of the righteousness of their union. She was wrapped up in her own happiness, as she wrote to her friend Allie a few weeks later:

> I am so absent-minded these days, that I am in doubt whether or not I mailed your letter. To be doubly sure I am scribbling a few lines to say that I am quite concerned [sic, contented] & happy & feel glad that I was brave enough to overcome my fears and doubts & decided to marry.
>
> I feel settled down and have such a domestic feeling about me. I am *so busy* helping my husband with his work, answering his correspondence and taking charge of all cablegrams & deciphering them into Chinese. And I hope some day that all my labors & sacrifices will be repaid by seeing China freed from the bondage of a tyrant and a monarchist and stand as a Republic, in the best sense of the word.

Talking about making 'sacrifices' for the marriage suggests that deep down Ching-ling knew that her marriage was irregular. She accepted this, telling herself that her action was for the greater good. Their marriage was real in all but a formal sense. Sun kept his vows and remained faithful; and Ching-ling was ready to give her life for him.

Meanwhile, President Yuan, popular and securely in office, started to yearn for something more. He had always hankered for the crown, and in 1915, announced that he was returning China to monarchy, with himself as the emperor. The aspiring monarch, however, was anxious about his own lack of legitimacy. In the Forbidden City, there was a carved dragon suspended from the ceiling over the throne, holding a large silver ball between its teeth. People believed that the ball would drop on anyone who sat on the throne if they did not belong there. Yuan was so troubled that the ball might crush him that he had the seat moved away from the carved dragon. Public opinion, which had been highly vocal for more than a decade, came out in force against turning back the clock. So did his colleagues and army chiefs. Republicanism was clearly there to stay. Eighty-three days after announcing his intention to become emperor, on 22 March 1916 Yuan called off the whole enterprise. He never made it to the throne.*

Yuan's unsuccessful bid to become emperor wrecked his reputation, and Sun Yat-sen was eager to exploit Yuan's vulnerability. Sun's worry was that Yuan might resign as president, in which case, as the constitution stipulated, Vice President Li Yuan-hong would automatically succeed and Sun would be deprived of a discredited and weak target. Li, the much-liked army chief who had helped lead the 1911 revolution, had emerged as an able and popular statesman. If Yuan were to resign, Sun would have no grounds to replace Li. It was critical that his men must act to overthrow Yuan at once. From Japan, Sun sent urgent cables to his followers in China, ordering them to create havoc immediately. He placed high hopes especially on Godfather Chen, and instructed him to organise uprisings in Shanghai right away.

Chen, in Shanghai clandestinely, was unable to do so. As well as the Beijing government, the Settlement authorities were after him. They were fed up with him for turning Shanghai into a battleground – in addition to making the city a paradise for gangsters. During the republican revolution in 1911–12, when the Godfather controlled the city, he had protected the gangs rather than suppress them, unlike many other republican provincial chiefs who turned on their former comrades. Gangsters had converged on Shanghai and flourished there.

Now the gangs themselves turned their backs on him. Chen had gone beyond the gangsters' normal trade and got involved in

---

* In July 1917, there was another attempt at restoring the monarchy, by General Zhang Xun, who, remained loyal to the Manchu throne. He and his troops kept the Manchu-style hair, the queue, and Zhang was nicknamed the 'Queue General'. His army entered Beijing and put Pu Yi, the last emperor, on the throne in the Forbidden City. But there was scant support for the restoration. Even the courtiers summoned to the palace to draft imperial decrees felt 'too irritated and upset to swallow' the royal lunch. Newspaper boys peddling the decrees cried, 'Buy antique! Antique for six coppers! This will be a piece of antique in a few days!' The charade lasted only twelve days.

politics – and emerged on the losing side. He was no longer a powerful godfather but only a failed revolutionary. Not only was he unable to bring off successful disturbances, he was unable to raise any funds. When he had been the boss of Shanghai, he had extracted huge sums from banks and businesses by intimidation. When the Shanghai manager of the Bank of China argued that he could not simply hand over the bank's money, the Godfather had had him arrested and the bank paid up. Now he could only dream of such easy solutions. He had no means to pay for revolts or mutinies, or as many assassinations as he would have liked. Indeed President Yuan had picked up his weapon and proved a far more desirable patron for hit men.

As Chen made little headway and produced only a string of failures, Sun Yat-sen grew impatient and scornful. He was furious that he now had to fund the Godfather, rather than the other way round. He sneaked into Shanghai to take personal charge, which was quite uncharacteristic and showed how much of a hurry he was in. Yuan might resign any minute, as he was under tremendous pressure to do so. Sun told off the Godfather in deeply wounding words when they met, leaving Chen dejected. Poor health had already been tormenting him, to the point that he had given up caring whether he lived or died. To people around him, he looked 'withered and spiritless like a skeleton'. Although on the wanted list, he was still strolling down the streets of Shanghai on his own, without a bodyguard. The fact was that he could not afford one. Then, almost casually, he walked into a fatal trap.

A fellow revolutionary who had secretly turned informer one day brought him a 'business deal' with a 'mining company'. The deal promised to add substantially to Sun's coffer, and Chen agreed to a meeting. On 18 May 1916, he went to a house that he often used to meet with the 'company representatives', and was alone in the sitting room with five of them. There he was shot in the head and killed, aged thirty-eight. He had no security men with him. The assassins had been let into the house without being searched for weapons. All this seems extraordinarily careless, particularly as he knew – and Sun knew – that the 'mining company' was a sham. Chen seems to have thought that if he was lucky, he would get the money for Sun; if not, he might as well die.

After he was shot dead, the owner of the house wanted his corpse removed at once. There had been a few comrades in another room, but nobody was willing to do the job. The later Generalissimo Chiang Kai-shek, who had killed a political rival of Sun's at the order of Chen, worshipped the Godfather as a mentor and loved him as a brother. He raced over and brought Chen's body to his own house, where he set up a mourning shrine. Few turned up to pay their respects. Sun Yat-sen, his own life in danger, did not come. The once fearsome Godfather had died a lonely man. His body was kept in storage, as his family could not afford a proper burial. Chiang Kai-shek was aggrieved. He wrote a bitter eulogy, much of it a cascade of loathing directed at Chen's 'friends'. Without mentioning Sun's name, he hinted that Sun had treated the man who had played an irreplaceable role in advancing his career shabbily, and that this had played a role in Chen's death.

When the news of the assassination of Godfather Chen reached Japan, Ching-ling jumped onto the next ship and raced over to Shanghai to be with her husband. She was worried sick and felt convinced that he would only be safe if she was there. She arrived early the next morning. When she walked down the gangway through the dispersing mist, Sun's familiar figure could be seen waiting on shore. It was most unusual for Sun to meet a ship – he was the 'Big Busy Man', as Ching-ling had fondly nicknamed him. And it was particularly risky for him at this moment. It seems that Sun was touched by Ching-ling's love and wanted to show his appreciation. She was moved by his gesture, and was also immensely relieved to see that he was unharmed.

Eighteen days after her arrival President Yuan died of uraemia, without resigning from office, at the age of fifty-six. Vice President Li succeeded him automatically. Sun had lost his discredited target. He suspended the war he had started, and contemplated how to deal with Li. For Ching-ling, her husband would now be safe. She felt very happy.

6

To Become Mme Sun

From past experience, Sun knew that President Li had no burning ambition to rule China. He sent good-will gestures to Li, hoping that Li would hand the top position to him. Li disappointed him; he only offered him a special title: senior adviser to the government. Sun turned it down in disgust, and tried to convince some Nationalist members of parliament to demand that he be made the president. As there was no constitutional basis for this move, the Nationalists declined to oblige. In the end, some tentatively suggested that perhaps they could propose Sun to be the *vice* president. When his emissary reported this, Sun flew into a towering rage and told him, 'You must be careful. I am going to start a rebellion now ... I will launch a military campaign. You lot had better be careful.'

Sun began preparing a war against the Li government. For this he needed money. The First World War gave him a chance. In early 1917, America broke diplomatic relations with Germany and invited China to take similar action. America had traditionally been China's friend, and promised China that it would have much to gain if it joined the Allies. The parliament debated the issue for weeks, with ministers from the Allies and Germany listening from the public galleries. On 10 March, it approved cutting off relations with Germany. Documents from German archives reveal that Germany had tried to bribe Beijing out of making the decision, and had particularly targeted Prime Minister Duan Qi-rui, a former soldier who spearheaded the move to join the Allies. The Germans offered

Duan $1 million for himself personally; Duan turned it down flat. (A former protégé of Yuan Shi-kai, Duan had also been instrumental in forcing his patron to abandon his emperor dream.)

Germany wanted to have Duan removed and the policy reversed. It started secret talks with Sun Yat-sen, through Sun's liaison Abel Tsao. The German consul general in Shanghai, Herr Knipping, reported to Berlin that Sun was eager to collaborate, and that in return, he 'demanded two million dollars'. The German chancellor agreed, and Sun got 1.5 million Mexican silver dollars (one of the currencies used in China at the time).* This was Sun's first big foreign sponsorship.

Sun planned to use the money to set up his base and settled on Canton, the prosperous southern coastal city cradled by low hills with a population of a million. In his youth Sun had shunned it for its feel of antiquity. Now modernisation had begun. Old alleys were being broadened into roads for automobiles. On the new, potholed avenues, cars rocked their passengers wildly on the satin-covered seats. For Sun, most importantly, a group of members of parliament from Beijing were there who could form his initial support base. China's first parliament had seemed chaotic and messy as reported by the free press, and there had been petitions for a fresh election. Under this pressure, President Li announced the suspension of parliament in June 1917 and called a new election – a move that was actually a violation of the constitution. Around a hundred members of parliament left Beijing in protest, and Sun Yat-sen, with the German money, was able to pay for most of them to come and operate in Canton. Also with the German money he persuaded a cash-strapped fleet under an old friend, Cheng Bi-guang, to follow him. In August, Sun formed a 'government' in Canton to rival Beijing, claiming he was defending the constitution.†

---

* The money was transferred to Canton through the Holland Bank and the Bank of Taiwan – according to a report by the American consul general P. S. Heintzleman.

† Having taken the German money, Sun's government declared war on Germany when it looked doomed.

To the assembled members of parliament Sun demanded to be made the 'provisional president' of China. They balked, arguing that according to the constitution their number was insufficient to elect Sun to office. It was not their aim to overthrow Beijing anyway; they only wanted the parliament to be reinstated. Sun erupted into one of his by now frequent mighty rages, and hurled insults at the Speaker. A compromise was reached and the title 'grand marshal' was bestowed on Sun (with the Canton government called a 'military government'). Sun assumed the title with much pomp, donning a gold-tasselled and red-sashed uniform, a plume, and a ceremonial sword.

Sun at once started a war against Beijing. Soldiers were paid fifteen yuan a month if they enlisted with weapons and ten yuan if without. His German funds depleted fast. The grand marshal had no authority to raise taxes, and when he ordered the Canton administrators to hand over money, they refused. Sun burst into another torrent of verbal abuse, and issued orders to the navy to shell the office building. The navy said no; Sun boarded a ship and fired the cannon into the city himself. This incensed and estranged the naval chief, Cheng Bi-guang. Before long, this old friend of Sun's was shot dead next to a pier. According to one of Sun's side-kicks who had been closely involved in this and other assassinations, Sun's secretary Zhu Zhi-xin arranged the killing. Sun was later reported to say that the death was 'an execution, for disobeying orders'.

The members of parliament were horrified by this heavy-handed 'dictatorship'. They regretted being associated with Sun and found a way to force him to leave. They voted to abolish the post of grand marshal, and replaced it with a collective leadership of seven men, of whom Sun was one. They had calculated that Sun would not tolerate shared leadership. Indeed, Sun resigned at once and left Canton on 21 May 1918. He had been the grand marshal for less than a year.

People who saw him at this time were struck by how shrunken he looked: at fifty-one: his hair thin and grey, his shoulders drooping, his expression spiritless. One eye was infected and badly swollen, leaking a trail of tears down his drawn face. He was gnawed by a deep grievance. He, the first man to advocate republicanism, had not been given his due. His greatness was not properly recognised, and what he deserved – to be president of China – persistently eluded him. He felt 'completely and helplessly alone', a situation which, he said, was 'not just my plight, but the plight of the republic'.

Ching-ling had mostly stayed in Shanghai while Sun was in Canton. Little Sister May-ling came home to Shanghai from America in July 1917, after an absence of ten years; then their father was in the throes of cancer and died on 3 May 1918. These events, and the fact that Sun was not in Shanghai, brought Ching-ling back together with her family.

When Canton threw Sun out, he wanted to come to Shanghai, and Ching-ling secured the French consul's consent that he could live with his wife in the French Concession. The Suns' home was a European-style mansion with a large garden. It sat at the bottom of a short cul-de-sac with just a couple of other houses in front – which made it relatively easy to guard. On the sitting-room wall was a picture of George Washington. Sun took it seriously when people sometimes said that he was China's George Washington.

The married Ching-ling grew more beautiful than before. Julian Carr, the tobacco magnate from North Carolina who had been her father's patron from the old days, visited Shanghai around this time, and commented that she was 'the handsomest young woman' he saw in China.

The Suns had many visitors, and she charmed them all. George Sokolsky, an American reporter who frequented the house, remarked that she had 'a personality so sweet and lovable' that she quite easily overshadowed her husband. Her 'presence in the room, her friendly laughter, her refined conversation left an impression more lasting than did the personality of the somewhat dour and always dreamy political leader'. For each visitor, Ching-ling 'had a warm welcome, a gentle manner, a kind word', but she was also 'there to save the doctor's time and energy, to safeguard his peace'. In the morning, she played tennis with him. After breakfast, he read and wrote, and she copied out his manuscripts. She worked as his secretary and was self-effacing. 'She appeared always on the scene; yet always she was behind the doctor, not beside him ... guarding the great man ... never once obtruding her personality in a manner to deflect even a ray of glory from her husband.'

With her as his secretary, Sun wrote a pamphlet grandly titled *The Sun Theory*, an *oeuvre* of which he was mightily proud. It contained one theme: 'It's easier done than said' (*xing-yi-zhi-nan*), a reversal of the old proverb 'It's easier said than done'. Sun announced that the old proverb was the source of all the ills of the country, and that his aphorism was 'the only way to save China', even 'the truth of the universe'. To argue his case, he started with stating the desirability of foods like bean curd, wood-ear fungus and pigs' intestines, followed by a spiel about the importance of money, with lectures thrown in about language, Darwin, science, Japanese reforms and the necessity of developing the economy. All these subjects were lumped together in no particular order, regardless of coherence or relevance.

With this hotchpotch Sun asserted the superiority of the man who had 'said' it first. By this, he meant himself, who had been the first to advocate republicanism. And he maintained that such a man must be obeyed. The leading liberal scholar of the day, Hu Shih, spotted what Sun was getting at and pointed out sharply: Sun wrote the book to say 'Obey me.' 'Do as I say.' 'After a careful study of this book, we cannot but conclude that this is the only possible explanation.'

Ching-ling, who had written impressively argued essays in her college days and liked to poke fun at self-importance, revered this stuff. Her sister May-ling, perceptive, with superb intuitive intelligence, observed to her friend Emma Mills: 'Do you know, I have noticed that the most successful men are usually not the ones with great powers as geniuses but the ones who had such ultimate faith in their own selves that invariably they hypnotise others to that belief as well as themselves.'

Ching-ling was certainly mesmerised by her husband. Writing to Allie, she said, 'I still retain my admiration for him, & am as much a devoted worshipper of his character as I ever was ... And the best thing I could wish for you, dear Allie, is that you may soon find your own ideals materialized into a human ideal & surely then happiness will come. Of course you are very happy now, too, but the happiness of a married life is different & much superior.'

Sun lived for more than two years in Shanghai. During that time, another general election was held, in 1918, which produced the next president, Hsu Shih-chang, a politician known as 'a scholar and a gentleman' and respected for his integrity. The election was boycotted by five Canton-influenced provinces, but the government elected by the rest of the country was recognised internationally. President Hsu made offers of peace and reunification to Canton, and people responded, with many in key positions leaving the southern city. Sun plotted to get back to Canton and continue his war, this time against President Hsu. For him power could only come through the barrel of the gun. When the nationalistic May Fourth student demonstration took place in 1919 (an event regarded as a milestone in Chinese history), some young people called to seek his advice. Sun showed scant interest in their movement, but said, 'I'll give you 500 guns to take care of the Beijing government. What do you say?' He sent three different groups of envoys to Germany to invite the German army to invade China and attack Beijing. The Germans thought he was 'crazy'. He implored Japan via its consul in Shanghai to back him in his war, offering to give Japan Manchuria and Mongolia when he succeeded. The Japanese ignored him.

It was now nearly a decade since China had first functioned as an electoral democracy. As the society was experiencing unprecedented freedom, smart ambitious people mulled over unconventional ideas about how the country should be run, trying to get their ideas put into practice. One such was Ch'en Chiung-ming, an officer of the Cantonese army. Before he embarked on a military career, he had trained as a lawyer and was elected a member of the provincial assembly in Guangdong in 1909. Officer Ch'en subscribed to the belief that China was too big to be run by a highly centralised government and a better alternative would be a federal system (like that of the United States). To start with, he believed, each province should have great autonomy and run its affairs well. To turn his vision into reality, Officer Ch'en set his heart on making Guangdong province, with Canton as its capital, a showcase for what he planned to do: build schools, houses, roads, parks and other public facilities. His problem was that he was only an officer, with no mandate to govern the province, and nobody would listen to him. He thought of Sun Yat-sen and fancied he could use Sun's name for his purpose. Sun seized the chance to get him to take over Canton, and arrived himself in November 1920.

Officer Ch'en soon regretted becoming bedfellows with Sun. His goal was poles apart from Sun's, which was to use Canton as a base to wage wars in order to rule the whole of China. A contest of wills quickly ensued. And in this, the officer was no match for Sun. In no time, Sun set up another government to rival Beijing. And this time, unlike in 1917 when he had only managed to be made grand marshal, he had himself declared the 'grand president of the Chinese Republic' on 7 April 1921. Thus Sun Yat-sen, the Father of China, split the country and formed a breakaway state, against the elected and internationally recognised government – something no other province did.

After visiting Canton and Sun, the US military attaché Major Magruder observed that Sun was driven by the 'one motive in life and that of self-aggrandizement', and that for this personal goal he would stop at nothing and would sacrifice anyone. Magruder's successor, Major Philean, made the same observation: 'His eyes are fixed on [Beijing] – his destination. He believes that the whole of China will be at his feet ... and the whole country will obey him.'

In May 1922, Sun began a military drive north to try to overthrow President Hsu, on the grounds that Hsu had not been elected by all twenty-two provinces. Hsu did not want another war and offered to resign, together with Sun, to pave the way for a new election. He tendered his resignation immediately after he completed a major diplomatic manoeuvre. The Japanese had been occupying a part of Shandong province since the First World War. At the post-war

Versailles Conference in 1919, China had failed to get it back, which triggered the nationalistic May Fourth student protest. Through skilful negotiations, Hsu's government successfully compelled the Japanese to return the territory in 1922. After he signed the ratification in Beijing on 2 June, President Hsu handed in his resignation the same morning, and left the capital in the afternoon. (This diplomatic victory has been airbrushed out of history books.)

Sun had not expected that Hsu would give up his presidency so easily and had rashly said that he would resign with Hsu. Now public opinion called on him to fulfil his promise, and to stop his war. He acted as though he had said no such thing. Officer Ch'en and his troops, who had long wanted peace, were fed up and made it clear that they would not fight for him; they demanded Sun's resignation in a press release. On 12 June, Sun called a press conference, at which he denounced the Ch'en army in yet another tirade of abuse. Threateningly, he declared: 'People say Sun Yat-sen is "a big cannon" [someone who brags wildly], I will show you what the big cannon really is this time. I will use eight-inch cannons to fire poison gas ... and reduce the sixty-plus battalions of the Ch'en Army to dust within three hours. It's true that to slaughter more than sixty battalions of army men, and frighten the inhabitants of the entire city, is too violent and cruel; but if I don't do this, they will not mend their ways.' He asked the newspapers to publicise his threats.

This was the last straw for Officer Ch'en. He made up his mind to drive Sun out. During the next few days, soldiers were deployed around Sun's 'presidential palace', which sat at the foot of a hill. Halfway up the low hill, at the end of a decorated covered walk, was his residence, an elegant villa in a lush garden. It enjoyed a wide view of the city streets below and the Pearl River beyond. From this presidential compound, Sun received messages urging him to leave. He refused.

About an hour after midnight on 16 June, a warning came that the compound would be attacked at dawn. Sun decided he had better escape. He put on a white cotton summer gown and a pair of sunglasses, and left with a few guards in plain clothes, taking with him the most secret documents. Once down from the house they were in the streets of Canton. They took rickshaws to the pier nearby, where they hired a motorboat which carried them to a gunboat loyal to Sun. In no time, within an hour and a half at the most, Sun was safe. He did not bring his wife with him.

At dawn, Officer Ch'en's army began to attack the Suns' house, unaware that the grand president had already gone. As Ching-ling was still in the presidential palace, Sun's guards, numbering more than fifty, vigorously fought back.

Ching-ling had volunteered to stay and cover Sun's flight. 'I thought it would be inconvenient for him to have a woman along with him, and urged him to leave me behind for the time being,' she wrote for a Shanghai newspaper immediately after the event. She said elsewhere that she had told her husband, 'China can do without me; it cannot do without you.' In love, she was ready to sacrifice herself for him.

What the young woman did not realise was that *after* he had reached safety, her husband still did not want her to escape. He was on the gunboat many hours before dawn, and well before the scheduled attack by Officer Ch'en's army. There was ample time for him to have sent Ching-ling a message telling her that he was safe – and that she could leave. But he did not. He had in fact dispatched a man back to the presidential palace – but only 'to reconnoitre', not to do anything else. So Ching-ling had no idea that her husband had reached safe haven, and she bravely stayed put.

As day broke, she wrote, the attackers began to charge at her house. Sun's guards fought back using 'rifles and machine guns, while the enemy employed field guns ... My bath was smashed to bits ... By eight o'clock our store of ammunition was running low, so we decided to stop shooting and preserve what was left until the last possible moment.' It was only then that she consented to depart. She and three attendants crawled along the covered walk to try to get down the hill. 'The enemy soon concentrated fire on this passage and flying bullets whistled about our ears. Twice bullets brushed past my temple without injuring me.'

Unlike her husband's smooth exit, her flight was 'a life and death struggle'. 'From eight in the morning till four that afternoon we were literally buried in a hell of constant gunfire. Bullets flew in all directions. Once the entire ceiling of a room I had left only a few minutes before collapsed.'

One of the attendants was struck by a bullet and could not go on. Wearing his hat and a raincoat of Sun's, Ching-ling made it into the streets with two other guards. She saw soldiers everywhere, 'who had by this time gone completely mad'.

I was absolutely exhausted, and begged the guards to shoot me. Instead they dragged me forward, one on each side supporting me ... Corpses lay about everywhere ... Once we saw two men squatting face to face under a roof. Closer observation revealed that they were dead, their eyes wide open. They must have been killed by stray bullets.

Again our way was cut off by a group of the mob running out of a little passage. The whisper ran through our party that we should lie flat in the street, pretending to be dead. In this way we were left unmolested; then we rose and continued our journey. My guards advised me to avoid looking at the corpses lest I should faint. Half an hour later, when the rifle shots were thinning out, we came to a small farmhouse. The owner tried to drive us out, fearing the consequences of sheltering us; his attempt was forestalled, however, by a timely swoon on my part.

I woke up to find the guards washing me with cold water and fanning me. One of them went out to see what he could of the way things were going, when suddenly there came a tattoo of rifle shots. The guard indoors rushed to shut the door; he told me that the other one had been struck by a bullet and was probably dead by this time.

While the firing subsided I disguised myself as an old countrywoman, and with the guard in the guise of a pedlar we left the cottage. I picked up a basket and a few vegetables on the way, and carried them with me. At last we reached the house of a friend ... we spent the night there. Shelling never ceased the entire night, and our relief was enormous when we heard cannon shots at last from the gunboats. Dr Sun, then, was safe.

So she did not know that Sun was safe until then. This was why she had stayed in the presidential palace when Officer Ch'en's army charged. Sun clearly intended to make his wife the bait so that the charge would develop into a heated battle. This gave Sun an excuse to bombard Canton from his gunboats. Scores of local and foreign representatives came to implore him to stop shelling, and he shut them up by pointing to the attack on his house by Ch'en's army. In a press release, he claimed that the attack had started 'several minutes after' he escaped and 'I ordered the navy to open fire because I am outraged and because I am determined that justice should be done.'

As his cannons roared, Sun was thrilled. People around him remembered that he 'chatted and laughed', and proclaimed that 'I am satisfied with the battle today!'

At this moment, his wife's life was hanging in the balance. After two hellish days and nights, she was at last able to make a telephone call to a friend, who managed to send a boat to collect her and escort her to Sun's gunboat. Throughout her escape from death, her husband did not lift a finger to help her. They met briefly, after which she left for home in Shanghai.

During her flight, Ching-ling suffered a miscarriage; she was told she would never be able to conceive again.

The blow was crushing. Ching-ling longed for children. Heartache would shadow most of her life. In the years to follow, close friends noticed that any talk to do with childbirth caused her to look 'pained' and to 'change the subject'. Her reaction was 'almost pathological'. Later, her unfulfilled need to have children would fundamentally affect her behaviour. In the immediate aftermath, she omitted to mention the miscarriage when she wrote her account. It was too raw. Her anguish was noticed by the American friend of her sister May-ling, Emma Mills, who was in

Shanghai at the time and saw Ching-ling arriving, incognito, in a peasant woman's outfit. 'Small, slight, very pale, and altogether the loneliest thing I have ever seen,' Emma wrote in her diary. (She stayed for supper and helped May-ling with a tailor who came by to put together some clothes for Ching-ling.)

What her husband did to her inevitably dawned on Ching-ling. She had very nearly died; she had lost her child and had no hope of ever having children. For Sun to use her to cover his escape may be excused, but for him to set her up as a target to bring about an enemy assault, knowing that she was likely to die – that was too much. Such behaviour would be enough to kill the love of any normal woman. And Ching-ling's love for Sun did not survive the ordeal. Later, her friend, the American journalist Edgar Snow, asked her how she fell in love with Sun. Snow recorded: '"I didn't fall in love," she said slowly. "It was hero-worship from afar. It was a romantic girl's idea when I ran away to work for him … I wanted to save China and Dr Sun was the one man who could do it, so I wanted to help him."'

The love-stricken letters she wrote tell a different story. She had been in love; it was just that the unreserved, whole-hearted love had died. The scales fell from her eyes and she saw the ugly side of her husband. He was no nobler, no better than she and did not deserve her sacrifice. Detachment replaced passion in her relationship with him. She did not wish to leave him, but she wanted to do 'deals'. And Ching-ling worked out exactly what she would ask for herself: she wanted to play a public role as his political partner. She would no longer go on as his secretary, typing away in the background when Sun and visitors were having discussions. She would join the talks. And she would appear in public side by side with him – she had made this request in the past but it had been turned down, on the grounds that the public were not used to seeing their leaders' wives. Now, she was determined to have her way. Most likely, she wrote the account of her escape for the Shanghai paper in order to show Sun and his associates what she had been through, and to prove to them she had earned the right to have her demands met.

Meanwhile, Sun's shelling of Canton failed to get him back to the city. In August he met up with his wife in Shanghai, and agreed to Ching-ling's demands. He seemed to feel he was in his wife's debt. In the future he would ask his associates to 'look after' Ching-ling. Those who had opposed her appearing in public as Sun's partner no longer did so; they were bowled over by her bravery and her self-sacrifice for Sun. They started to treat her reverently.

From now on, an assertive Ching-ling emerged in the public eye, and gained a high profile in her own right (starting the practice of a leader's spouse being a public figure). She wrote to her American friend Allie on 15 September: 'Will you do me a great favour? I am in need of some visiting cards of the latest fashion. Will you please order 200 cards for me *at once* from Tiffany's or any other good engraving store. Please choose the style of type that is simple yet beautiful. Simply the name on the card: Mrs SUN YAT-SEN.'

Later, the simple 'Mrs' was deemed inadequate for the status of the consort of the Father of China. The French title of respect, 'Madame', replaced it, and Ching-ling became known as Mme Sun Yat-sen.

'I wish to follow the example of my friend Lenin'

It was after Sun was driven out of Canton in summer 1922 that Russia started to play a big part in the lives of both him and Madame Sun.

He had established contact with the new Bolshevik state by cabling Lenin in 1918. This time, having escaped onto the gunboat in June, he sent a messenger to see Moscow's men in Shanghai, scribbling a few lines on a page torn from a student's exercise book. The note was addressed to Chicherin, People's Commissar for Foreign Affairs, ending with 'Best regards' to Lenin. Sun wrote it in English: 'I suffer a grave crisis brought about by [Officer Ch'en], the man who owes me absolutely everything.' Russia responded with alacrity. It needed him, right at this moment. It was negotiating the establishment of diplomatic relations with Beijing, and there was a sticking point: Mongolia. This vast land was Chinese territory but occupied by Russian troops. The Beijing government rebuffed Russia's attempt to annex it, and demanded instead that Moscow withdrew its troops. Moscow could now play the Sun card.

Russia's negotiator, Adolf Joffe, sent a Dutch Communist known by the pseudonym 'Maring' to talk to Sun in Shanghai. After their meeting on 25 August, Sun wrote to Joffe to say that he agreed that the 'Soviet army should stay' in Mongolia. Moreover, he suggested, the Russian army should take the 'historical route' of invasion and seize Beijing. Joffe reported to Moscow that Sun's advice to Moscow was that they should first 'occupy Xinjiang and organize an army for him there'; and then 'he himself would go to Xinjiang, where he would establish any political system agreeable, even a Soviet system.' To help the Russians make up their minds, Sun informed them that in Xinjiang 'there are only 4,000 Chinese troops, so there cannot be any resistance'. As a further enticement, he reminded the Russians that the province was 'rich in mineral resources', which they could extract. Sun's price for the whole scheme was '2 million Mexican dollars maximum (the equivalent of roughly 2 million gold roubles).'

Moscow found Sun very useful and became committed to him – especially as the Chinese government refused its demand to annex Mongolia. Joffe, having failed his diplomatic mission in the capital, came to Shanghai and clinched a deal with Sun, with a declaration on 26 January 1923. Joffe's reports were discussed among Soviet leaders, including Lenin, Trotsky and Stalin. Sun Yat-sen 'is *our man*' (italics in original), Joffe told his bosses. 'Isn't all this worth 2 million gold roubles?'

A Soviet Politburo meeting approved giving Sun 2 million gold roubles annually. This was Sun's second huge foreign sponsorship, after the 1917 German cash. But with this sponsor, it was not a one-off sum. Moscow decided to back Sun comprehensively and for the conceivable future.

With this guaranteed vast income, Sun persuaded army chiefs of neighbouring provinces who coveted Canton to invade the city. Officer Ch'en, who had no stomach for a war that could wreck Canton, resigned and left. In triumph, the future Father of China returned to Canton in February to set up yet another breakaway government. And this time, his prospects were more promising than ever before.

At Stalin's nomination, Mikhail Borodin – a Belarusian and veteran Soviet agitator who had done clandestine work in America, Britain and Mexico – was appointed Sun's political adviser. Tall, with what May-ling (who met him later) described as 'a leonine head, with a shock of neatly coiffed, long, slightly wavy dark brown mane that came down to the nape of his neck', Borodin cut an impressive figure. He spoke 'in a resonantly deep, clear, unhurried, baritone voice', and 'gave the impression of great control and personal magnetism'. When he arrived in Canton, Sun gave him a rapturous welcome. As Borodin wrote to Moscow, Sun 'fixed his gaze at me for several seconds without a blink', and 'asked every detail about Lenin, enquiring about Lenin's health like a doctor'.

An outstanding organiser, Borodin taught Sun the Leninist way to fulfil his dream. He reorganised the Nationalist party on the Bolshevik model, and masterminded a Soviet-style first party congress in Canton in January 1924. Moscow bankrolled and trained an army for Sun, and established the Whampoa, a military academy, on a pretty island in the Pearl River some ten kilometres from Canton.

Although they had committed to Sun, the Russians knew that he was not a believer in Communism, and that he could not be relied on not to double-cross them. Moscow ordered members of the Chinese Communist Party (CCP) – a minuscule group it had founded in 1920, and had also been funding – to join the Nationalist party and help steer it in accordance with Moscow's orders. Among the Communists who joined the Nationalists was Mao Ze-dong, whose political career would take off inside the Nationalist party before he became the leader of the CCP.

The future of China, the ideology, who the bedfellows were – none of these now mattered to Sun. As he said in an interview with Fletcher S. Brockman, an old American acquaintance, 'I do not care what they are if they are willing to back me against Peking [Beijing].'

The Beijing government, which Sun was soliciting the backing of all sorts of foreign powers to overthrow, had been consistently working to protect China's interests. Having taken back Japanese-occupied Shangdong in 1922, it compelled Russia to recognise Mongolia as part of China in 1924 (establishing diplomatic relations with Moscow only after this). It was, above all, the only demo-cratically elected government in the history of China. Elections, however imperfect, were held, and a parliament functioned. Yuan Shi-kai's sabotage, and various other setbacks, did not change the democratic nature of the country. The most famous scandal involved the overambitious Cao Kun, who bought votes from some members of parliament and had himself elected president in 1923. But hundreds of other members, as well as public opinion, furiously denounced him and he remained in office for barely a year. Under the Beijing government, free speech, including a free press, thrived. So did competing political parties. An independent legal system was working. Private enterprise flourished. And a host of literary and artistic giants flowered. Creativity was at a height unsurpassed to this day. The modern Chinese language was born, ensuring that average men and women could read and write.* President Hsu Shih-chang, who himself was a noted classics scholar, was instrumental in promoting the modern language, signing a law that obliged all primary schools to give emphasis to its teaching. Women's liberation, which had started with Empress Dowager Cixi (heralded by her edict against foot-binding in 1902), gathered stunning pace. Within a couple of generations, women went from being prisoners in their own homes to appearing in public linking arms with men; and from being kept largely illiterate to enjoying equal educational opportunity. The Soong sisters were the first generation of women to have benefited from the reforms: Ching-ling went to America on a government scholarship and was escorted to America, with other scholarship students and May-ling, by a government delegation. When the sisters returned to China, in the new republic, their Westernised style was not at all unusual.

In this period, tolerance of dissent was extraordinarily high: Sun Yat-sen, leading a breakaway government, went on being treated with genteel courtesy. The control exercised by the central government was relaxed and loose, and the provinces had more autonomy than before. As provincial chiefs grew powerful and assertive, some of them took to arms to settle disputes with their neighbours. A few resorted to wars to try to gain influence over Beijing. They

---

* The artistic achievements of this period are later attributed to 'the May Fourth Movement'. In fact, they had little to do with the nationalistic demonstration that took place on 4 May 1919.

were later termed 'warlords'. Sun was not considered a warlord, even though he owned an army and occupied Canton. The warlords all recognised the elected Beijing government. Conflicts between them were reported in great detail in the press, giving the impression that the country was in utter confusion and chaos. In fact, the fighting was sporadic and small-scale, and most outbursts lasted no more than a few days. The style of fighting seemed half-hearted to Western observers. The soldiers, in grey uniforms, marched to the field of battle, waited, and then let off a few haphazard shots. Occasionally, cannons roared, but they rarely hit their targets. Fatalities were low. Some armies hired coolies to carry coffins, to reassure the soldiers that, if killed, they would be properly buried (which was of paramount importance to the Chinese). The troops also brought with them, amongst other essentials, tiny teapots and wax paper umbrellas. At the first drop of rain, fighting stopped and the umbrellas were opened, turning the battlegrounds into fields of colourful mushrooms. These were the kind of troops that would have to face the Soviet-trained military force that Sun Yat-sen was building.

The warlord 'kings' and kingmakers in Beijing could not compete with Sun, either, for single-mindedness in the pursuit of power and for total disregard for scruples. The most prominent of them was Marshal Wu Pei-fu, a fine-boned, poetry-loving ex-scholar, whose army was stationed in north China, including the areas around Beijing. For years he was thought to be 'the strongman of China', and his portrait adorned the cover of *Time* magazine in September 1924. *Life* magazine remarked, 'If an old-style warlord could have united China then, Wu would have done it. He was the only one who was personally fearless and incorruptible, who never offered or accepted a bribe. A little, brown-eyed, mild-mannered man, he had absolutely no personal ambition.'

Indeed, Wu categorically rejected proposals to nominate him as president, for fear that this would make his effort at uniting the country seem self-seeking. The marshal had a good name and held it dear. He took no concubines, lived simply, and his troops were disciplined. The West respected him, regarding him as 'China's honest warlord' and 'a democrat'. The Chinese liked him for his legendary patriotism: although he was no xenophobe and was courteous when dealing with foreigners, he would on principle not seek asylum in the foreign-administered Settlements in cities like Shanghai, even if his life was threatened, because the Settlements had been forced on China after the Opium War in the nineteenth century.* Marshal Wu's cherished principles tied his hands when he faced Sun's war. The Beijing government lacked funds; but enlisting foreign help in a civil war was anathema to him. The Russians had wooed him; he rebuffed them because of their designs on Mongolia and their ideology. The Japanese courted him and offered to help him defeat Sun; he rejected them too because he knew there were strings attached.

Sun Yat-sen did not have any of the marshal's qualms. Embracing Russian money and arms and taking their orders, he was busy building up a military machine in Canton – one that would eventually defeat Marshal Wu and overthrow the Beijing government.

Ching-ling was at all Sun's meetings with Moscow's men, and came under the influence of Borodin. The Belarusian and his wife Fanny had spent time in America, where they had learned to speak English with a Midwest accent. Ching-ling felt at home with them, and was close to them. As the little group had English as their common language, Sun joked that 'the language of the colonialists . . . proved to be an excellent means of transmitting the experience of Russian revolutionaries to Chinese comrades'.

Ching-ling had been interested in politics from her school days; now she was in the thick of the action. She loved it. Leninism cast a spell on her and brought out her fierce, steely side. She became a committed Leninist and a believer – Red Sister – unlike her husband, who was actually more interested in using the Russians for his own ends.

---

* Later in 1939, in Japanese-occupied Beijing, he rebuffed Japan's approaches for collaboration and died of what was widely believed to be poisoning by the Japanese.

In 1924, the merchants of Canton revolted against Sun. His war had been putting a heavy burden on them and they felt they were being bled dry. A series of strikes by shop owners culminated in a general strike in August. Sun made up his mind to use force to suppress the strikers, who had their own armed squad and enjoyed the sympathy of the army units brought over by Sun. Ching-ling wrote to Borodin on 13 October, 'Dr Sun has decided to act at once ... [Sun's troops] need more training in street fights, so Dr Sun hopes you will get your experts to give them some training in this respect ... The object of this fight is to crush the traitorous army and the rebellion's merchant volunteers.' Using Leninist language, she told Borodin, 'the people in Canton are hostile towards us', therefore 'only fear and a reign of terror' could save Canton.

At the time, Soviet-trained cadets were being turned out by the Whampoa Academy. They were instrumental in wiping out the armed merchants, confiscating their shops, goods and houses. The shop owners who were not involved were ordered to open for business at once or face execution. In this crackdown, hundreds died and thousands of houses were burnt. It was widely condemned; but it secured Sun's base.

More good news came for Sun – this time from Beijing. On 23 October, a coup ousted President Cao Kun, who had already been discredited and much weakened from vote-buying. The leader of the coup was the man dubbed 'Christian General', Feng Yu-xiang, who legendarily baptised his troops en masse with a fire hose. A receiver of huge Soviet arms supplies like Sun, he invited Sun to Beijing to 'preside over the country'. The dream Sun Yat-sen had been pursuing all those years seemed to be within reach. Sun replied at once that he was coming.

Borodin, Moscow's enforcer, laid down the rules. Before leaving Canton, Sun must issue a manifesto with slogans like 'Down with the imperialists!' (i.e. the Western powers) and condemn the West publicly wherever he went, not least in the capital. Sun had to go to Beijing as Moscow's protégé.

Sun duly issued such a manifesto. Mouthing Kremlin slogans, he left Canton on 13 November and reached Shanghai on the 17th, accompanied by Borodin. From there it was forty hours by train to Tianjin, the main port and business centre of north China, on the doorstep of the capital. In a matter of days his dream could be fulfilled. But Sun paused – and made a detour to Japan for thirteen days.

Sun had been calculating. Borodin had made sure that he stuck firmly to the 'anti-imperialist' rhetoric. Sun had been speaking exceptionally sharply against the West, especially in Shanghai, where he threatened to abolish the Settlements as soon as he came to power (in spite of the fact that all his life, whenever he was in Shanghai he had stayed in and operated from the Settlements so as to be protected by Western laws). Soviet-style rallies had greeted him, chanting anti-West slogans. It was clear that he was making enemies of all the Western powers and tying himself to Russia alone.

The spectre of Communism scared the general public, including most of the Nationalists. Sun Yat-sen being seen as Moscow's man would be sure to alienate them as well as the foreigners. If Sun continued to be under Borodin's control, it was doubtful whether he could assume the presidency (however hard the Moscow-funded Christian General Feng might be promoting him). And even if he did make it, he might not occupy the position for long. But going against Borodin's wishes was unthinkable. With the Russians bank-rolling him and arming and commanding his army, Sun was totally beholden. His only alternative was to find another powerful patron. Sun's thoughts swung back to Japan.

Borodin saw through Sun and could have vetoed the detour, as he told the Kremlin. But he decided to let Sun go. He was confident that Sun was too committed to Russia to get anywhere with Japan; the trip would only finish off Sun's illusions and solidify his commitment to Moscow. Indeed, the Japanese government rejected Sun's express wish to visit Tokyo and to meet officials. A senior Japanese diplomat told Sun's envoy that Japan would help Sun only if he abandoned his Soviet line. Sun returned from Japan empty-handed. He was dejected and 'extremely reluctant to talk about his trip', Borodin reported to Moscow.

Sun landed in Tianjin, and stayed in the city's Settlement, which looked like a European city and was policed by turbaned Sikhs from British India. It was now well over forty days since the coup by Christian General Feng. While Sun was absent, the general showed that he was incapable of managing the situation and was sidelined by the prestigious former prime minister Duan Qi-rui, who had turned down hefty German bribes and ensured that China sided with the Allies in the First World War. Duan formed a caretaker government. Borodin noticed the gloom with which Sun greeted the news. Duan was a much admired man, and commanded respect from people of different walks of life, including Sun's brother-in-law and Big Sister's husband H.H. Kung, who observed that Duan was 'a good man' and 'tried his best' for the country. Duan and other major players were still respectful to Sun, referring to him as the founder of the republic. Repeatedly they invited him to Beijing for a unity conference, to produce a new government. There was still hope for Sun to become president.

But Sun knew he had an insurmountable hurdle. To be endorsed by power players and public opinion, as well as by Western allies of China, Sun had to distance himself from Moscow. This was something he was unable to do. With virtual control of Sun's army and about 1,000 agents in Canton, and with Borodin and his men surrounding Sun, Moscow was, in Borodin's words, the master of Old Man Sun.

Upon arriving in Tianjin on 4 December 1924, Sun had a meeting that he had much anticipated with one of the most important players, Zhang Zuo-lin, the strongman of Manchuria known as 'the Old Marshal'. Starting first as a common soldier, then a bandit, and rising to be the chief of this gigantic and much-coveted region, the Old Marshal was a most impressive man, with an astute, pragmatic and yet imaginative mind (once he commissioned thinkers to invent a political ideology for him). He had made a spectacular success of Manchuria, and was now a kingmaker of China. He told Sun that he could endorse him, but only if Sun broke from Moscow. This was a big blow, and Sun collapsed. Vomiting violently, he writhed with pain in the liver area, sweating so much that two large towels were soaked. The next morning, the pain did not subside, and he had to miss the welcome rally that had been carefully organised many weeks before, to which he had so much looked forward. The doctors' diagnosis, which Borodin presented to Moscow, made clear Sun was suffering from grave liver disease. Sun's illness became public and many said that his days were numbered.

While Sun was bedridden and suffering acute daily pain, on 10 December Ching-ling wrote to her American friend Allie Sleep an entirely cheerful and chatty letter:

> Dearest Allie,
> Since writing you last I have been traveling from one end of the country to the other. I was so happy on my arrival here to read your letter … It is really a pleasure to read that your health has improved so wonderfully that you have gained in weight.

Evidently, Ching-ling was not insensitive to health issues. But her husband's intense suffering seemed to have no effect on her. She referred to him, but only in terms of the adulation he had received and the good time she had had as a result:

> We received a wonderful reception in Japan and in Tianjin. Over 10,000 were at the pier to meet my husband with banners and cheers. We are living now in an old monarchist's house which the government has fixed up for our residence. It is a lovely place, full of interesting things. Everything is new and beautiful, for 20,000 dollars was spent in decorating the place. I am wondering how it'd feel to live in one of the palaces at Peking! However, I am sure I should be spoiled and humble …
> Day before yesterday I was the guest of honor at ex-President Li Yuan-hung's house, for my husband too was there to attend. The dinner was given in the ballroom of his private theater, a magnificent building which cost him 800,000 dollars. During

the dinner an orchestra of fifty velvet-uniformed men played. For the first time in my life, I ate with gold knives, forks & spoons which the ex-president informed me were especially ordered from England. Exotic flowers and fruits were in gold vases & stands.

So she went on with other details of a lunch that must have been an ordeal for Sun: that morning, the pain had been so unbearable that he had to stay away from the grand welcome rally. Throughout this period, when Sun was in tremendous pain, Ching-ling appeared to be oblivious to his agony. She described to Allie her 'delight' and 'pleasant surprise' when some old friends visited her: 'my how we chatted in that hour of visit'. One friend 'made a special trip from another city to call on me. I have learned so many things about my father, what smart & witty things he said when he was a boy, how he played tricks on the teachers at Nashville, Tennessee, what arguments he made to mortify this professor who taught philosophy.' She informed Allie, 'We are all going to Peking in a week's time. Great preparations are being made to welcome my husband. Over 150,000 men will make a welcome demonstration.'

Sun was moved to Beijing on the last day of 1924, partly for treatment. Doctors in Tianjin had pronounced his condition incurable. In the capital, a surgeon operated on him and found advanced liver cancer. All his comrades were devastated. So was Ching-ling. Perhaps only now did it sink in that Sun was dying. This was the man she had once loved so much that she was willing to die for him, but he had let her down. Now her feelings for him was bound to be complicated. In his final days before he died in March 1925, she was seen weeping and fussing over him devotedly. But their last conversation, recorded by Sun's manservant Lee Yung, who was present, suggests that Sun was well aware that Ching-ling had little love left for him. Seeing her in tears, he said, 'Darling, don't be sad. Whatever I have will be yours.' He thought Ching-ling was in distress because she feared he might not leave her anything. On hearing this, Ching-ling's lips quivered, and she stamped her foot on the floor. Sobbing wildly, she said, 'I don't love any of the things. I only love you.' Sun replied, 'That is hard to say.' Ching-ling wept uncontrollably. Before he died, Sun called out 'Darling'. And when he breathed his last, Ching-ling cried until she fainted. Afterwards, she tenderly closed Sun's eyelids.

When she had realised that Sun was dying, Ching-ling informed her sisters in Shanghai and they set off at once for Beijing. The railway line that linked the two cities was not operating at the time, as the result of bandit troubles (one group had hijacked a train and taken more than a hundred foreign and Chinese hostages). To go by ship via Tianjin was impossible as the port at the northern city was iced up. But the sisters were determined to come, and embarked on a journey over 1,000 miles long not knowing exactly how or even whether they would get there. The trip involved changes between many forms of transport, without food or heating in the carriages in the depth of a winter so harsh that water froze in the pipes. They had never experienced this level of hardship in their lives. Finally, though, they made it to Beijing and stumbled out of the station, exhausted and frozen.

Ching-ling needed them and other members of her family around for moral support, and to protect her interests. Borodin's deputy and Sun's heir apparent, Wang Jing-wei, was a man she did not trust and called a 'snake'. Wang overtook other old associates of Sun's partly thanks to his republican credentials. With soft and appealing feminine looks, he had actually started his career as a notable assassin and had spent time in a Manchu prison under a sentence of life imprisonment, for trying to assassinate the last emperor's father. He was also smart and approachable. But the clincher was that Borodin gave him his blessing. A committee with Borodin as the ultimate decision-maker prepared a 'Testament' for Sun when his terminal illness was diagnosed. Wang wrote it.

In addition to the political Testament, Wang wrote another, private, will for Sun. It left all Sun's possessions to Ching-ling. Sun's children were there, and they raised no objection. They had never benefited from their father, and were not about to quibble over inheritance. (Ching-ling appreciated the spirit of generosity of the Sun family and maintained a close and affectionate relationship with them for the rest of her life.)

On 24 February 1925, Wang read out the two documents to Sun in the presence of four of Sun's relatives – his son Fo, daughter Wan, and brothers-in-law T.V. Soong and H.H. Kung – and, tentatively, he asked Sun to sign them. Sun nodded agreement to the contents, though he declined to sign, telling Wang to 'come back in a few days'. He still hoped he might recover.

The Testament reaffirmed the Borodin-directed policies. Sun Yat-sen, dying yet still lucid, registered this when it was presented to him and said to Wang, 'You've made it so explicit; this is dangerous. My political enemies are waiting for me to die to soften you up. That you are so uncompromising and firm is bound to bring you danger.' At this Wang replied, 'We are not afraid of danger. We will follow our declared objectives.' Sun nodded, 'I approve.'

Borodin noted Sun's commitment to Soviet Russia, and went one step further by having his English-language secretary, Eugene Chen, write in Sun's name a 'Deathbed Letter to the Soviet Government'. Eugene, born a British subject in Trinidad of mixed Cantonese and African ancestry, spoke no Chinese; but this did not prevent him from being appointed the foreign minister of Sun's government. He had been trained as a barrister in London, and had been much wounded by the racism of the day. Those offended sensibilities had found an outlet in the revolution. The Chinese translation of the letter was alien to a Chinese – the long and convoluted sentences (the golden rule in Chinese writing was brevity), the foreign vocabulary, the quintessential Soviet style. Even its title was a mouthful: 'To the Central Executive Committee of the Union of Soviet Socialist Republics'. And its ending went far beyond what even Sun would have said: 'In bidding farewell to you, dear comrades, I wish to express the fervent hope that the day may soon dawn when the USSR will greet, as a friend and ally, a strong and independent China and that the two allies may together advance to victory in the great struggle for the liberation of the oppressed peoples of the world.' It could have come straight out of a Moscow dossier.

On 11 March, when it looked likely that Sun could die at any time, more witnesses gathered around his bed. Ching-ling supported Sun's right hand and guided it to sign the Testament and the private will. Then T.V. Soong, American-educated, read out the letter to Moscow in English, and Sun signed it, also in English. How much Sun took in the content of the long letter was unclear. But there was no doubt he grasped and endorsed the gist. He died the following morning, 12 March 1925, at the age of fifty-eight.

Ei-ling and her husband H.H. did not like Communism, and tried hard to prevent their brother-in-law from being seen as a Communist. They persuaded Ching-ling to hold a Christian service for him in the hospital chapel – 'to prove that he was not a Bolshevik', Ching-ling said wryly.

Sun was not a Bolshevik. He just needed the Russians in death, as he had in life. Only they could immortalise him the way he desired. They would not only put his party in power but also teach the Nationalists how to build his personality cult. Sun had told the party through Ching-ling: 'I wish to follow the example of my friend Lenin, to have my body embalmed and placed in the same kind of casket.'

Lenin had died the previous year. His embalmed body had been put in a specially made transparent crystal coffin in a mausoleum. Hundreds of thousands of people were said to have filed through and paid respects to him in a matter of weeks. A huge personality cult swept through Russia, and Lenin was elevated to divine status. His portraits, posters and busts were obligatory in all public places, from offices to classrooms, streets to parks, always signalling to the people that he was their omnipotent saviour.

Sun had decided that this was what he would like to have in death. Indeed, after he died, the Russians made a Lenin-style coffin for him. The only snag was that it was deemed unusable. The glass top was apparently unsuitable for the heat of a Nanjing summer. Sun's body was not laid out for display like Lenin's.

But the other parts of his wishes were amply fulfilled. The Nationalists began a Lenin-style cult straightaway. The title 'the Father of China' was used for the first time. In the ensuing years, especially when the Nationalists conquered China in 1928 and needed Sun's name to claim legitimacy, the Cult of Sun reached fantastic dimensions. Statues of him were erected in cities and towns; his every word, however banal, was treated as gospel, and no one was allowed to say anything irreverent about him. Soviet-taught Nationalist propagandists called Sun 'the liberator of the Chinese nation', 'the greatest man in the 5,000-year history of China' and, even, 'the saviour of all oppressed nations'. These words were later appropriated by Mao for *his* cult.

The biggest symbol of the cult was the Sun Yat-sen Mausoleum. Before he died, Sun had specified that his resting place must be 'on the Purple Gold Mountain in Nanjing, because Nanjing was the founding place of the interim government'. This was the only government in which he enjoyed the title of 'interim president', even if only for forty days. The Purple Gold Mountain was also where the founding emperor of the last Han dynasty, the Ming, was buried. Sun Yat-sen, who had harboured a competitiveness with this emperor, Zhu Yuan-zhang, had stressed that his own tomb must be next to the emperor's, but a great deal grander and taller, and in such a position that 'no one else can build a tomb at a higher place'.

The Ming tomb occupies an area of 1.7 million square metres and is already one of the largest for Chinese emperors. Sun's, built by the Nationalists, is 90 metres taller, with 392 steps, and covers over 30 million square metres, encompassing a large part of Purple Gold Mountain. To make room for it, villages were destroyed and many thousands of residents were forced to sell their land and houses to the government. The locals petitioned in desperation: they 'lost the roofs over their heads, became homeless and had to sleep rough; some even committed suicide because they would rather perish with their homes.' Each of the announcements for the continuous expansion of the site 'threw hundreds, even thousands, of people who were about to lose their homes into utter panic, as if they were about to lose their parents. They begged Heaven and Earth, and had nowhere else to turn.' The petitioners argued that their misfortune seemed to contradict what is still known as Sun's motto: 'Everything under the heaven is for the people' (*tian-xia-wei-gong*). Nationalist officials merely told them: 'You must make it the goal of your life to sacrifice everything you have' for the Father of China.

PART III

The Sisters and Chiang Kai-shek (1926–1936)

8

Shanghai Ladies

Before she returned to China in July 1917 at the age of nineteen, Little Sister May-ling had spent a decade in America and grew into a fun-loving and carefree young lady with little interest in politics. After finishing high school at Wesleyan in Macon, Georgia, she went on to the east coast to attend Wellesley College, Massachusetts. There she studied English language and philosophy, taking, amongst a variety of courses, Old Testament history. Outgoing and gregarious, May-ling was far more integrated into American life than her two sisters. Wesleyan contemporaries agreed that 'She was the friendly one, seeming to like everyone and interested in everything, always gay and talkative.' 'May Ling used to come to my room and lie on the little baby pillow on my bed while she talked.' Described as 'chubby' and 'fat', she was 'intensely alive and into mischief every minute'. She was bursting with energy and 'used to be allowed to go out and run around the campus in the middle of her French lesson because her restless little body could not be still so long.'

At Wellesley, she kept a 'confession book', like other girls, and like them she showed hers to others. One entry went: 'My one extravagance, clothes ... my favourite motto, don't eat candy – not one piece ... my secret sorrow, being fat.' She had to watch her weight very carefully all her life.

After graduation she headed home with her brother T.V., who had been studying economics at Harvard and Columbia. Unlike his outgoing sister, T.V. was shy and adopted a distant and aloof expression, which contributed to his reputation of being haughty. He and May-ling were devoted to each other. Later Little Sister fondly reminisced to him 'how I used to cook cocoa for you in the early mornings before your classes'.

Together they journeyed in the summer of 1917 by train across Canada to Vancouver to board a steamship for China. In Vancouver she wrote to her friend Emma Mills, 'Brother & I went to the best shop, trying to get some things; but to our disappointment, the store was terrible. Someone said that there isn't a well-dressed Canadian woman here; I did think that was an exaggeration. Now, however, I am inclined to think that there is some truth to that. The women here look like dowds!'

Chinese affairs did not preoccupy her. When they did confront her, her reactions were instinctive, and somewhat unexpected: 'we saw a train-load of Chinese coolies who are being shipped to France as laborers. If one of them should die, his family gets $150.00! Such is the price of life to them! If ever I have any influence, I shall see to it that no coolies are being shipped out, for China needs all her own men to develop the mines.'

She wrote her first letter from Shanghai to Emma three weeks after her return. With excitement she boasted about her home:

We live way uptown. The further up the more exclusive. It is lovely here: but it is so far from the shopping district and the theatres and eating houses! We have a lovely carriage and two coachmen etc.: but horses are such bother. One can only use them just so much. Next week we are going to get an automobile for running around town, and let Mother keep the carriage for her private use. We have a beautiful garden, lawn tennis [sic], croquet ground. The house is one of the loveliest in Shanghai ... We have verandahs, sleeping porches and whatnot. The house has three stories and has 16 large rooms not counting the kitchen, baths etc. ... By the way, I am taking charge of the house now. We have five maids and seven menservants. Let me tell you it is no joke! ... I am so tired now from running up and down inspecting the house ...

Mother still has charge of the financial end for which I am duly grateful!

It is very annoying sometimes, as I forget myself and speak in English to the servants ... At times I cannot express myself in Chinese; then I ring for the butler who acts as interpreter! ... Since I have returned home, it seems to me that I am always buying clothes ... I have been to a great many dinners and teas, & other affairs.'

She found herself in the warm embrace of her family. Ching-ling was in Shanghai waiting for her (while Sun Yat-sen was in Canton), and Ei-ling had come with her children from her home in Shanxi in the north-west. The two older sisters lavished affection on Little Sister. May-ling told Emma that they constantly said to her, 'Oh we saw the most adorable dress at so & so a place. You must have one like it ... They enjoy dressing me up, as I am the youngest & the only unmarried one.' They were so happy to be together that Ei-ling started thinking about moving to Shanghai, even planning for the whole family to live under one roof. They went to see a house together. It was 'a 30-room house (not counting servants quarters). It is really an immense mansion of five floors with roof garden. To tell the truth, I don't care for it: it is too huge, and the ceilings are so high that I feel lost in it. It is like a huge hotel and very formal although elegant. It is "too much" for a girl just graduated from Wood Barn to live in! ... I do hope that we won't decide to move to that huge place they are considering. Of course, I should like to have sister [Ei-ling] live with us – at the same time 30 rooms will be no joke! I am rather plebeian in my taste – at least the family think so!' They did not buy it, but living in different houses was no barrier for Ei-ling and May-ling, who saw each other all the time.

May-ling also now had the company of her two younger brothers, T.L. and T.A. Her fondness for them showed through her claims of treating them strictly:

Both my little brothers flunked last year, & the family is furious. The poor kids have two tutors (an English & a

Chinese) to come every day. And believe me, they are working! I am also teaching them English grammar. One of the poor kids is learning to punctuate, & the other is learning spelling with me watching them now ... Mother is so disgusted that she handed them over to me bodily. They are hard to manage, because they are deucedly clever and lazy at the same time. I have whipped the younger one several times, & they both are afraid of me. You don't know what a good disciplinarian I can be!

May-ling was madly in love with her family. 'It seems very queer to have a family. I am so used to doing what I please without consulting anyone that it is rather hard to remember that I am not at college and cannot do and think what I please. Of course, though, I am very happy at home.'

Already, there were suitors:

H.K. has been here from Peking, and so has Mr Yang. I like them: but that's all. Oh, Emma, I might as well tell you that on board ship, I lost my head over a man whose father is Dutch and mother a French. He is an architect and was going to Sumatra. He asked me to marry him, and the family here is greatly wrought up! I have been having a rather uncomfortable time. Remember that this is a secret: don't tell it to a single soul, for heaven sakes [sic]! ... Tonight, a Frenchman I met on the boat is coming to see me. We speak nothing but French ... And for love of Pete do not tell anyone what I have told you ...

When this cheerful, chatty and highly informative long letter eventually came to an end: 'By the way, will you subscribe the *Literary Digest*, the *Scribners* and a magazine on child psychology & how to take care of them etc. for me. The last mentioned is for Mrs Kung [Ei-ling] as she has two growing kids of about 2 and 1 yr old. But send it in my name, & tell me how much the whole thing is & I'll refund the money.' Requests to buy American magazines and run other little errands became a staple in her correspondence with Emma.

★

Every morning, May-ling took Chinese lessons. The old tutor 'taught me when I was eight years old, and if I remember correctly, he administered the stick on my palm once when he found out that I had been eating candy all the time pretending that it was the "foreign devils'" cough drops. Now however he is so polite to me.' She learned the language fast, finding the very complicated classical written forms easy. The rest of the morning she mostly wandered about the house, 'in and out among the rooms fixing the flowers, picking up a book here and there'.

At lunchtime, she rang a bell. A servant looked after the floor she shared with T.V.,

whose only duty is to keep these rooms in order, and answer my bells. Often I have my luncheon sent up here on the porch. I have dismissed my maid: I have found that I simply did not need her, as Mother's maid does all my mending and picks up my clothes for me, and it grated on me to have my maid around when I could execute my own orders in less time than it takes for me to explain to her what I want done. You see, all the years in democratic America have their effects on me. I am quite contented with this one servant who attends to Brother's and my wants. He polishes our shoes, dusts, sweeps, and make up the beds etc. ... The afternoon usually rounds up with a tea somewhere or tea at home.

As for dinner: 'I have been so busy. During the last 2 weeks there was only one evening when we either did not give dinners or were not invited out!' When dinner was over: 'we usually go for a spin in the car and carriage, or else take a walk, or go to the theatre'. 'We have been having Russian Grand Opera here and I have been to six or seven different performances.' The Chinese theatre remained an un-acquired taste; she described it as 'tooth and nail cries'. Long midnight rides were frequent. 'And of course we never returned until after mid-night. Is there any wonder then that I am tired?'

In this pampered existence, her chief problems were things like 'we have ordered our Buick car – but tough luck, the next shipment won't be in until another week'. One day, she discovered an infection on her face. This was a major disaster. 'You cannot imagine how I have cried out of pure nervousness ... But now at the end of this week, I shall be able to go to a party!' 'Since I have shut myself up at home, life has become dull – dull, dull! I am seized with such unreasonable and unreasoning fits of temper that sometimes I think I am going insane.'

Shanghai parties were on a grand scale: a reception for over 1,000 people, a wedding for 4,000. 'I am enjoying myself tremendously ... Only sometimes I become quite conscience-stricken when I think how little time I stay with Mother ... You would think that I am a regular butterfly.'

Tragedy soon marred this picture of fun, when Charlie died in May 1918, less than ten months after she came home. He had been suffering from kidney disease. In the last weeks of his life, May-ling looked after him like a well-trained nurse and with great affection. She gave him a massage with olive oil every night as his skin became dry as parchment. In hospital, while her mother or other members of the family kept Charlie company during the day, May-ling spent the nights with him. Gazing at his swollen face in his sleep, she felt 'almost more than I can bear'.

When the doctors pronounced that his chances of recovery were about twenty per cent, Mrs Soong brought Charlie home, in spite of doctors' objections. She belonged to the Apostolic Mission Faith, which believed in the power of prayer. Her fellow disciples filled their house and prayed for him night and day.

After Charlie's death, his wife arranged a quiet and simple funeral for him, with only his closest friends notified. He was buried in the new International Cemetery, where the family bought enough land for all of them. He was the very first person to be buried in what became a prestigious cemetery. May-ling was comforted, 'he liked being the first in any kind of competition; so I know that if he knew this, he would be awfully pleased'.

May-ling mourned her father for a long time: 'With Father's death, the family does not seem real at all – We all miss him greatly: he was such a companionable father.' 'He has been such a wonderful father to us! And we love him even though he is no longer with us.'

That she had only months to spend with her father after she had been absent for ten years remained a lifelong regret for May-ling. This, and the fact that she had missed a home during her adolescent years, gave her love for her family a special intensity. Barely in her early twenties, she concluded that: 'friends are very nice, but remember when you actually really get to a hard fix, the family is the one that will stand by you. Coming from me, who has spent a greater part of my life thousands of miles away from my family, this may sound green. But honestly, you will find that I am right.'

A cousin who had returned from America found life with her family unbearable. May-ling observed, again unusually mature, 'I think the whole trouble lies in this: the family and she expect too much of each other ... What a very different homecoming this is compared to mine. My family took me for granted, good and bad. And although we did not always agree, we respected each other and compromised.'

She saw her mother as the person who made her family the way it was: 'not every one is so fortunate in having such a good mother as I have. Really my mother is so considerate of me that every day I am ashamed of myself, and of my behavior.'

Mrs Soong's love was that of an exceptionally strong mother. She could steel herself to send her nine-year-old daughter across the ocean for a decade for a superior education; yet throughout that time, she missed her daughter intensely. When May-ling visited Ei-ling in Shanxi, she wrote to Emma, 'Mother in her heart of hearts did not want me to leave her and yet she did not want to stand in the way of my going.' 'Mother is so afraid that sister will make me stay longer. Poor dear! She'll be lonesome without me.' 'Mother is so good to me, and does lean on me so much that I really hate to think of leaving her.' When she grew thin, Mrs Soong reacted like a most traditional parent (who always wanted their children to put on weight): 'Mother cried the other night, because she said that it hurts her to see me looking so pale & wan.' The weight loss was in fact intentional. Little

Sister, who had been fretting about her figure, went from 130 lb to 107 lb in a matter of months, and was transformed into a slender woman (she was about five foot three and looked much taller).

Deeply attached to her mother, May-ling gladly did what she wished her to do. Because of Mrs Soong's objection, she gave up dancing, even though she had loved it at college. Mrs Soong gave much time and money to charities. In order to please her, May-ling became involved in charitable work. She taught at a Sunday school: 'Mother is happy beyond words at my consent. There is so little I can do for her that I am eager to do anything I can.' She fundraised for the Shanghai Young Women's Christian Association. She visited slums: 'I do hate nasty smells and dirty sights. But I suppose somebody has to see the dirt if it is ever going to be cleaned up.' Shanghai society considered her public-spirited and able, and fit to be an executive in a major charity organisation.

Next to her mother, Big Sister was the person she esteemed most. She told Emma, 'I wish you could know her, for she is undoubtedly the most brilliant mind in the family, and is unusually keen + quick witted, vivacious, quick, and energetic. She is not the sort I would consider at all fanatical; and yet she is deeply religious.'

For several years after Ei-ling had returned to China in 1914, she went through a depression. The purpose in life that she had found working for Sun Yat-sen had turned into disappointment. She was discontented, then, with her married life in a provincial city. Having thrived at the centre of the action, she felt dissatisfied just being a schoolteacher, a wife and a mother. At the time of the births of her first two children, Rosamonde in 1915, and David in 1916, she was restless and miserable. As May-ling told Emma, 'she has gone through periods of agony ... misery and sufferings'. She even lost faith in God, 'even denied the existence of a god, and whenever religion was mentioned in her presence, she either shunned the topic or else plainly said that it was all old women's nonsense'. Although she helped her husband make a fortune – and discovered her own talent in finance – contentment eluded her, as she saw the whole activity as purposeless.

The return of Little Sister brought a ray of sunshine into Ei-ling's life: she now had an intimate friend and confidante, and this helped her clear her mind and recover her equilibrium. She realised that she needed her religion. By the time she had her third child Jeanette in 1919, Big Sister had gone back to her God, repenting that she ever doubted Him. When her youngest son Louis was born in 1921, she told Little Sister she had at last 'found solace in life and faith in living'. As May-ling wrote to Emma, 'She now prays to God to help the solution of her problems. More than this, she has found peace, such peace as she has never known.' She 'is just as gay, and goes out to parties etc. just as much as before'. But 'somehow or another, there is a difference in her. She is a great deal less critical, more thoughtful, and not so intolerant of the short comings of others.'

Ei-ling tried to persuade Little Sister to be more religious. At this stage, May-ling resisted, telling Emma, 'You know Dada [May-ling's pet name for Emma], I am not a religious person. I am too darned independent and pert to be meek or humble or submissive.' She thought that Ei-ling 'intentionally drugged her mind', and was irritated with her, telling her 'to keep still'.

As they argued, their lives grew more intertwined. Little Sister often babysat Ei-ling's children and doted on them. Writing to Emma: 'it certainly is a job looking after them. They are hungry from morning till night in spite of the amount of food they eat. As sister gave strict orders not to give them rich food, I think that is the reason why they feel the need and insistent craving for candies etc. all the time. Lately I have been giving them one piece of candy each day and that seems to allay some of their perpetual demand for food between meals.'

Ching-ling was more distant from these two, mentally as well as physically. But whenever they were together, they always had a good time. May-ling wrote: 'My sister Mrs S. was in Shanghai from Canton for two weeks. During that time, life was a perpetual whirlwind of social gaieties.' 'My sister Mrs Sun is giving a very large reception on the tenth of October which is a national holiday in Celebration of the Republic. I shall help her receive. I am a bit tired.' She visited Ching-ling in Canton, and found walking on the city's hilly streets in high heels rather trying.

In those Shanghai years, a main activity for May-ling was her busy romantic dalliances, which were documented in detail in her letters to Emma. Starting with the Dutchman on the ship home, a string of suitors appeared – and then disappeared. Her family objected to any man who was a foreigner, and May-ling readily gave in to their feelings. There was a brief encounter with a Mr Birmeil: 'I only met him the night before I sailed from Hong Kong at a friend's house, and altho we were on board ship together only three days, we became very good friends. The day we arrived in Shanghai was his birthday; and so in spite of the fact that I had been away from home these months, I spent the day with him ... We had a beautiful time together, and I am so glad I was so rash for once in my life.' The family reacted with fury 'and was scandalized ... They were also furious because he is a foreigner. They literally accused me of "picking" him up on board ship ... Since he left Saturday afternoon, I have received two wireless messages from him saying how much he misses me. The family tried to keep the wireless away from me, but did not succeed ... In a way, I am glad he is not here, for I do not know how his presence might affect me.' But he was soon forgotten, like the Dutchman, without much pain.

Another man for whom she professed she cared 'more than words can tell' was not a foreigner – but he was married. 'For the past few months, we both have been too miserable for words ... you know how my family feels towards divorce, and besides there is nothing the matter with his wife except that he does not care for her ... it is terrible to care so much. I never knew before what it means ... But everything is hopeless.' Again, she got over him easily.

Little Sister relished her conquests. When one man said he had not heard from her for ages and was 'worrying to death', she wrote mockingly to Emma, 'The [First World] war is killing so many people that one more or less dead doesn't make much difference, does it?' She would moan: 'Oh deliver me from such trouble! I wish the man had sense enough to leave me alone or go hang himself.' She would sniff: one man had taken 'on a most irritating and aggravating turn of falling in love and bothering me'. And another 'showed decided symptoms of proposing'; but 'I guess I have gotten rid of him for good.' The 'town of Shanghai is at present is [sic] full of rumors about my being engaged, each rumor roping in different men ... What makes the situation so funny is that none of the men are either denying or acknowledging the rumors. I am quite put out.'

Though not a great beauty, Little Sister had abundant charm and allure. She had other more tangible, even pragmatic, attractions, about which she was completely frank: 'I am also known as being "intellectual" and "brainy", rather proud but pleasant ... a good sport but somewhat apart from the "common herd" because of my family's position, and because of the fact that I dress very well, and in foreign clothes, ride around in a motor, and does [sic] not have to teach to get my living.'

As time went by, a frantic social and romantic life lost its attraction. May-ling began to be filled with discontent: 'I am busy all day yet I don't seem to get anywhere.' 'I am bored, horribly and unspeakably so.' She could see that there was 'so much sickness in China ... so much misery is everywhere! Sometimes, when I look at the dirty, ragged swarming humanity in our slums, I feel the sense of bitter futility in hoping for a great and a new China, and the sense of my own smallness. Dada, you cannot conceive how useless one feels in such surroundings. The percentage of poor here is greater than any you could conceive of in America.'

Voluntary work failed to satisfy her. It 'is not real work, it is too much of a makeshift ... I simply am not able to feel that I am accomplishing anything.' 'We do a lot of gabbing; but I see no practical results. Oh, I suppose we do some good; at the same time there is nothing tangible.' She yearned 'to get a real size [sic] job and try to find some satisfaction out of living', and longed to 'amount to something'.

At one point, the idea of returning to America to study medicine occurred to her, but it came to nothing. She did not want to leave her mother, and the family could no longer afford to fund her studies. In 1921, her mother lost a large sum of money on the gold exchange, which affected the Soongs' lifestyle.

May-ling wanted marriage and children. 'I think women lose interest in life ... if they do not marry ... And then too, really what has one to look forward to if one does not have children?' But she did not envy any of the married women she knew. 'I cannot see ... that they are any better satisfied or had gained something more precious from life. They seem cramped, either indifferent, lackadaisical or bitter. Their lives seem so empty – empty.'

She was tormented by bouts of 'agony'. Ei-ling asked her to give religion another try. May-ling wrote to Emma: 'She told me that the only way for me to conquer this lassitude of mind is to become religious, and to really commune with God.' May-ling conceded to Emma, 'now I am trying her advice, and so far I cannot say how it will work out. I will say this, though, since I tried her advice, I feel a great deal happier – as though I no longer am carrying a heavy bundle alone. When I pray now, I am in a receptive mood, so to speak.'

Still, discontent shadowed her. She remained 'so tired of life', and felt 'so keenly the futility'. She yearned for 'that vibrant joy of life, and of living'. Ei-ling realised what Little Sister needed: a suitable man, the man who could give her a purpose and fulfilment.

So she looked out for that man. In 1926, Ei-ling brought her twenty-eight-year-old sister together with Chiang Kai-shek, who at thirty-eight had just been appointed commander-in-chief of the Nationalist army. A whole new world opened up to Little Sister.

9

May-ling Meets the Generalissimo

Chiang Kai-shek, known as the Generalissimo, was born in a hilly town called Xikou in Zhejiang province near Shanghai in 1887. His family could not have been more dissimilar from May-ling's. His father, a small-town salt merchant, died when he was eight, and his widowed mother struggled to bring up him and his sister. Chiang's childhood was soaked in his mother's tears: over the death in infancy of her youngest son, over the lack of help from relatives in raising her young family on her own, over people's apparent indifference when floods threatened to destroy their house, over a failed lawsuit about a legacy – and over many other misfortunes. The grief-stricken woman roused a fierce attachment in her son – to the extent that as a teenager, he was distraught whenever he had to leave home, and his mother had to drive him out of the door with stern words, even striking him with a cane.

When he was fourteen, in keeping with tradition his mother arranged a marriage for him, with a girl five years his senior named Fu-mei. On the wedding night after the ceremony, the newly-weds went into Mrs Chiang's bedroom to present tea to her. She lay in bed with her back to them, weeping and refusing to accept the tea. Chiang knelt in front of the bed and cried his heart out, one of the three bitterest cries in his life, he later recalled. Neither mother nor son had pity for the bride, who got off to such a bad start. The marriage was punctuated by rows, during which Chiang, in violent fits, beat his wife. Sometimes he dragged her down flights of stairs by her hair.

Mrs Chiang had no kind words to say about her daughter-in-law, but she would not allow them to divorce. Chiang took a concubine, Zhi-cheng, who fared little better as his passion quickly turned to loathing, partly as a result of his mother's constant complaints about her. In 1921, when he was thirty-four, his mother died. (Chiang was bereft, and mourned her throughout the rest of his life. He put up pagodas in many beauty spots to commemorate her, and turned a whole hill into her mausoleum.) Her death released Fu-mei from the unhappy marriage, as Chiang divorced her. Chiang gathered together close relatives, including Fu-mei's brother, and asked for their consent. They gave it readily. Chiang married another woman, Jennie, after whom he had been lusting for several years since she was thirteen. Chiang regarded her as a concubine, although she was addressed publicly as Mrs Chiang.

Even by his own admission, Chiang had always been something of a lecherous lout. When he was young he frequented whorehouses and picked drunken fights. Neighbours avoided him and relatives were ashamed of him, regarding him as a disgrace to the family. Deeply affected by the ill feelings towards him from all quarters, Chiang was determined to make a success of himself and chose a military career. In 1907, the Ministry of the Army under the Manchu government gave him a scholarship to study in Japan to be an officer cadet. There he met Godfather Chen and followed him into the Green Gang – and the ranks of the republicans. When the republican revolution broke out in 1911, Chiang returned to China to take part. His most notable act was that at the behest of the Godfather, he assassinated Tao Cheng-zhang, opponent of Sun Yat-sen, and helped Sun secure his position as the interim president. As Chiang sensed, this brought him to the favourable attention of Sun.

After Godfather Chen was gunned down in 1916, Chiang, mourning his mentor and resenting the way Sun had treated Chen, kept his distance from Sun, and although Sun repeatedly solicited his assistance, Chiang did not respond, despite the fact that he did not have a proper job (at the time he was working unsuccessfully as a stockbroker). He also did not get on with the people around Sun. His foul temper was legendary – he would hit rickshaw men, servants, guards and subordinates, and shower verbal abuse on his colleagues. (He was sensible enough, though, to confine his rage towards his superiors to his diary.) Such behaviour was universally abhorred.

Chiang kept open the option of serving Sun. After Sun was driven out of Canton in June 1922, the gunboat he was on was mutinous, and he was desperate. On learning about Sun's plight, Chiang raced to him, proving that he was a dependable friend. Sun was so relieved at the sight of Chiang that he burst into tears and found himself incapable of uttering a sound for quite a few moments.

Chiang escorted Sun to Shanghai in August. That month Sun clinched his deal with Moscow, and Russia's full sponsorship, including founding an army, was soon confirmed. Sun's future looked promising. Chiang made up his mind to throw in his lot with Sun, after Sun assured him that he would be made the chief of the army. As a prelude, he was appointed to head a military delegation to Russia in 1923.

Chiang was a sharp observer and a man with his own principles. During the trip, he was repulsed by the Soviet practice of 'class struggle' and horrified by Red Russia's attempt to turn China communist. He decided he did not want to collaborate. He considered leaving Sun and held off reporting to Canton after he came back to China, in spite of Sun's repeated summonses. Finally, Chiang spelt out his thoughts to Sun's close aide Liao Zhong-kai, who was corresponding with him on Sun's behalf: 'In my observation, the Russian party has no sincerity whatsoever towards us ... Its only goal in China is to bring the Chinese Communist Party to power, and it has no intention for the CCP to cooperate with our party in the long term ... Russia's policy concerning China is to make Manchuria, Mongolia, the Muslim area and Tibet all parts of the Soviet Union; it quite possibly covets China proper as well ... The so-called internationalism and world revolution are nothing but different names of Kaiser-style imperialism.'

In his reply, Liao did not address Chiang's views about Russia, but pressed him more urgently to hurry to Canton, telling him that his delay was causing Sun a great deal of pain. The message seemed clear: despite Chiang's opposition to Russia, Sun still wanted him, perhaps even more so. Chiang went to Canton and had a secret talk with Sun (the content of which has never been revealed). Undoubtedly, Chiang was reassured that Sun did not disagree with him. Sun, it would seem, was only trying to use the Russians. Chiang stayed in Canton and, in 1924 when the Whampoa Academy was set up there by the Russians to train officers for Sun, he was appointed its head. Sun meant for the anti-Soviet Chiang to control his army.

Over the next three years, Chiang concealed his views and used the Russians to build up the Nationalist army. All the while, he honed the skills of a consummate schemer and waited for the day when he could break from Moscow's hold over his party. Equally success-fully, he hid his own political acumen, presenting himself as an apolitical soldier. There was a strong anti-Russian faction in the Nationalist party, but Chiang steered clear of it. Borodin, naturally, was checking on him. The Chinese Communists reported that 'Chiang is an ordinary soldier; he has no political ideas at all.' And Liao, the recipient of Chiang's letter that revealed his real thoughts, told Borodin that Chiang was very sympathetic to Russia and was full of enthusiasm after his visit to the Soviet Union.* As a result, the Russians trusted Chiang. (Liao was assassinated in Canton in August 1925. Who did it remains a mystery. His widow believed that Chiang was responsible. Whether or not this was the case, the man who knew Chiang's true colours held his tongue forever.)

Borodin was taken in, he confessed later. Chiang 'seemed so amenable, so obedient, so modest'. He told Moscow that Chiang was 'completely trustworthy'. Russia poured money and expertise into Whampoa, along with arms including cannons and airplanes. In one shipload, weapons worth 4 million rubles were dispatched.

---

* Liao had given this false information to the Russians before he received Chiang's letter; but he did not correct it afterwards.

In January 1926, Moscow virtually hijacked the Nationalist party at its second congress, which produced a leadership dominated by CCP members and pro-Russia Nationalists. Red Sister Ching-ling became one of the leaders: a member of the Central Executive Committee. (Mao was an 'alternate member' of the Committee.) As his party was now almost totally in the hands of the Russians, Chiang judged that the time had come for him to act. First, he moved to get his foes to lower their guard further. He made a request to go to Russia 'to study how to make revolution'. He even put this request in his diary. (Chiang kept a diary for fifty-seven years and was always aware that it could be read by those who wanted to find out about him.) He also wrote an ostensibly private letter which he knew the Russians would read, all but declaring himself a Communist. Having laid this smokescreen, Chiang pounced in a surprise attack on 20 March. Using a pretext, he arrested dozens of Communists and disarmed the guard of the Soviet advisers, who themselves were placed under surveillance. In one stroke, Chiang had torn control of the Nationalist army away from the Russians.

Having accomplished this quasi-coup, Chiang managed to lead the Russians into misreading him. They thought what he had done was the outburst of a proud Chinese general offended by bossy Russian advisers trying to force a strange Soviet system onto his army. They decided that the best thing to do was to mollify Chiang – and so withdrew his chief Russian advisers. The Russians were still convinced that 'Chiang Kai-shek can work with us, and will work with us', although they were also getting prepared to 'eliminate this general' at some stage. Above all, Chiang made them believe that Borodin, who was not in Canton at the time, could sort out everything, as the Soviet representative exercised 'truly extraordinary personal influence' over him. The Russians had no inkling that the coup had been premeditated and was part of Chiang's stratagem. As a result, far from being punished, Chiang was promoted to commander-in-chief of the Nationalist army.

Wang Jing-wei, head of the Nationalist party, had had to stand by and watch Chiang getting away with it all. He feared for his life,

went into hiding and soon fled abroad. And so Chiang, the quintessential schemer, rose to become the most powerful man in the
Nationalist party.

One woman quietly took note of this dramatic turn of events, and
saw its potential significance. Ei-ling had a keen political sense,
'very much keener than I, a really brilliant woman', said Little
Sister. Big Sister was passionately anti-Communist, and had been
opposed to Sun's Soviet policy. After Sun died, she and her husband
had insisted on a Christian funeral to counter Sun's Bolshevik image.
Ei-ling saw that Chiang had kicked out a host of Soviet military
advisers, and sensed that the new commander-in-chief was changing
the Nationalist party. She was delighted. Her sister Ching-ling and
brother T.V. were both in the Nationalist government, with T.V.
being the minister of finance. (T.V. managed to calm down the
resentment of the locals by doing away with extortionate taxes –
thanks to the vast input of Russian money, as well as his abilities.)
Big Sister loathed seeing her siblings working under Moscow's
command. Chiang Kai-shek's action kindled her hope and her
enthusiasm.

It then occurred to her that the young commander-in-chief could
be a candidate as a husband for Little Sister, who had by now
exhausted the eligible pool in Shanghai. Although there was a 'Mrs
Chiang', to Ei-ling who was determined to find a husband for Little
Sister, she was only a concubine, not a proper wife, and could be
pushed out of the way with relative ease. To find out more about
Chiang, Ei-ling took Little Sister to Canton in June 1926. The
subtropical city was in the grip of an intense heatwave. But the
sisters had a purpose. They stayed in the house of the manager of
Standard Oil, who was in New York on vacation. It was a detached,
two-storey white villa shaded by cedar trees and a tropical garden.
On 30 June, Ei-ling gave a dinner for Chiang. Jennie, the then Mrs
Chiang, was also invited, and instinctively felt that the dinner would
change her life.

Chiang was tremendously excited by the invitation. He told
Jennie, 'I have position, but I lack prestige,' and it was extremely

important 'to get closer to the Soong family'. According to Jennie, 'He spoke as he walked up and down the room in great excitement. His throat seemed contracted with tenseness. "An invitation!" he repeated to himself. " ... at last, after all this time, you and I have a chance to dine with this great personage."' Chiang meant Ei-ling, who was considered a grande dame in Shanghai society. 'It is really too wonderful to be true,' he told Jennie, who wrote that 'He strutted the floor like a peacock and refused to sit down. He seldom behaved in this agitated manner.'

Jennie arrived earlier than her husband, who was delayed by work. It was a small dinner for just six, the other two guests being Mrs Liao Zhong-kai whose husband had been assassinated a few months before, for which she privately suspected Chiang, and the Trinidadian Eugene Chen, foreign minister of the Canton government. There had been much speculation about a possible match between Eugene and May-ling, but 'judging by their behavior toward one another in the drawing room, the rumor probably was unfounded', Jennie concluded. Indeed, May-ling could not stand Eugene. In a letter to Emma, she had said he 'was at one of the dinners and sat beside me. He is very clever, and brilliant, but horribly egoistic and vain. He has such horrible shrugs of shoulders which almost drove me wild! He is coming to call on me this week: and I hope I won't be rude.'

Jennie, young and innocent, came from an average family and did not have a cosmopolitan upbringing. She eyed the two sisters not without jealousy. Both wore chic bright silk cheongsams; their hair, styled in the 1920s fashion, was sculpted into waves and pulled back into a chignon at the base of the neck. They looked like figures stepping out of a Shanghai fashion magazine.

The heat and humidity were wearing everybody down. With three electric fans going at full blast, May-ling still kept fanning herself with a large, carved-ivory silk fan, and Ei-ling 'patted the perspiration from her forehead with her lace handkerchief'. While Little Sister complained about it being 'so sticky and utterly miserable' and was looking forward to going 'back to Shanghai on the *Empress of Japan* next week', Big Sister questioned Jennie closely about her husband. 'Kai-shek is well known for his horrid temper. Doesn't he ever scold you? ... No? Then you must be patience personified ... According to Dr Sun, Kai-shek flairs up at the slightest provocation. Is that so? ... Tell us about the first wife ... And what about the second wife? ... What is she like?' The questions might sound tactless. But Jennie was regarded as too simple a young girl to need tact – and Ei-ling was not known for her subtlety.

Chiang Kai-shek arrived and was seated between the sisters. The dinner party provided Big Sister with much information about the new commander-in-chief. More importantly, May-ling seemed rather taken with him. He had a soldierly bearing, and his thin brown face looked sensitive and alert. Little Sister was charmed by his conversation, so different from the usual chatter in her Shanghai circle. At the end of the dinner, she gave him her address in Shanghai.

Chiang registered May-ling's interest in him and was ecstatic. His relationship with Jennie had been based more on sex than deep love, and he would not hesitate to drop her. Now it seemed he had a chance to link his name to Sun Yat-sen – not to mention to make a 'grande alliance' with a beautiful and sophisticated lady, to whom Jennie, in his view, could not hold a candle. This piece of good luck came at a propitious time for him as he was on the threshold of fulfilling his political ambition. Chiang was about to launch the Northern Expedition, his military campaign against the Beijing government, and he was confident he could win and establish his own regime. A woman like May-ling by his side would add a great deal of lustre to the future ruler of China. She could also help him make friends with Western powers, as he was preparing to ditch the Soviets.

Before May-ling left for Shanghai, Chiang wrote in his diary that he was already missing her. Soon after she left, Chiang sent messengers to Big Sister Ei-ling and older brother T.V. (whom he also knew) to express his amorous intentions. T.V. was against Chiang's proposal. But Big Sister overruled him. Ei-ling decided that the new most powerful man of the Nationalist party was certainly worth considering. But for now, she was non-committal.

Chiang was still wrapped in his pro-Russian camouflage and sending out conflicting messages. Ei-ling could not be absolutely sure what he really stood for. Any inclination towards the Reds would not do. In addition, Big Sister and her husband H.H. Kung never identified with Sun Yat-sen's Canton, a breakaway regime Sun had set up to rival Beijing purely because he wanted to be president. The Beijing government was democratically elected and internationally recognised, and it commanded the Kungs' allegiance. When Sun had originally declared himself the grand president of China in 1921 in Canton, Little Sister had happened to be there staying with the Suns, and she had hoped to attend the inauguration. But Ei-ling and their mother had sent three urgent telegrams ordering her not to do so but to return to Shanghai at once. A younger brother was dispatched to Canton and 'literally dragged me home', May-ling told Emma.

H.H. had always felt 'like a fish out of water' in Canton and had declined job offers from Sun, telling Sun that he was 'for national unity'. He remained an admirer of Beijing's leaders. Of Marshal Wu Pei-fu, he said: 'he was really a good man. He was patriotic and he had principles.' President Hsu Shih-chang had got on with the Kungs well and invited them to the president's receptions, and he had consulted H.H. on matters of state. Much of the Kungs' life was spent in Beijing. After entertaining Chiang, Ei-ling returned to the capital, not Shanghai, sending her children to the American School there.

Now the Nationalist army might defeat the Beijing government. The pragmatic Big Sister had to accept this reality. But she also wanted to see how Chiang treated the Beijing leaders. Chiang rightly surmised that Big Sister's reservation had to do with politics. He put his pursuit of May-ling on hold and waited until his true colours – and his abilities – could be seen.

In the meantime, he led a successful Northern Expedition against Beijing and took a series of provinces. In November, the *New York Times* devoted a full-page article to Chiang, under the headline: 'New Strong Man Holds Half of China'. On 21 March 1927, Chiang's army seized Shanghai. In April, he publicly broke with the Communists and Russian control, issuing a wanted list that was headed by Borodin (and included Mao). Borodin fled back to Russia through the Gobi Desert. Sleeping in the desert in a tent one night, he ruminated about his mistake of trusting Chiang. The Generalissimo gave orders to suppress Communist-led rebellions. It became clear that the Communists, not Beijing, were his real enemy. The Shanghai business community and Western residents, who had been living in panic fearing mob rule and lynchings, breathed a long sigh of relief. They began to feel favourably disposed towards Chiang, appreciating, even admiring, what he was doing. It was only now, when he had shown his real political position, established his credentials and become an object of admiration among May-ling's friends, that Chiang resumed his courtship of Little Sister.

Though endowed with great intelligence, Little Sister initially had rather vague political views compared to her two older sisters. This changed in the winter of 1926–7, before Chiang Kai-shek broke from the Communists in April 1927. Chiang's army had taken Wuhan, the strategic city on the Yangtze River, and the Canton government had moved there. Red Sister, a Nationalist leader, and T.V., the finance minister, were in this temporary Nationalist capital. May-ling went to visit them together with her mother and Big Sister and stayed for three months. They saw a 'Red' city. One obvious sign was the gigantic wall posters everywhere, showing scenes like Chinese masses pushing bayonets into fat and ugly foreign capitalists cowering on the ground, drawing blood. Other inescapable signs were: frequent strikes, mass rallies and demonstrations, and the conduct of students and trade unionists which, as the eyewitness and left-wing journalist Vincent Sheean observed, suggested 'a highly organized social revolutionary movement that might, at any moment, seize the machinery of production and proclaim the dictatorship of the proletariat'. The 'froth of the brew' was the many foreign revolutionaries crowding the streets, as delegations from Europe, America and other parts of Asia came to see Red Wuhan and be inspired.

In Red Wuhan, Red Sister lived the most active and radical phase of her life, endorsing the violence rampant in and around the city. But May-ling was appalled by what she saw, as were her mother and Big Sister. Outside her window, 'Never a week passed when there was no demonstration of thousands upon thousands of Communist union-controlled workers shouting slogans of down with such and such a person, some tradition or mores, or some imperialist country ... For hours on end one could hear the deafening shouting of thousands reach a crescendo as each unit marched past ... The cacophony of noise made by bugles, drums, gongs and brass cymbals was drowning.' She abhorred 'indiscriminate arrests, public lashings, illegal searches and seizures, kangaroo courts and executions'. She was outraged: people were 'tortured and killed because they dared to dispraise the Communists' and were terrorised by the '"open trials" of landlords, officials and even of their kith and kin such as their mothers'.

Borodin, the architect of the Soviet-style 'red terror', was in Wuhan before he fled back to Moscow across the Gobi. May-ling asked him how he could justify all this. Borodin was apparently keen on May-ling. A servant had spotted a piece of paper in his bedroom, from his blotter, on which he had written over and over 'Mayling, darling. Darling Mayling'. Out to dazzle her, hoping even to convert her, he put on his full thinker-orator mannerisms and delivered long monologues to her. He would pace to and fro in T.V.'s living room, ponderously or swiftly as the mood of his arguments dictated; every now and then he would lift a clenched fist and suspend it in the air as a punctuation mark, before bringing it down and slamming it into the palm of his left hand for emphasis. Little Sister only felt that 'my nature and instinct, in effect my whole being, and my convictions were revulsed [sic] and repelled by what Mr Borodin propounded'.

Returning to Shanghai in April May-ling totally agreed to Chiang Kai-shek's move to expel the Reds from the Nationalists. With encouragement from Big Sister, she was ready to join her life with Chiang's. In May, when the commander-in-chief wrote and sent her his photo, she responded positively. They started to see a lot of each other, talking deep into the night, going out to the country where they ate in small, atmospheric restaurants, and taking midnight rides by car. They were in love, perhaps not head over heels, but as two mature adults with shared views, who knew what they wanted in life and were delighted that they could find fulfilment in each other. As the spouse of the future leader of China, May-ling felt she could at last do things that would make a difference with her boundless energy.

Chiang had already been divorced from his wife Fu-mei. He now made arrangements for his two concubines, who had no alternative but to consent to leave him. He undertook to support them for life. Jennie was put on a ship to America. On board, she was spotted 'fashionably gowned', but crying. Chiang placed a notice for three days in the main Shanghai paper to state that he was unattached.

On 27 September 1927, May-ling and Chiang Kai-shek were engaged at Big Sister's house, where they had their engagement photograph taken. The next day, Chiang went to meet May-ling's mother, who was in Japan at the time. Mrs Soong had clearly delegated the whole matter to E-ling. Still, she wanted to have a look at her future son-in-law. She was pleased by how the commander-in-chief looked and behaved and gave him her consent to his face. Chiang was elated. As soon as he returned to his lodging, he took up a large brush and wrote four giant characters: 'Conquering in one sweep a thousand armies' (*heng-sao-qian-jun*).

Mrs Soong came back to Shanghai to supervise the preparation of the wedding, which took place on 1 December 1927. That day, the bridegroom published an article in the Nationalist newspaper expressing his joy, while the bride told friends she felt 'dazed'. After a Christian ceremony at her home, more than 1,000 people attended their civil wedding at the Majestic Hotel, a splendid chateau-like edifice set in a large garden. It was the best venue in town, and 'anybody who was anybody was present', May-ling wrote to Emma excitedly. 'It was the biggest wedding Shanghai ever saw!' The press reported every detail. One paper described her European-style wedding gown: 'The bride looked very charming in a beautiful gown of silver and white georgette, draped slightly at one side and caught with a spray of orange blossom. She wore also a little wreath of orange buds over her veil of beautiful rare lace made long and flowing to form a second train to that of white charmeuse embroidered in silver which fell from her shoulders. She wore silver shoes and stockings and carried a bouquet of pale pink carnations and fern fronds.' As pure white was the colour of mourning in China, May-ling introduced a lot of silver into her outfit.

After the wedding, Chiang had long talks with Big Sister – rather than his wife – about the current situation and what he planned to do. Ei-ling's sympathy with the Beijing government undoubtedly influenced Chiang's stance towards it. After he defeated it, Chiang showed respect and good will towards its officials and continued to employ many of them. He referred to former prime minister Duan Qi-rui as his 'mentor', and praised Duan for his 'undeniable great contribution' to the country. He arranged a state funeral of enormous scale for warlord Wu Pei-fu.

Big Sister was now acting like an adviser to Chiang. And she felt she ought to keep the newly-wed on his toes. One day, he went out riding with May-ling for a whole afternoon. That evening, when he called on Ei-ling, she told him off for indulging in pleasure and not taking his political responsibility seriously. Chiang was hurt and wrote in his diary that Big Sister underestimated him and failed to appreciate his soaring potential. He resolved to prove himself to her. From now on, as people close to them testify, Ei-ling would exercise a bigger influence than anyone else on the Generalissimo.

Married to a Beleaguered Dictator

Discord between May-ling and her husband started early. By the end of December 1927, the month they were married, the newly-weds had already had a flaming row, in Shanghai. Chiang came home during the day and found that May-ling was out. He was used to women who were always on standby waiting for him. He was annoyed. When May-ling came home and offered no apologies, he flew into a rage. She was astonished and fought back. He found her unbearably 'arrogant', and took to bed to nurse some unspecified 'illness'. She ignored him and stormed off to the Soong house, letting it be known that she, too, was ill. In the end, Chiang climbed down. He came to May-ling in the evening – 'in spite of my own illness'. May-ling told him she was 'sick of losing her freedom', and proceeded to advise Chiang that he should improve his character. They made up. That night, he was too shaken to sleep, feeling his 'heart shivering and flesh jumping'.

Chiang Kai-shek had married a tigerishly strong-willed and independent woman. For the first time in a relationship, it was he who had to say sorry. During the sleepless night, he realised he had no choice but to accommodate May-ling. He needed her in many ways, not least for her connection with Sun Yat-sen, whose heir he claimed to be. But Chiang also found that he 'rather agreed with her', and that he should change his ways. The next morning, rather than rising at dawn as he usually did, he stayed in bed and made lingering and amorous love to her until ten.

May-ling was quick to respond in a conciliatory manner. She was feeling greatly excited at being Mme Chiang, and thought, as she recalled later, 'Here was my opportunity. With my husband, I would work ceaselessly to make China strong.'

May-ling believed that Chiang's victory would end internal strife and bring peace to the country. She resolved to help him win and be a good first lady. She put away her Western clothes and adopted the traditional silk cheongsam. With embroidered flowers, and the skirt slit on both sides halfway to the knee, it became her 'uniform'. She wore her hair in the Chinese women's style of the day, straight and with a neat fringe. When her brother T.V., who had become Chiang's finance minister, wanted to resign, she persuaded him to stay. While Chiang was at the front of the Northern Expedition, she bought medicine for wounded soldiers, procured large quantities of clothes and bedding, and secured Red Cross doctors and nurses. She delivered his message to Western consuls, assuring them that the Nationalist army would protect their colleagues in the war zones. She was like Chiang's special representative, performing tasks that others could not. Chiang wrote in his diary that half of his victory was due to his wife. Equally importantly, May-ling introduced humanitarian practices into Chiang's army, and was, all in all, a civilising influence on the Generalissimo. It was she who founded a school for the children of dead soldiers and officers, a first in Chinese wars. She devoted herself to them over the years, and they remained her 'children' to the end of her life.

Chiang Kai-shek defeated the Beijing government and entered the Northern Capital on 3 July 1928. The Nationalist regime was established, its capital Nanjing. The Generalissimo made himself the chairman.

An epoch of seeking democracy in China was over. This period, 1913–28, is often described negatively in history books as a period of 'warlords fighting'. In fact, the longest and most significant wars throughout those years, even if intermittent, were not waged by the warlords but by Sun Yat-sen, followed by Chiang Kai-shek. The wars between the warlords were much shorter and more limited, causing much less upheaval; life went on as usual for civilians, as long as they were not caught in the crossfire. Above all, the warlord rifts ended with renewed efforts to strive for parliamentary democracy. Chiang's last target, Marshal Wu Pei-fu, for instance, was well known for his commitment to democracy, and his final act before exiting the political arena was to pay the fares home for the hundreds of members of parliament who had stayed in Beijing in the hope that he might win and the parliament could be reconvened. Chiang's victory ended China's journey along this course and set the country on the path of unapologetic dictatorship.

And yet, even though Chiang embraced dictatorship and inherited some of the Leninist 'methods of struggle' – Soviet-style organisation, propaganda and control mechanisms – as Borodin put it, he rejected Communism, and did not go on to build a *totalitarian* state, unlike Mao, who later overthrew him. The Generalissimo's regime kept many of the country's freedoms. Although May-ling did not make policy, her influence was very much present in the dictator's more humane decisions.

Chiang's biggest problem was legitimacy. His predecessors in the republic had all been elected, however problematic some of the elections might have been. Chiang's conquest did not win the hearts and minds of the population and he was not seen as the liberator. When his army had marched down Beijing streets, they were greeted with 'thunderous silence' by expressionless onlookers, noted one observer. The Beijing leaders, on the whole, enjoyed a far better reputation than him. Nor did his victory convince people of his military genius. Many believed that Beijing was defeated by Soviet military might rather than by him. The fact that Chiang had broken the Russian hold on his party was only grudgingly appreciated. Other Nationalists had been acting against Moscow's control while Chiang was ostensibly pro-Russian. To these men, the Generalissimo was an opportunist.

Chiang claimed to be the heir of the Father of China, and promoted Sun to divine status. At his own wedding, an enormous portrait of Sun hung on the platform, flanked by the flag of the

Nationalist party and that of the country he was about to rule. The flag of China was basically a duplication of the party flag on a red background, symbolising Sun's vision that his party would dominate the nation. Everybody – the newly-weds and their over 1,000 guests – bowed three times to Sun's portrait, introducing a ritual that would become ubiquitous in ceremonies across China.

As a matter of fact, Sun was far from godlike in the Generalissimo's private thoughts. Once with May-ling and Big Sister, he talked about how Sun's Russia policy would have led to a Communist takeover of his party and country, and would have doomed both – had he, Chiang, not saved the situation by stratagem. But for political reasons, he needed Sun's deification.

He also needed an ideology from Sun for his regime. Sun had produced a sort of ideology: the Three Principles of the People (*san-min-zhu-yi*). This was an imitation of Lincoln's 'government of the people, by the people, for the people'. Roughly, the principles were nationalism, the people as the masters, and the welfare of the people. They were as vague and mercurial as Sun's real-life beliefs. Talking about them to camera for a three-minute English newsreel, Chiang, his interpreter and May-ling gave different definitions. The first lady was meant to talk about how Sun's principles had liberated Chinese women. This was something so intangible that she had to memorise her lines by rote. As a result, having talked fluently about women's role in China as she saw it, she got stuck when it came to Sun's supposedly great contribution; she could not remember what she had to say. Haltingly she stumbled on: 'Dr Sun has given women economic ... and ... economic ... and ...', and she ground to a halt. Giggling embarrassedly but sweetly, she turned to her husband, who had been looking on with palpable anxiety and who now whispered in her ear. She completed the sentence: ' ... has given women economic and political independence.'

Nevertheless, that the 'ideology' was vague and open to interpretation did not matter in the grand scheme of things. It was benign and worthy. The problems started when Chiang aimed for precision and announced that the political system under him would

be 'political tutelage' (*xun-zheng*), which was the not very euphe-
mistic name Sun had given to his brand of dictatorship. The word
xun brings to mind the image of a superior lecturing inferiors. Sun
had said this was how the people of China should be treated by
him and the Nationalists. The Chinese were slave material and unfit
to be the masters of the country; 'so we revolutionaries must teach
them', 'lecture them', 'using methods of force if necessary'. A
propaganda poster illustrated Sun's words: China was pictured as
a toddler being pulled to a higher state of existence by Sun. This
was a drastic departure from Chinese culture, which frowns on
openly holding ordinary people in contempt.

The Generalissimo dictated that no one was allowed to be irreverent about Sun. In organisations like schools and offices, people
were made to gather once a week to commemorate Sun. They had
to stand in silence for three minutes, read Sun's deathbed Testament,
and be lectured by their bosses. All this was alien and off-putting
to the population. They had never had to do this under the
emperors. And for nearly two decades, they had been living in a
form of civil society with a multi-party political system, a reasonably fair legal system and a free press. They had been able to
criticise the Beijing government publicly without fear of retribution.
In 1929, a number of prominent liberals spoke out in a collection
of essays called *On Human Rights*. Hu Shih, the leading liberal of
the day, wrote that his fellow countrymen had already been through
a 'liberation of the mind', but now 'the collaboration of the
Communists and the Nationalists has created a situation of absolute
dictatorship and our freedoms of thought and speech are being
lost. Today we may disparage God, but may not criticise Sun Yat-sen.
We don't have to go to Sunday church services, but we have to
attend the weekly [Sun] Commemorative Service and read the Sun
Yat-sen Testament.' 'The freedom we want to establish is the
freedom to criticise the Nationalist party and to criticise Sun Yat-sen.
Even the Almighty can be criticised, why can't the Nationalists and
Sun Yat-sen?' And, 'The Nationalist government is deeply unpopular, partly because its political system fell far short of people's
expectations, and partly because its corpse-like ideology failed to

attract the sympathy of the thinking people.' These publications were confiscated and burnt; Hu Shih was forced to resign his job as the chancellor of a university.

Things could be worse, Hu Shih observed. Anyone could lose their freedom and property on charges of being 'a reactionary', 'a counter-revolutionary' or 'a Communist suspect'. There was not much respect for private property. Wellington Koo, once prime minister of the Beijing government, had a splendid mansion in Beijing, bought by his wife's father, a rich overseas Chinese businessman. The Koos loved the house. During Sun Yat-sen's final trip to Beijing, it was lent to him and he died there. After their victory the Nationalists simply took over the house and turned it into a shrine for Sun – to the gut-wrenching distress of the Koo family. They were also dismayed that the new masters proceeded to cover the original colour of the house, a beautiful old Beijing red, with a coat of gloomy grey-blue, to show this was a sad place.*

Chiang regarded what belonged to the country as his own. He created a major bank, the Farmers' Bank, with funds from state taxation. When he wrote his will (in 1934), he put the assets of the bank under the heading 'family matters', below the item telling his sons that they must regard May-ling as their real mother.

As a dictator, the Generalissimo could boast enemies in all directions. Province potentates from east, west, north and south were rebelling against him. So were a large number of his Nationalist colleagues from the left, right and centre. They had one thing in common: they refused to recognise Chiang's authority. Some took to extreme measures. Assassinations, which had been rare under the Manchu dynasty, were the de rigueur way of solving problems by the republicans, Sun and Chiang both being old hands. Now the sword was dangling over the Generalissimo – and May-ling.

---

* Chiang later employed Koo, an outstanding and cautious diplomat. Decades later, when he spoke about this episode for the oral history project of Columbia University, New York, a flustered Koo abruptly halted the taped interview and told the interviewer to switch off the recorder, 'This is to be closed. It casts a reflection on the Kuomintang.' Then he changed the subject. Clearly he decided that it was wiser to pull his punches.

One night in August 1929 in her Shanghai home, May-ling was woken by a nightmare. As she wrote later, an eerie, ghostly figure appeared in her dream, a man with 'a coarse and brutal face' and 'an expression of evil intent'. 'He lifted his hands and in each was a revolver.' She screamed, and Chiang sprang from his bed and ran to her side. She said there might be thieves downstairs. Chiang went out of their bedroom and called for the guard. Two answered, and he went back to bed reassured, though thinking that it was a bit odd two men responded as only one was supposed to be on duty.

A few days later, the two guards tiptoed into the bedroom and were about to pull the trigger when Chiang turned and coughed loudly. Startled, they crept out. Meanwhile, the guard who was not supposed to be on duty had roused the suspicion of the taxi driver who had brought him to the residence. The taxi driver noticed that the man was trying to conceal his military uniform with a slouch hat and a raincoat, and found the way he was greeted at the gate fishy. The driver called the police, who came to the house at once. The guards were taken away. They had been two of Chiang's oldest and most trusted bodyguards; and yet they had accepted the commission of one group of Chiang's numerous enemies.

As a result of these assassination attempts, May-ling suffered a miscarriage. She was 'unbearably disraught', and 'in extreme agony', Chiang wrote in his diary. Chiang stayed by her side for seventeen days, leaving his work unattended, which was unusual for him. After the miscarriage, she was told she could never conceive again. Like her sister Mme Sun, Mme Chiang would have no children of her own.

May-ling was in a state of constant fright and suffering from extreme nervous tension. In yet another nightmare, she saw a stone in the middle of a stream, with blood flowing all round it. As Chiang Kai-shek's name contains the word for 'stone' (shek), for days she was expecting something terrible to happen. As it turned out, what did happen was that the neighbouring province, Anhui, broke from Chiang and shelled the capital, Nanjing.

But Little Sister stood by her man, in spite of the dangers and her reservations about his ways. In 1930, some prominent Nationalist generals and politicians (including the man who had written Sun's deathbed Testament, Wang Jing-wei) banded together and formed a rival government in Beijing. Chiang waged a war against them. Known as the Big War of Central China, it lasted for months. During that time, May-ling was in almost daily cable communication with her husband and showed him much love and support. Worried that Chiang, at the front, might not eat well, she offered to send her cook to him. When the weather became extremely hot, she enquired anxiously how he was coping. Fearing that he might be lonely, she sent her youngest brother T.A. to bring him letters and presents. She was again Chiang's most dependable logistics manager. One consignment she arranged contained 300,000 tins of meat, bamboo shoots and sweets, 150,000 hand towels and large quantities of medicine for the troops, which she chartered a special railway carriage to deliver. When T.V. became fed up with Chiang's endless demands for vast sums of money and tendered his resignation as finance minister, she again talked him round.

Some of the money went through her hands personally and quietly. The strongman in Manchuria was now Zhang Xue-liang, the Young Marshal, son of Old Marshal Zhang Zuo-lin.* In this conflict the Young Marshal decided to lend Chiang a hand – for a price. After secret negotiations, a colossal payment in the region of $15 million was agreed upon. The sum was so large that it had to be drawn over several years, during which the Young Marshal made occasional trips to Shanghai and Nanjing to collect the instalments. On 18 September 1930 May-ling wired $1 million to the Young Marshal, with a promise to send the remaining $4 million of the first instalment in the following days. That day, the young warlord sent troops south from Manchuria to form a pincer attack with Chiang against the rebels. This doomed the rebel army.

---

* The Old Marshal was briefly in charge of the Beijing government in June 1927, at the last stage of Chiang Kai-shek's Northern Expedition. The Japanese offered to help him stop the advance of Chiang, in exchange for substantial rights in Manchuria. The Old Marshal told them in so many words: 'I do not sell out the country.' The Japanese planted dynamite on a railway bridge, killing him in his train on 4 June 1928. His death helped secure Chiang's victory over the Beijing government.

In this period, May-ling stayed with Ei-ling and their mother. While Mrs Soong gave her moral support, Big Sister provided her with detailed advice. Chiang was immensely grateful to both women, and asked after them practically daily. As always he was deferential to Ei-ling, never failing to address her respectfully as Big Sister, even though he was older than her. When he was told Mrs Soong was ill, he wanted to know every detail and told May-ling to convey his pledge: 'please rest reassured that your son-in-law is carefully following your teaching and behaving responsibly'.

As a gesture of gratitude to Mrs Soong and Big Sister, after the war was over Chiang was baptised on 23 October 1930, in a ceremony that took place at the Soong home in Shanghai. From then on, he was increasingly influenced by Christianity.

The war was over but those opposing the Generalissimo had not finished. They shifted their base to Canton and set up another rival government the following year, 1931. One of the members was Fo, Sun Yat-sen's son. In Nanjing, Sun's old associates remained deeply and openly contemptuous of Chiang. Chiang put some of them in prison, but he had to pretend that he only kept them locked up in order to listen to their advice.

Chiang felt he was besieged by ill will as he had been in his youth, and raged against practically everyone around him. His diaries are littered with remarks like: 'there is no genuine friendship or kindness or love under heaven, the relationship between mother and son is the only exception'; 'I can't stop feeling rage and anger ... most people are false friends ... and selfish ones ... I want to cut myself away from all of them'; 'People's hearts are all devious and ugly. Those who fear me are my enemies; those who love me are also my enemies, as they only want to use me for themselves ... My wife is the only person who loves me and supports me sincerely'; 'It is the nature of human beings that nobody treats others in good faith, except one's parents, wife and children.'

Beset by these grim thoughts, the Generalissimo remained a loner and a one-man band. To him 'China has too few talents. If you give people responsibility, they just fail'; 'Of all the people I employ, in all the organizations, almost not a single one's work is to my satisfaction'; 'Apart from my wife, not a single other person can share a little responsibility or a little work with me'; 'I have to deal with everything myself, domestic or foreign policies ... civil or military matters.' Indeed, at key moments when China needed international support such as the lead-up to the Japanese invasion in 1931, he had no ambassadors in Western countries.

Chiang's small inner circle mostly consisted of the extended Soong family. In his own family, he had always loathed his half-brother: 'How I detest him and feel disgusted towards him.' He also scorned his sister. One day he dropped in to see her with May-ling and saw her guests playing cards noisily. Chiang 'felt ashamed' and feared his 'beloved' would despise him for his relations.

His strong emotional relationship with his mentor Godfather Chen gave him another 'family'. Chen's two nephews, Guo-fu and Li-fu, founded and ran his intelligence system. But even they did not have his full trust. The Generalissimo was suspicious and worried that they might become too powerful, and created another intelligence agency to limit their influence.

Only the Soong family enjoyed Chiang's total confidence. They could be relied on not to cheat him, and he depended on them to manage the lifeline of his regime: money. He created an authority for China's major banks – the United Office of the Four Banks – and made Ei-ling's husband, H.H. Kung, the overlord. Mainly for H.H., who was his most obedient servant, and also for his other brother-in-law, T.V., Chiang reserved the very top posts: finance minister, foreign minister, prime minister. H.H. stayed on in the last post for well over a decade, near the end of Chiang's regime.*

The person Chiang heeded most was Big Sister Ei-ling. Her ideas on political and financial affairs, told to Chiang either by herself or through May-ling or H.H., always had the Generalissimo's ear.

---

* In the Confucius clan chronicle of the 1930 edition, H.H. Kung was listed as a descendant of Confucius, with whom he shared the same surname. As he was in power then and supervised the writing of the chronicle, some questioned the validity of the claim. Ching-ling referred to him sarcastically as 'the Sage'.

Her husband's prolonged occupation of top posts was largely due to Chiang's reliance on Ei-ling.

Outside the tiny family circle, the Generalissimo trusted or listened to few people. There were no proper debates among the top echelon. Meetings were a cheerless affair, at which Chiang would assume a pose of aloofness and harangue his subordinates and colleagues. The more civilised members of his audience found it hard to bear and only refrained from fighting back out of fear. The less cultured followed his lead and treated their own underlings similarly badly, generating resentment down the line.

Under such a boss, few officials cared to contribute to policy-making. Even his senior officials seldom offered suggestions. Ei-ling, who exerted most influence on him, was smart, but she did not have the mind of a political leader. And she had a fatal lack of empathy with the common people. As a result, Chiang's regime failed to present an agenda that would enthuse or give hope to the general population. The absence of inspiring policies was so keenly felt that Hu Shih, the leading liberal, called on Chiang to 'do the minimum of the minimum and learn from the autocratic emperors: issue some degrees from time to time asking the population to make outspoken suggestions!'

For Chiang this was water off a duck's back. Even worse, he gave the impression that he actually held the population in contempt. The Chinese, he said in public, 'have no shame, no morals'; they were 'lazy, indifferent, corrupt, decadent, arrogant, luxury-loving, incapable of enduring hardship, unable to keep discipline, [had] no respect for law, no sense of shame, no idea what morality is'; 'Most of them are half-dead-half-alive, neither-dead-nor-alive ... "walking corpses".'

Lifting the population out of poverty was not on his agenda – a catastrophic failure he regretted too late, when he was being driven out of mainland China. There had been a proposal to reduce the rent peasants had to pay to landowners, but it was only tried out in a couple of provinces and was abandoned when it met with tough resistance. The Communists were keen to take advantage, and claimed that their goal was to give people a better life. The

Reds' influence grew, as did their territory. With Moscow's backing, they formed a 'Soviet republic' in 1931 in south-east China, a rich part of the country not far from Shanghai. At its height, this breakaway state controlled a total area of 150,000 square kilometres and a population of over 10 million. A major threat to Chiang grew right under his nose.

Confronted with a multitude of horrendous problems, May-ling lost her initial optimism about achieving great things as Mme Chiang. She later wrote in 1934: 'During the last seven years I have suffered much. I have gone through deep waters because of the chaotic conditions in China.' In addition to the ceaseless internal strife, there were other disasters: a drought in Shaanxi in the north-west in 1929 resulted in a famine that killed hundreds of thousands; prolonged storms in the north-east in 1930 made millions homeless; and in 1931, 400,000 died from floods in the Yangtze valley and other regions; Japan was aggressively flexing its muscles on the border. 'All these things have made me see my own inadequacy ... To try to do anything for the country seemed like trying to put out a great conflagration with a cup of water ... I was plunged into dark despair. A terrible depression settled on me.'

Her darkest hour came when Mrs Soong died of bowel cancer on 23 July 1931. May-ling had cared for her through her long illness and stayed with her during her last days in Qingdao, a seaside resort where they had gone to escape Shanghai's stifling summer heat. Little Sister was inconsolable. She said that her mother's death 'was a terrible blow to all her children, but it hit me perhaps even harder than the rest, for I was her youngest daughter and had leaned on her more heavily than I realized.' She remembered particularly a moment shortly before Mrs Soong's death: 'One day while talking to her, a thought which I considered quite bright occurred to me. "Mother, you're so powerful in prayer, why don't you pray to God to destroy Japan in an earthquake so that she can no longer harm China?"' She remembered her mother 'turned her face away' and refused, telling May-ling that even suggesting the idea was unworthy of her. This point of view influenced May-ling throughout her life and made her admire her mother even more intensely. When Mrs Soong died, she felt lost: 'Mother was no longer there to pray me through my personal as well as other troubles. I had a lifetime to face without her. What was I to do?'

On the day of her mother's death, May-ling's brother T.V. narrowly escaped an assassination attempt by a group of young left-wing Nationalists. Their target was actually Chiang Kai-shek, but they picked T.V., Chiang's 'money man', as a rehearsal. They had studied T.V.'s movements and knew he regularly came to Shanghai from Nanjing, the capital, on the night express on Thursdays for long weekends. On this particular Thursday, they waited for him at Shanghai North Station. Wearing a smart suit and a white topee, and over six feet tall, T.V. cut a conspicuously dapper figure. As he made his way through the crowd, followed by his secretary and bodyguard, the men shouted 'Down with the Soong dynasty!' and started firing. Bullets ricocheted off the walls and through the windows. T.V.'s secretary, walking next to him, was killed. One eyewitness, a stallholder close to the scene, told the newspapers afterwards that the assassins 'were wearing Sun Yat-sen costumes of a greenish grey'. (This outfit, later called the 'Mao suit', was an adaptation of the Japanese cadet uniform and was first worn by Sun. At the time of the shooting, civil servants of the Nationalist government were required to wear it.)

After the shooting started, two bombs were detonated. According to the eyewitness, this 'caused much white smoke so that you could hardly see Mr Soong. I hid under my counter.' Taking advantage of the smoke, T.V. leaped behind a pillar, simultaneously drawing his revolver. One of the railway police on duty rushed over and told him, 'Throw your hat away, Mr Minister. Stoop down so that they can't see you so well and follow me. I will take you to safety.' T.V. groped through the fog of smoke, avoiding the bodies on the ground, and followed the policeman to a boardroom upstairs. Seeing that he went to the upper floor instead of an exit, the assassins gave up the pursuit. After more exchanges of fire with his bodyguard, they dropped their weapons and disappeared into the station crowd, who were fleeing in all directions, screaming. They got away – to plot against their real target, the Generalissimo.

Before this group had even got home, other gunmen fired at Chiang in a park. They missed, and Chiang was unharmed. Not wishing to make May-ling more distraught, Chiang cabled her to say that the news was only a rumour. May-ling knew it was not and was in anguish. Repeated assassination attempts haunted her for life; in her old age, she could not sleep peacefully without a trusted security man in the next room.

To top all these calamities came a national catastrophe: in September 1931, Japan invaded Manchuria and occupied this enormous and rich part of China. May-ling, as she recalled, slid into 'the depths of despair'.

11

Ching-ling in Exile: Moscow, Berlin, Shanghai

While Little Sister was struggling to cope with the perils of her married life, Ching-ling, Red Sister, was living in self-imposed exile, first in Moscow.

She went to Russia after Chiang Kai-shek broke with the Communists in April 1927. Her mother and sisters used every argument to stop her from going, and indeed tried to talk her out of her Red belief. May-ling came to Wuhan again with a letter from her mother. But Ching-ling remained the headstrong young woman who had run off to marry Sun Yat-sen twelve years before, and refused to listen. From Wuhan she went to Shanghai to wait for a ship to take her to Russia. There were more furious confrontations with her family. Finally, in the company of a group of comrades, and under the disguise of a poor woman, she clandestinely left Shanghai and boarded a Russian steamer for 'the capital of the world proletariat'.

Her thirty-two-year-old brother T.V. decided to side with Chiang Kai-shek. T.V. had been vacillating between the anti- and pro-Chiang camps. The journalist Vincent Sheean, who knew him at the time, said that he was

unable to make up his mind between the horrors of capitalist imperialism and the horrors of Communist revolution ... in China it was impossible to step out of doors without seeing evidence, on every hand, of the brutal and inhuman exploitation of human labour by both Chinese and foreigners. T.V.

was too sensitive not to be moved by such spectacles. And yet he had an equally nervous dread of any genuine revolution; crowds frightened him, labour agitation and strikes made him ill, and the idea that the rich might ever be despoiled filled him with alarm.

One day in Wuhan a mob squeezed up against his car, shouting menacing slogans and cracking one of the windows. This gave him a dislike for mass action for life – although it did not kill off his sympathy for the left.

Like T.V., most of the Nationalists in Wuhan chose Chiang. The seemingly gigantic tide of the Soviet-style movement died down as suddenly as it had risen, its popularity turning out to be illusory. Ching-ling was devastated. She did not expect the revolution to crash so drastically and thoroughly. She loathed the man she held responsible, Chiang Kai-shek, and before her departure for Moscow, issued a statement condemning Chiang in the fiercest language.

She arrived in Moscow on 6 September. Vincent Sheean came to call soon afterwards:

The door at the end of the darkened reception room on the second floor of the Ministry of Finance opened, and in came a small, shy Chinese lady in a black silk dress. In one of her delicate, nervous hands she held a lace handkerchief ... When she spoke her voice almost made me jump: it was so soft, so gentle, so unexpectedly sweet ... I wondered who on earth she could be. Did Mme Sun Yat-sen have a daughter of whom I have never heard? It did not occur to me that this exquisite apparition, so fragile and timorous, could be the lady herself, the most celebrated woman revolutionary in the world.

Enamoured of her and struck by 'the contrast between her appearance and her destiny', Sheean became one of a small group of loyal friends around Ching-ling in Moscow. The Soviet government treated her royally as a guest of the state. Servants were assigned to look after her and normally unavailable apples and grapes from the Caucasus were delivered to her table. She was put up in the Metropol, the grandest hotel in town – and home to a large number of contented bedbugs. Borodin was also staying there. But the old friends avoided seeing each other: the days of merry get-togethers were over.

A purge was looming. Stalin was locking horns with Trotsky in a power struggle, in which the catastrophe in China was a major issue. In the lead-up to Stalin gaining the upper hand, Ching-ling witnessed the last attempts to defy him by Trotsky and his supporters. On the anniversary of the October Revolution, she was invited to Red Square to watch the parade. It was one of those bitingly cold days of the famous Russian winter. She stood with the Soviet leaders on the old, original wooden mauso-leum for Lenin, wearing thin leather-soled shoes inside rubber overshoes, frozen in the falling snow. She had not learned the trick of putting newspaper under her feet to keep them warm. Down the rostrum in the parade, some Chinese students unfurled banners with slogans hailing Trotsky. Afterwards, Ching-ling walked back to the Metropol off Red Square, and saw crowds listening to people speaking. The police surged out from an alley, dispersed the listeners, and took away the speakers. Trotsky and his fellow opponents of Stalin were trying to reach out to the Muscovites. A week later, Trotsky was expelled from the party before being exiled, first internally, then abroad; until finally, in 1940, he was killed in his villa in Mexico City by Stalin's assassin, using an ice axe.

Anyone who had been in China or connected with the Chinese revolution was in a perilous situation – except Borodin who, as Stalin's man, was safe. Despite this, he still felt the need to distance himself from the Chinese, any Chinese, including Ching-ling. Others were not so lucky. The man who had made the initial deal with Sun Yat-sen four years before, Joffe, was loyal to Trotsky. He shot himself days after his friend's expulsion from the party, leaving at his bedside a letter addressed to Trotsky: 'You have always been right politically ...' Karl Radek, the head of Sun Yat-sen University in Moscow, which had been set up to train Chinese revolutionaries, was expelled from the party together with Trotsky and exiled to Siberia. The new provost of the university mounted a purge among the students.

Such an atmosphere was enough to frighten away most who had a choice. But Ching-ling was not faint-hearted, and chose to live a life of high risks. It was also true that, if one was not on the receiving end of the purges, life in wintry Moscow could be fascinating. Conversations were not about money or careers, or other mundane matters of a bourgeois society – full-time activists debated how to change the world, reorganise society and remould people like clay. And they did create waves around the world, even if they themselves could sometimes be submerged by them. Ching-ling was in a unique position that allowed her to ride the waves and enjoy the exhilaration with relatively little danger of going under: she was Mme Sun Yat-sen, widow of the dead Father of China, and as such she was untouchable – provided that she operated skilfully. She deftly avoided the Stalin–Trotsky rift and hid her sympathy for the latter. Students from Sun Yat-sen University eagerly sought her views, but after one speech in the early days of her exile, she declined to visit the campus ever again and kept a total silence. In this way she preserved herself and lingered in the Russian capital for eight months – and she loved her time there. Later when she returned to Moscow she wrote to a friend, 'It is lovely to be back. Life is full of interest and activity here ... I feel sorry to be leaving.'

As her life so depended on being Mme Sun, any danger of losing this status panicked her. While she was in Moscow, the *New York Times* and a few other papers ran a report alleging that she had married the Trinidadian Eugene Chen, ex–foreign minister of the Nationalist government: 'according to an official Soviet dispatch, the couple will spend their honeymoon in China and start a new revolution ... the Red International is said to have given a large check to finance the political activities of the bridal couple'. It made a point of mentioning that Eugene's previous wife had been 'a woman of negro descent'. The article may have been short, but it had an 'annihilating force' on Ching-ling, her friends saw, sending her into 'a state of collapse', and she was bedridden for three weeks. She feared that the news item was part of a stratagem to cut her off from Sun's name.

Another blast followed when Little Sister married Chiang Kai-shek, thus connecting Chiang to her late husband. The man who had robbed her of the victory of her revolution now promised to snatch from her the ownership of Sun's name. She would say to friends that the marriage was 'opportunism on both sides, with no love involved'.

To add to her distress, Stalin did not seem to think much of her. He only met her once, together with Eugene Chen, who was also in exile in Moscow. The meeting lasted just over an hour, during which Stalin hardly said a word, gazing inscrutably around the room and puffing on his pipe. When he did open his mouth, it was to tell her that she should return to China soon. He had sized up Ching-ling and concluded that she was not cut out to be a political leader. He declined to give her any backing of the kind that he had given her late husband. Ching-ling was told that the Comintern (Communist International), Moscow's arm that directed revolutions abroad, would give her instructions through 'its messengers to China'.

The Comintern held a special meeting to discuss Ching-ling's future role. Its proposal contained a number of points that began with 'Use Soong Ching-ling ...' Red Sister would be used to blow Russia's trumpet, to entice over bigwigs in the Nationalist party, and to put pressure on Chiang to be more friendly with the Soviet Union. She could help the Chinese Communists in ways big and small.

Ching-ling considered returning to Shanghai. She also wanted to see her mother. She had left her family acrimoniously and, when Mrs Soong wrote telling her to come home, Ching-ling had ignored her. She now longed to go back to Shanghai to explain to her mother and make up with her.

While she was pondering what to do, in February 1928 a friend by the name of Deng Yan-da – a fellow left-wing Nationalist leader and the former chief of education at Whampoa – wrote from

Berlin. He had also fled China and had been in Moscow, where he had talked to Ching-ling about forming a Third Party as an alternative to the Nationalists and the Communists. Now he pleaded with her to go to Berlin so they could resume their discussion.

A little younger than Ching-ling, tall and broad-shouldered, Yan-da was an 'exceptionally genuine, open and charming' man by consensus. He had great charisma. Even Mao felt his attraction, later reminiscing that Yan-da 'was a very nice man, and I liked him very much'. (Mao never used such expressions, or such a tone, to describe anyone else.) People were drawn to Yan-da by his transparent warm-heartedness and consideration for others, and by his liveliness and sense of fun. And yet underneath one could sense 'tremendous toughness and willpower'. The combination of these qualities was so rare and powerful that many young people looked up to him as their idol. He was often described as a 'natural leader'.

He impressed Stalin too, who talked with him one night from 8 p.m. to 2 a.m. Afterwards Stalin accompanied him to the outer gate of the Kremlin, which was a marked sign of respect. Stalin also thought Yan-da had leadership quality and proposed setting him up as the head of the CCP. Yan-da protested that he was not even a member – to which Stalin said, no matter, the Comintern could fix it. But Yan-da did not believe in Communism, which to him stood for 'destruction' and 'violent dictatorship', and would 'make Chinese society poorer and more chaotic'. The Third Party he wanted to form would aim for 'peaceful struggle', 'construction' and 'a quick establishment of a new orderly society'. It would also be 'nationalist' and would not take orders from Moscow, unlike the CCP.

These ideas – and to have said no to Stalin – made Yan-da fear for his life and he quickly got out of Moscow and went to Berlin. Stalin soon settled on Mao to lead the CCP.

From Berlin, Yan-da wrote Ching-ling letters that exuded his passionate and affectionate personality. Could 'Sister Ching-ling', his 'dear comrade', please come and discuss matters relating to forming a Third Party – since he was unable to go to Moscow? Everything was '120%' and exclamation marks were frequent: 'I must discuss with you in detail this matter which is 120% important'; 'naturally all the programs, policies, slogans and organisational matters will be 120% specific'; 'I long for you to feel 120% at peace and ease and to use your determination and courage to comfort your dear mother!'; 'There are so many things I want to talk to you about in person; I wish I had wings so I could fly to you this minute!!!'

Ching-ling arrived in Berlin at the beginning of May 1928. This was the Golden Twenties, with explosive innovations in every field: literature, film, theatre, music, philosophy, architecture, design and fashion. People in the city were friendly, and, Ching-ling noted, one could live well there very cheaply. She rented an apartment, comfortable though by no means grand. Every day an assistant came to help her with household chores and paperwork. Lunch was generally in a small restaurant which served a set dish of meat and potatoes or rice and vegetables, costing one mark. Dinner was cooked at home. She lived as a private citizen under unobtrusive German government surveillance.

A month later, Chiang Kai-shek successfully deposed the Beijing government and established his regime in Nanjing. The news ought to have been crushing for Ching-ling, and yet it hardly affected her mood, which was one of contentment and serenity. Another, simultaneous blow which might also have been devastating was that her mother seemed to have disowned her. In a letter dated June 1928, she wrote, 'Dear Mother, I have written you so many letters but have no reply. This is another of the "refused" ...'

The envelope, addressed 'Care of Mme Kung' and bearing Berlin and Shanghai postmarks, was returned from Shanghai in July – unopened. Mrs Soong was immensely distressed by her favourite daughter's embrace of Communism and decision to live as a Red exile – and wanted nothing to do with her. During this period of her anguish, Ei-ling and May-ling grew closer to her than ever, and Big Sister became the linchpin of the family.

Despite her family's rejection, Ching-ling remained tranquil and content. She said later that she had never felt so at home as when she was in Berlin at this time; indeed she was more at ease there than she had ever been in Shanghai.

What gave her this peace of mind, happiness and strength was undoubtedly the fact that Yan-da was with her. In Berlin they saw each other every day, talking for hours and taking long walks. He was her teacher in history, economics and philosophy, as well as the Chinese language. She was an eager pupil, excited by his intellect and personality.

Both in their thirties, both of passionate temperament, spending so much time alone, planning action for the future of their country together and adoring each other – here were all the ingredients for a burgeoning love. Ching-ling was widowed and Yan-da was in a miserable arranged marriage that he had been struggling to end. In a letter to a friend from Berlin in late 1928, he said that although he cared about his wife, he had been living separately from her for years, and had only kept the marriage going for fear she might commit suicide if he left her. 'I believe deeply that Chinese women – naturally including her – are living inside prisons enduring pains unendurable to others. We should be liberating them and helping them ... This is why I oppose all "fashionable men" abandoning their wives to marry "fashionable women". And this is why I have been enduring years of lifelessness.' After much agonising, he eventually wrote to his wife and ended their relationship. She was sad, but did not kill herself, and they maintained fond feelings for each other.

The way Yan-da treated his wife was highly unusual, and in marked contrast to Sun Yat-sen's behaviour. That he should win Ching-ling's heart was the most natural thing. And yet their liaison could not flourish – because she must remain Mme Sun. If she, or Yan-da (who described her as 'the symbol of the Chinese revolution'), wanted any political role, she had to bear that name. And in her kind of politics, the title was of overriding, life-and-death importance.

Rumours that they were lovers spread quickly. So, it seems, they decided to stay away from each other. Ching-ling left Berlin in December 1928 and did not return until the following October. She went to Moscow, and then to China to attend Sun Yat-sen's entombment in June 1929. The gigantic mausoleum for Sun in Nanjing had finally been completed and his corpse was moved there to be buried in a grandiose ceremony. Just before she arrived back in Berlin, Yan-da went to Paris and London, where he conducted their discussions about forming the Third Party by correspondence. In the end Ching-ling declined to be part of the Third Party, as it was condemned by Moscow. But she also refused Moscow's order to denounce it.

In 1930, Yan-da returned clandestinely to China to organise the Third Party. Before he set off, he went to Berlin to say goodbye to Ching-ling. Although danger and death hovered over him – he told her that these could be their last days together – they had a wonderful time. It seems that they went to the cinema to see the film *The Blue Angel*, a tragicomic love story starring Marlene Dietrich in which she sings her signature song 'Falling in Love Again'. More than two decades later, Red Sister asked her German friend Anna Wang to buy the record of the song for her, telling her it had a very special meaning for her.

Sun Yat-sen's entombment in 1929 had been staged by Chiang Kai-shek. It was the Generalissimo's show and Ching-ling's presence only seemed to add to her glory. Red Sister felt that she was being used, and boycotted many functions, but her absence was greeted with indifference. As Chiang was effectively turning himself into Sun's heir, she lived in virtual seclusion in her Shanghai house in the French Concession.

Her hoped-for reconciliation with her mother did not happen. After two years of separation, she felt more alienated than ever. Her family was now at the core of Chiang's regime. Ei-ling's husband H.H. Kung was the minister of industry and commerce, and T.V. was the finance minister. Mrs Soong was referred to as 'the Mother-in-law of the Country'. (When she died in 1931, her coffin was draped with the Nationalist flag, and the funeral cortege included a full military parade.) The family saw little of Ching-ling. The French Concession police, who kept tight surveillance on her, recorded few visits from her mother and sisters.

Frustrated and furious, Ching-ling wanted to lash out. At this moment, Soviet Russia invaded Manchuria in a dispute over the

Russian-built Chinese Eastern Railway. While Nationalist fervour ran high, Ching-ling openly parroted Moscow's line and blamed the invasion on Chiang's government. On 1 August 1929, a Comintern front organisation in Berlin published a piece by her which attacked Chiang in unprecedentedly strong language: 'Never has the treacherous character of the counter-revolutionary Kuomintang [Nationalist] leaders been so shamelessly exposed'; they had 'degenerated into imperialist tools and attempted to provoke war with Russia'. No Chinese newspapers dared or wanted to publish it, but it was printed in leaflets and thrown from the roofs of high-rises in the centre of Shanghai.

Chiang Kai-shek was incensed and, in a rare move, wrote a stinging reply. He wanted to break completely with Red Sister. Ei-ling counselled restraint, arguing on political as well as personal grounds. Chiang took her advice and did not send the letter (although he did have it framed).

Red Sister's political position had been well-known. Now as she openly sided with Russia against her own country, she became extremely unpopular. She felt the tension and told a friend that she wished to be in a country where there were no Chinese. The whole family were united in criticising her. Emotional strain drove her back to Berlin in October.

Her stay in Berlin this time was a very different experience from before. Yan-da was not there to comfort and support her, though they did have their wonderful few days together when he came to say farewell. The German Communists looked after her, sending a housekeeper and arranging for luminaries to befriend her, including the playwright Bertolt Brecht. But the Golden Twenties were over. Unemployment rose alarmingly; beggars knocked on her door six or seven times a day; theft was rife. Jobless actors wandered the streets and violinists played outside cafés in snow and frost for a few *Reichspfennig*. Like her German friends, she was full of apprehension that the Nazis were gaining momentum, and wrote in a letter in February 1931 that a Nazi win was 'unavoidable in the near future'. In this environment, her commitment to Communism strengthened.

In April, she received a telegram from her family saying that her mother was gravely ill. Still furious with them, she did not go home. She would never see her mother again. In July, Mrs Soong died. Neither of her sisters wrote; clearly they were angry with her for not returning to visit their dying mother. Ei-ling's husband telegrammed, and a few days later T.V. cabled, telling her 'Please come back at once.' Mrs Soong was to be buried in Shanghai in a public ceremony, and it would not look good if she did not attend. Ching-ling set off home, with a Chinese assistant who was an undercover Communist. Their first stop was Moscow, where Ching-ling stayed for a day and held a secret meeting with Soviet leaders. When the train entered China, she was given a stately reception and provided with a special train. A government official, who was a relative, came to the border to escort her southbound. He described to Ching-ling her mother's illness and death. At last it sank in that she had come too late, and she cried the entire night. When she saw the house where her mother had died, she sobbed uncontrollably. And she wept throughout the funeral.

But with the pressure of her mother's disapproval lifted, Red Sister settled back in Shanghai, leaving her voluntary exile in Europe and entering self-imposed exile in her home city.

The day before her mother's funeral, Yan-da, who had now organised an underground Third Party in China, was arrested. He and Ching-ling had not had the chance to meet up. Of all Chiang's opponents, who at the time included Sun Yat-sen's son Fo, Yan-da was the biggest threat to the Generalissimo. Not only did he have charisma and leadership qualities, he also had a well thought-out political programme, which Chiang lacked. He had travelled in Europe and Asia to study how different countries were run and had produced a detailed policy agenda, at the core of which was the alleviation of the peasants' poverty. The biggest headache for Chiang, though, was Yan-da's influence in the military, where he had legions of admirers. Chiang ordered that Yan-da be executed in secret in Nanjing on 29 November 1931.

The news leaked out. Hoping against hope that this was just a rumour, Ching-ling went to Chiang in Nanjing to plead for Yan-da's release. This was the only time she appealed to her brother-in-law in person for anything. She was at her most amiable to the Generalissimo, saying: 'I've come to mediate your differences with Deng Yan-da. Send for him and we can discuss everything.' Chiang was silent for a while before muttering, 'It's too late ...' Ching-ling exploded, screaming, 'You butcher!' The Generalissimo hurriedly left the room. Ching-ling departed for Shanghai in a state of despair. She penned a tirade against the Nationalist party and, for the first time, publicly called for its 'downfall'. Also for the first time, she openly hinted that she might switch her allegiance to the Communists. The article drew much attention. It took up two pages in the *New York Times*, and the caption under a wistful picture of her read: 'I Speak for Revolutionary China'. Its Chinese translation was published in an influential Shanghai newspaper, the *Shen-bao*. For this and other acts of defiance against the Generalissimo, the managing director of the newspaper, Shi Liang-cai, would be assassinated.

It was in the aftermath of the death of Yan-da that Ching-ling approached the secret Comintern representative in Shanghai and requested to join the Communist Party. She was already working for the Communists: the Comintern was using her as planned, so there was no need for her to become a party member. Indeed, if she joined she would have to subject herself to the orders and disciplines of the Communist organisation, and would run much higher personal risks – both vis-à-vis Chiang and in inner-party struggles, which she had witnessed first-hand.

But Red Sister was determined. All she was thinking of was how to get Chiang. She told the Comintern representative that she was 'willing to give it all', and that she 'understood profoundly' the implications of clandestine work in Shanghai. The representative hesitated, and she insisted. In the end, her wish was granted. Afterwards, the Comintern thought this was 'a big mistake': 'once she became a party member, she would lose her unique value'. It kept her membership a secret.

It became one of the best-kept secrets in modern Chinese history and was not revealed until the 1980s, after she had died, by Liao Cheng-zhi, son of Liao Zhong-kai, the assassinated old faithful aide of Sun's. Liao junior was an underground Communist himself. One day in May 1933, he recalled, Ching-ling came to his house. With some pretext, she deftly sent his mother, who was her own best friend, out of the room and talked to him alone. Her opening words were, 'I am here on behalf of the Supreme Party.' 'The Supreme Party?' he stared at her in astonishment. 'The Comintern,' she clarified. He nearly cried out in disbelief. 'Calm down,' she said. 'I have just two questions for you. First, can our clandestine network continue to function in Shanghai? Second, I want a list of the names of the traitors you know.' She told him he had ten minutes to write down the names and, taking a cigarette out of her purse and lighting it, she got up and walked into his mother's room. Ten minutes later, she emerged and Liao handed her the list. She opened her purse again for another cigarette, picked a little tobacco out of it, nimbly rolled the list into a very thin tube, and pushed it into the cigarette. Then she left. Liao wrote in his reminiscences, 'Although nearly 50 years have passed. I remember totally clearly every minute of that brief meeting of less than half an hour.' Ching-ling had even received training as a secret agent.

In the years to come, Red Sister stood as the most prominent dissident openly challenging Chiang's regime, right under its nose in Shanghai. She gave whatever help the Chinese Communists asked for: transferring large sums of money to the CCP, or finding the right escorts to take their emissaries to Moscow. When their radio links with Moscow were cut off, she transmitted their messages through her own secret wireless. One particular service she performed was to arrange for the American journalist Edgar Snow to interview Mao and his colleagues in the Red area. The result was the international bestseller *Red Star Over China*, which introduced Mao to the West as a highly likeable man.

Ching-ling formed a front organisation in Shanghai for the Comintern: the China League for Civil Rights. It consisted of a group of like-minded radicals, foreign and Chinese, who were her friends in her seclusion. They held long meetings in her sitting room and shared earnest discussions over her dinners. The young activists adored her. One, Harold Isaacs, wrote in later life:

I was smitten hard by this beautiful great lady, as who could not have been, it seemed to me then, and seems so to me now ... I was twenty-one ... and enormously impressionable; she was about forty and enormously impressive as a woman and as a person. For her beauty, her courage, her queenly espousal of just cause, I came to love her like a young knight pure in heart. In return she bestowed on me an ever correct yet warmly personal affection. Make what one might of that now, that is how it was.

She was a thorn in Chiang's side. Chiang's intelligence agents sent her bullets in the post to try and scare her into silence. An intimate friend Yang Xing-fo, chief executive of her League for Civil Rights, was shot dead near her house in a car, together with the driver, and Yang's fifteen-year-old son narrowly escaped. A 'car accident' for her was discussed, even rehearsed. But the Generalissimo ultimately vetoed it. Of all the considerations, his wife's reaction, backed by Big Sister, was paramount. In spite of everything, May-ling remained deeply attached to her sister as well as fiercely committed to the Soong family. Ching-ling had taken her to America when she was nine, and she had many sweet memories of Ching-ling's loving care towards her. Little Sister had missed rice and Ching-ling had devised a way to cook it in her room. She put it in a flask filled with boiling water, it slowly cooked overnight, and they ate it the following day. May-ling would absolutely not allow her sister to be harmed, however annoyed she might be with her. The first lady even felt a respect for the way Red Sister 'stood alone', defying the world.

May-ling also sympathised with her sister's unremitting hatred for Chiang because he had killed Deng Yan-da, the man she knew Ching-ling cared for deeply. In particular, many people said that

Chiang had had Yan-da cruelly tortured before having him shot. The Generalissimo assured his wife that there had been no torture, and May-ling believed him. But she could not convince her sister, who absolutely refused to trust Chiang. May-ling wanted the world to know that her husband was not a torturer. Towards the end of her life, she made a point of stating that Chiang had not had Yan-da tortured before having him shot.

Thanks to the protection of May-ling – and Big Sister – Ching-ling lived through her internal exile unscathed.

The Husband and Wife Team

The Japanese invasion in September 1931 brought Chiang Kai-shek an external enemy and an opportunity to break out of his political isolation. He pleaded for national unity and invited opponents to join his government. (The invitation did not include the Communists, who were regarded as 'bandits'.) Some responded – on condition that he resign as government chairman. Chiang did so – though not before seeing to it that two lightweights were made the chairman and the prime minister. The latter was Sun Yat-sen's son, Fo, who lacked his late father's killer instinct. Chiang would claw back these posts later. For now, he called the shots as the military chief, the Generalissimo.

Chiang relaxed repression and won over many critics. The leading liberal, Hu Shih, was invited to be the minister of education. Although he declined, he became better disposed towards Chiang. The Generalissimo, Hu observed, had grown 'considerably more tolerant of dissent than before'. In this shift, one could detect the influence of May-ling and Big Sister.

Red Sister Ching-ling inadvertently helped push Hu into Chiang's arms. Hu had joined her League for Civil Rights, as he shared its ostensible goal to fight for freedom of speech and human rights. One day in 1933, the league arranged for him to visit a prison and afterwards published a letter implicitly in his name, charging the government with using gruesome forms of torture. Hu Shih was alarmed. He had not found signs of torture in the prison and nor had he written the letter. He wrote to Ching-ling asking for a correction, and then gave frank interviews to the press. Ching-ling denounced him and expelled him from the league. Hu Shih realised that the league was a front for the Communists, who were trying to use him. He began to think that Chiang was the only acceptable leader around and, moreover, the Nationalists had the potential to move from dictatorship to democracy. His criticisms of Chiang became noticeably restrained.

Yet some die-hard dissenters continued to plot against the Generalissimo; in 1933 another breakaway government was declared in the coastal province of Fujian. Chiang defeated it. He also waged 'extermination campaigns' against the 'Communist bandits' who held huge hunks of land in China's rich south-east, and drove them out in 1934.

May-ling had been in the depth of depression following her mother's death in 1931. Her husband was determined to pull her out of it, and had a special gift made for her in 1932. It was no ordinary present – it was a necklace made out of a mountain. The gemstone of the pendant is actually a beautiful villa with emerald-green glazed roof tiles, nestling in the midst of the Purple Gold Mountain. The chains of the necklace are long rows of French plane trees that line the driveway from the villa to the entrance gate. Their leaves are a different colour to the surrounding native forest, and in autumn, the contrast is particularly spectacular when they become a unique shade of yellow-red. Taking a ride in a private plane, May-ling could have a magnificent view of her present, with the brilliant green roof tiles of her villa shining and sparkling like a giant emerald.

A large portion of the Purple Gold Mountain, the pride of Nanjing, was now the mausoleum for Sun Yat-sen's corpse. Chiang had the villa built as 'the residence for the chairman of the Nationalist government' – when he was the chairman. After he left office, it did not house the next chairman, but remained at the Generalissimo's disposal. When he presented it to May-ling, it was adorned with dozens of carved phoenixes, the symbol for an empress. It became known as the 'May-ling Palace'.

With this 'necklace', Chiang also hoped that his wife would stay more often with him in Nanjing. May-ling had been reluctant to come, preferring to stay in Shanghai. The capital seemed to her to be 'nothing but a little village with one so-called broad street', and primitive, uncomfortable houses. But Chiang needed to be in the capital, and would miss her. He said that he only felt 'reassured' waking up in the middle of the night with her sleeping next to him.

As the 1930s unfolded, May-ling spent increasingly more time with her husband. When Chiang drove the Reds out of their territory in south-east China in 1934, she went with him to some of the recently vacated areas. The Reds' occupation had lasted several years, and together with their battles against Chiang's army, had created a vast wasteland. She wrote at the time: 'thousands of *li* of fertile rice fields are now devastated ruins; hundreds of thousands of families have been rendered homeless'. In the villages, empty houses 'stood with doors gaping wide. Inside mutilated pieces of furniture sprawled in confusion. The walls were scorched and blackened from hurried attempts to destroy them ... Everything that could be carried away had been damaged. Devastation and death silently pervaded the whole hamlet.' Once she stubbed her toe on a human skull. Another time, she passed by a small pagoda and saw a young man lying in its shadow, his eyes open, looking ill and emaciated. She told one of her guards to go and see what they could do to help; the guard returned and said, 'He is already dead!' In her sleep, May-ling was 'haunted by the deserted farms and ravaged villages I saw during the day'. There were more shocking scenes. One day, Chiang's army surrounded a Red unit that had been ordered to stay behind to fight a guerrilla war. The Red soldiers offered to surrender and, to prove that they meant it, killed their commander, severed his head and brought it to Chiang.

May-ling had several brushes with death. In the middle of one night at Chiang's field headquarters in Nanchang – capital of the province of Jiangxi, which had housed the centre of the Red state – she was woken up by gunshots from the direction of the city wall. Communist guerrillas had staged a surprise attack. She threw on her clothes and started to sort out 'certain papers which must not fall into enemy hands. I kept them within reach to be burnt if we had to leave the house. Then I took my revolver and sat down to wait for what might come. I heard my husband giving orders for all available guards to form a cordon, so that we could shoot our way out if we were actually surrounded by Communists.' She was not frightened. 'I had only two things on my mind: the papers giving information of our troop movements and positions, and the determination, should I be taken captive, to shoot myself.' As it happened, the attack was repelled, 'and we went back to sleep'.

Little Sister was jolted back to life. She yearned to help her husband, and searched for an answer about what she should do. She had always looked to her mother for guidance; Big Sister Ei-ling now stepped into that role after their mother's death. Ei-ling had been trying for years to persuade May-ling to become more religious, sometimes to Little Sister's irritation. Now she carried on with their mother's weekly prayer group sessions in the old family home, and encouraged May-ling to join in as a way to mourn their mother. The effect on May-ling was miraculous. She wrote, 'I was driven back to my mother's God. I knew there was a power greater than myself. I knew God was there. But Mother was no longer there to do my interceding for me. It seemed to be up to me to help the General spiritually.' She decided 'to try with all my heart and soul *and mind* to do the will of God', and prayed hard 'that God will make His will known to me'. And God, she felt eventually, spoke to her. 'God has given me a work [sic] to do for China.' That work was to champion the New Life Movement.

The idea had come to her husband when he was travelling in the former Red territory. There, Communist ideology, especially the concept of class struggle – which had so repelled him during his visit to Moscow a decade before – had been the order of the day. The poor were told it was right to rob the rich; employees were encouraged to betray or even kill their employers; children were urged to denounce their parents. To Chiang, these 'struck at

May-ling and Chiang on their honeymoon, beginning a long, eventful and extraordinary marriage.

Ei-ling and her husband, H.H. She exercised a greater influence on Chiang Kai-shek than anyone else; H.H. was Chiang's prime minister and finance minister for many years.

Red Sister – Ching-ling – went into exile in Russia in 1927, and fell in love with Deng Yan-da (to her left, in this photograph, in the Caucasus). Deng went on to form a Third Party and was executed by Chiang Kai-shek in 1931.

Chiang Kai-shek (second from right) and May-ling (next to him), sightseeing near Xian, in front of the Tomb of King Wu (first king of Zhou dynasty, 1046–1043 BC), late October 1936. The Young Marshal Zhang Xue-liang (centre, with puttee, smiling), was their host. Scarcely a month later, he launched a coup against Chiang and detained him. General Yang Hu-cheng, his co-conspirator, is on the far right, standing to attention.

May-ling risked her life to help secure her husband's release, and the Chiangs flew home in December 1936.

May-ling visiting wounded soldiers: after all-out war with Japan broke out in 1937, Chiang led the country in resisting the Japanese.

Ching-ling (front chair) and May-ling (behind) being carried up to the war capital Chongqing, 'City of Mountains', in 1940.

In Chongqing in 1940 the three sisters showed a united front and appeared in public together for the first time in more than ten years. Big Sister (left) and Little Sister (centre) were very close, whereas Red Sister (right) stayed slightly apart from them.

The sisters with Chiang Kai-shek at a reception in Chongqing, 1940 (from left: May-ling, Ei-ling, Chiang, Ching-ling). Ching-ling always kept a distance from her brother-in-law, whom she loathed.

The sisters visiting a military hospital in Chongqing, 1940.

The Chiangs with Captain Claire Chennault (left), leader of the American Volunteer Group, or 'Flying Tigers', during the Second World War. Chennault said of Little Sister: 'She will always be a princess to me.'

For the American general Joseph Stilwell, Ching-ling 'is the most simpatico of the three women' (early 1940s, Chongqing).

Chongqing, 1942: May-ling (centre) charmed Wendell Willkie (to her right), Roosevelt's personal representative, who invited her to America. Ching-ling (second right), complained privately that she could not get a word in with Willkie. H.H. Kung is between the sisters.

May-ling had a triumphant official visit to America in 1943.
The highlight was addressing Congress, 18 February.

May-ling (centre, with flowers on her lap) spoke to a crowd of 30,000 in the Hollywood Bowl in Los
Angeles, 1943. She brought Ei-ling's children, David (second from the left) and Jeanette (far right),
on the American trip and gave them prominent exposure. Second from right is the outstanding
diplomat Wellington Koo (who had been acting president of China in 1927).

The Chiangs with President Roosevelt and Prime Minister Winston Churchill
at the Cairo Conference, November 1943.

T.V. Soong (right), China's wartime foreign minister, with President Roosevelt
and US Postmaster General James Farley in Washington in 1942. A commemorative stamp
was issued on 7 July that year in recognition of the Fifth Anniversary of Chinese
Resistance to Japanese Aggression.

The Soong brothers, T.A. (far left),
T.V (centre) and T.L. (far right), with
their wives, celebrating Christmas in
Washington D.C., 1942.

The Chiangs eating under his
portrait, early 1940s.

all the fundamental principles' of traditional Chinese ethics. He took it upon himself to resurrect the ethics of old China, in which loyalty and honour were essential. The Generalissimo launched the New Life Movement in spring 1934 in Nanchang.

May-ling threw herself into the project, although to her the movement meant something else. During her travels with her husband in the heartland, she saw real China for the first time in her life. Like a Westerner who had just strayed outside the gilded screens of Shanghai, she found the place filthy, smelly, chaotic and aggressive. Men walked around half naked. Boys, even grown-ups, urinated at street corners. To her as to many foreigners, China appeared 'old, dirty, and repulsive'. May-ling found herself 'more disturbed as I traverse the crowded, dirty streets of an interior city than I am by the hazards of flying with poor visibility'. She longed to change her country into a place of which she could feel proud. For Little Sister, making the whole population adopt good manners was essentially what the New Life Movement was about.

Husband and wife put their heads together and agreed that the 'Movement should start from the simple and proceed to the complex, advance from the practical to the idealistic'. First of all, they attempted to tell the population how to behave. May-ling asserted that 'if a man were sloppy and careless about his personal appearance, about his bearing ... he would also be untidy in thought'.

So, from the ruins of the ravaged former Red land, the land that had been through so much terror and slaughter, the Generalissimo told the Chinese that a better future lay in injunctions like: 'Do not make noises while drinking and chewing'; 'Do not shout and laugh loudly in restaurants and tea houses'; 'Correct your posture'; and 'Do not spit'. Coolies were forbidden to bare their torsos. And all should button up their shirts. Pedestrians were told to 'walk on the left-hand side of the street' (to which some wags replied 'Won't the right-hand side of the streets be empty?').

The New Life Movement became the Chiangs' pet project, and the regime's signature domestic policy. It was promoted as the cure for all ills, guaranteeing a glorious future for the country. This grand claim was patently untrue, even though nobody would deny that decorum, orderliness and good manners were essential to a civilised society. Commenting on a government pamphlet that laid down fifty-four rules and forty-two hygienic requirements, Hu Shih, the leading liberal, wrote that mostly they were 'a basic common sense way of life for a civilised person; there is neither any panacea to save the country nor will there be any miracle cure to revive the nation'. He pointed out that many bad habits were 'the products of poverty. The average people's living standard is so low that it is impossible for them to develop good manners.' 'When children were scouring rubbish dumps to find half a burnt-out coal, or a bit of filthy rag, how could you accuse them of dishonesty if they pocketed a lost item they had picked up?' asked Hu Shih. (One of the New Life rules was to 'return lost items you found'.) 'The first responsibility of the government is to make sure the average man can live a decent life ... To teach them how to lead this so-called new life can only be the last thing.'

Hu Shih's sensible voice was drowned by vilification from Chiang's propaganda machine. May-ling would 'refute this argument' with what she called 'the very evident fact that, if everyone from the highest official to the lowest wheelbarrow coolie would conscientiously practice these principles in everyday life, there would be food for all'. Although this was plain wishful thinking, Hu was not able to argue back. He was not persecuted either. Little Sister just indignantly dug in with her assertion that the movement was her husband's 'greatest and most constructive contribution ... to the nation'. As for herself, her action was directed by God and could not be questioned. 'I seek guidance, and when I am sure, I go ahead, leaving the results with Him.' Energetically, she selected foreign missionaries as advisers, wrote rules and tried to enforce them, 'like the president of a really first-rate American women's club', observed one American. At her disposal were paid staff and hundreds of thousands of volunteers. The couple's efforts solved few real and urgent problems and petered out – even though they did produce some civilising effects.

But for May-ling the movement was life-changing: 'despondency and despair are not mine today. I look to Him who is able to do all things.'

This joint venture brought May-ling and her husband closer than ever, and they felt a new degree of affection for each other. On Christmas Day 1934, they travelled over 500 kilometres south and flew to Fujian province. There they were driven into the most mountainous region of eastern China, on a new military road. Thousands of men had sliced whole sides off high cliffs with primitive hand tools. Sometimes the Chiangs 'motored along the edge of a plateau where the least swerve would have flung us over the precipice'. At journey's end, 'my husband began to reproach himself for submitting me to such hazards'. May-ling reassured him that personal danger meant nothing to her, and that she was actually absorbed by the beauty along the route. Range upon range of mountains were covered with fir trees 'in their Christmas green, brightened here and there ... by a single candleberry tree of flaming red'. 'It was gorgeous, unlike anything I have ever seen.'

On New Year's Eve, the couple took a walk in the mountains. They paused to admire a young tree heavy with white plum blossom. In Chinese literature the winter plum is the symbol of courage: it flowers in the coldest weather. Chiang carefully broke off a few twigs with clusters of blossom and carried them back. That evening, when candles were lit and they sat down to supper, he had the twigs brought to the table in a little bamboo basket. In the candlelight, the shadows of the branches on the wall made large bold strokes, while the blossoms spread their delicate scent. Chiang presented the basket to May-ling as a New Year present. She was moved, and wrote, 'My husband has the courage of the soldier, and the sensitive soul of the poet.'

Getting Chiang's Son Back from Stalin's Clutches

In the days after his baptism in October 1930, Chiang Kai-shek had travelled to his birthplace at Xikou to supervise the expansion of his mother's tomb. Having built a vast mausoleum for the Father of China, he now felt he could give his own late mother a more fitting resting place. Though not nearly as big or grand as Sun's, this mausoleum would nevertheless comprise a whole hill, commanding a magnificent panoramic view of the east China countryside. The entrance was at the top of a climb of nearly 700 metres through pine trees.

May-ling and Ei-ling went with him. On the first day of the trip, they bought up a subject that was the closest to his heart: how to get his son Ching-kuo back from Russia. Ching-kuo, the Generalissimo's son with his first wife, had been held hostage by Stalin for the past five years.

Born on 27 April 1910, Ching-kuo was fifteen when Chiang sent him to a school in Beijing. The young man's dream was to learn French and then study in France. But as his father's star rose among the Nationalists, the Russians were eager to get their hands on Ching-kuo, and diplomats in the embassy quickly befriended him. According to Ching-kuo's own account of his life (which at his request was made public after his death in 1988), they 'persuaded' him that he 'should go to Russia to study'. Stalin kept children of foreign revolutionary leaders in Russia as potential hostages, while giving them an education. The impressionable boy was keen to go. And Chiang, who was pretending to be pro-Russian at the time, could not object.

Within only months of arriving in Beijing, Ching-kuo was taken to Moscow by a Red mole working inside the Nationalist party, Shao Li-tzu. Shao had been a founding member of the CCP in 1920, but had been told by Moscow to keep his identity secret and to operate as a Nationalist. He brought along his son, who was the same age as Ching-kuo. When Ching-kuo completed his studies at Sun Yat-sen University in Moscow in April 1927 and asked to return to China, he was not allowed to leave. His father had just broken with the Communists and Stalin was holding him hostage. Moscow told the world that the young man refused to go home, since his father had 'betrayed the revolution'.

The seventeen-year-old was 'isolated completely from China', and was 'not even allowed to mail a letter'. He missed home day and night: 'I did not know how to stop thinking of my parents and my native country.' He felt he was 'in the mire of distress and homesickness'. Many times he asked to be allowed to go home, or just to send a letter; each time the request was turned down. Sometimes, he feverishly wrote letters to his father, only to destroy them later. He did keep one letter and managed to give it discreetly to a fellow Chinese to take to China (after he sold some belongings to help raise funds for the journey); but the man was arrested near the border.

In captivity, and with no hope of breaking out, the young man developed a tough resolve and bided his time. He withdrew from a Trotskyist organisation which he had joined in his student days and volunteered to be a member of the Russian Communist Party. He enrolled into the Red Army and proved himself to be a brave soldier. As a result, he was allowed to live in Russian society rather than a prison cell, but Moscow decided where he should live and how.

In October 1930, at the time May-ling and Ei-ling talked to his father about getting him back, Ching-kuo was sent to work in a power plant as a labourer, working from 8 a.m. to 5 p.m. non-stop except an hour's break for lunch. As he was unaccustomed to heavy manual labour, his arms swelled, his back was so sore that he could not stand up straight, and he suffered from constant pain and exhaustion. Food was in great shortage and very expensive; his pay was not enough to feed himself, and he was permanently half starved. 'I often went to work on an empty stomach,' he recalled. He had to take on an extra job to earn more money, so his working day was extended to 11 p.m. He gritted his teeth and told himself that 'hard work would be a good way to discipline myself'.

After the factory, he was sent to do 'labour reform' in a village outside Moscow. There he learned to plough the fields and slept in a hut that even a peasant found unfit for the night. The fields he was working in reminded him of the green rice paddies around his native town, and tears 'rolled down my cheeks'.

Chiang Kai-shek missed his son acutely, particularly as he knew that life for his son in Stalin's hands must be hell. Over the years, in his diary, he described his yearning for Ching-kuo time and again. Ching-kuo was Chiang's only blood offspring. May-ling was unable to conceive after her miscarriage and, although Chiang adopted another son, Wei-go, Ching-kuo was his real son and heir. To have a male heir was the most important thing for a Chinese man. One of the worst curses in China was: 'May you have no heir!' 'Heirlessness' (*jue-hou*) was also deemed to be the greatest hurt one could inflict on one's parents and ancestors, and Chiang's obsessive love and mourning for his late mother made his agony about his son all the more intense.

When May-ling and Big Sister began talking to Chiang about seeking Ching-kuo's release in 1930, China and Russia were still in dispute over the Chinese Eastern Railway. This had been such a hot issue that Russia had invaded China a year before and diplomatic relations had been broken. Ei-ling made a suggestion: perhaps Chiang could make some compromise over the railway in return for his son? Chiang was touched by the sisters' concern and wrote in his diary on 1 November, 'Big Sister and my wife would not forget about my son Ching-kuo. I am so moved.' But he decided not to take the advice. Moscow was demanding something that was an infringement of China's sovereignty. To give in would cause a public outrage. But the idea of doing a deal for his son with Moscow germinated. He decided he needed to think and plan carefully. 'We should not try to solve this matter in haste,' he wrote in his diary.

A year later, Moscow itself proposed a swap. The head of Comintern operations in the Far East, going by the pseudonym Hilaire Noulens, had been arrested and imprisoned in Shanghai together with his wife. As they knew so many secrets, Moscow was eager to get them out fast. A host of international stars, including Albert Einstein, were mobilised to pressure Nanjing for their release. Red Sister added her voice. And it was she who brought Moscow's plan for a hostage exchange to Chiang in December 1931. Chiang turned it down. The swap was quite impossible. The imprisonment of the two agents was a high-profile public affair; they had been openly tried and sentenced to death (commuted to life imprisonment). Any horse trading would be exposed and would wreck Chiang's reputation.

But Moscow's offer unleashed a torrent of anguish in the Generalissimo. It was now clear that Ching-kuo was a hostage and could return only at an extremely high price. The Russians might well demand something else in the future. Day after day, Chiang wrote in his diary. 'In the past few days, I have been longing to see my son more than ever. How can I face my parents when I die?' 'I dreamed of my late mother and cried out to her twice. After I woke up, I missed her so much. I have committed a great sin to her.' 'I am unfilial to my mother and unloving to my son. I feel I am a worthless man and I wish the ground would open up and swallow me.'

It was at this time that the Red mole, Shao, who had taken Ching-kuo to Moscow, lost *his* son. Shao had brought his own son to the Red capital with Ching-kuo. His son had since returned to China, and later went to Europe. He was shot dead in a hotel room in Rome. Shao and his family were convinced that he had been murdered by Chiang's agents.

With its offer rebuffed, Moscow threw Ching-kuo into the gulag in Siberia in 1932. In a gold mine he did back-breaking labour, always hungry, always cold. Among his fellow labourers were 'professors, students, aristocrats, engineers, rich farmers and robbers. Each of them had had an unlooked-for, unexpected misfortune which had sent him into exile.' Sleeping on his left side was a former engineer; he would say to Ching-kuo before retiring at night, 'A day is over. I am moving one day nearer the recovery of my freedom and the return to my home.' Ching-kuo held tight to the same hope.

In December 1932, Chiang's government resumed diplomatic relations with Russia. A mutual enemy, Japan, made an amicable relationship imperative. Japan had attacked Shanghai; the Japanese puppet state, Manchukuo, had been set up in Manchuria; and the Japanese were encroaching further south. A full-scale conflict looked unavoidable. China needed Russia. Russia, the historical rival of Japan in the Far East, needed China: Stalin's most dreaded scenario was that Japan would take over China and then use its resources and a porous 7,000-kilometre border to attack the Soviet Union. He wanted the Chinese to fight and bog down the Japanese so they would not turn on Russia. As the foes were gingerly becoming friends, Chiang started to plan in earnest about getting his son back. He knew he had to offer the Russians something that mattered to them dearly, and his thoughts turned to the Chinese Reds.

At the time, the Generalissimo was waging wars against the breakaway Red state in south-east China. He had surrounded the Reds, and had been determined to stamp them out. Now he began to think that instead he could just drive them out of the rich south-east near Shanghai, then herd them north-west into barren and sparsely populated North Shaanxi on the Yellow Earth Plateau. He could deplete them along the way, while taking care to preserve the Communist leadership. At the destination, he could box them in, let them hover on the edge of survival, and make sure they could not expand. He reckoned that when the war with Japan started, they would go into battles (Stalin would want them to do so), and there would be a strong chance that the Japanese would wipe them out. Meanwhile, because he had let the Chinese

Communists survive, Stalin, who cared very much about them, would release his son.

Such was the Generalissimo's calculation.

In autumn 1934, Chiang drove the Reds out of China's rich south-east. Their flight came to be known as the Long March. It is generally recognised that the Reds were defeated and were fleeing, but few realise that the fact that the journey took place at all, and that the Reds were able to survive it, was fundamentally thanks to Chiang Kai-shek's design to have his son released.

The Long March took a year and covered 6,000 miles (far longer in both time and distance than Chiang had intended – thanks to Mao's machinations on the March*). The Marchers went through tremendous hardships and were much diminished. At its end, Chiang told himself that the CCP was 'showing signs of willingness to surrender' – whereas in fact the opposite was true. Desperate to get his son back, the Generalissimo was deluding himself.

Chiang's 'Reds for Son' deal could not be spelt out, even to Moscow, and Chiang had to send Moscow implicit but unambiguous signals. At each moment of the Long March when the Reds accomplished a key objective, he would let Moscow know that it was he who was responsible for it and he would ask for the return of Ching-kuo. Just before the start of the Long March, Chiang sent the first formal request for Ching-kuo's release through diplomatic channels, which he recorded in his diary on 2 September. After the Reds had successfully passed through layers of his painstakingly constructed blockades, Nanjing repeatedly asked for Ching-kuo. There were many documents in Russian Foreign Ministry files reporting: 'Chiang Kai-shek requests the return of his son.' Each time, Moscow pretended that Ching-kuo did not wish to go home. 'There is no end to the Russian enemy's revolting deceit,' Chiang wrote in his diary.

---

* For details of Mao's machinations on the Long March, see Jung Chang and Jon Halliday, *Mao, the Unknown Story*, Chapters 12–14.

The Generalissimo accomplished another goal through the Long March. To the west of the emptied Red base were two provinces, Guizhou and Sichuan, which kept their own armies and paid Nanjing lip service. Chiang wanted to bring them under firm control. To achieve this he had to have his own troops on the spot, but the provinces did not welcome them. Now the Generalissimo pushed the Red Army into the provinces. The local chiefs were frightened of the Reds settling in their territory and allowed Chiang's army in to chase the Reds out; so Chiang was able to establish control over the provinces. Sichuan, in particular, would become his base in the war against Japan, with its biggest city, Chongqing, serving as the wartime capital.

This scheme of Chiang's was easy to spot. In case Moscow missed his more important goal, Chiang let the Reds escape after he had conquered the two provinces, and, moreover, let Mao's group join forces with another Red branch in June 1935. Right after this, Ei-ling's husband H.H. Kung, at the time vice premier (Chiang had taken back the post of prime minister), called on the Russian ambassador, Dmitri Bogomolov, and told him that Chiang wanted his son back. His visit made Chiang's horse-trading intention clear.

On 18 October 1935, the day the Long March ended for the CCP leadership, Chiang saw Bogomolov himself for a friendly meeting. He did not mention Ching-kuo, but immediately afterwards sent Chen Li-fu, nephew of Godfather Chen, to the ambassador to make the request. That Chiang intended to exchange the Reds for his son was all but spelt out.

Because the deal was still implicit (and not agreed on beforehand), Moscow played deaf and dumb. Stalin now knew about the Generalissimo's weakest spot, and held onto his hostage in order to get more out of Chiang. Bogomolov and everyone else contacted by Chiang's emissaries gave the same old lie that Ching-kuo did not want to leave Russia.

Meanwhile, thanks to his incredible value, Ching-kuo was given better treatment. He was released from the gulag and assigned a job as a technician in a machinery plant in the Urals. There, he led a more or less normal life, studying engineering in an evening school, and even rising to be the assistant director of the plant. He fell in love with a Russian technician called Faina Vakhreva. 'She understood my situation best and was always there to sympathize and help me whenever I had difficulties. When I felt sad for not being able to see my parents, she tried to soothe me.' They were married in 1935. The first of their four children was born in December that year, into the same captivity that Ching-kuo would continue to endure.

14

'A woman protects a man'

In October 1936, the three major Red Army forces, with tens of thousands of men, all completed their Long March and converged in their new 'home' in north-west China. Again, Chiang asked Moscow to give back his son. May-ling spoke to the new Chinese ambassador to the Soviet Union, telling him to press the matter hard. But there was no sign of Ching-kuo. The Generalissimo decided to put pressure on Stalin and ordered the Nationalist army surrounding the Reds to relaunch his 'extermination campaign'. The Reds were now in deadly trouble. They were on the Yellow Earth Plateau, where the loess, the most highly erodible terrain on earth, created a barren landscape. Here, it was impossible for a large army to survive, let alone build a base.

But the chief of the local Nationalist army declined to carry out Chiang's orders. He had his own agenda. This was Zhang Xue-liang, the Young Marshal, former warlord of Manchuria. When the Japanese invaded the region in 1931, he had retreated into China proper, taking with him 200,000 troops. Chiang stationed him and his troops in the province of Shaanxi, whose capital, Xian, was some 300 kilometres to the south of the Reds.

Zhang's American pilot, Royal Leonard, gave this description of him: 'here was the president of a Rotary Club: rotund, prosperous, with an easy, affable manner ... We were friends in five minutes.' He had a reputation for being a playboy, who 'does nothing with his troops. Just flies around in his private plane.' Known as the Flying Palace, this luxury Boeing may well have been bought with

Chiang's multimillion-dollar bribe (for helping Chiang defeat his party rivals in 1930). The Young Marshal often piloted it himself for fun, his long robe tucked up around his knees and his cap awry. But this frivolous image masked a man of boundless ambition and gambler-like daring. Like so many other provincial potentates, he did not think much of Chiang's ability and believed he could do a better job. He aspired to supplant the Generalissimo, and the arrival of the CCP gave him a golden opportunity. Anyone who wanted to be the 'king' knew that Stalin was the kingmaker, and the route to Stalin's favour was through the CCP. The Young Marshal got in touch with the Reds, provided them with desperately needed food and clothing, and began to plot with them against Chiang. Moscow encouraged these machinations, in order to get the Young Marshal to keep helping the Red Army. Mao went a step further and spurred him on to get rid of Chiang. The Young Marshal was led to believe that Moscow would back him to replace Chiang. Under this illusion he hatched a plan to stage a coup – with the expectation that once that happened, Moscow would announce its support for him.

The Young Marshal lured Chiang to Xian by telling the Generalissimo that the troops would not obey his order to wage war against the Reds in Shaanxi because they wanted to fight Japan instead in their homeland, Manchuria, and he asked Chiang to come to Xian to persuade them himself. The Generalissimo duly went at the beginning of December 1936.

At dawn on 12 December, Chiang had just finished his routine exercises and was getting dressed when he heard gunfire. Some 400 of the Young Marshal's men were attacking his quarters. Many of Chiang's guards were killed, including his chief of security. Chiang managed to escape into the hills behind and hid in a crevasse, clad only in his nightshirt in the bitter cold, with no shoes or socks. He was lucky to be alive, but he was captured by a search unit. The Young Marshal publicly declared that he had taken the action because he wanted to force Chiang to fight the Japanese. He wired Nanjing his demands, the first being 'reorganisation of the Nanjing government'. He assumed that the CCP and Moscow would propose him to head the new government, as Mao had led him to believe.

Vice Premier H.H. Kung was in Shanghai when he heard the news of Chiang's arrest. He went at once to inform his sister-in-law. To May-ling, this was 'like a thunderclap out of a clear sky'. They went back to the Kungs' house to discuss with Ei-ling what to do. The only non-family member there was William Donald, Sun Yat-sen's old Australian adviser now serving May-ling. He had previously worked for the Young Marshal and had helped the playboy kick his opium addiction. Among the many remarkable qualities that enabled him to move through the powerhouses of China were Donald's sound judgement, and his ability to level with the powerful without angering them. The fact that he had made a point of not learning Chinese was, paradoxically, seen as an advantage, as this made it unlikely he would intrigue with Chiang's colleagues. May-ling asked Donald to hurry to Xian to find out what had happened. It was obvious to him that she did not trust a Chinese for the mission.

May-ling, Big Sister, H.H. Kung and Donald took the overnight train to Nanjing, arriving in the capital at seven in the morning. The four of them were having breakfast when the minister of war, General Ho Ying-ching, came to report the outcome of an emergency top-level meeting during the night. The participants in the meeting had not waited for Vice Premier Kung because he had been such a negligible figure in decision-making in Chiang's one-man dictatorship. In the name of the Nanjing government, the meeting had publicly condemned the Young Marshal and sacked him from all posts, promising severe punishment. They threatened war against Xian. May-ling was hugely upset. War against Xian would effectively mean dropping bombs on her husband. His safety was her absolute priority. That the top officials had made the decision to attack and announced it before H.H. Kung and she had arrived in Nanjing only added to her fury and roused her worst suspicions. She told Donald to go to Xian to see the Generalissimo first. General Ho, who disliked Donald on account of his influence with the Chiangs, objected to him going. May-ling brushed his protest aside, and gave Donald a letter to carry to her husband, telling the Generalissimo to take care and to let her know the lie of the land.

May-ling tried to compose herself. She did not want to be 'regarded as a woman who could not be expected to be reasonable in such a situation', but she was boiling with rage at the top officials in Nanjing. She was convinced that her husband's many foes were using the crisis to have him killed, and insisted on flying to Xian to persuade the Young Marshal to release Chiang. The Nanjing leaders regarded her confidence in her own powers of persuasion as fantasy.

In fact, the Young Marshal did not need to be convinced to release Chiang. Two days after the Generalissimo's capture, he realised that he had made a catastrophic mistake – and he was already planning to release Chiang, and even to go to Nanjing with him. On that day, 14 December, Moscow used the harshest language to condemn his actions, accusing him of helping the Japanese, and emphatically endorsed the Generalissimo. Moscow had realised that Chinese public opinion showed an almost universal support for Chiang. People were aware that Chiang's troops were at this very moment putting up stiff resistance against Japan's encroachment in Suiyuan, north China. They saw that the Generalissimo was a staunch opponent of Japan and that his demise would only facilitate Japanese conquest. Nobody thought that the Young Marshal could step into his shoes.

H.H. Kung, now the acting prime minister, contacted influential people across the country inviting their help – and most of them reacted positively. One of the few who did not cooperate was Red Sister Ching-ling. When H.H. called on her for support, she told him that she was delighted that Chiang had been caught, that the Young Marshal's actions were entirely right, and that 'I would have done the same thing if I had been in his place. *Only I would have gone farther!*' But she did not express these sentiments publicly: Moscow would have been furious.

H.H. sent a message to Stalin that 'word was around' that the CCP was involved in the coup, and that 'if Mr Chiang's life were endangered, the anger of the nation would extend from the CCP to the Soviet Union.' This, he strongly implied, could lead to the country joining hands with Japan against Russia. Stalin escalated the condemnation of the Young Marshal and ordered the CCP to help secure Chiang's release.

It could not be clearer to the former warlord that the game was definitely up. Moscow had denounced him. Mao had tricked him. He had to find a way to save his own skin. His only option was to stay with Chiang Kai-shek. But the Nanjing government was sure to have him shot. Not only had he staged a coup, he had killed many Nationalist officials (and soldiers) in the process, including high officials. Their families and colleagues would all be calling for his blood. His only hope was that the Generalissimo would spare him if he was released. But knowing how stubborn Chiang was, the Young Marshal could not count on Chiang to agree to a deal, and even if Chiang did agree, he could not count on the Generalissimo to keep his end of the bargain. The only person who could do a deal on Chiang's behalf and make Chiang honour the deal was May-ling. And the Young Marshal felt he could trust her. The two had genuinely got on well, both speaking English. More importantly, he knew that she was straightforward and fair, and that if he did a deal with her she would not double-cross him. Her Christian faith also meant that she would be inclined to forgive him, if he presented himself as a repentant sinner.

From 14 December, the Young Marshal sent May-ling a string of messages through Donald, beseeching her to come to Xian. He said he had only tried to pressure Chiang to fight the Japanese, and that he had realised what he had done was wrong, although it was 'with good motives'. He vowed that he had no intention of harming her husband – in fact he wanted to release him and go to Nanjing with him. But first of all please could she come so they could sort things out together.

Nanjing found the Young Marshal's words bizarre and untrust-worthy, and refused to let May-ling risk her life by going to him. The ex-warlord was told just to set Chiang free, or face war. But May-ling's powerful instinct told her that he did intend to set her husband free, and that somehow she needed to be there to make this happen. The officials in Nanjing remained unconvinced: it could be a trap; she would be walking into a lynch mob and still would not be able to save her husband. But May-ling insisted, and Nanjing finally gave in. On 22 December, Little Sister boarded a plane heading for Xian.

Donald had come back to escort her there. In the plane, he pointed out Xian to her. Gazing at this square walled city in the embrace of snow-covered mountains, May-ling was overwhelmed with emotions. When they approached the opening of the valley leading to the city, she handed Donald her revolver before disembarking, and made him promise that 'if troops got out of control and seized me', he would shoot her 'without hesitation'.

When Chiang saw his wife walking into his room, it was his turn to be overcome with emotion. 'You have walked into a tiger's lair,' he burst out, in tears. He then told his wife that he had opened the Bible that morning, and he had been drawn to these words: 'The Lord has created a new thing on the earth: a woman protects a man.' May-ling thought that these words conveyed a double message: that she was coming, and that 'All is right.' May-ling's words came from a Robert Browning poem: 'God's in His heaven – / All's right with the world'. This gave her great hope and she comforted her husband with her optimism. Seeing that he was 'lying there injured and helpless, the shadow of his former self', she felt 'an uncontrollable wave of resentment against those responsible for his plight'. As he was 'agitated and upset', she opened the Bible and read Psalms to him until he calmed down and drifted off to sleep.

The Young Marshal did a deal with May-ling and T.V., who had come to Xian a day before her. The former warlord claimed that he had only seized Chiang on a moment of impulse, 'we tried to do something which we thought was for the good of the country. But the Generalissimo would not discuss anything with us ... I know I have done wrong, and I am not trying to justify myself or this action.' He tried to flatter May-ling, saying: 'You know I have always had great faith in you, and my associates all admire you.

When they went through the Generalissimo's papers after he was detained, they found two letters from you to the Generalissimo which caused them to hold you in even greater respect.' Her words 'moved us', he claimed, before producing the clinching argument, 'especially when you wrote that it was by God's grace that more mistakes were not made than had been made, and that you felt you should pray more for divine guidance'.

With his safety promised, the Young Marshal was ready to set his prisoner free. There was just one last hurdle to cross. The Communists demanded that Chiang talk to its emissary in Xian, the later famed diplomat Zhou En-lai, who had been in the city for some days. Chiang categorically refused to see Zhou, even though the Young Marshal told him that without the meeting he could not leave. The guards and the troops around had been thoroughly infiltrated by the Reds. For the Generalissimo to see Zhou would be like, in modern-day terms, the US president meeting the representative of a notorious terrorist group. But on Christmas Day, Zhou did walk into Chiang's bedroom. He brought with him a message fresh from Moscow: Ching-kuo, Chiang's son, would come home. Moscow knew that this was the one thing for which Chiang would compromise.

The Chiang–Zhou meeting was brief: the Generalissimo merely asked Zhou to 'come to Nanjing for direct negotiations'. But these words changed the status of the CCP. From this moment on, it stopped being officially regarded as a bandit organisation to be exterminated, and was treated instead as a legitimate and signifi-cant political party. Negotiation duly ensued, which led to the two parties forming a 'united front' as equal partners when the war against Japan started, within months. During the war, Chiang gave the CCP all sorts of concessions, which enabled the Red Army to grow enormously, so that after the war it was in a position to turn on Chiang and beat him. Chiang's desperation to get Ching-kuo back had led to him fatally underestimating what Stalin and Mao combined could do. The Generalissimo paid a huge price for his son. But he got Ching-kuo out of Stalin's clutches. The hostage was released and left Russia for home with his family in

March 1937, having survived his twelve-year ordeal, including hard labour in the gulag.

On Christmas Day 1936, after the meeting with Zhou, the Chiangs hurried away with the Young Marshal, flown by his pilot Royal Leonard. They had to spend the night in the city of Luoyang. Leonard recorded the moment when his passengers disembarked:

> As I landed the narrow, sand-swept field was filled with students and soldiers running towards us. When they saw Madame step out of the door they halted in a spray of dust and came to attention. They saluted as she set foot on the ground, and two of the officers came forward to assist her. The Young Marshal followed her. As he stepped to the ground four soldiers pointed their rifles at him.
> 'Should we kill him?' said one of the soldiers.
> 'No!' said the Madame emphatically. 'Let him alone!'
> She put her arm around him, and the Young Marshal put his arm around her ... After Madame's command he was treated like a guest of honor.

When they returned to Nanjing, the Young Marshal turned his charm on Ei-ling, who he knew had great influence on the Generalissimo. He had already formed a good relationship with her, addressing her as Big Sister and 'confessing' to her that she commanded his 'greatest respect'. He had even proposed a marital alliance between their children. 'Please forgive me,' he now implored Ei-ling; and she was softened. She said later, 'I wanted to – well, to punish him for what he'd done, and yet he was so sorry.'

In the end, the Young Marshal's only punishment was a comfortable house arrest, under which he was also protected. Over half a century later, after the deaths of both Chiang and his son, he was freed and moved to Hawaii, where he died in his bed in 2001, aged one hundred.

Chiang's popularity reached its peak after this personal ordeal. At the Luoyang airfield, when he was carried out of the plane,

Leonard saw that 'those who came to greet him went wild with excitement. They threw their hats into the air ... Some of them had tears in their eyes.' When his car drove into Nanjing, spontaneous crowds lined the streets to cheer him. Fireworks crackled all night. The Chinese wanted Chiang to lead the fight against Japan. From now on, plotters against the Generalissimo significantly dwindled in number and action.

This nationalist passion also helped Chiang overcome a strong undercurrent of resentment among his colleagues against himself and his straight-talking wife.

After returning to Nanjing, May-ling was still seething with indignation against Nanjing leaders for threatening war against Xian when her husband was there. She wrote an account of the event, in which her hostility was directed squarely at them, with not a bad word about the Young Marshal or the Communists. The picture she painted gave the impression that Chiang's colleagues were the villains responsible for his misfortune. Their action had been 'precipitous' and 'intolerable', and there had been an 'unhealthy obsession on the part of leading military officers'. The credit for Chiang's release belonged to her – and she said as much. Not only did she make a detailed inventory of the Young Marshal's flattery of her, which boiled down to saying that he had freed Chiang due to his admiration for her, she did not hesitate to offer her own conclusion: 'Mr Donald had laid the foundations, T.V. had built the walls, and it would be I who would have to put on the roof.'

The Generalissimo had his wife's article published in a booklet together with his own account of Xian, thus giving her accusations against his colleagues his stamp of approval. In one go, the couple managed to hurt and enrage virtually all of Chiang's team outside the Soong family. People tolerated May-ling: after all, she was the wife whose priority was her husband's safety, and she had no malice. But they found Chiang's behaviour unforgivable. As the leader of their party and the country, he ought to know that Nanjing's hard stance towards the Young Marshal was the only response possible from the government. Close associates like Chen Li-fu fumed for decades to come. The biggest loss for Chiang was the alienation of Dai Ji-tao, Chiang's old 'buddy', whose illegitimate son Chiang had adopted as his younger son, Wei-go. Dai had provided Chiang with much valuable frank advice over the years. This time, as he had been a major advocate for the hard stance, he bore the brunt of May-ling's ire. Sensing the Generalissimo's suspicion, Dai, like others, clammed up. Chiang Kai-shek, who had had very few dependable friends and advisers, ended up with even fewer. Loyalty, already scarce, became scarcer. Once the Japanese threat was removed, many colleagues would betray him.

But May-ling was right to feel that the crisis had been resolved thanks to her. Indeed, if she had not gone to Xian, the Young Marshal would not have been reassured about his safety under Chiang, and would not have released him. A war between Nanjing and Xian would have resulted and Chiang would almost certainly have been killed, if not by Nanjing's bombs then by the Young Marshal – who had considered this scenario – and by the Reds. (Zhou En-lai had brought to Xian a team of professionals from the Communist security apparatus, to 'assist' the Young Marshal to kill Chiang.) China would have sunk into chaotic civil war, which for Japanese invaders would have been an undreamed-of opportunity. May-ling, it could be said, saved her country as well as her husband.

PART IV

The Sisters in Wars
(1937–1950)

15

Bravery and Corruption

In July 1937, Japan occupied Beijing and Tianjin. In mid-August, all-out war broke out in Shanghai. The Chinese army fought bravely, but suffered catastrophic defeat. Over 400,000 men were wiped out, along with virtually all of the country's nascent air force and most of its warships. At this critical moment, Generalissimo Chiang Kai-shek called on the nation to resist Japan at any cost.

To set an example and to raise the morale of the troops, Mme Chiang and her sisters went to the front, made rousing public speeches, and mobilised women to train as nurses and care for orphaned children. They wrote to the foreign press, gave interviews to journalists flocking to China, and delivered broadcasts to America in perfect English.

Ei-ling focused on setting up hospitals, one of which was in the Lido Cabaret, formerly a popular dance hall which Big Sister converted into a well-equipped ward of 300 beds. With her own money, she also bought ambulances and trucks for transferring the wounded.

For the first – and perhaps only – time, Red Sister put aside her loathing for Chiang Kai-shek and asked the public to rally round the Generalissimo. She declared that she was 'extraordinarily excited, extraordinarily moved', indeed 'moved to tears' when she read Chiang's speech that called for unity with the Communists so the country could fight Japan together. She promised to 'leave behind all past grievances and grudges'.

Little Sister May-ling visited wounded soldiers devotedly. One day she was driven to a hospital in an open-top car, accompanied by her Australian adviser Donald. It was a dangerous trip as the roads were pockmarked with shell craters and Japanese planes looked out for cars, which were used only by bigwigs. Dressed in blue slacks and a shirt, May-ling was chatting to Donald animatedly when the car hit a big bump and the rear tyre blew. The car ran off the road and overturned. May-ling was hurled out over Donald's head. She landed in a ditch some twenty feet away and was knocked unconscious. When she came to, looking sick and complaining that her side hurt, Donald asked her, 'Do you want to go on and visit the soldiers?' She thought for a moment and answered, 'We'll go on.' They made the rounds of a few camps. Later doctors found that she had a broken rib and concussion.

In mid-December, Nanjing, the capital, was lost, and the conquerors carried out a massacre. The Japanese army then took all China's seaports and most key cities on the railways. Its reputation for brutality to civilians preceded it, and 95 million people fled in panic – the biggest number of refugees in history. Chiang was forced to move his government to Wuhan, 600 kilometres up the Yangtze, before settling further west in Chongqing, the 'City of Mountains' in Sichuan province. Surrounded by high peaks, with the Yangtze at its feet, navigable only to small boats, the capital of unoccupied China was well protected from the invaders. The Generalissimo ran the war from here for the next seven years.

The relocation of the government from Nanjing to Chongqing went amazingly smoothly. Under constant Japanese bombardment, hundreds of thousands of people – office workers, hospital staff, teachers and students – trekked some 2,000 kilometres, having patiently packed their precious equipment, machinery and documents into crates. The goods were then transported by (valuable) trucks when absolutely necessary, by carts when any could be found, but mostly by labourers. Machines were pulled by manpower over wooden rollers onto boats to travel up the Yangtze. In the Central University, one piece of equipment weighed seven tons, and there was no crane. By hand the students moved it inch by inch and loaded it onto a boat. The boats then had to pass through the perilous Yangtze Gorges, where the river was squeezed into a raging funnel by perpendicular cliffs bearing down from both sides, obscuring even the sky. The water seethed and roared as it was forced into whirlpools around submerged rocks. In some places, the boats had to be pulled up the rapids by boat-pullers, who worked with superhuman effort, bent double with thick ropes taut on one shoulder. To coordinate and sustain them, they grunted a hard, monotonous tune in unison.

In this manner the university managed to transfer all its movable possessions, including its substantial library – along with two dozen corpses for anatomy lessons. Its agricultural college shipped one animal from each species they owned in a boat, nicknamed by students *Noah's Ark*. The rest of the farm animals were herded by staff overland, like a nomadic tribe. The journey took a year, as the precious cattle, introduced from Holland and America, moved at their own leisurely pace, occasionally objecting angrily at having to carry chickens and ducks in bamboo cages on their backs. At the end of the trek, not one animal had been lost; there was even an addition: a calf had been born on the way.

Arriving at various stages in Chongqing, over 1,000 students and teachers found welcoming accommodation and classrooms – all dug out of the cliffs of a mountain. The new campus had been completed by 1,800 labourers in twenty-eight days, with the supervision of engineering professors who had flown there ahead.

Although the war brought great upheaval and privation to their lives, people endured stoically, and supported Chiang's decision to fight. The Generalissimo was absolutely unwavering. Although he had no idea exactly how he would win, he made it his strategy to 'outlast the enemy'. China's immense size, its mountainous terrain without roads made it impossible for Japan to occupy the whole country and gave him enough room to retreat and tough it out. Fierce nationalist sentiments sustained him. He was also bitterly upset by the death of his first wife, Ching-kuo's mother, who was killed in a Japanese bombing raid in December 1939.

The Generalissimo's hatred of Japan, where he had learned some of his martial craft, was visceral and longstanding. In May 1928, the Northern Expedition he had conducted was blocked by the

Japanese at Jinan, the capital of Shandong province. After some unsuccessful protests, Chiang had to accede to Japanese demands, which included him apologising, and took another route to Beijing. In the eyes of the country, he was caving in to the Japanese. From then on, Chiang nursed a profound grievance which lasted throughout his life. That month, he started the extraordinary practice of beginning each day's diary entry with the words 'avenge shame' (*xue-chi*). He did this every day for more than four decades. There was no way Chiang would ever kowtow again.

Now, Chiang's uncompromising stance won him great prestige. In the spirit of national unity, all the provinces surrendered control of their armies to him so they could fight the war as one force. This was when Chiang Kai-shek came the nearest to uniting the country in essence as well as in name. The only force that kept itself outside his control was the Red Army, which maintained its own separate command and only nominally took orders from him. They were able to do so thanks to Stalin, who had signed a treaty with Chiang as soon as all-out war broke out, becoming literally Chiang's sole source of arms. Another concession Chiang made was to agree to the Red Army only fighting a guerrilla war behind Japanese lines rather than at the front. These privileges made a world of difference to the Reds. By the time the war ended in 1945, Chiang's other challengers had seen their armies destroyed by the Japanese. Mao would emerge as the Generalissimo's only rival.

May-ling arrived in Chongqing with Chiang in December 1938, after two months' touring war fronts from the north to the south. She acted as a true wartime first lady, dealing with a million matters, exhausted but stimulated. Writing to her American friend Emma Mills, she exclaimed, 'What a life! When the war is over I think my hair will turn white, but there is one comfort: I am working so hard I am not in danger of ever becoming a nice, fat, soft, sofa cushion, or having a derriere.' In another letter, again, 'What a life! But we will not stop resisting.'

Chongqing was a hard place to live in. It was well known as the 'Furnace of China' for its oppressive humidity and heat. Vapour from the Yangtze below was trapped by the mountains, shrouding the city like a suffocating damp towel. In the long summer months, it was like a pressure cooker. Winter brought little relief, with a heavy mist hanging over the city, giving it another nickname: the 'City of Fog'. The fog was so thick that sometimes one could not see one's own hand. To go about in the city involved trudging up and down hundreds of steep stone steps. Those who could afford rode in chairs, carried by coolies, and there were only a few relatively new roads in downtown Chongqing where one could use rickshaws and motor cars. Everything was in short supply, and the whole infrastructure was groaning under the burden of the millions of extra people who suddenly crowded into the city. Dysentery and malaria were rampant.

The Japanese started bombing in May 1939, when the fog lifted. There were only primitive air-raid shelters dug into the cliffs. Ventilation was almost non-existent; when an air raid lasted a long time, the air inside became foul and suffocating. One night, after hours of bombing, hundreds of people rushed out of a crammed tunnel for fresh air, when suddenly another wave of planes flew over, dropping bombs indiscriminately. In panic, people tried to force their way back to the dugouts; over 500 were killed in the stampede.

May-ling suffered from the skin allergy hives, or nettle rash, which was made much worse by Chongqing's extreme humidity. Sitting for hours in the bomb shelter was torture. 'I am covered with water blisters which itch like Job's old sores!' she wrote to her brother T.V.

She witnessed horrendous suffering all around her. The city was densely packed with timber houses, some perching on long poles on the sides of cliffs. Each bomb would detonate an avalanche of fire which raged for hours. One day after a raid, May-ling went out to see what rescue work was being done. Large sections of the city were like 'raging infernos', she wrote to Emma. As there was little open space, it was hard to escape the fire and smoke. People tried to climb up the old city wall, but the flames caught many of them. Thousands died. Burnt bodies were pulled from the smouldering piles. 'Relatives and friends are still digging furiously.' 'The cries

and shrieks of the dying and the wounded resounded in the night
... the stench is increasing and living in the vicinity is impossible.'

She herself had a narrow escape from a bomb. In the air-raid
shelter, to keep her mind occupied she was taught French by a
Belgian priest, Father Weitz. One day, after spending most of the
day cooped up in the dugout, she said to him, 'Let us continue our
lesson outside.' Minutes later the emergency alert sounded again
and Chiang called out for them to return to the shelter. Just as they
entered the tunnel, a bomb dropped near the place where they had
been sitting. They were hurled forward onto their faces, their bodies
covered with rubble. The French-grammar book she had left on
the spot was sliced through by a piece of shrapnel.

The first lady was thrown together with the average men and
women and she started to refer to them as 'our people'. When
winter descended, she would think how this 'intensifies the suffering
of our homeless and wounded people'. She was moved and inspired
by the morale: 'It is to the credit of our people that they were
uncowed, for after each bombing, scarcely had the all-clear siren
trailed off its last thin echo before the surviving householders
returned to their burned shops and homes and began to salvage
whatever they could. A few days later, temporary shacks and
building would make their appearance on the old sites.' 'Our
women were wonderful. ... when they would justifiably be allowed
to succumb to hysteria and nervous prostration, they have held out
and have been cheerful and indefatigable ...'

May-ling wrote to Emma: 'we shall fight on.' Chiang Kai-shek's
high prestige at the time was substantially due to his wife's brave
presence.

May-ling carried the grand title of 'Secretary-General of the
Aviation Commission': she had helped build the Chinese air force
in the mid-1930s. It was she who scouted and invited Captain Claire
Chennault to China in 1937, who then founded the American
Volunteer Group or 'Flying Tigers', a crack force of over a hundred
American pilots. They destroyed hundreds of Japanese planes.
Chennault was a brilliant fighter pilot with imagination and daring;

his flair entered legend after a stunt he performed in the early 1920s near El Paso, Texas. A large crowd had gathered to watch the Fort Bliss Air Force manoeuvres, when an old woman in a long dress tottered onto the airfield, her bright headscarf fluttering in the wind. The loudspeaker announced that Grandma Morris, aged eighty, was eager for a ride in a plane, and that the air force had decided to grant her wish. The crowd cheered. Grandma Morris was hoisted into the cockpit. The pilot, standing outside, buckled her up and started the engine. She waved to the crowd. Just as the pilot was about to climb in, the plane jerked forward, throwing him onto the ground. The crowd, terrified, shouted for Grandma Morris to jump out. But the plane started taxiing and soon took off unsteadily, narrowly missing rooftops. In the air it rose and dipped and turned wildly, finally plummeting in a nosedive. The crowd screamed and yelled. The plane brushed past the field and again rose to loop and roll in the air, before it tailspun earthward again – only to make a perfect landing. Out of the cockpit leapt Grandma Morris, peeling off her wig and headscarf and dress to reveal a laughing, uniformed Captain Chennault.

The captain had a very craggy face, possibly from having spent so many hours flying in an open cockpit. Apparently Winston Churchill muttered about him, 'My God, that face; glad he's on our side.' Chennault was definitely on May-ling's side. 'She will always be a princess to me,' he wrote in his diary. 'Madame Chiang repeatedly risked her life by coming to the airfield – always a prime target – to encourage the Chinese pilots, for whom she felt responsible. It was strong medicine even for a man – the grim and hopeless manner as they went off to face ever lengthening odds, the long nerve-racking waiting, and the return of bloody, burned, and battle-glazed survivors. It always unnerved her, but she stuck it out, seeing that hot tea was ready and listening to their stories of the fighting.'

The American airmen admired her too. One, Sebie Biggs Smith, recalled driving to the airfield after an ugly air battle:

We get out there to survey the damage, but before we get out of the auto we see Madame Chiang out walking around an airplane that had been severely damaged. She had beaten us to the airport. Again I have to say she was a mighty brave woman. She was taking chances all the time during the war, as if she was one of the soldiers herself. After each air raid she seemed to hasten to the airport to count the boys when they came back in, and she insisted on there being coffee for them and was trying to do what she could to make it as easy as possible for these brave boys that were fighting against odds and without replacements, and each one knew every morning when they'd go to the airport that it might be their last trip.

Donald worked closely with May-ling. Together they unearthed a 'squeeze' involving exorbitant commissions on government purchases of aircrafts and aviation equipment. The middleman was an American called A.L. Patterson. US ambassador Nelson T. Johnson wrote in a memorandum after a conversation with a member of his staff: 'Wing Commander Garnet Malley … was satisfied that Patterson had doubled, and in some cases trebled, the price of American aircraft sold to the Chinese Government.' In one case, the price was 'four times the right price'. May-ling was horrified and gave orders 'to sift the matter to the bottom'. But quickly it was discovered that Big Sister was implicated. A 'General Tzau had been mentioned for some time as the agent of Mrs H.H. Kung in collecting "squeeze" on the purchase of airplanes,' wrote the American ambassador in the memo.

In mid-January 1938, May-ling flew to Hong Kong for treatment of her injury from the recent car accident. But she was also there to have a word with her sister. Ei-ling lived in Hong Kong much of the time, where she managed her large array of businesses from her house on a cliff overlooking the ocean. The neighbourhood consisted of terraced gardens and well-tended tennis courts. Her evenings were often spent playing bridge. May-ling stayed longer than planned. She cabled her husband that Ei-ling had had a fall and hurt herself. Then she herself took to her bed. Chiang sent solicitous wishes, asking May-ling specifically 'not to worry about that business of the Aviation Commission'. But in mid-February

he sent two urgent cables: 'I expect you have recovered.' 'The
Aviation Commission is being reorganised. Important. Please return
at once.'

During her lengthy stay, May-ling was persuaded by Big Sister
that her business practice would make no difference to the outcome
of the war, but would be vital for the personal and political life of
Little Sister and her husband. Her argument was that she had to
meet the Generalissimo's political needs, provide for Little Sister,
and, especially, prepare for the first couple's rainy day. Ei-ling had
to look after the future of her whole family. As the war wore on
and years progressed, May-ling would see her sister's logic. Right
now, even if she was not fully convinced, she bowed to Big Sister's
authority. When she returned to the temporary capital, she resigned
her post as the Secretary-General of the Aviation Commission. Her
husband halted the investigation of the scandal.

Ei-ling's reputation as someone who took advantage of China's
war to line her pockets had already been doing the rounds. All
agreed that she was the brain behind key financial decisions by her
husband, H.H. Kung, who held the key to the country's coffers.
As he later told the Oral History Project of Columbia University,
New York, the real budget of the country (which he called the
'secret budget') was decided by two people: himself and Chiang
Kai-shek: 'only two signatures were required for the secret budget'.
This position gave the Kungs a tremendous financial advantage. In
1935, H.H. reformed the Chinese currency by creating the *fabi*;
when the war started two years later and he knew there would be
inflation, the family changed all their *fabi* into gold and kept their
wealth intact, while the average Chinese saw the value of their
assets plummet. During the war, as the government was spending
large sums of money buying arms, the Kungs took significant
kickbacks. H.H. appointed their son, David, a graduate barely in
his twenties, the joint managing director of the Central Trust
Company, the purchasing agent for government supplies. As the
army's appropriation was mostly in Chinese dollars and the muni-
tions had to be bought with foreign currency, the purchase involved

currency exchanges from which large sums of money were made
– by David. In addition, the young man set up his own import and
export company, the Yangtze Trading Corp., which functioned as
the agent in China for major Western manufacturers. When
America joined the war in 1941 and American supplies began to
arrive, the Kungs and their cronies inserted themselves as intermedi-
aries, and made fortunes. Even the Chinese banknotes, which were
printed by foreign companies designated by H.H.'s ministry,
brought the Kungs commissions.

John Gunther, an American journalist, wrote of Ei-ling in 1939:
'She is a first-rate financier in her own right, and takes a fierce joy
in business manipulations and enterprises. To her shrewdness, her
financial ability, the growth of much of the great Soong fortune is
attributed.' 'There is talk of malign influence of "squeeze". Efforts
to abolish corruption in office have at times been unaccountably
blocked. The Kungs are of great importance to the Generalissimo,
and they know it. So does he ... they control the national finances.'

These and similar descriptions annoyed Ei-ling so much that in
spite of her dislike for publicity, she agreed to the request of the
writer and journalist Emily Hahn to write her biography, in an
effort to clear her name. ('Mme Kung's voice shook' when she
talked about Gunther, Hahn noted.) Ei-ling spoke to Hahn of her
contributions to the war: she had bought three ambulances and
thirty-seven military trucks for the army, donated a further twenty
trucks to the Aviation Commission (when it was headed by
May-ling), and paid for 500 leather coats for airmen. Out of her
own pocket, she had converted the Lido Cabaret into a field hospital
of 300 beds and set up a children's hospital with a hundred beds.
There were other charitable activities, but these paled in comparison
with the huge hoard generated by her 'squeeze'. Eventually, the
wealth amassed by the Kungs may have reached, or even surpassed,
$100 million.

People knew about the colossal corruption at the centre of power,
even if they did not know the detail. They even coined a phrase
for the practice: 'making fortunes out of national catastrophe'
(fa-guo-nan-cai). The Kungs were constantly under fire from the

press, the public, the Nationalist grandees, and the American government. But Chiang kept his brother-in-law on as his 'financial tsar' and declined to do anything. H.H. did much to ensure that unoccupied China's finances held up under the monumental strain of the war when it was cut off from virtually all its economic bases. He felt, justifiably, that he had done 'wonders keeping the war going and maintaining the currency'.

The main trick, he revealed in his memoirs, was that he 'made the Land Tax a national rather than a provincial tax', with the result that 'receipts covered more than fifty per cent of the expenditure'. Taking what was traditionally an income for the provinces and putting it into the central government coffers, from which his family could help themselves, H.H. Kung made many sworn enemies for the regime among the provincial chiefs. He blithely dismissed them: 'Some provinces were of course more difficult to deal with than others. This was due to self-interest or plain ignorance.' But the fact was that many an embittered foe would later clandestinely help the Communists bring down Chiang Kai-shek.

To the Generalissimo, H.H. was his faithful and obedient servant – and also his convenient lightning rod. Anger about corruption focused on the Kungs, leaving Chiang to enjoy the reputation of a spartan soldier. In fact, the money in the Kungs' pockets was effectively money for the Chiangs. Big Sister particularly had her sister's welfare in mind. The first lady was unafraid of death but could not stand discomfort. Indeed she was addicted to a grand style of living. She toughed it out in the first few years of the war, but the hardship tested her endurance to the limits, and whenever possible she would escape to the luxury of Hong Kong and America, where she would stay for months at a time. Her trips were extremely costly. On one occasion she stayed in the New York Presbyterian Hospital for months and took an entire floor for her staff. It was impossible for the Chinese government to pay all her expenses, and Ei-ling footed a big portion of the bill. For the rest of her life, May-ling continued to depend on her sister financially. Later, outliving Chiang for nearly three decades, she lived in New York and was sumptuously provided for, partly by the Kungs.

May-ling was grateful to Big Sister and always defended her vehemently. William Donald, close to May-ling, was once rung up by the president of a missionary university. 'Someone has to tell the Soongs and the Chiangs to put a stop to this nonsense. Some of their official family are making money hand over fist in the exchange market. Lord, haven't they any sense of decency!' Donald decided he had to have a word with the first lady. One day in 1940, he gently took her arm, walked her into the garden, and asked her to do something about the Kungs. May-ling turned on him in a blaze of anger and told him in so many words, 'Donald, you may criticize the government or anything in China, but there are some persons even you cannot criticize!' This made up Donald's mind to leave the Chiangs' service. He said goodbye to the country where he had lived and worked for thirty-seven years.

May-ling had a very special bond with Big Sister and her family. Their home was her home, where she felt more relaxed than with Chiang. Unusually, Ei-ling brought up her children to be as close to May-ling as possible, even closer than to herself. Two of them, David and Jeanette, were truly like May-ling's own children, the children she was unable to have. They called her *niang* ('mother'), and made sure that every wish of hers, however tiny, was catered to. Their devotion to her was exceptional. Neither of them married, and their lives revolved around her. Ei-ling had given Little Sister a family, and filled the childless void that might otherwise have left her dissatisfied (a dissatisfaction Red Sister suffered most of her life).

Ei-ling's daughter Jeanette managed May-ling's household, and was addressed by the staff as 'General Manager'. She was blunt and overbearing with them, and they disliked her. May-ling, who cared about good manners, turned a blind eye to her niece's rudeness and even worse behaviour. One night in Chongqing Jeanette drove to her parents' country house during a blackout. All cars had to drive slowly according to regulations; but Jeanette drove fast. When a traffic policeman stepped into the street to try to stop her, she accelerated right at him, swearing 'Fuck off!' The car brushed past the policeman and there was blood on the street. Her aide-de-camp got out and arranged for the policeman to be carried to the hospital, while she stayed in the car apparently unperturbed.

(Jeanette was fiercely strong-willed. She was a lesbian and defiantly flaunted it by always wearing a masculine haircut and men's clothes, which was most unusual in those days. Either in a Western suit or a traditional men's gown, the white silk lining of its long sleeves turned out, with a man's hat posed at an angle, she looked like a young man. She made no concession for an official visit to Washington with her aunt, and caused President Roosevelt to address her as 'my boy'. At least two women were well known to be her live-in partners. Only she did not present them to her aunt, and May-ling looked the other way, never raising the subject.)

David was at the centre of the corruption charges against the Kung family. But the ire against him did not stop at money matters. Neither he nor his younger brother, Louis, went anywhere near the battlefield in China – in common with the offspring of most of the elite. That the rich and powerful refused to risk their lives in the fighting was a constant source of revulsion and resentment. One day at a dinner party, when a toast was proposed to the 'Old Hundred Names' – the ordinary people – who bore the brunt of the war, US Ambassador Johnson, who was present, felt that the general attitude was 'Let us fight to the last drop of coolie blood' while 'in the midst of it all the Soong family carries on its intrigues which sometimes disgust me completely'. A favourite retort among Hong Kong foreigners when asked for relief funds was: 'Why aren't all these young men we see at the swimming pools and the movies doing something for their own country?' President Roosevelt's personal representative, Lauchlin Currie, complained to the Chinese government about the Kung children.

Louis was a graduate from Sandhurst military academy, and was a captain in the British Army. When Britain was at war with Nazi Germany, he was about to be sent to the front. But H.H. cabled the Chinese ambassador and told him to speak to the British government. According to H.H.'s memoir, 'I told him I was not thinking of my son's safety but of those seven hundred men under his care.

He was quite young. I was worried about his having to take command of seven hundred men. I said I would prefer that they gave him another job ... Later, he was assigned the task of training soldiers in England.'

Of Ei-ling's children, the one people found most likeable was Rosamonde, her first child, who grew into a quiet and gentle woman. She fell in love with a man of whom Ei-ling disapproved, because his father was a 'lowly' conductor in the orchestra of a dance hall. The young couple went to America and married there. Belatedly, Ei-ling accepted their marriage and airfreighted them large quantities of luxury goods as Rosamonde's 'dowry'. The plane crashed and the silks were found, exposing Ei-ling once again to public outrage at her widely perceived wartime extravagance and corruption.

Over the years, Ei-ling developed a conviction that it was her mission in life to look after and provide for her illustrious sisters, especially Little Sister. This was what God wanted her to do, she believed; and making money was her way to fulfil this role. Having this conviction gave her a purpose in amassing a fortune and forti-fied her against the incessant accusations. Later, on the eve of the collapse of Chiang's regime in mainland China, Ei-ling was ill and thought death was imminent. She saw this as God calling her to His side, because there was no more she could do for Him on earth. She felt peaceful and was ready to die.

Red Sister's Frustration

Before the fall of Hong Kong to the Japanese in 1941, the British colony of Hong Kong was the favoured destination for those who did not want to stay in China and who had the means to get out. Ching-ling, who loathed living in Chongqing, Chiang Kai-shek's wartime capital, made her home there after she evacuated Shanghai. Mme Sun's decision to seek safety and comfort outside her country while it was fighting a brutal war raised eyebrows – many expected the torchbearer of the Father of China to be a bomb-defying heroine. The Japanese press sneered too. But Ching-ling was perfectly at peace with herself. To her, the decision was about not living in the same city as Chiang.

Ching-ling's revulsion towards the Generalissimo had not lessened in intensity over the years. When the war began in 1937, out of patriotism, and because Moscow issued a stiff order to cooperate with Chiang, Red Sister was briefly nice to her brother-in-law. But her compliments were barbed: 'It is a matter for congratulation that General Chiang Kai-shek has stopped further civil warfare.' Anyone who knew her was aware that her distaste for Chiang remained.

In Hong Kong, she was busy with her own war relief work. She set up a China Defense League to give publicity to the Communists, fundraise for them, and buy and transport supplies to their bases. It was a small outfit, a group of volunteers with two or three paid staff each drawing a basic living wage. Its impact in material terms was negligible, but it gave Ching-ling her own organisation. She attended to all details, signing the receipts for all donations, however small, and writing to thank the donors personally. Ching-ling was contented with her modest set-up. This struck Major Evans Carlson of the US Marines, assistant naval attaché in China, who wrote that she had 'a peace of mind, an utter self-assurance which lacked egotism'. Indeed she did not seek power for herself, and nor was she deluded about her own limited abilities.

Inside the organisation she generated an atmosphere of camaraderie. Israel Epstein, a volunteer who became a lifelong friend and her biographer, described his experience: 'With co-workers, high or low, she was warm and democratic, making all feel equal and at ease. The league's weekly meetings, in our cramped Hong Kong headquarters at 21 Seymour Road, was intimate and informal, amid work-piled desks and, often, mounts of supplies stacked for sorting on the floor. We were of different nationalities, positions and ages. I was 23 and the youngest. Soong Ching Ling, presiding, never lectured.'

The staff liked her sense of humour. One day she was told that the British politician Sir Stafford Cripps (later a member of Churchill's War Cabinet) was in Hong Kong and would like to meet her. She invited him to dinner at her home. A small banquet was prepared. Just before the distinguished guest was scheduled to arrive, she learned that he was a vegetarian. The cook had to start all over again. Then the additional information was delivered that he was a raw-food vegetarian. At this Ching-ling threw up her hands and declared, 'We'll just have to turn him out on the lawn to graze!'

In February 1940, May-ling flew to Hong Kong to have a cauterisation for a bad sinus problem. She stayed with Ei-ling in her ocean-facing mansion. Touched by her fragility, Ching-ling also moved in, and for over a month the three sisters spent every day together, something they had not done for many years. The wartime united front allowed them to set aside momentarily their political differences and indulge their fondness for each other.

Ching-ling had in the past criticised Ei-ling's methods of accumulating wealth and had told the journalist Edgar Snow, 'She's very clever, Ei-ling. She never gambles. She buys and sells only when she gets advance information ... about changes in government fiscal policy ... America may be able to afford rich men, but China cannot. It is impossible to amass a fortune here except through criminal dishonesty and misuse of political power backed by military force.' But now, she was wallowing in the affection lavished on her by Big Sister and chose not to be critical of her. She also had kind words to say about May-ling. Edgar Snow, who was in Hong Kong at this time, noticed that she 'somewhat changed her mind' about May-ling's marriage. Before, she had told him it was 'opportunism on both sides, with no love involved'. Now she said, 'It wasn't love in the beginning, but I think it is now. Mei-ling is sincerely in love with Chiang and he with her. Without Mei-ling he might have been much worse.'

One night that month, the sisters went out to the hottest night-spot in town, a dinner-dance restaurant at the Hong Kong Hotel. This was perhaps the only time they ever did anything like this. Such places were deemed not quite suitable. Like royals, the sisters confined their socialising to formal functions or private parties. But this evening, dressed up in splendid cheongsams, they sat with their backs to the wall and watched the glamorous or wicked Hong Kongers gliding past. Ching-ling, in black, wore an amused look. She actually loved dancing, particularly waltzes, but her status had long prevented her from stepping onto a dance floor. Dancers stole glances at them to check it really was the three sisters, speculating in whispers about what political message was embedded in the meal.

Emily Hahn came to the restaurant with an RAF officer. Ei-ling had tipped off her biographer about the dinner. Although she normally did not seek the limelight and preferred to stay in the background, Big Sister knew how to send a signal. The message was that the 'united front' was solid. Meanwhile, the sisters were at last able to have a good time with a free conscience.

Unity was indeed in crisis right now. The number two in the Nationalist government, Wang Jing-wei, who had written Sun Yat-sen's will, had defected to Japanese-occupied territory and was about to set up a puppet government as an alternative to Chongqing. Wang was a long-term rival to the Generalissimo. In 1935, at the opening of a Nationalist congress, when the VIPs gathered to have a press photo taken, Wang was shot by a gunman and badly injured. The gunman had actually intended to kill Chiang Kai-shek, whose seat was in the middle of the front row. But the Generalissimo's powerful sixth sense alerted him and he decided at the last minute not to appear for the photo. The assassin emptied his pistol at Wang, the next highest official, before being fatally wounded himself. Everyone suspected Chiang, finding his eleventh-hour change of mind otherwise inexplicable. Chiang did his best to persuade people it was not his doing by conducting a vigorous investigation. Still, a cloud of doubts lingered.

Wang was pessimistic about the war. He also blamed Chiang for the defeats, saying that the loss of Shanghai and other major cities and huge swathes of land in an abysmally short time was the result of Chiang's 'corrupt and dark ... one-man dictatorship'. Wang saw Chiang as someone who harboured perennial suspicion of rivals and treated them unfairly. This view was shared by many. Joseph Stilwell, the US military attaché, noted from Chongqing in 1938 that Chiang 'wanted to keep all his subordinates in the dark because he didn't trust them ... The same old mistrust kept him from making his army efficient.'

Wang felt China could only be preserved by seeking 'peace' with the Japanese. At the end of 1938, he sneaked out of Chongqing for Shanghai, via Hanoi, surviving more assassination attempts by Chiang's agents. (His bullet wounds ultimately led to his premature death six years later.) A puppet regime headed by him was established in Japanese-controlled Nanjing in March 1940.

Wang had been Sun Yat-sen's original successor, and Sun had trumpeted 'Great-Asianism', which was the current slogan of the occupying Japanese. This helped Wang's claim that he was Sun's authentic heir – and posed an unprecedented challenge to the Generalissimo. To assert his own legitimacy, Chiang Kai-shek formally bestowed on Sun the title 'Father of China' (although the logic was somewhat bizarre, as all Sun had done vis-à-vis Japan was encouraging its aggressive ambition towards China rather than rejecting it).

The day Wang was sworn in in Nanjing, Ching-ling made an impromptu decision to go to Chongqing and show solidarity with the Generalissimo. Little Sister had suggested the trip and Big Sister evinced great enthusiasm; Red Sister wanted to please them, as well as to tell the world that the widow of Sun was opposed to Wang's regime. The three sisters flew to the wartime capital the next day.

Red Sister was greeted like a queen, a goddess and a film star all rolled into one. The headline of the influential *Ta Kung Pao* read: 'Welcome, Madame Sun'. Another newspaper gushed about her black cheongsam and grey-blue flat-heeled shoes which, it declared, showed off her illuminating elegance and beauty. It was said that 'tens of thousands of women thirst to gaze and marvel at Madame Sun's magnificent bearing'. In the following six weeks the sisters led a whirlwind tour visiting bombsites, relief projects, and homes for war orphans. They looked happy together when they reminisced about the old days. Emily Hahn, who followed them, observed, 'I grew sentimental when they giggled and chaffed, thinking of their lives long ago, in the school town in Georgia.' Ching-ling joined Ei-ling in expressing amazement at how much Little Sister had done and how she had kept going in the past three years and was 'not already dead and buried'. May-ling and Ching-ling fulsomely praised Big Sister's charitable work. Reporters, photographers and a film crew accompanied them, recording the historic moments.

But Ching-ling meticulously maintained her distance from the Generalissimo and took care not even to smile when he was nearby. In one rather typical photograph she was next to a beaming Chiang with her lips tightly pinched, looking guarded. At a tea party, Chiang stood like a flag pole by her side for well over ten minutes, clearly willing her to turn round and talk to him so the guests could see how amicable they were. But Ching-ling remained resolutely turned away. To her close German friend Anna Wang, who was in Chongqing at the time, she said she felt she was being used by Chiang and was itching to get back to Hong Kong.

Meanwhile, the united front between the Communists and the Nationalists was slowly crumbling. Chiang had assigned the Red Army to fight a guerrilla war behind Japanese lines. Also operating in these areas were Nationalist forces. The idea that these guerrillas might unite against a common enemy proved illusory. They were busy fighting each other in increasingly large battles, with the Reds more often emerging as the winner. Some months after Ching-ling returned to Hong Kong, in January 1941 there was an ugly clash along the Yangtze River. The facade of the united front all but collapsed.

Ching-ling longed to use the opportunity to launch a stinging attack on Chiang, partly to vent her frustration at having been used by Chiang through her trip to Chongqing. But she was only able to send a public telegram to the Generalissimo telling him to 'stop suppressing the Communists'. Moscow would not allow her to do more than that, least of all to condemn Chiang by name. Her frustration deepened in November, the tenth anniversary of Deng Yan-da's death. The murder of the man she had loved hopelessly and intensely remained the key to her unrelenting hatred of the Generalissimo. But she could only hint at her bête noire obliquely in her article commemorating Yan-da. Perhaps thanks to this restraint, her article had no rancour or Communist-style jargon, unlike her other public statements. It had uncommonly personal expressions. Yan-da, under her pen, was 'the last beautiful flower to grace our revolution'.

On 7 December 1941, the Japanese attacked Pearl Harbor, and then bombed Hong Kong. As the planes roared menacingly overhead, Ching-ling hurriedly climbed up a bamboo ladder over an old wall to the garden of the house next door, where there was an air-raid shelter. The blitz, she wrote to T.V. afterwards, 'made me extremely nervous. I was quite ill the first week.' Not forgetting her sense of self-mockery, she added: 'My hair comes out by handfuls – soon I shall be bald, I fear.'

T.V. was sympathetic to Ching-ling and her cause, and had lent his name to her Defense League as the president. Chiang had been furious and cabled him several times demanding that he withdraw. T.V. had stalled with various excuses until an ultimatum came. He resigned from Ching-ling's organisation, but his affection for Red Sister had not dimmed. Nor had Ching-ling's for him.

On the day Hong Kong was bombed, T.V. was in the United States as Chiang's personal representative to President Roosevelt. He cabled May-ling: 'Urgent. To Madame Chiang: Hong Kong perilous. Would it be possible to send a plane at night to try to get Second Sister out of danger? Please reply.'

Chongqing dispatched a plane, but Ching-ling stubbornly refused to leave. She would rather stay in Japanese-occupied Hong Kong than live in the same city as her loathed brother-in-law. Ei-ling, who was also in Hong Kong, tried and failed to talk Ching-ling round and, at her wits' end, said that in that case she herself would not leave Hong Kong either. Ching-ling yielded at the last minute. She had made no preparations for the evacuation and her maid grabbed a few old clothes in the darkness of the blackout before they raced to the airport. At dawn on the 10th, just before the Japanese took over, the sisters flew to Chongqing.

The reception in the wartime capital was very different from a year before. It was downright hostile, which took Ching-ling by surprise. She wrote to T.V. with indignation, 'the *Ta Kung Pao* welcomed us by pri[n]ting a libellous editorial accusing us of bringing tons of baggages [*sic*], seven milk-fed foreign poodles and a retinue of servants', when in fact, 'I could not even bring along my documents and other priceless articles, let alone my dogs and clothes ... For one who writes everyday, I was without even a pen ... I wanted to answer the editorial ... but was told to hold a dignified silence.'

In fact Ching-ling was entirely left out of the criticisms. Big Sister took all the bullets – together with her husband H.H. Kung, who was not even on the plane. Students in several cities took to the streets to demonstrate (uncommon during the war) against the couple. The charges included: 'When Hong Kong was falling, the government sent a plane to bring over officials; but it brought back only Mme Kung together with 7 foreign dogs and 42 suitcases.'

The demonstrators shouted 'Down with H.H. Kung who used the plane to transport foreign poodles! ... Execute H.H. Kung!'

However well she knew that the accusation was untrue and that it hurt Ei-ling, Ching-ling said nothing to help her sister. The saint-like prestige she enjoyed among the students would be in jeopardy if she stuck her neck out, so she kept quiet.

She maintained a similar silence when she began her Chongqing life staying with Ei-ling, in the Kungs' mansion sporting tall red pillars and large windows overlooking a river. There she was said to be kept a prisoner by her wicked sister. Zhou En-lai, the Communist representative in Chongqing, reported to Mao in Yenan that Ching-ling was 'unable to receive visitors; moreover, using the excuse that there is a housing shortage, [the Kungs] are making her share her room with someone, who is there really to keep her under watch'. In fact Ching-ling occupied a whole floor and could see whoever she liked. As she told her brother T.V., 'The sisters are so kind to me.' But publicly she acquiesced with the rumour.

Ei-ling did not ask her sister to speak up. Indeed, she made things easier for Red Sister by telling her that she did 'not care about correcting rumors'.

Soon Ching-ling moved into her own place in Chongqing. She saw her sisters, but avoided functions where Chiang might be.

Life was hard compared to Hong Kong. Her staff shopped in the market, which was subject to the scarcity and hyper-inflated price of such basics as onions, sugar and even salt. There was no place to buy stockings or shoes, and an ordinary cheongsam which in pre-war Shanghai had cost just eight yuan was selling for over 1,000. Months went by without her tasting her favourite drink, coffee, and after an official reception, her most cherished memory was of having potato salad and watermelon there. Friends gave her presents like a tin of sardines, or a few apples, or stockings. In summer, she sat in her bathtub filled with cold water.

She was surrounded by her usual small circle of young, loyal and left-wing friends, Chinese and foreign, much like when she was in Hong Kong. As her circle was so small, there was much mystique about her. She became something of a 'tourist attraction', and many who were visiting the city sought an audience with her. More often than not, she declined.

Her League continued its work, and her primary interest at this time was in getting American aid to Communist-controlled areas. To this end she made friends with American officials and journalists and never missed a chance to denounce the Generalissimo. She told them that Chiang was 'nothing but a dictator', and even claimed that there was 'close contact between the puppet officials and the [Chongqing] administration'. They noticed her 'deep resentment', and that she 'was very outspoken in her criticism of the Generalissimo'. Many were sympathetic. But to her immense frustration, she had to ask for her remarks to be kept 'in strict confidence'.

General Joseph Stilwell, at the time chief of staff to the Supreme Commander China Theater (i.e. to Chiang), did not see eye to eye with Chiang, but thought Red Sister was wonderful. Stilwell had served in China on and off since the 1920s, and knew the country well. He was a man of the people. A sketch he wrote about his travels in China gives a glimpse of his personality. At a country food stall, he saw the cook dish out noodles into 'a bowl which has just been used by a previous customer and which he cleans by wiping with a dark object like a piece of garage waste. He wipes a pair of chopsticks on his trousers, puts them in the bowl, hands it to a serving boy who presents it with a flourish to the customer.' Stilwell was not disgusted, unlike many a Westerner; he made his request to clean his bowl and chopsticks in his own way. He asked for a bowl of boiling water, which he pretended he was about to empty on the cook's head. This brought a round of laughter. With this joke, he was 'accepted by all present as a great fellow with a keen sense of humor and thereafter can do as he likes, even to scraping the chopsticks with a penknife before using them.'

Stilwell wrote of Ching-ling in his diary: 'Madame Sun is the most simpatico of the three women, and probably the deepest. She is most responsive and likeable, quiet and poised but misses nothing.' When he was recalled by Roosevelt and went to say goodbye to her, she, as he wrote in his diary, 'cried and was generally broken up ... Itching to go to the US to tell FDR the fact [about Chiang] ... Wants me to tell FDR the real character of CKS [Chiang Kai-shek]. "He is a paper tiger." ... "Why doesn't the US put him in his place."'

Other Americans thought differently about Red Sister. The US diplomat John Melby wrote in his diary after a meeting with her: 'The famous charm was there, but she seems to me basically a cold, hard, ruthless woman who knows what she wants and how to get it.'

She also could not compete with Little Sister, China's wartime first lady, for glamour and status. In 1943, May-ling made a triumphant tour of the United States, and this stirred up quite a bit of jealousy in Red Sister. In a letter to a friend, Ching-ling allowed herself to be acidic while trying to be restrained and fair:

> May-ling looks so Fifth Avenue and behaves so '400'* that we have found she has undergone a great physical change ... Whatever one may say, she has given widest publicity to China's cause and as she herself remarked to a gathering of admiring throng, 'I have shown the Americans that China is not made up entirely of coolies and laundrymen!' I suppose China must be grateful for that ... The crew of her plane related what a lot of trunks she brought in, and the amount of tinned food, etc. But I haven't seen a single can of baked beans or ... pair of shoes. I am told that she has no room for them so my shoes will be brought on 'the next plane'. Hooray! ... after the war, I suppose.

May-ling's present to her was a small plastic mirror, something that was unobtainable in Chongqing. But she longed for nylon stockings. One evening, after slapping a mosquito on her ankle, she said to her guest with a smile, 'No stockings, you see. I'm

---

* A famous list of New York society during the late nineteenth century.

breaking the rules of the New Life Movement, but I can't get nylons from America the way my little sister, the Empress, does.'

In 1944, her sisters went to Brazil and Ching-ling went to the airport to see them off. She was much impressed by the plane they had chartered: 'I never saw such a huge plane. It was like a Pullman car [i.e. the luxurious train carriage].' To American friends she said disapprovingly that her sisters had 'run out' on China's war, something she would not do herself.

Ching-ling kept her sarcasm towards her sisters strictly private and took great care to maintain a congenial appearance in public. Her close friend Anna Wang commented: 'She had no illusions about the role of the "Soong dynasty" – detested Chiang Kai-shek's dictatorialness, was well aware of Mme Kung's speculations and Mme Chiang's appetite for luxuries. With good friends, she would make acerbic remarks about these matters. But amazing political skill and self-control, learned over many years, prevented her from proclaiming her views too early.' Indeed Ching-ling waited, in frustration as well as determination, for the war against Japan to end, for the war by the Communists against the Generalissimo to start, and for the Chiang regime to be thoroughly destroyed, even if this meant disaster for her family and her sisters.

17

Little Sister's Triumph and Misery

In October 1942, Wendell Willkie, the 1940 Republican presidential nominee, came to Chongqing as Roosevelt's personal representative. To date, he was the most important visitor to the wartime capital and was taken to the front. He liked what he saw and was particularly taken with May-ling. With a flurry of compliments he invited her to America for a goodwill tour. She had 'brains, persuasiveness and moral force ... wit and charm, a generous and understanding heart, a gracious and a beautiful manner and appearance, and a burning conviction ... Madame woud be the perfect ambassador.' On the eve of his departure, Willkie asked May-ling to fly with him to Washington 'tomorrow'. (There is no evidence they had an affair, as some have claimed.)

This ardour, coming from somebody close to the White House, made up May-ling's mind to visit the United States. The idea had been mooted since the early stage of the war. She had hesitated, not out of fear of lack of attention, but of too much attention from the Americans. She told Emma Mills: 'I visualize what would happen. All the friends I have, all the thousands of people who have written letters and contributed money, and the hundreds of thousands of curious people, to say nothing of the thousands of newspaper men and people of importance who would want either to speak to me or me to speak to them, would overwhelm me within the first few hours of my arrival.' She was afraid she might not be able to cope well (she had been working flat out and felt she had 'no reserve left') and would let down the American people as well as her country. As she told Emma, she was 'afraid of the sympathy and the goodwill of Americans'. If Emma did not think this was how the Americans would act, May-ling said, 'Emma, you do not know your own people.'

May-ling had foreseen an extremely warm welcome – but its intensity far exceeded even her expectation. Her words to Emma had been written in 1939 – before Pearl Harbor. Since then, American sympathy for China had skyrocketed. This poor and mysterious country had been fighting Japan, a fearsome evil enemy, for the past four and a half years, alone. May-ling was the representative of that heroic nation. She was a beautiful woman – and she was *American* in all but her face – a face of 'ivory satin skin' at that. The reception was stupendous. When she arrived in Washington DC to start her official visit in February 1943, she was met at the train station by Mrs Roosevelt herself, who took her arm and brought her to meet the president, who was waiting in a White House car outside the station. May-ling spoke to a rally of 17,000 in Madison Square Garden in New York, to 30,000 in the Hollywood Bowl in LA, and was greeted by wildly excited crowds from city to city. When she addressed Congress – a big honour – on 18 February, just the sight of her, dressed in the traditional, alluring cheongsam, looking petite and delicate, amidst all those big men under the magnificent ceiling, was awe-inspiring. And her speech, in impeccable American English, moved many a powerful man to tears. The standing ovation lasted four minutes.

For May-ling, all this did not come without a great deal of effort. A perfectionist, she exhausted herself writing and rewriting her speeches. At some events, she was so drained she nearly fainted. When her husband watched a newsreel of her in Chinatown, New York, he was worried that she looked ill and was struggling to cope. She had been in poor health before her trip, with hypertension and stomach trouble that was suspected to be cancer (it was not). To have her ailments fixed before the official visit – and to indulge herself a little – she had come to America three months before and checked into the Presbyterian Hospital of New York. She was able to look her best in front of the American public, won their goodwill and got the American government to redouble its aid. The trip was a triumph.

There were criticisms, some from the White House staff. She had brought her own silk sheets and had them changed once a day, or twice if she took a nap. Actually, this was largely due to the hives that had been tormenting her, which improved when she had fresh sheets. The Americans who came into contact with her group were also put out by the bad manners of her nephew David and niece Jeanette, whom she brought as her assistants. Emma, for instance, described David as 'gross' and Jeanette 'weird'. The White House staff found them imperious, and the Secret Service detail was irked by their rude demands. But they were devoted to their aunt and looked after her as nobody else could. May-ling relied on them.

Stepping out of the train in Washington for her official visit, May-ling had David by her side. He appeared in many press photos – in spite of the fact that he was not a government official. Nor was he the dashing nephew an aunt might want to show off, portly and distinctly unprepossessing as he was. Still, he was introduced as her 'secretary', and signed his name on telegrams thanking people like the governor general of Canada who had hosted her. For her nephew to sign such communications rather than herself was against protocol and impolite, and much upset Chinese diplomats. But May-ling ignored their objections. She doted on her favourite nephew and niece, and also wanted to please Ei-ling, to whom she felt deeply in debt. Big Sister was paying a large part of her bills for the trip while under attack for being corrupt. As David was also under fire, giving him prominent exposure was May-ling's way of demonstrating her support for Big Sister and her family.

The American trip was not only a great success for China – May-ling herself had a fabulous time in the country where she felt most at home. She was there for eight months and did not return to Chongqing until July 1943 – in spite of her husband's repeated entreaties to come home.

The Generalissimo had been writing to tell her that he missed her: how sad he had felt when she had boarded the plane to depart and how lonely he had felt on both Western and Chinese New Years. The day May-ling returned, Chiang came home and saw her lying on the bed (with a stiff neck), her two sisters and his two sons all present. He said he felt joy at this rare family scene. After the others had gone, May-ling related to him what she had achieved during her trip, and his happiness was complete.

But gloom soon marred the reunion. Gossip had reached the the first lady that while she was in America, the Generalissimo had been seeing other women, especially his ex-wife, Jennie, who had settled in Chongqing. People vouched that they had often seen Jennie in the swimming pool of the Army University, with Chiang sitting by the pool, watching. May-ling stormed off to Big Sister's. It took her several months to come round and accept Chiang's insistence that the story was unfounded. What was true was Chiang's self-confessed battle against his hankering for sex while he was separated from his wife.

May-ling's bitter mood persisted, and she succumbed to a series of illnesses from dysentery to iritis, which caused pain and sensitivity to light. Her hives also got worse in the damp fog of Chongqing. Scarlet patches puffed up her face as well as her body. During fitful nights she tried to suppress the urge to scratch, snatching only moments of sleep and relief.

She was in a bad way when she had to accompany her husband to Cairo for a conference with President Roosevelt and Prime Minister Winston Churchill, set for 22–26 November 1943. The Cairo Conference would not only make decisions about the war and post-war Asia, it would visibly put Chiang on a level with the heads of America and Britain. It fell on May-ling to carry out negotiations on her husband's behalf, as well as interpreting and socialising for him, as he didn't speak English. On the plane to Cairo, her face looked more swollen than ever, and the itchiness allowed her little sleep. She seemed to be on the verge of collapse and Chiang was anxious. Miraculously, luck and willpower combined to reduce the swelling before the plane landed. Still, her doctor had to dilate the pupils of her eyes. As she later wrote to her friend Emma, she 'had a particularly thin time' in Cairo.

Being the only woman amongst a large gathering of high-powered men, she attracted much attention. General Sir Alan Brooke, in his famously 'indiscreet, malicious and true' diaries, described her as: 'Not good-looking, with a flat Mongolian face with high cheekbones and a flat, turned up nose with two long circular nostrils looking like two dark holes leading into her head.' But the general credited her with 'great charm and gracefulness, every small movement of hers arrested and pleased the eye'. In the official photographs, she was seen chatting gracefully with Roosevelt and Churchill, elegant in a dark-coloured cheongsam, a white jacket and shoes decorated with pretty bows. She looked completely at ease, showing no trace of physical strain. The continuous itchiness only caused her to arrange and rearrange her feet a little more frequently than usual as she sat through long meetings. This movement, revealing her shapely legs, was interpreted by some as being done deliberately to distract the men from her husband's poor performance. Brooke wrote, 'This caused a rustle among those attending the conference, and I even thought I heard a suppressed neigh come from a group of some of the younger members!'

Future British prime minister Anthony Eden, in Cairo as Churchill's lieutenant, took away a pleasant impression of her: 'Madame surprised me. She was friendly, a trifle queenly perhaps ... but an industrious and earnest interpreter and neither sprightly nor touchy as I had been led to expect.' Eden found the Generalissimo impressive. 'He would be difficult to place in any category and does not look a warrior. He has a constant smile, but his eyes don't smile so readily and they fix you with a penetrating unswerving look ... His strength is that of the steel blade ... I liked them both, Chiang particularly, and I should like to know them better.'

Together the Chiangs achieved much. The Cairo Declaration is considered 'a triumph for Chiang Kai-shek'. Indeed it spelt out that 'all the territories Japan has stolen from the Chinese, including Manchuria, Formosa [Taiwan], and the Pescadores, shall be restored to the Republic of China'. This had been on Chiang's wish list, which he had given to May-ling to take to President Roosevelt when she visited America.

On the last day of the conference, Chiang wrote in his diary:

This morning my wife went to see Roosevelt about economic matters and returned at 11 to talk to Hopkins [Harry, Roosevelt's confidant]. Until he left in the evening, for 10 hours she had practically not a minute of relaxation and was totally focused on everything under discussion. Her every word was said with the fullest concentration. At 10 o'clock at night, I could see that she was utterly exhausted. With her bad eye trouble and the ever-present itchiness, that she could work like this is really something. Truly no average person can be like her.

One evening Winston Churchill came over, and Chiang saw his wife laughing and talking animatedly with him. Later he asked her what they had been talking about; she told him that Churchill had said to her, 'You must think of me as the worst possible old man, am I right?' (This, if said, was probably a reference to Churchill's response to Chiang's demand to return Hong Kong: 'Over my dead body.') May-ling, according to her husband's diary, told the great British prime minister, 'You must ask yourself whether you are a bad man.' Churchill was said to have replied, 'I am not evil.' Chiang concluded that his wife had thoroughly chastised Churchill. Whether or not this version of the conversation was accurate, May-ling had earned Chiang a great deal of face, and he was proud of her.

Returning from Cairo in excitement, Chiang took his wife to picnics in the wintry hills around Chongqing. 'What joy,' he wrote on New Year's Eve 1943.

May-ling was not so cheerful. Her hives got worse. In Cairo she had consulted Churchill's physician, Dr Moran, about it, and he had told her that there was nothing wrong with her and that 'you will only get better when the strain of your life is relaxed'. But life only became more stressful. An immediate and major problem was her husband's relationship with the most important American in

Chongqing, General Stilwell, who held him responsible for the disasters on the battlefield. He reported to Washington that 'The Chinese soldier is excellent material, wasted and betrayed by stupid leadership.' Nicknamed 'Vinegar Joe' for his quick temper,* Stilwell had many rows with Chiang, and openly refused to take the Generalissimo's command.

May-ling, together with Big Sister, tried to patch up the relationship; they got nowhere. Stilwell's deep-rooted antipathy towards Chiang's regime could not be charmed away. Vinegar Joe did not have much empathy with the two women anyway, and preferred Red Sister.

A crisis point was reached in April 1944, when the Japanese launched a major offensive code-named ICHIGO, which linked up occupied north China with the occupied south. Chiang Kai-shek's troops, including some of his best, collapsed like a house of cards. The Americans were once again dismayed by the fact that Chiang did not seem to have any 'plan or capacity to hamper Japanese movement'. Distaste for the Generalissimo reached new heights. President Roosevelt, feeling 'the case of China is so desperate' that 'radical and properly applied remedies' must be 'immediately effected', wrote to Chiang on 6 July, telling him bluntly to hand over military command to Stilwell. Roosevelt demanded that Stilwell be placed 'in command of all Chinese and American forces and that you charge him with full responsibility and authority for the coordination and direction of the operations required to stem the tide of the enemy's advances'. The Generalissimo would not concede to this, even if, as he stated, it meant a split with America.

There was nothing May-ling could do. She was besieged by nightmares all pointing to an ominous future and longed to get away. She decided to leave China on the grounds of ill health. This

---

* About his own temper, Stilwell told a story against himself. A Chinese merchant bowed and greeted him: 'Good day, Missionary.' 'Why do you address me as "Missionary"?' he asked with a terrible scowl. 'Because you look like one,' the man replied, before elaborating, 'because of your calm benign expression, sir.'

was seen by insiders as 'an attempt to get away'. Mindful of what people would say, Chiang refused to let her go. May-ling was desperate, and when the US vice president Henry Wallace came to China, she approached a member of his mission and begged him to ask Wallace to bring up the issue of her health with her husband. She even pulled down her stockings to show the red patches of hives on her legs.

At last Chiang allowed May-ling to leave and she flew to Rio de Janeiro in early July with Ei-ling, niece Jeanette and nephew David. Just before her departure, she told her husband tearfully that she was worried that they might never see each other again. She promised that she loved him, that she would never forget him for a moment, and that he must never doubt her love. He wrote in his diary that he was so sad that he couldn't think of anything to say.

Chiang gave a farewell party for her, at which he made a bizarre speech. In front of more than seventy Chinese and foreign dignitaries and journalists, he vowed that he had never been unfaithful to May-ling. To explain himself publicly was embarrassing, but the couple judged it to be necessary. Rumours about Chiang's alleged infidelities had grown louder and more lurid, entertaining everyone in the City of Fog at teas and suppers. May-ling's departure on yet another trip, with no set return date, would seem to confirm that their marriage was over if they did not issue a denial. May-ling also made a speech at the party, declaring her total trust in her husband.

When the trip was announced, May-ling's destination roused interest and suspicion. While some kindly suggested that the first lady was going to Rio to seek treatment for her skin trouble from a renowned doctor, many, including future US president Harry S. Truman, believed that the Soong family had stolen American aid money and invested it in real estate in Brazil. No proof has surfaced to justify either claim. It may well be that the sisters chose Rio because the city was the most pleasant and glamorous place to be at the time. To go to America would have been unwise: Little Sister's image there had taken a knock. Instead of the American press lavishing superlatives on her as they had done only a year before, they now focused rather unsympathetically on 'her priceless sable coat and muff, adorned with diamonds and jade worth a king's ransom'.

May-ling was in Rio for two months before she went to New York, where she stayed in the Kungs' mansion and kept a low profile. She told Emma that she felt she was 'suffering the tortures of the damned'. As time went by she started to enjoy life again and had great fun. She spent much time with Emma, talking 'girl talk'. After one dinner, they drove to Broadway to see a film, accompanied by two Secret Service men, entering through an exit door. They visited the Bronx Zoo incognito, to see the pandas that May-ling had given to New York in appreciation of its support for China's war. She feasted on ice-cream sodas, which she confessed she had sorely missed. One source of pleasure was acquiring a Packard limousine (most likely paid for by Big Sister), which she drove round New York. Secret Service men taught her how to drive, and sat next to her.

China's first lady was away from her country and its war for over a year. Chiang remained devoted to her. He wrote to her frequently, asking after her health, telling her, almost pathetically, how much he missed her – on her birthday, on their wedding anniversary, on Christmas Day, and on every other conceivable occasion, not least the anniversary of her departure for Rio. He begged her to come home soon. She replied with her usual list of sicknesses.

Chiang was dependent on May-ling not because he needed her to keep a good relationship with America. During her long absence, that relationship actually took a turn for the better. President Roosevelt recalled Stilwell in October 1944. His successor, General Albert C. Wedemeyer, and the new ambassador Patrick J. Hurley both got on well with the Generalissimo and were supportive of him.

On 12 April 1945, President Roosevelt died of a massive cerebral haemorrhage. May-ling drove to his New York estate, Hyde Park, to visit Eleanor. The next president, Harry S. Truman, continued to support the Generalissimo and gave him a personal plane, an elegantly and comfortably equipped silver C-47. Chiang named the plane *May-ling* – even though it did not bring back his wife.

*

May-ling was particularly angry with her husband at this time because of how he was treating Big Sister's husband. H.H. Kung had come to America on official business as vice premier and finance minister in mid-1944 and had stayed on, claiming that he needed medical treatment in the US. In spring 1945, a corruption scandal erupted involving bonds worth more than $10 million. H.H. was accused of pocketing over $3 million. The Nationalist rank and file seethed with rage, and Chiang was forced to order an investigation. He sent H.H. a string of cables, each more insistent than the last, telling him to get back to China to answer questions. H.H. was compelled to return in July. He was fired and had to hand back some of the money he had misappropriated.

Chiang made his other brother-in-law T.V. Soong the next prime minister. This soured the relationship between T.V. and the Kungs. From then on, H.H. lost no opportunity to denigrate T.V.; and Ei-ling only half made up with her brother late in their lives.

Ei-ling was furious with Chiang for what seemed to her to be shabby treatment of her husband and, by extension, herself. Behind closed doors she talked emotionally to Little Sister. Emma noticed the mood in the house. Like most Americans associated with China, she felt an aversion for the Kungs and wrote in her journal that her friend was too much 'under the influence of Mrs Kung. I wish she had almost anyone else with her.' May-ling took her sister's side entirely and stopped answering Chiang's telegrams. To Emma, she hardly ever mentioned him.

On 6 and 9 August 1945, the United States dropped atomic bombs on Hiroshima and Nagasaki. On the 8th, the Soviet Union declared war on Japan. On the 10th, Japan announced its intention to surrender, sparking celebrations around the world. May-ling was in New York and did not race back to China to share the moment of victory with her husband. She drove to Times Square where she got stuck in a huge boisterous throng, and watched the crowds roaring with joy, waving American flags. She identified with this place and had no wish to go back to China. Given the choice, she would much prefer to stay in New York with Big Sister.

18

The Downfall of the Chiang Regime

On 10 August 1945, Chiang Kai-shek, in Chongqing, learned about Japan's willingness to surrender in an unusual way. Tokyo made the announcement in a broadcast in English. As May-ling was in New York, he had no English-speaker with him who could listen to the radio and monitor the news. (Such was the man's isolation.) According to his diary, at about 8 p.m., he heard loud cheers and then firecrackers in the American army HQ near his residence. He sent a messenger (a relative) over to ask 'what is the noise about', and this was how the historic news reached the Supreme Commander China Theater.

Chiang's reaction was not euphoria but extreme tension. The moment had come for his showdown with Mao over who would rule China. Stalin had just sent 1.5 million troops into northern China along a huge front stretching more than 4,600 kilometres. The territory they occupied (eventually larger than the entire land under their occupation in central and eastern Europe) could be turned over to Mao's men if Chiang did not act immediately. Mao's army had been tiny before the war, but was now over 1 million, nearly a third the size of Chiang's forces. Chiang wanted to deploy troops at once. That evening, he was entertaining the Mexican ambassador, and he felt tremendous irritation because the ambassador kept on talking rather than leaving him alone to cable his commanders.

America wanted peace in China and compelled Chiang to invite Mao to Chongqing for peace talks. Mao had no wish to set foot in

Chiang's territory, knowing well the Generalissimo's track record of assassinations. But Stalin wanted Mao to play the negotiation game: he was not sure that Mao could beat Chiang militarily. After Stalin cabled him three times ordering him to go, Mao reluctantly departed his base, Yenan, on 28 August. He flew to Chongqing in an American plane accompanied by Ambassador Hurley – the Americans had also guaranteed his safety. Chiang was pleased that Mao had 'come as summoned', as he put it in his diary of 31 August. He wrote that it was his 'moral authority and powerful aura' that had done the trick, in addition to 'God's will'. He felt confident that he could handle Mao.

Chiang had sent a plane to New York to fly his wife back. May-ling did not want to come, telling Emma: 'I don't feel ready to go, Emma. But my husband needs me in the coming crisis with the Communists. I hope and pray the country can avoid armed conflict and achieve national unity. I will miss you. And might never see you again. The Communists might "get" me.' The first lady seemed to be already anticipating defeat. Still, she arrived in Chongqing on 5 September. Chiang met her at the airport. There was no expression of any emotion in his diary about the reunion after fourteen months, quite unlike after her trips to the US before.

Chiang was, of course, preoccupied with his meeting with Mao. In Chongqing, the Communist leader went around exclaiming 'Long live Generalissimo Chiang!', but he was determined to unseat Chiang through war. Indeed, he had planned an offensive against Chiang's forces just before his departure, which was being fought while he was in Chongqing in September and October. This battle, at Shangdang in Shanxi province, was the overture to the CCP–Nationalist civil war. Chiang, gearing up to defend his reign tooth and nail, poured his hatred of Mao into the pages of his diary. During the whole time that Mao was in Chongqing, he never invited Mao to meet May-ling. The Generalissimo clearly decided he did not want Mao to be the recipient of his wife's charm.

After Mao had been in Chongqing for nearly a month, Chiang felt unable to suffer his guest any longer, and took May-ling to Xichang, a remote region of Sichuan on the eastern edge of the

Himalayas. This was the place he had earlier earmarked to be his next capital if Chongqing fell to the Japanese. An airport on a narrow stretch of flat land 6,000 feet above sea level had been prepared, and a cluster of houses built.

Chiang's abrupt departure sent Mao into a panic; he suspected this was the prelude to a hit job targeting him. He sent Zhou En-lai to ask the Russian embassy to let him stay there – and was angry when the request was denied. People around Chiang had indeed urged him to assassinate Mao; but Chiang decided against it, as he was afraid of losing American aid.

The Chiangs spent a week in Xichang, a place of strange beauty. Frequent earthquakes had torn apart the surrounding rocky mountains, which made the canyon walls look like giants' bared teeth. These savage-looking canyons cradled a lake, as still as an immense mirror. The Chiangs reclined on a boat under a crystal-clear high sky, basking in the dazzling sunshine and crisp fresh air, so different from humid and stifling Chongqing. In those seven days, Chiang let himself relax totally, not even shaving, which was unusal for him. After his return to Chongqing, on 10 October, he signed an agreement with Mao. Neither man intended to keep it, and both escalated the preparations for all-out war.

Mao started to issue battle orders as soon as he returned to Yenan on 11 October. His army was not only much smaller than Chiang's, it had not had the experience of fighting tough battles against the Japanese as Chiang's had. It had only won conflicts against weak regional Nationalist units. Now it was facing the cream of Chiang's battle-hardened, US-trained forces. Before long Mao found to his dismay that the performance of his army fell far short of his hopes, and that Stalin, who was giving him covert backing, seemed to be keeping his options open. After a series of blows, in late November 1945 Mao collapsed with a nervous breakdown and took to his bed with cold sweats and convulsions.

While Mao was laid low, Chiang toured the country as the victorious war leader. When he entered cities like Beijing, Shanghai and his old capital Nanjing, 'it was as if Julius Caesar were entering

Rome', eyewitnesses observed. He was greeted by crowds numbering tens of thousands, hailed as the man who had won the war against Japan. The atmosphere was heady, and the Generalissimo revelled in his glory, evidently agreeing with the crowds that it was he who had beaten the Japanese. Standing tall and waving majestically, he gave every impression that he was 'infallible like God', his personal pilot commented. Those in the know felt he was seriously deluded. But no one levelled with him.

In triumphant mood, Chiang treated himself to a new presidential aircraft: the state-of-the-art C-54. One of these had been chartered to carry May-ling and Ei-ling to Rio in 1944, and it had wowed everyone who saw it. Chiang now ordered one for himself, even though his personal plane, the C-47 that was a gift from President Truman, had been in service barely a year. The new carrier, named *China–America*, was fitted out under the supervision of people who knew the Chiangs' taste. The cost, $1.8 million, was met by a reluctant finance ministry. Those who thought this extravagance inappropriate, given the crisis they were facing, kept their own counsel.

As if taking their cue from their leader, Nationalist officials sent to take over ex-Japanese-occupied cities and towns indulged themselves with little restraint. They had suffered deprivation for years; now they grabbed houses, cars and other valuables. Anyone unfortunate enough to own things they coveted could be designated a 'collaborator' and have their belongings confiscated. Regarding themselves as victors, these officials often treated the locals with open contempt and called them 'slaves who have no country of their own' – simply because the locals had lived under foreign occupation. People in large parts of China who only days before had welcomed the Nationalists as 'liberators' now cursed them as 'robbers' and 'locusts'. Within a very short time, the enthusiasm and admiration for Chiang Kai-shek and his regime evaporated, replaced by powerful disgust. 'The calamity of victory' was how the influential *Ta Kung Pao* described the takeover. In terms of popularity, Chiang stood at the peak of glory only briefly before the plunge began.

★

In the war itself, Chiang fared better. For more than a year, his army was winning on almost all fronts. The most critical theatre was Manchuria on the border with the Soviet Union – if the Communists seized it, they would be able to receive vital Russian arms and military training. In June 1946, Chiang's troops were on the verge of driving out the Reds, when the Generalissimo made a fatal mistake. He suspended his pursuit and ordered a ceasefire that lasted four months – under pressure from General George Marshall, who had come to China to try to stop the civil war. The ceasefire allowed Mao's army to establish a solid base larger than Germany on the borders with Russia and Russian satellites North Korea and Outer Mongolia.★ It was able to take full advantage of Stalin's priceless all-round backing, including, critically, repair of railways, which ensured speedy transport of heavy weapons and large numbers of troops. Chiang's disastrous decision changed the outcome of the war. By spring 1947, the tide had turned.

Chiang made this and other fatal errors partly because he did not have a team to assist him in decision-making. Whereas Mao had two able assistants, the strategist Liu Shao-qi and the first-rate administrator and diplomat Zhou En-lai, Chiang's remained a stubbornly one-man show. At this stage, he did not even have the counsel of Big Sister as he had alienated her by firing her husband.

Chiang never consulted his new prime minister T.V. Soong on military matters, and put him in charge of the economy. But although T.V. was a graduate of economics from Harvard and Columbia, and despite the fact that he was an outstanding diplomat, the economy fared disastrously under him. He was faced with an impossible task: a mammoth civil war was raging. His personal flaws did not help. T.V. was a foreigner in his native land. He had spent most of his life either abroad or in a privileged cocoon at

---

★ Chiang had recognised the 'independence' of Outer Mongolia in January 1946, in the vain hope that Stalin would hand over Manchuria and other Soviet-occupied territory to him, rather than to Mao.

Chiang's portrait on Tiananmen Gate, Beijing, after China's victory against Japan, 1945–6.

May-ling (centre, in floral dress) returning to Chongqing from New York on 5 September 1945.
As Chiang was having peace talks with Mao, she was met at the airport by Ching-ling (to her left).
H.H. Kung is next to Ching-ling; Kung's daughter Jeanette is to the right of May-ling.

Three sisters (from left: Ching-ling, Ei-ling, May-ling), possibly at Ei-ling's house in Chongqing during the Second World War. Soon they would be torn apart by the Nationalist–Communist civil war and would never see each other again.

Chiang Kai-shek's family celebrated his birthday in Nanjing, 1946. (The big character in the background – 'shou' – means 'longevity'.) He and May-ling are seated; Chiang's two sons stand behind them: Ching-kuo (left); Wei-go, (third from left). Between them is Ching-kuo's wife, Faina Vakhreva; the couple had met and married in Russia when Ching was kept there by Stalin as a hostage. Their four children are also in the picture, with a toddler on May-ling's lap.

A downcast Chiang Kai-shek visiting his ancestral temple for the last time
before leaving Mainland China in 1949, with his son and heir, Ching-kuo (front in hat).
May-ling was not with her husband in those last days.

In Taiwan in 1956, Big Sister, Ei-ling, was Chiang's guest of honour at his birthday dinner.

Chiang meeting May-ling at Taipei airport in 1959, when she flew back from New York.
They were ecstatic, as America had become more committed to defending Taiwan as a result of
Mao's recent sabre-rattling.

Red Sister became Communist China's vice chairman. Here she is visiting Moscow in 1957 as Mao's deputy. The post-Mao paramount leader, Deng Xiao-ping, is sitting on the other side of Mao (far left).

Ching-ling with Mao on Tiananmen Gate, October 1965. From right: Mao, Princess Monique (wife of Prince Norodom Sihanouk of Cambodia), Ching-ling, and Prime Minister Zhou En-lai.

Ching-ling (the shortest in the line-up of leaders, seventh from the right) at the memorial service on Tiananmen Square for Mao, who died on 9 September 1976. When the service was held on 18 September, the Gang of Four – Madame Mao and three other assistants of Mao's – were present. By the time this photograph was published shortly afterwards they had been arrested, and their images were removed, leaving conspicuous gaps.

Ching-ling entertaining guests with her adopted daughter,
Yolanda (first left), at home in Beijing in the 1970s.

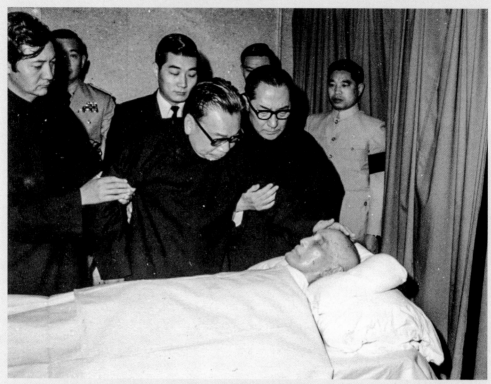

Ching-kuo stroking the forehead of his deceased father, Chiang Kai-shek, Taiwan, 1975. He was about to change his father's legacy and lead Taiwan towards democracy.

Ching-kuo and his wife Faina Vakhreva, a former Russian technician, whom he had met in Russia when he was kept there as a hostage by Stalin.

home, and had never attempted to be in touch with the average Chinese person. Although he had a strong sense of duty for the country, he knew little about the real China. His economic policies may have looked fine on paper but in practice were unworkable.

Instead of making an effort to redress his weaknesses, T.V. almost flaunted his wilfulness and hauteur. At the time of the Japanese surrender, Wellington Koo, Chinese ambassador to Britain, gave a big reception in London to celebrate. Among the guests were the then British prime minister Clement Attlee and foreign ministers from major countries including the US and Russia (Vyacheslav Molotov), who were in London for a conference. The entire diplomatic corps was there. T.V., prime minister of China, was in the embassy itself, but he declined to show up. Ambassador Koo and the Chinese foreign minister tried hard to persuade him to come downstairs, but he refused to budge, or even give his excuses. Ambassador Koo, an old-school gentleman and diplomat, had felt great exhilaration at the news of Japan's surrender and had at once ordered the Chinese flag to be hoisted outside the embassy. He wrote in his diary that 'at last the moment to which I had been looking forward and about which I had dreamed and worked has arrived'. He could not fathom why T.V. was behaving this way and in his memoirs permitted himself to vent his exasperation by remarking that 'It must have been considered a little awkward that Dr Soong stayed away.' A less restrained diplomat wrote sarcastically that the prime minister 'must have been fatigued from working too hard'.

More significantly, T.V. lost faith in Chiang and his regime just a year or so into the civil war. On 29 December 1946, very seriously and with obvious emotional emphasis, he spoke his mind to US adviser John Beal and told him, 'we are in a blind alley ... This isn't like America, where you can say, "All right, let the Republicans run the country for a while." The alternative here is Communism. If China collapses, the Communists will take over.' He began contemplating an alternative to Chiang and sounded out Beal about America's position on a possible 'liberal bloc'. This did not come to anything. In early 1947, when public opinion called on him to resign as prime minister, he stepped down promptly.* He was posted to Canton as the provincial governor. There he held secret discussions with Chiang's Nationalist opponents based nearby who were plotting to oust Chiang. He ultimately balked at joining them because they planned to collaborate with Mao. 'We cannot work with the Communists,' he said.

Ei-ling was apprehensive about the outcome of the civil war from the beginning. Knowing Chiang Kai-shek well, she did not think he would succeed. By spring 1947, she was in such despair that she felt she was terminally ill. Cancer was suspected and, although doctors told her there was no sign of it, Ei-ling remained gripped by a sense of her own impending death. In June, she wrote a will-like letter to her Red Sister, who had moved back to Shanghai when the war against Japan ended, telling her how much she loved her, now more than ever. Ei-ling seemed to be expecting a Communist takeover, and envisaging that life under the Communists would be hard, even for Mme Sun, she was making material preparations for Red Sister. In her role as the 'provider' for her sisters, a function she believed was assigned to her by God, she said she had asked May-ling's pilot, who was flying to Shanghai, to take a parcel of shampoo and other daily necessities, which she hoped would sustain Ching-ling for a long while. She told Ching-ling that every night as she lay in bed, the thought that preoccupied her was whether her dear sister had everything necessary to make her life comfortable and pleasant. 'If something happens to me, please remember that I love you very much.' Her other messengers brought Red Sister eyebrow pencils, textiles, chic jackets, handbags and jewellery, including gold earrings. There were also treatment sprays that promoted hair growth. Big Sister asked Red Sister to let her know the moment she needed money.

---

* There were allegations that T.V. massively looted the till. But compared to those against H.H., the charges lacked telling detail, and people in financial institutions generally refrained from making the accusation. Still, by his own account, T.V. was worth more than $5 million in 1943, and this had much to do with his privileged positions.

Under Big Sister's influence, May-ling also saw the writing on the wall fairly early on. While Chiang was relishing his victory tours just after the war against Japan, May-ling felt weary rather than elated. She complained to Emma: 'The last few months have been nothing but travel, travel, travel and then more travel. We have just come back from my second visit to Manchuria. It is strange that, in spite of all these years of air travel, I have never become immune to air sickness.'

She behaved very differently in this war than in the last. Then, she had toured the front, comforted the wounded, made passionate speeches and acted as a superb public relations figure. As John Beal recalled, 'She had addressed Congress, she charmed everyone she met. She talked fluent English and discussed with senators and representatives the substance of war and post-war problems in social conversation. To Americans she was a live, gracious, magnetic presence.' Now Beal noticed that she did not wish to do anything. He talked to her on 1 July 1946 about 'what a lousy press' her husband's government was getting. She agreed, but said immediately, 'I know what you want me to do. You want me to be there [at Chiang's meeting with the press] and interpret. I did that during the war, and I'm tired of it, and I'm not going to do it any more.' Beal wrote in his diary that May-ling 'went off in such a rush it rather surprised me, especially since I hadn't been thinking of that role for her, though it would have been a good touch'.

All Little Sister hankered for was 'dear old New York', and her American friends were constantly in her thoughts. A letter to Emma was full of nostalgia: 'Just imagine, about a year ago I was in New York and we were having such fun together.' Another urged Emma to write to her: 'What are you doing and how are you getting along? Write and tell me all the news.' She craved letters from her friend: 'This is just a short note to tell you to keep on writing to me although, Heaven knows, I treat you badly enough by not answering you adequately.' In the thick of a bloody civil war, she busied herself with pretty gifts to her friends on the other side of the ocean: 'I am sending you [Emma] a kimono and also some kimonos to various other friends. I am enclosing a list of their names. Will you please address them and have them mailed or delivered? ... I am again imposing on your good nature, but you are always so good to me and so sweet about doing things for me, that I know you will not mind attending to this'; 'I am sending a check for US$100.00 for the Alumnae Fund and the Class Reunion Fund. Please give it in whatever proportion you think suitable.'

May-ling did willingly perform one service for her husband. At the end of 1947, she invited Red Sister for an outing to the nearby beauty spot Hangzhou. There, strolling alongside the great peaceful lake, she asked Ching-ling frankly what the Communists' bottom line was for a settlement to stop the war. This straightforward question took Ching-ling aback. The sisters had always avoided talking about their political division. At the same time as doing her best to help Mao beat Chiang, Red Sister was sending delicacies like freshwater prawns to the Generalissimo's wife, who returned the gesture with ginger cake and cheese biscuits. She offered remedies for Ei-ling's eye trouble, and airmailed books to T.L.'s daughter – as if the raging battles all round them were irrelevant to their lives. May-ling's question brought home the stark reality. What was more, Ching-ling had been keeping up the pretence that she was an independent sympathiser, and not a member of what was to the rest of the Soongs an evil organisation. Now Little Sister's question signalled that the pretence was over; all Ching-ling's brothers and sisters knew that she was a key member of the organisation that set out to destroy them all. Hurriedly, Red sister replied, sticking to the same old make-believe, that she had nothing to do with the Communists and how could she know what their bottom line was? She left her sister and boarded the next train to Shanghai, where she immediately informed the CCP of the conversation between her and Little Sister. She did not want the party to think that she was doing deals with her family behind its back.

For his wife to enquire about their enemy's bottom line revealed Chiang Kai-shek's desperation. Indeed, throughout 1947–8, he suffered a series of catastrophic defeats. His chief US military adviser, General David Barr, put the responsibility squarely on the Generalissimo. In his report to Washington on 18 November 1948, Barr commented: 'no battle has been lost ... due to lack of ammunition or equipment. Their military debacles in my opinion can all be attributed to the world's worst leadership and many other morale-destroying factors that lead to a complete loss of will to fight'. Most morale destroying of all were perhaps some spectacular and miraculous Communist victories in key battlegrounds such as Manchuria and the region where Mao's HQ was. Red moles, who had gained Chiang's trust and top army positions, delivered Chiang's troops to the Reds to be wiped out piecemeal and en masse. Chiang Kai-shek rarely trusted people, but when he did, his trust was sometimes fatally misplaced – which is a comment on his judgement.

In summer 1948, the Generalissimo started preparing to 'move house' to Taiwan, the island of 36,000 square kilometres and a population of 6 million. He made a plan to extract as much gold, silver and hard currency as possible to take to Taiwan. The extraction went under the name of a 'currency reform': everyone was told to exchange their liquid assets for a new paper money called the 'gold yuan'. Failure to comply was punishable by death. While petty officials in the provinces went from door to door trying to scare people into parting with their life's savings, Chiang's son Ching-kuo was sent to Shanghai. There he blamed the raging hyperinflation and the general economic crisis on the business community, and ordered them to register all their assets. This was a prelude to confiscation. Businessmen who declined to cooperate were called 'tigers', and in an operation called 'tiger-beating', they were harassed, arrested and even executed.

To browbeat the businessmen into toeing the line, Ching-kuo arrested a son of one of the biggest Shanghai gangsters, Big-Eared Du. When the son's photograph appeared on the front page of the Nationalist mouthpiece, the Central Daily, Big-Eared Du took to his bed for days. He had considered himself a friend of the Generalissimo and did not think he deserved this. He resolved to fight back. Before long, the press began to expose the Yangtze Trading Corp., the company that belonged to Ei-ling's son, David. It was accused of hoarding imported goods illegally. The police raided and sealed off its warehouse. David faced heavy fines, even imprisonment. In truth, thanks to his insider connections and his mother's financial acumen, David had registered those goods (which were in any event only a fraction of his wealth), and so strictly speaking he broke no law. But public anger boiled over. Even the *Central Daily* condemned the 'capitalists with state power', in language that was normally seen in Communist propaganda. Ching-kuo felt like being in the middle of a tornado. If he pressed on with getting people to hand over their possessions, he just had to make an example of his cousin. And he was inclined to do so.

David pleaded with his aunt May-ling, who was outraged. She summoned her husband, who was away inspecting the military front in the north. Her words and tone left no room for hesitation, and he flew to Shanghai at once. May-ling confronted him with what amounted to an ultimatum: she would be with the Kungs against him if he were to sacrifice them. The Generalissimo told his son not to touch David. Ching-kuo left Shanghai and the 'tiger-beating' stopped. Ching-kuo's job was – and still is – portrayed as an anti-corruption operation by the Chiang father and son; it was in fact the Generalissimo's extortion spree. Thanks to May-ling's determination to protect her nephew, it petered out – and the middle class managed to keep what remained of their assets (for now; soon Mao took them all). But Chiang had extracted a lot, and this, together with the government gold reserves, tided the Nationalists over the initial period in Taiwan after they fled there.

To the general public, the 'tiger-beating' anti-corruption drive had failed because of May-ling, and people turned their anger on her. In November, Chiang noted in his diary several times that 'all the Nationalist party members', as well as society at large, blamed his wife and the Kungs and Soongs. He mentioned an attack on himself and his son, but hastened to add that this was 'entirely because [we] were tarnished by association with Kung senior and junior'.

May-ling had already been devastated by the impending collapse of the regime. Now she was bitterly upset that everyone was pointing the finger at her family. It was particularly galling that her husband and his son were ready to make her family the scapegoats, even sending her nephew to jail. She confronted Chiang, sobbing and yelling uncontrollably, which startled Chiang as he had never seen her like this before. He tried to calm her down, but Little Sister was inconsolable. She could not wait to get away from him, from the accusations, and from the mess the country was in. On 28 November 1948, she left China for New York. She was prepared never to see her husband again.

As she would soon learn, President Truman held the same abysmal view of her family and herself. The president later told the writer Merle Miller that 'any money we spent to support them [China] ... a good deal of it would end up in the pockets of Chiang and the Madame and the Soong and Kung families. They're all thieves, every damn one of them.'

May-ling was convinced that her family was not the cause of the downfall of Chiang's regime. 'Time and God will vindicate them,' she believed fervently.

On 21 January 1949, Chiang Kai-shek was forced to resign as president in favour of Vice President Li Tsung-jen. He 'retired' to his birthplace at Xikou. There, he stayed by the mountain-sized tomb that he had built for his mother. On 23 April, the Communist army took Nanjing, in effect ending twenty-two years of Nationalist rule over the mainland. On 19 May, Chiang reached Taiwan. During his last months on the mainland, Chiang was without his wife's company. He had repeatedly asked her to return. Her excuses ranged from the usual health issues to the need for her to keep working on Washington. Ching-kuo wrote and told her that his father was facing the gravest moment in his life and depended on her to support him. She replied: 'I wish I could fly back like an arrow. But right now my return does not help the difficult situation. So I plan to stay here for a while. I am sure this will benefit the party and the country.'

During this period, Ching-kuo, approaching forty, was with his father daily. Father and son developed an extremely close bond. When May-ling suggested – rashly, as she would soon realise – that Ching-kuo come to America to brief her about the exact situation in China and discuss what she could do in America, Ching-kuo replied that he could not possibly leave his father alone. The father–son relationship grew to replace the Generalissimo's attachment to May-ling.

Chiang's telegrams to May-ling became distant and businesslike. Sensing her husband's coolness – and feeling guilty about not being by his side at this 'crisis hour' – May-ling acted somewhat ingratiatingly towards him, something she had not done before. She eagerly expressed concern about his safety and well-being, reported her lobbying work in America, and ever so gently suggested that Chiang come to her and travel the world with her. Chiang absolutely refused to go abroad, and vowed to live or die in Taiwan. Almost bluntly, he told May-ling to join him there ('On which day do you plan to leave for Taiwan?').

Ei-ling advised Little Sister not to go. She would 'protest' whenever May-ling suggested leaving New York. To her, Chiang did not deserve their loyalty for all the outrage he had committed towards their family, in addition to his disastrous incompetence. But above all, Ei-ling cared about her sister and did not want to see her flying into almost certain death. The Communists were making plans to seize Taiwan, and, with Stalin's help, aided by the strategically placed moles on the island, they would quite likely succeed. As the Generalissimo refused to leave Taiwan, Ei-ling did not want Little Sister to die with him. And yet, she was painfully aware that for a wife to desert her husband in need was bad form. She must also have known that Chiang would never forgive May-ling if she left him – and that Little Sister could well come to share the fate of the many whom Chiang did not forgive. Usually assured about her own mind, Ei-ling was now unusually torn.

May-ling was in turmoil. She felt guilty about even entertaining the thought of leaving her husband at this juncture – and she knew this would hand the Communists a propaganda coup. If she deserted him, she would never be able to forgive herself. On 1 December 1949, Chiang cabled May-ling to say that he regretted not being able to celebrate their twenty-second wedding anniversary with her. The reference to their marriage seems to have opened a floodgate of memories for May-ling about her life with the Generalissimo. She remembered that 'I had accompanied my husband on his campaigns. We had lived in mud huts, in railway stations, in trains, through the hot stony sandy formations of the Northwest, in primitive barracks, and in tents ... I had started schools, orphanages, hospitals and opium-cure clinics ... I had even gone into military service as Secretary General of the Air Force.' Her full and exciting life would never have been possible without her marriage to Chiang. She asked herself: 'How could I let my husband face the greatest setback of his life without me at his side?'

She could not sleep and was unable to stay still during the day. She tried to talk to Ei-ling and clear her mind. Big Sister told her, 'Keep on praying and be patient. I am certain He will open a way.' May-ling had been praying hard for months, and had come to feel that 'my prayers had become somewhat mechanical and repetitious'. Still she persevered. 'Then one morning at dawn, unaware whether I was asleep or awake, I heard a Voice – an ethereal Voice saying distinctly: "All is right."'

This slight variation on Browning's line had occurred to May-ling before. In December 1936, when Chiang Kai-shek was kidnapped, she had flown to Xian to share his fate. On that occasion, Chiang had told her that God had signalled her arrival through a passage in the Bible he was reading. She had then interpreted this 'remarkable thing' as God sending her husband the message: 'All is right.' Speaking these words to her now, it seemed to her God was making a comparison with 1936 and telling her to go to her husband again.

'Fully awakened by the words, I immediately rose and went to my sister's room. She looked up from her bed. She was not surprised by such an early visit because during those troublous days when I was beset with insomnia, I often disturbed her, day or night.' Ei-ling saw that May-ling's face was 'radiant', and understood immediately. 'I told her that I had heard God speak to me ... [and] announced that I was going home by the first available plane, she helped me to pack. No longer did she protest.'

May-ling arrived in Taiwan on 13 January 1950. In his diary that day, Chiang wrote blandly and formally that after she had a rest, he 'listened to [her] report' about her work in America.

However, the significance of May-ling's return soon sank in. The situation in Taiwan was critical: 2 million troops and civilians had fled with him from the mainland, flooding an island with only 6 million inhabitants. Taiwan was facing a big economic crisis. The US was standing aloof. There was no US ambassador, only a second secretary. The Communists had announced their determination to take Taiwan. Everyone thought the island would fall before long. Everyone was in a state of panic. And anyone who could leave was rushing to do so. And yet, May-ling flew the other way. This was a huge boost for the Nationalists' morale. When the news that she was coming leaked out, crowds made their way to the airport. The Generalissimo came to appreciate what his wife did. In his diary, he compared May-ling to legendary heroes who came to the rescue at the most dangerous moment.

PART V

Three Women, Three Destinies (1949–2003)

19

'We must crush warm-feeling-ism': Being Mao's Vice Chairman

Days before the Communists seized Shanghai in May 1949, May-ling, in America at the time, sent Red Sister a letter that was full of concern. Ching-ling was constantly in her thoughts, she said; she so hoped that her sister would be safe and everything would go well. Little Sister was most anxious that she could not do much to help as the ocean now separated them; but please could Ching-ling write and tell her how she was. At this time May-ling was on the Communists' list of 'war criminals', together with her husband, and she considerately avoided sending the letter just in her name. It was co-signed with brother T.L., whose daughter had received some books from Ching-ling.

Red Sister did not reply. Nor did she answer any of Ei-ling's letters. In the lead-up to the Communist takeover, while her exiled sisters wrote with constant expressions of love and affection, she sent not a word of good wishes to them. She was unmoved – or perhaps even offended, for they seemed to assume that her chosen future was one of hardship and trouble. Ever since she decided to throw in her lot with the Reds, Ching-ling had steeled herself to cut her sisters out of her life. Her earlier fond and intimate gestures towards them were more a mechanism to protect herself against possible harm from Chiang Kai-shek than a reflection of her deep feelings. She had long resolved to live without the family into which she was born.

Her adopted family were her comrades and close friends. With some of them she celebrated the Communist takeover of her city.

'The day we have been fighting for has at last come!' They gathered in her house and told each other. Smiling excitedly, Ching-ling pushed a red rose into a visitor's buttonhole.

Mao chose Beijing to be his capital, and wrote to urge her to come and join his government. The language the Chairman used was courteous and respectful: please could Mme Sun come and 'guide us on how to build a new China'.

Ching-ling thanked Mao profusely, but she declined to go to Beijing. She said she was suffering from high blood pressure and other ailments and needed treatment in Shanghai. The new prime minister, Zhou En-lai, tried to persuade her, so did some old friends. She politely said no to them all.

She was not playing hard to get. Apart from the fact that Shanghai was where she wanted to live, she wisely decided it was best to stay away from the centre of power, where she might be sucked into Party intrigues. Ching-ling had no illusions about the cruelty of her chosen system. She had witnessed Stalin's bloody power games first-hand and knew about Mao's brutal purges (in which even Zhou En-lai had been a victim and had had to grovel). At times, the future seems to have scared her, and she briefly contemplated going to live in Russia, 'for medical treatment'. What she really wanted was just to run her small operation, now renamed China Welfare, in the company of her intimate friends in her home city.

Mao dispatched Zhou's wife, who knew Ching-ling well, to Shanghai to reissue the invitation in person. To keep saying no would be a snub. Ching-ling accepted the invitation from Mrs Zhou. Meanwhile, Zhou made arrangements for her future life with his trademark attention to detail. He inspected the house that had been readied for her, and informed her that it was more spacious than her residences in Chongqing and Shanghai and that it had two floors, which was rare for Beijing, where most houses were single-storey. The interior had been decorated under the supervision of her old friends, the prime minister added, not forgetting to suggest that she bring her own cook. Ching-ling had made some complaints, and they were all resolved to her satisfaction. An old servant of Sun Yat-sen's who had been arrested was released. The house of her favourite (and apolitical) brother, T.A., had been confiscated (like all her family's properties), and was given back to her for safekeeping on his behalf.

In late August, Ching-ling set off for Beijing. During the two-day train journey, she gazed out of the window at the changing landscape, of fields and villages and towns, from the south to the north, and she thought 'how our homeland could become prosperous. We have all the conditions ... . We have great resources ... no success is beyond our capacity ... .'

Mao came to the railway station to meet her. Children presented her with flowers – Soviet-style. At the age of fifty-six (eleven months older than Mao), Red Sister became the vice chairman of Mao's government. When Mao proclaimed the People's Republic on 1 October 1949, she walked right behind him onto Tiananmen Gate. While her sisters were living as exiles, she was at the pinnacle of her life.

That life was singularly privileged. Red Sister had enviable houses in both Beijing and Shanghai. The one in Shanghai, confiscated from a prominent banker, was a European-style villa with a large well-groomed lawn lined with rare trees and exotic flowers. Her successive Beijing houses were even more magnificent. The final one was a palatial mansion that had belonged to a Manchu prince, and Pu Yi, the last emperor, had been born there. Among the favoured possessions of the royal household was a gnarled 140-year-old pomegranate tree which still bore several fruits a year. As her late husband was presented as the selfless leader of a great revolution that had overthrown the imperial family, the irony that she should move into this palace did not escape the many sceptics and idealists. Ching-ling felt uneasy and attempted a form of apology to friends: 'I am really getting royal treatment, altho' am unhappy because others *far more deserving* [her emphasis] live in simple little houses.' Her houses were well staffed, and the servants addressed her in the pre-Communist style: Taitai ('Ma'am').

She was not a member of the CCP, strictly speaking. In the 1930s she had enlisted in the Comintern, which was directly under

Moscow authority; but Moscow had then decided that she should stay outside the organisation as a secret member. After the Comintern was dissolved in 1943, Red Sister had been treating the CCP, together with Moscow, as her 'Organisation', even though formally she was not a member. In Communist China, she was not involved in policymaking, which suited her well. Having no personal political ambition and accepting her own limitations, she was satisfied just to be in charge of her own small outfit, China Welfare, now housed in her old family home, which she donated to the Communists, together with all her family's properties. China Welfare was allowed to run a hospital for women and children, a kindergarten and a Soviet-style 'youth palace'. There was a playhouse for children. But it had to cease performing a major function: famine relief. Officially, there was no such thing as famine in Communist China. When Voice of America reported that she had been helping famine victims, she wrote to Zhou En-lai at once and offered to denounce this 'shameless falsification of facts' publicly.

She published an English-language magazine, *China Reconstructs*, but Party censors carefully screened every issue. The Party inserted new men into China Welfare, while thoroughly vetting its old staff. Some close friends found the changes unbearable and left. But Ching-ling accepted them without demur. She adjusted quickly.

The adjustment included being surrounded by bodyguards who had been Communist soldiers. They often came from poor peasant families, and found much to disapprove of in her lifestyle. And they would make blunt comments to her in a way her old servants would not. The Communists made a particular thing about 'equality' with the staff, making this a key part of its claim to be 'democratic'. One day in 1951 she went to the East German embassy for a reception. Afterwards, some of her bodyguards criticised the women's long evening dresses for being wasteful: 'All that good silk and textile unused!' Ching-ling spent a lot of time explaining to them that fashion and adornment were important in people's lives. Whether this convinced the young men or not she did not know.

A Christmas party was no longer a natural thing. When she invited her friends for Christmas Eve in 1951, she had to tell them to keep quiet and not to tell anyone it was a party. Celebration would cause 'misunderstanding'. In later years, she celebrated New Year's Eve instead, although with a Christmas tree.

She learned to be cautious about things she did not used to have to worry about. When she forwarded a letter from her old American friend Edgar Snow to Mao at Snow's request, she felt it necessary to stress that 'I do not know whether his recent thoughts are still correct, as I have not read his works for a long time.' Writing to friends, she often asked them to 'burn' or 'destroy' the letters after reading.

In 1951–2, Mao launched a campaign called 'the Three Antis' (anti-corruption, waste and bureaucracy), targeting officials who handled money. People in China Welfare were told to denounce others as well as come clean themselves. Ching-ling found herself on the receiving end of unsavoury accusations. One referred to a building contractor who was a relative of hers, who had built and maintained houses for her family and friends, including the one that she donated to China Welfare. Just before Chiang Kai-shek lost Shanghai, there had been speculation that Chiang might kidnap Mme Sun and take her to Taiwan. This relative had stayed at Ching-ling's house and acted like a bodyguard for her. She felt grateful and close to him and every now and then they exchanged presents. Now rumours suggested that she was receiving bribes from him. She had to go through the indignity of arguing that the presents they had given each other were no more than cakes and biscuits, and that if his gifts were costly, such as two bottles of red wine, she would give him far more expensive gifts in return. She vowed that she could produce witnesses to back her up, and even tried to dissociate from him, demanding that he be subject to a thorough investigation and punished if found to be corrupt.

As more political campaigns followed and one friend after another got into trouble, Ching-ling ruminated that she had always been inclined to trust people rather than suspect them, and that this was now a quasi-crime: 'the right-wing way of thinking'.

Nevertheless, in those initial years, Red Sister's equilibrium remained more or less intact. She went on giving parties for her core circle of friends, and they danced and listened to old Western gramophone records. Mao designated Zhou En-lai, the most urbane and charismatic face of the rigid regime, to keep in contact with her. Other high officials she dealt with, especially in Shanghai, were old friends who had been underground Communists. They formed a pleasant cocoon around her. All manner of honours were showered on her, not least the much trumpeted Stalin Peace Prize given by the Kremlin. Two renowned writers, Ilya Ehrenburg from the Soviet Union and Pablo Neruda of Chile, flew to Beijing to make the presentation. There were new pleasures. She travelled to many countries, feted as the gracious and illustrious representative of China. Life for Ching-ling was not at all bad, and she was reasonably contented.

In 1956, Red Sister had her first – and quite possibly the last – direct confrontation with the Party. That year, a new executive committee was imposed on China Welfare, headed by the Party secretary of Shanghai, Ke Qing-shi, one of Mao's favourite cronies. Although Ching-ling was still the 'chair', it was obvious that this was no more than an honorific title. She had lost her 'baby' altogether, and was deeply upset. In private letters, she vented her vexation, referring to the Party as 'they': 'I was never consulted on anything & in fact ... I had no idea they've decided to ...'

In November she exploded. That month was the ninetieth anniversary of Sun Yat-sen's birth, and Beijing was planning a big commemoration. Ching-ling wrote articles about Sun for the *People's Daily*, the Party's mouthpiece. She portrayed Sun as China's Lenin, saying that the CCP 'took over his mission' after he died.

As before, Ching-ling sent her draft to Beijing for approval. Normally, she communicated with Zhou En-lai, whom she respected. This time, Zhou was frantically preoccupied with something more urgent. The Communist world was in upheaval. The Hungarian Uprising was breaking out in Europe, following protests in Poland, and Mao was rattled. At the same time, he was trying to take advantage of the crisis and supplant Nikita Khrushchev as the leader of the Communist camp. (Stalin had died in 1953.) How to handle the situation consumed all the time and energy of Mao and his lieutenants. For days and nights, they were immersed in meetings.

Zhou En-lai had no time to read Ching-ling's articles, and the job fell on more junior censors. Without Zhou's tact, the officials asked Ching-ling straightforwardly to make changes and emphasise the guiding role of the CCP in Sun's career. Ching-ling was told that she should say: 'Dr Sun's anti-imperialist work, etc. developed as an outcome of seeing Li Ta-chao and Chiu Chu-pak [two early CCP leaders].' Ching-ling was incensed. She wrote to a friend on 8 November that Sun had had his revolutionary ideas 'early in life ... before he met any CP'; 'I am not belittling their contributions, only as we value truth and facts, we must record them truthfully even if the facts are not what some people wished to see.' As was by now her habit, she asked the recipient, 'Please kindly destroy this note.'

She insisted on her version, and the lesser censors, having no authority to overrule her, let her articles be published as written. When they read her words, the Party leaders were annoyed and decided to teach her a lesson. On 11 November, when the commemoration of Sun was held – a grand affair attended by Mao himself, together with the whole of the CCP leadership – Sun's widow was nowhere to be seen.

Meanwhile, a rumour was flying around that Ching-ling was having an 'illicit affair' with her chief bodyguard and could no longer be regarded as Mme Sun. A cousin of hers heard the rumour and wrote to tell her. Ching-ling was beside herself with rage and replied that if anyone said this again, 'take him to the police!' The cousin asked why then did she not attend the commemoration. She had to say that she absented herself because she was worried she might not be able to control her grief and might lose her composure, which would not look good. The truth was that she was not invited, or even told about the occasion.

Ching-ling did cherish – and show – an uncommon fondness for her chief bodyguard, Sui Xue-fang. Sui was a handsome young man, a good shot, a skilled driver, a talented photographer and a gifted dancer. At Ching-ling's parties, when she occasionally danced, he was her partner. More often they played chess and billiards together. Ching-ling, who was generally kind and considerate to her staff,* perhaps treated Sui like the son she could never have. In fact, she was also affectionate to Sui's deputy, Jin Shan-wang, whom she fondly nicknamed 'Cannon'. She taught Jin how to play the piano, and even deputised him to make informal speeches on her behalf. The two young men competed for her affection, sometimes in a petulant and wilful way. And she would act vivaciously and mischievously like a younger woman. The atmosphere in Ching-ling's household took on the semblance of a family, with affection and laughter, as well as sulks and rows.

Gossip was inevitable, but in this case, most unusually, it spread to the general public. The private lives of the country's leaders were normally kept under the thickest blanket of secrecy. Other top officials might have affairs but none ever reached the ears of anyone outside their guarded elite compounds. Ching-ling alone was widely talked about.

The rumour – and being excluded from the commemoration of Sun Yat-sen – alarmed Ching-ling. She realised that she could very well be deprived of the title of Mme Sun that was vital for her survival. There had been rumours like this before, under Chiang Kai-shek; but then she could always speak out and refute them. Some newspaper would publish her story, or else she could have it printed as leaflets and thrown from the rooftops of Shanghai's high-rises. Now she no longer had any outlet for her voice – even if she was the vice chairman of the country. She had no way to defend herself in public and was completely at the mercy of the Party. If the Party said she was no longer Mme Sun, she would no longer be Mme Sun – even if she remained his faithful widow.

This frightening realisation forced the headstrong Ching-ling to yield. She found a way to demonstrate her submission. In April 1957,

---

* I interviewed two key long-term members of Ching-ling's staff: assistant Li Yun and deputy chief bodyguard Jin Shan-wang; both made a point of telling me how kind she was to her staff and asking me to mention this quality of hers. Such a request was unique among the staff of leaders whom I interviewed.

Mao's number two, President Liu Shao-qi, was in Shanghai and visited Ching-ling with his wife. The intelligent and elegant Mrs Liu came from an eminent old family and had graduated in physics from the Catholic University in Beijing in the pre-Communist days. Ching-ling got on well with the couple. She saw the Lius' visit as a signal that the Party wanted to make up with her, and she seized on the opportunity. She told Liu that she wished to join the CCP. Mrs Liu noted the earnestness with which she made the application. Her husband was delighted but, weighing every word, he replied that he would report to Mao as this was 'a very big thing'. Liu soon returned to Shanghai with Zhou En-lai, the number three, and told Ching-ling that the CCP felt she could help their common cause more effectively by staying outside the Party. The Party would inform her of all major issues and she would participate in decision-making. Ching-ling nodded; tears came to her eyes and she seemed very emotional.

Indeed, Mao and the leadership had no wish to alienate Ching-ling. Mao himself had a rather good personal relationship with her, calling her 'Dear Elder Sister' and writing to her in a playful manner. Politically, she was priceless. China's non-Communist neighbours feared Red China, and Ching-ling could help the CCP win them over. President Sukarno of Indonesia, whom Mao particularly wanted to cultivate, was attracted by the good-looking and graceful Ching-ling and sang her praises – literally, in a song dedicated to her and sung by himself. Mao made a point of telling Red Sister that he was very pleased with the impact she made on Sukarno.

Ching-ling was even more valuable in Beijing's design to take Taiwan. US president Harry S. Truman had initially distanced himself from the Chiang regime; but after Mao backed North Korea to invade the South in June 1950, starting the Korean War, he dispatched the US Seventh Fleet to the Taiwan Strait to protect the island from any possible invasion. Mao's army was unable to conquer Taiwan by force. His only option was to lure Taiwan into capitulation. And who had more clout to sway the Nationalists than Mme Sun? Ching-ling dutifully wrote to Ei-ling in New York, urging her to come for a visit 'at once', before they were both too old. Ei-ling had written Ching-ling several letters in the past few years without any reply. Tactfully, she explained that she had cataracts and was about to have an operation; she promised that once her eyesight recovered, she would come to see her dear sister as soon as possible. And of course she missed Ching-ling all the time and wished they could be together like before. She sent Ching-ling some cashmere garments. But she never went to Communist China.

Mao made another goodwill gesture to Ching-ling, to compensate for her humiliation. He took her as his deputy to Moscow in November 1957 for the celebration of the fortieth anniversary of the October Revolution. Ching-ling, for her part, signed up to the Party line on Sun Yat-sen wholesale before the trip, by writing that Sun had only developed 'the correct view about the Chinese revolution after he met with the representatives of the CCP'.

Meanwhile, Sui, her chief bodyguard, married a factory worker. Ching-ling gave a dinner to celebrate their wedding and, as the newly-weds were not assigned a flat, offered them rooms in the staff quarters of her Shanghai mansion.

The episode was resolved adroitly on both sides. But the rumour about Ching-ling's relationship with Sui persisted. Like others growing up in China in the 1960s and 70s, I often heard that Ching-ling had secretly married her chief bodyguard, and that 'Mme Sun Yat-sen' was only a facade, which the Party kept for her to save her face. People believed the rumour. Many still believe it today.

The upshot of the whole event was that Ching-ling stopped acting independently altogether, and became a pure decoration for the Party, visiting foreign states and entertaining overseas visitors on its behalf. There were no more overt critical remarks, not even in private. In public, she echoed the Party's voice unfailingly. In 1957, during the 'Anti-Rightist' campaign, hundreds of thousands of educated men and women who had accepted Mao's invitation and spoken up about the country's problems were condemned. (Mao's invitation was bait to lure out potential critics.) Among the victims were many of Ching-ling's old friends and acquaintances who had fought Chiang Kai-shek with her. They lost their jobs and were sent to do manual labour. Some were packed off to the gulag; others driven to suicide. This ruined far more lives than anything Chiang Kai-shek had done. But Red Sister was silent. (That year, she was struggling for her own survival.) Their misfortune did cause her pain, but she battled to harden her feelings. In an article, she quoted a Party slogan to advise her readers and herself, 'We must crush warm-feeling-ism ...'

In 1958, Mao launched the grandiose 'Great Leap Forward', which in reality was his bid to build a whole range of military industries at breakneck speed. Steel was in demand and Mao, who was completely incompetent about economics, ordered the whole population to make steel. Backyard furnaces sprouted across China, and Ching-ling built her own with members of her staff in her garden. To make room for the monstrosity, she had to have some beautiful old trees cut down. The *People's Daily* announced that she held down a red-hot lump of steel for young men to hammer. She was unhappy, but did not protest.

The monumental waste of human and natural resources of the Leap played a big part in causing a nationwide famine, which lasted four years, 1958–1961.* Some 40 million people perished. Even in Ching-ling's privileged world, people were hungry. At one point, she gave the order to kill a pet goat to supplement her staff's diet. Facing misrule of such unthinkable dimensions, some old Communists rebelled – most noticeably Marshal Peng De-huai, the defence minister. Peng was denounced in July 1959. (He later died in incarceration.) Ching-ling, who had admired the marshal, was shaken. Writing to an old trusted friend, she revealed, 'I feel very tense and am having nightmares.' The recipient was told to 'burn the letter after reading'.

It was at this point that Red Sister might have contemplated leaving China, using health problems as a pretext. She had arthritis and had the best possible medical attention; but in a letter to her German friend Anna Wang on 27 July 1959, she claimed to have

---

* The main cause was that Mao exported food to Russia to pay for military industries – food that the Chinese were dependent on for survival. See Jung Chang and Jon Halliday, *Mao, the Unknown Story*, Chapter 40.

been informed that only by staying abroad could she get the right treatment and care. This looks like a hint to Anna to try and find a health-related way to get her out. It was more wishful thinking than a serious plan. But just to hint at it to a good friend made her nervous. Her letter was written as if she sensed some Big Brother looking over Anna's shoulder reading it. While making the sounding, she simultaneously retracted it by adding that she was in pain and it was hard for her to travel abroad – and that her problem seemed insurmountable.

Ching-ling's anxiety over her letters did not stop at expecting them to be read; she feared they might be intercepted, and would anxiously wait for her friends' confirmation that the letters had arrived. Only occasionally did she permit herself to voice some complaints. Loudspeakers (a feature of the Great Leap Forward) screaming ecstatically from dawn to nine o'clock at night were driving her crazy; social life of a pleasurable kind had disappeared, replaced by dreary official functions; and there was an acute shortage of daily necessities. To Anna she wrote that mothers with newborn babies had to beg others shame-facedly for used sheets to make nappies, and that she herself had given away her spare sheets and old clothes. She was in urgent need of materials to make shirts and trousers. Could Anna please send her some materials (from East Germany)? Anything would do, as 'beggars can't be choosers'. Anna also sent her elastics for her underwear, socks, and a mirror with a stand for her dressing table.

Admirers of Mme Sun, wishing desperately to see some defiance from their heroine, often claim that she wrote to protest to the CCP leadership many times. There is no sign of this. But the evidence only shows her endorsing the Party line and pledging to stick to it.

During the famine, something happened to Ching-ling so she was able to close her eyes and her mind to reality. When the 1950s turned to the 1960s, she informally adopted two daughters, who filled her life.

They were the children of Sui, her chief bodyguard and co-victim of the scandalous rumour. At the end of 1957 his first child, a girl, was born, and he brought her to show Ching-ling – something staff usually did to please her as she loved children. Ching-ling sat the baby on her knees and cradled her in her arms. The infant did not cry, but smiled at her. They looked each other in the eye. The baby then proceeded to relieve herself on Ching-ling's starched gown. Other members of staff, knowing that their mistress was fussy about cleanliness, lurched to try to snatch the baby away. But she stopped them: 'Let her finish her pee, otherwise it would be bad for her.' The warm pee stirred to life a sensation inside Ching-ling, something she had not experienced and had been thirsting for: being a mother. From now on the dark shadows of politics began to recede, as Ching-ling, in her mid-sixties, became absorbed in motherhood.

20

'I have no regrets'

The little girl of Sui's who peed onto Ching-ling grew to be a cute toddler. Ching-ling gave her an English name, Yolanda, but called her 'my little treasure'. Given that Ching-ling was by this time in her late sixties, people told the child to address her as 'Grandmother', or 'Taitai' ('Ma'am'); but Ching-ling wanted to be called 'Mother'. As if sensing what was on her mind, the clever child muttered to her 'Mama-Taitai', which delighted Ching-ling and solved the problem. She promptly gave instructions that all children brought to visit her address her so. Behind closed doors with Yolanda, she referred to herself as Mama, and the child called her Mama.

One day in 1961, the three-year-old Yolanda danced for Mama-Taitai. Ching-ling could hardly contain her pride, and showed her off to friends. Yolanda was invited to dance at a big celebration of Children's Day (1 June) that year, wearing a pretty Korean costume. When Ching-ling watched her on television (a television set was a rare luxury available only to a tiny group of the elite), she was enthralled. In particular, she felt that, incredibly, Yolanda looked like her. (Others thought so too.)

Ching-ling had also unofficially adopted Yolanda's sister, Yong-jie, born in 1959. When the baby was five months old, a photo was taken of her. Ching-ling so loved the picture that she asked for it to be published on the cover of the official women's magazine, *Women in China*. (Her request was not granted.)

The two little girls were in and out of her house, which was nothing short of paradise to them, as they lived in the basic and cramped staff quarters. Life was hard for their parents, the body-guard and the factory worker, especially during the famine. The couple had many mouths to feed: after Yolanda and Yong-jie, they had two more children, a son and a daughter. It was not a happy family, either. There were frequent quarrels, and much yelling. Mrs Sui did not like Ching-ling's presence in her family, and in fits of frustration and rage, would smash bowls and plates, all precious items. Once she chased her husband to his boss's house and swore at the august Mme Sun, blaming her for the tension in the Sui household. Ching-ling was shaken and ordered accommodation to be found for the family at once. They soon moved out.

In 1963, Sui suffered a stroke and was partially paralysed. Ching-ling wrote to an old friend: 'The news made me very unhappy & up to now I have not gathered enough courage to visit him. I am afraid my emotion might cause him unhappiness & and make him worse. I have sent 2 of his children to the kindergarten where the influence is better than his home. The children are extremely clever. I visited them at the kindergarten upon my return & found them quite accustomed to their new routine & surroundings.' She would collect them and bring them to her home and they started to stay with her regularly.

Although their mother resented this, she accepted that this was the best for her children. Yolanda and Yong-jie maintained their relationship with their parents, but spent much time with Mama-Taitai, who gave them otherwise unobtainable food and undreamed-of gorgeous clothes, including the softest fur coats made of baby lambs' wool, which thrilled them to bits. Ching-ling dressed their hair in the morning with colourful silk bows shaped like butterflies. She watched them play on her large lawn, sitting on a bench waiting for them to race into her arms. On the lawn were two big geese, and the girls, in her embrace, would feed them as they waddled over. Mama-Taitai taught the girls the etiquette of meeting VIPs and introduced them to visiting dignitaries. In one picture, a beaming Zhou En-lai took their hands and strolled in the garden with them.

The girls completely occupied Ching-ling's life and engaged her attention. Yolanda later remarked that Ching-ling's previous devotion to her work may have been to fill the hollow inside her created by being deprived of motherhood.

When the Cultural Revolution started in 1966, Red Sister could no longer ignore the reality outside her mansions. In this, Mao's biggest purge, President Liu Shao-qi was the prime target, because he had ambushed Mao and managed to slow down Mao's breakneck military industrialisation (thus halting the famine).* Mao hated being thwarted and ensured Liu died a wretched death in prison. Mrs Liu was thrown into prison on the outlandish charge of being 'a CIA and Nationalist spy'. Alleged Liu followers were condemned in the tens of millions all over China, with labels like 'capitalist-roaders', 'ox-devils and snake-demons', and other equally bizarre and deadly tags. Prime Minister Zhou En-lai hovered on the edge of survival by serving Mao slavishly.

Ching-ling was spared, again thanks to her value as Mme Sun Yat-sen. Indeed, she headed a list of people singled out to be protected from the violence of the Red Guards, Mao's task force. Nasty things happened to her, but they were mere nuisance by comparison. Her parents' tomb in Shanghai was ransacked; but after she sent Zhou En-lai the pictures, it was restored – although the names of her brothers and sisters were chiselled off the tombstone. A new chief bodyguard made her life miserable, but after she complained to Mrs Zhou about him, he was removed. (The Maoist zealot was sacked in dramatic fashion. He was walking back to his own room in the grounds, humming a song composed to a quotation of Mao, when a subordinate saluted him and asked him to step into an office for some urgent consultation. No sooner did he walk in than two other guards leapt out from behind the doors and grabbed him by the arms, one removing the pistol from his belt at the same time. He was escorted out of the gate and rode away on his bicycle.)

But Mao wanted everybody to be scared at least a little. So Red Guards were allowed to set up camp outside the crimson walls of

---

* For detail, see Jung Chang and Jon Halliday, *Mao, the Unknown Story*, Chapter 44.

Ching-ling's residence in Beijing (where she was told to remain and not to go to Shanghai). Their loudspeakers blasted blood-curdling slogans over her wall. They subjected their victims to violent 'denunciation meetings' outside and cries of pain would sometimes reach her ears. She was terrified. There had been nothing like this in Stalin's purges or Chiang Kai-shek's white terror, or Mao's own previous political campaigns. Fearing that the Red Guards would be let into her house and torture her for possessing beautiful hand-bags, shoes and textiles, which were designated 'bourgeois', she threw them into the stove. When she read a newspaper article that condemned keeping pets including pigeons and goldfish, she instantly put down the paper and told her staff to kill all her pigeons. Luckily for the birds, this matter was reported to Zhou En-lai, who gave an order to leave them alone. Once, Ching-ling impulsively described her fears to her old friend, the pro-Mao American journalist Anna Louise Strong. But as soon as she posted the letter, she was seized by a greater fear and rushed off a second letter telling Strong to destroy the first. Strong assured her: 'on the same day that I received your second note I personally tore the first letter into small pieces and flushed it down the drain ... Nothing of the correspondence remains.'

Life became a daily bulletin of horrible news. Friends and relatives were tortured at denunciation meetings; they were thrown out of their homes, imprisoned, died violent deaths. A close friend and old associate, Jin Zhong-hua, until now a deputy mayor of Shanghai, was accused of being an 'American spy' and was put through intense and brutal interrogations. His house was raided, and some eighty letters from Ching-ling were found. Ching-ling had asked him to destroy the letters, but he had treasured correspondence from her and had not done so. Although the letters contained nothing remotely offensive to the regime, the former deputy mayor was consumed by anxiety that they might for some unexpected or unfathomable reason have disastrous consequences for Ching-ling. The tension was too much to bear and he hanged himself in 1968.

Virtually all Ching-ling's relatives were subject to appalling treatment, just for being related to the Soong family. A cousin on her mother's side, Ni Ji-zhen, was turned out of her house in Shanghai by Red Guards, and beaten and trampled on. In great pain and spitting blood, she appealed to Ching-ling for help. In one letter, dated 14 December 1966, she recounted in detail what she was going through and wrote: 'I don't know how long I can go on with all this suffering and fear ... I will try to live on (I hear that if you kill yourself you will be deemed a counter-revolutionary). I haven't broken any laws and I will not seek death ... Would you please please write me a few words when you receive this letter so I know you've received it? That would give me some comfort.' After signing her name, the cousin added, 'The daughter-in-law of the Gans committed suicide, with gas. Of the people I know, eight have done so.'

Ching-ling, who was still under orders to live in Beijing, did receive the letter. She did not reply, but quietly asked an old subordinate in Shanghai to take some money to the homeless cousin. She said that 'apart from being born into a bourgeois family, my cousin has never been involved in politics, and has never done anything bad. She has always done what she was told to do.' The subordinate was heard of no more and Ching-ling later learned that she had been thrown into one of the ad hoc prisons set up by virtually all organisations in China – probably for delivering her money. Red Sister had to stop trying to do anything to help her cousin. In May 1968, the much tortured and desperate cousin pressed the doorbell of Ching-ling's Shanghai mansion. She was told that Ching-ling was in Beijing and was turned away. The cousin crossed the street and went into a building opposite; there she leapt off the roof terrace and killed herself.

The death haunted Red Sister, who felt that she was 'partly responsible' for it, and often saw the cousin in her dreams. Finally, she could not bear the nightmares any more and unburdened herself to a long-time intimate friend, Cynthia, who as a child had been at her wedding to Sun Yat-sen. The letter was frank with anger and revulsion at the cruelty and atrocities all around. And she did not ask for the letter to be destroyed. Written in February 1971, this was the closest she came to protest against the Cultural Revolution. Red Sister was at her wits' end.

In those hellish years, she was also forced to stop seeing her two adopted daughters. The old rumour about her relationship with their father, Sui, resurfaced, and this time insinuation was loud and official. Militants publicly accused her of giving Sui a large amount of gifts, including a camera – a big luxury at the time – and a collection of clothes. She had to try to clear herself by writing to the authorities in October 1969: 'The truth is that his clothes were provided by the government when he went on several official visits abroad with me. I have not had one single item of clothing made for him. That camera is my gift to him.'

As before, the authorities concluded that it was not a good idea to make an enemy out of Mme Sun. Ching-ling saw her adopted daughters for the first time in years at the beginning of 1970. Her heart swelled when the teenagers appeared. Gazing at them, she noticed how much they had grown. Yolanda was now taller than she was and her feet were so big she had to wear men's shoes. Ching-ling felt she loved them more than ever. It was now that they moved in with her definitively.

The girls had had little education: schooling had been stopped, and children had only been going to their school buildings to denounce their teachers, or to fight each other in Red Guard factions, or just to fool about. Now Mao had decided to dissolve the Red Guards and pack them off to villages to work as peasants. This future was the only one available for the vast majority of the country's youth. Ching-ling was determined that it would not be for her 'daughters'. She pulled strings to enrol them in the army, an alternative only available to the elite. In the army, Yolanda trained as a dancer, and Yong-jie worked in a hospital.

In September 1971, a monumental event took place. Army chief Lin Biao, who was Mao's number two in the Cultural Revolution, died in a plane crash while fleeing China, having fallen out with Mao. Mao could no longer trust Lin's men who had been running the country for him, and was forced to reinstate some former officials he had purged, including Deng Xiao-ping, an old lieutenant who had declined to collaborate with him in his great purge. Things eased up palpably. In fact, in high circles, the Cultural Revolution began to be referred to as China's 'holocaust'. In this new atmosphere, Ching-ling felt able to speak more freely. She wrote in June 1972 to a relative and trusted friend, 'It was good I could open up my heart a bit to you last evening. A revolution does bring up some bad elements to the surface, but also, at the sacrifice of <u>so many good</u> lives! <u>Capable cadres</u>!' The underlining spoke volumes about the intensity of her feelings.

In the following years, many of Ching-ling's friends were released from prison. Among them were her old friends Israel Epstein and his wife, who had been languishing in jail under false charges for five years. When the news of their release came, Ching-ling was thrilled. But she also felt the need to enquire, indirectly to the authorities, whether she could treat them in the same way as before.

She started her parties again, at which the old friends who had been through so much and who had not seen each other for years chatted and laughed. Before the parties, she would carefully dab a little powder on her face and trace her eyebrows with a drawing pencil. There were still many things that infuriated her. A close friend was prevented from coming to a dinner she gave (she was told he was ill and could not come, and he was told she was ill and could not see him). Indignantly Red Sister wrote to him: 'This is <u>no</u> way to treat an old party member, and one that has always been loyal to the party.' She had enormous trouble finding a maid who could pass the security vetting, which dictated that their family backgrounds had to be politically acceptable. One maid who had passed the vetting process was assigned to her, but she had bound feet and could hardly walk. Ching-ling was cross. 'They said she came from a good family background. But must one be responsible for one's ancestors!'

In January 1976, Zhou En-lai died of cancer, aged seventy-seven. Ching-ling grieved for him. Zhou had still been smoothing her life even when he had only a few months to live. On one occasion, Yolanda was beaten by a man who claimed that she had borrowed money from him and refused to pay it back. Ching-ling immediately put pen to paper and reported the man to the authorities. When Zhou heard about it, he ordered the man to be detained for a week

Big Sister, Ei-ling, 'the most brilliant mind in the family' according to May-ling, was one of the richest women in China.

Red Sister, Ching-ling, vice chairman of Communist China.

·Little Sister, May-ling, first lady of Nationalist China.

Ching-ling in exile in Moscow, 1927–8.

Chiang Kai-shek's present to his wife in 1932 was a necklace made out of a mountain.
The gemstone of the pendant is actually a beautiful villa known as the 'May-ling Palace'.

May-ling in America, where she was given a fantastic reception in 1943
as the first lady of wartime China.

Ei-ling in Taiwan in 1969, with her daughter-in-law Debra Paget, former Hollywood star and leading lady in Elvis Presley's first film *Love Me Tender*. Debra is holding her son Gregory Kung, who is the only descendant of the three Soong sisters.

May-ling left Taiwan for good in 1991 and disassociated herself from the politics of the island. Seeing her off was President Lee, who in 1996 became the first democratically elected president.

May-ling aged around 100, in her Manhattan apartment. She died in 2003, aged 105.

A 1912 postcard showing the three most important founding figures of the Chinese Republic.
From left: Li Yuan-hong, Sun Yat-sen, and Huang Xing.
The caption reads: 'Congratulations to the creation of the Republic of China.'

More than 150 statues of Chiang Kai-shek and Sun Yat-sen from the days of
their personality cult have been removed and placed in a 'statue park' outside Taipei.
Behind these statues is a restaurant.

and to write a letter of apology. When Ching-ling then had a fall, Zhou telephoned more than once to ask after her.

On 9 September, Mao died. Ching-ling was in Shanghai at the time, and was informed by a long-distance call. Apparently, tears rolled down the face of the eighty-three-year-old. But she said nothing and did not discuss this event with anyone. Rather, she seemed to be preoccupied with suspicion that letters to her had been intercepted and blocked just after the death. A month later, Mao's four assistants closest to him in his last years, the 'Gang of Four' headed by his wife Jiang Qing, were arrested. They were blamed for all the atrocities in the Cultural Revolution, which now ended officially. At this, Ching-ling began to come to life.

For all her loathing of the Cultural Revolution, Red Sister was reluctant to blame Mao. To confront his responsibility would involve reflection on her own decisions, and might even lead to the thought that her whole life had been a mistake, and that she had chosen the wrong God. She was determined not to allow this to happen. 'I made my choice and I have no regrets,' she told people close to her. The fall of Mme Mao, whom she never liked, gave her a convenient scapegoat, and restored her equilibrium.

In fact, Jiang Qing originated no policies; as she herself said, 'I was Chairman Mao's dog; whoever Chairman Mao asked me to bite, I bit.' She had been an actress in Shanghai in the 1930s before she went to Yenan with some other left-wing artists. There she caught Mao's eye and he married her in 1938, divorcing his (third) wife. Over the years, Mao noticed that she had a lot of venom and liked venting it. 'Jiang Qing is as deadly poisonous as a scorpion,' he once observed to a family member, wiggling his little finger, like a scorpion's tail. He used her to spearhead the Cultural Revolution and got her to do much of his dirty work. Mao knew how much she was hated. Near the end of his life, he suffered an incurable disease and feared a coup; so he repeatedly sent a message to his opponents, 'Leave me to die in my bed, and then do whatever you want with my wife and her Gang.'

After Mme Mao was slung into prison, Red Sister was joyful. She exclaimed to a friend, 'The party is too generous for such a wicked slut! Also, she demanded her wig back as the weather is unbearably cold!' During the trial of the Gang of Four in 1980, she wrote to Anna Wang that the worst thing Mme Mao did was to soil her husband's name by claiming that everything she did had been on his orders. 'What a horrible woman!' Mao's vice chairman exclaimed. She felt able to go into raptures about Mao again, even in private communication: 'To me, he was the wisest man I ever had the good fortune of meeting – his clear thinking and teaching ... we must follow faithfully for they lead us from victory to victory.' This eulogy was followed by an afterthought: '(One thing that I wondered though, <u>why</u> he never cut off his relations with [Jiang Qing] at one stroke, so as to prevent her from making troubles?)' Red Sister seemed genuinely to think that the 'holocaust' of China was all this unlikeable woman's doing.

A new era began. Deng Xiao-ping took charge, and the country entered the phase of Reforms and Opening Up to the Outside World. This transformed the face of China. Deng laid down the line that the Communist Party and Mao must not be questioned. For Red Sister, this was the perfect line. She was now at peace and was 'very relaxed', 'very contented' in the last years of her life.

Yolanda and Yong-jie added sunshine to Ching-ling's life in those years. She was in her eighties and very frail. Like her sister May-ling, she was permanently tormented by hives, and her skin was prone to being covered by blisters like strings of red cherries. Her health problems could have driven her to suicide, she once told a friend, if she had not been so tough. Having her adopted daughters around gave her diversion and laughter. She appreciated them and found them intelligent and fun. Indeed she doted on them and provided them with whatever privileges were available to the top circle.

Towards the end of the Cultural Revolution, China allowed a small number of foreign visitors into the country. To cater for them, desirable goods were put on sale in the 'Friendship Store' in the capital. At the time everyone in the country wore uniform-like blue jackets and baggy trousers. Yolanda and Yong-jie were mesmerised by all the beautiful new things. They badgered Ching-ling to get her foreign friends to buy goodies for them. Once it was nylon stockings, which they saw their friends wearing; another time it was hair curlers. (Women were not permitted to style their hair or use make-up.) They wanted to visit the fabulous store themselves. Ching-ling sympathised and indulged them. Several times she let them use her car to go shopping, which raised eyebrows. She bought pretty clothes and shoes for them, and a bicycle each. For Yolanda's fifteenth birthday, she asked a friend in Hong Kong to buy the girl a watch –a hugely expensive luxury, even though she specified that it should be 'an ordinary worker's wristwatch ... strong and not fancy'. Two years later, when Yolanda had to end her dancing career as the result of an injury and became a film actress, Ching-ling asked the friend to buy her another, more stylish watch, for her new job.

By her own account, Yolanda was vain and a show-off in those days. She was unpopular, and provided much fodder for gossip among the Beijing elite. Israel Epstein, Ching-ling's authorised biographer, dismissed her with disdain in his book, calling her and her sister 'the importunate girls'. A woman in Beijing went so far as to give the exalted Mme Sun a piece of her mind. Ching-ling wrote that the woman 'upbraided me for not teaching [Yolanda] better manners, and it is true that I cannot control [the] haughty ways of Y'. The chorus of disapproval made Yolanda only more rebellious, and she would exaggerate her arrogance. In frustration, Ching-ling would tell her 'Not to come back.' But Yolanda always returned, to the embrace of her Mama-Taitai.

Before she was eighteen years old, in 1975, Yolanda had acquired a boyfriend. Ching-ling warned her to be careful but, when Yolanda refused to heed her advice, let her be. The relationship excited the girl's many adversaries, who spread lewdly embellished stories. Ching-ling was upset on behalf of her adopted daughter, and took it upon herself to set the record straight among her friends. In a letter to a friend, Ching-ling declared, 'I love Yolanda. I know she is innocent, even though she has shortcomings.'

After the death of Mao, the Chinese began to shed the puritanical straitjacket forced upon them. Yolanda, entering her twenties, enjoyed life frantically. She was perhaps the country's first good-time girl. She went out day and night, invited by visitors from abroad to fancy restaurants and clubs that were starting to bring colour to the drab capital. Fox Butterfield, the *New York Times*'s first correspondent in Beijing since the Communist takeover, saw her in the Beijing Hotel in 1980: 'She was dressed in a short, hip-hugging wool skirt, high brown-leather boots, and a bright-orange blouse. Yolanda was ... slender, and very tall for a Chinese, about five feet eight. She had on heavy eye shadow and lipstick; not pretty, but haughty, striking, and sexy. She looked like a film star from Taiwan or Hong Kong.'

At that year's ceremony of China's version of the Oscars, 'Yolanda was outfitted in a red silk blouse and a long, embroidered red-print skirt, a dazzle of colour and style in a forest of baggy blue. She was also smoking a cigarette, something very few young Chinese women do in public. When a Canadian television crew also noticed her, she pulled a compact out of her handbag and checked to see if her nose was shiny. Inside the bag, I saw, was a pack of Marlboros; foreign cigarettes are not available in regular Chinese stores.'

Ching-ling tolerated all this. She did not mind that Yolanda relished the Western lifestyle and was 'dazzled by ... talk of how grand life is in the US'. She and Yolanda even teased each other about 'love', an unmentionable word in those years. One day, Yolanda caught Ching-ling gazing at a photo of the young Sun Yat-sen, and cried out, 'Waw! Mr Sun was so handsome. If I were there, I would also be chasing him.' Ching-ling, face flushing with pride, said, 'You are too late, I have got him! This man is mine. You won't be able to lay hands on him now.' Yolanda noticed that when Ching-ling talked about Sun, she behaved like a young girl in love. It seems that having become a 'mother', with the wound of losing her child perhaps healed to some extent, Ching-ling redis-covered her love for her dead husband.

Yolanda was courted by many men. Like a real mother, Ching-ling was anxious. The young woman seemed to be flaunting her sexuality: her sweater was too tight, for instance, and showed too much of her full breasts. Ching-ling would sigh with exasperation,

'I hope somebody eligible will soon relieve me of this burden of watching over her like a mother hen! The frequent telephone calls back and forth give us all headaches. Perhaps she is responsible for my frequent attacks of hives.'

In 1980, the film actress chose her future husband, a dashing fellow actor fourteen years her senior. Ching-ling had someone else in mind, and did not approve of the marriage, but she said nothing to oppose it. The only thing by way of a warning, which she said to Yolanda the day before the wedding, was: 'One thing you must not tolerate for even a second: if he hits you, even just one slap, divorce him and come home straightaway.' Ching-ling gave a tea party to celebrate the wedding, for which she sent out a red invitation card with golden characters. At the party, Yolanda wore a white cheongsam and a veil, looking fabulous. Ching-ling's heart brimmed with a mix of emotions, and she left the room abruptly. When Yolanda came after her, she turned round and gripped the bride's arm, bursting into tears.

After the wedding, for months Ching-ling felt unwell and had many check-ups. There was nothing particularly wrong with her health. She told Anna Wang ruefully, 'Perhaps the psychological cause is bigger.' She continued to fuss over Yolanda, and helped the newly-weds acquire a hard-to-get small flat in one of the new tower blocks built in the early 1980s. For more than a decade, little accommodation had been built, while a generation had grown up and were getting married and having children. These new tower blocks were keenly fought over. They had been hastily built. The rooms were tiny, the floors were bare cement – to Ching-ling's consternation. The lift stopped operating at 9 p.m. and the couple's flat was on the eighteenth floor. When they worked night shifts and got home at 3 a.m., they had to start climbing the stairs. They had barely moved in when Ching-ling started planning to move them to a better flat.

Mama-Taitai was equally protective about her other adopted daughter, Yong-jie, for whom she had secured a place in an army hospital. But then she found that the girl had no chance to study medicine, but was assigned a clerical job and spent her days copying documents. Ching-ling believed the job was a punishment which over the years had damaged Yong-jie's eyes. To friends she wrote, 'Don't believe the malicious rumours spread by their [the two sisters'] enemies. I love them, and I am prepared to do everything I can not to let the element of envy destroy their future.' She pulled strings to get Yong-jie into the prestigious Beijing Foreign Language Institute to learn English. In 1979, Yong-jie won a scholarship and went to study in America. Ching-ling spent much money kitting her out. She sold her furs, which her mother had left her, and some valuable wines inherited from her father. Before Yong-jie even got to America, Ching-ling had begun to miss her and to plan ways to get her back for the summer holiday.

Harold Isaacs, once a young activist working with Ching-ling in the early 1930s, revisited her in 1980. 'There was much I had hoped to ask her about,' he wrote after the meeting; but 'she was obviously going to talk now about what *she* wanted to talk to us about, and that was a little packet of pictures she had ready on the low table before her.' The pictures were those of Yolanda and Yong-jie. To Isaacs' surprise, the once renowned 'Joan of Arc of China' started 'a very parental conversation' with him. 'I want to tell you about my family,' she said. She talked about Yolanda's wedding and how Yong-jie, back from America briefly, ably arranged the whole thing. 'She spoke of Yoland[a] with the pain of maternal loss and of [Yong-jie] with high maternal pride,' Isaacs noted. He was asked to bring a package of magazines to Yong-jie, then at Trinity College in Hartford, Connecticut.

Months later, in May 1981, Yolanda was shooting a film on the southern coast, when a telegram came for her to return to Beijing. She flew home at once and found Ching-ling drifting in and out of consciousness. Yolanda took Ching-ling's hand to her cheek, calling out 'Mama-Taitai!' Ching-ling opened her eyes and stroked Yolanda's cheek, murmuring, 'My child, my Little Treasure, you are back at last.' Yong-jie raced back from America.

In the small hours of 15 May, after receiving reports that Ching-ling's life was in danger, the Chinese Communist Party decided to make her a member formally and openly. That Red Sister did not apply at this time did not matter. She had done so a quarter of a century before, in 1957. Mrs Liu Shao-qi, who had witnessed that occasion, and who had just survived Mao's prison (her husband, the late president, had not), was dispatched to Ching-ling's bedside. Mrs Liu said to her, 'I remember you once asked to join the party. I wonder whether you still have the same wish?' Ching-ling nodded. Mrs Liu repeated her question three times, and each time Red Sister nodded affirmatively. So the formality was completed, and that afternoon, Deng Xiao-ping presided over an emergency politburo meeting which 'unanimously decided to accept Soong Ching-ling as a member of the CCP'.

The next day, 16 May, Ching-ling was given the title 'Honorary President of the People's Republic of China'.

As she lay dying, the Party invited her relatives to come and see her in Beijing. Top of the invitation list was Mme Chiang Kai-shek, who was urged to pay her dying sister a last visit. When Mrs Anna Chennault – the Chinese wife of the US pilot Claire Chennault, who had set up the 'Flying Tigers' in the Second World War – delivered the message to May-ling, now living in New York, Little Sister refused to reply.

Ching-ling died on 29 May 1981, aged eighty-eight. Beijing again invited anyone of 'the family' to attend the funeral, offering to pay for all travel and other expenses. These gestures were met with a resounding silence from the Soongs, the Chiangs and the Kungs. The closest relatives who did come and were photographed at her bier were grandchildren of Sun Yat-sen by his first marriage.

Yolanda and Yong-jie were not seen. Harold Isaacs, who had seen Ching-ling the year before and saw how she regarded them as her own daughters, was 'astonished to discover that these two young women appeared in none of the photographs taken of family and friends at the funeral ... I can only imagine how sad and painful this must have been for the two young women for whom, as she made plain to us when we saw her, she cared most in the world.' Indeed, the sisters wept very hard as they bid farewell to Ching-ling's body, the last in a long line, after the staff. Then they were led away. Their identity remained unmentionable for three decades. While Yolanda continued her acting career in Beijing, Yong-jie departed for America after the funeral and has not been heard of since.

The official anonymity of Ching-ling's two adopted daughters was only in small part to do with the fact that their adoptions were informal. The main reason was that they did not fit in with the Party's agenda. The Party wanted to stress the blood bond of Ching-ling's extended family in its continuous efforts to bring Taiwan into its fold. The girls were, inconveniently, not members of that clan.

Old age had actually rekindled Red Sister's affection for her natural family. She put her mother's portrait prominently on the wall in her home and brought guests to pay respects. She gave instructions to be buried by her parents' tombs because, she told people close to her, she wanted to keep apologising to her mother. 'I acted badly towards her. I have been feeling so guilty.' Red Sister also felt bad about the way she had attacked her sisters in the past. In the 1930s, she had made harsh remarks to Edgar Snow about Big Sister's moneymaking skills, and Snow had published what she said. In 1975, it seems she was remorseful for having made those comments, and accused Snow of putting 'offensive words about my elder sister' in her mouth. She insisted on Snow's widow taking them out of his book.

In spite of all these feelings, Ching-ling had nevertheless got on with her own life and built her own family. Apart from her adopted daughters and close friends, whom she called 'my sisters and brothers', a key member of her household was her housekeeper of over fifty years, Sister Yan-e, who devoted her whole life to her mistress. Ching-ling repaid her loyalty with loyalty. When Sister Yan-e was suffering from cancer and in great pain, Ching-ling was anguished. She paid for the best and most expensive treatment available and, when Sister Yan-e died (a few months before herself), gave instructions to bury her next to her own future tomb, in the Soong family burial ground. It was never Ching-ling's wish to enter Sun Yat-sen's grandiose mausoleum.

Nor did Red Sister regard herself as belonging to the Party totally. For all her lifelong association with the Communists, she still saw herself as having a separate, private identity. She had carefully prepared her will (with no lawyers involved; there was then no such profession), bequeathing her personal possessions, things that she regarded as her own and not those of the state, to individuals she specified. This was a most unusual act for a Communist at the time – if they made a will at all, they usually gave everything to the Organisation. Ching-ling left members of her staff sums of money. One friend in Hong Kong, Ernest Tang, was particularly remembered. Over the years he had bought many things for her which she could not get in China (including watches for Yolanda). Although she had always thanked him profusely and sent him valuable gifts such as brandies and whiskies collected by her father and gold earrings from her mother, she felt she had not thanked him enough, and bequeathed her library to him in 1975, in a document headed 'My Testament'. She posted the document to Ernest with a letter explaining that these books did not belong to the state but were her own collection since her student days, and that he could pack them in wooden cases and ship them home. For now, she told him, he should keep the will to himself. She was worried things might go wrong. Things did go wrong after she died. Ernest was by her side in her last days, but after her funeral, he was not allowed to return to Hong Kong and was kept in Beijing ('staring at the ceiling [of his hotel] all day,' he would write). Eventually, under pressure, he made a statement, declaring that he wished 'not to accept the books and to let the government decide what to do with them'.

Yolanda and Yong-jie were the chief beneficiaries of the bequest of their Mama-Taitai. Treating them as her own daughters, she left them furniture, paintings, clothing and jewellery – and sums of money that were huge for the time. Yolanda was to receive 5,000 yuan and Yong-jie 10,000 yuan. They were simply told that they would not receive any of the things except the money and a few items of clothing as keepsakes.

Although Ching-ling's dying wishes were largely ignored, she died a serene woman. Her mind was not at odds with her faith. Physically she was well looked after by devoted medical and domestic staff. Above all, she had found fulfilment as a mother.

Taiwan Days

For Ching-ling's sisters, the last three decades had been very different. As the Communists took China in 1949, and as Red Sister became Mao's vice chairman, Ei-ling and May-ling were thrown out of the mainland together with the rest of their family and Chiang Kai-shek's regime. At the beginning of 1950, May-ling joined her husband in Taiwan.

As soon as she arrived, Little Sister plunged into a flurry of activity to boost the morale of the Nationalists who had retreated to the island. She travelled from the north to the south, visiting the wounded and the sick and cheering up the troops. She presided over a housing project to accommodate the new arrivals, and started a Women's Anti-Communist League to oversee the production of hundreds of thousands of garments for the army and their families. She paid personal attention to those garments, checking carefully whether they were properly sewn.

When she was alone, she contemplated questions such as: 'Why had the Communists prevailed?' 'Wherein have I personally failed? Could I have done more?' Her conclusion was: 'I had not been working directly for God, under God, and with God.' She formed a prayer group, which began with six earnest Christians. Eventually, she believed, the nation would pray together, which would solve all the problems.

On 25 June that year, the North Korean army under Kim Il-sung invaded the South, with the backing of Stalin and Mao. The Korean War started. Two days later, US president Truman reversed the policy of 'non-intervention' towards Taiwan and committed to defending the island. This commitment secured the future of Taiwan. American aid began to arrive and Chiang's crisis passed. May-ling was elated. In spite of the weather ('horrible, terrifically hot and muggy'), and her skin trouble ('I have been breaking out in prickly heat and humidity rashes'), she was cheerful: 'My head is busy with ideas of enlarging the work, with new projects.' 'I have faith that before the end of the year [1951], we shall be back on the mainland.'

In an optimistic frame of mind, May-ling started to learn to paint in the Chinese style. In her fifties (long past what was conventionally seen as the age to begin learning), she found that the ink and brush came to her surprisingly easily: 'it is no effort to me at all to paint'. She fell in love with her new hobby. 'Painting is the most absorbing occupation I have known in my life. When I am at work, I forget everything in the world, and I wish that I could spend all my time in doing nothing but painting and painting.' Five months later, she boasted to Emma, 'all the artists and connoisseurs of Chinese painting say that I have the possibilities of a great artist. Some even say, perhaps the greatest living artist.' Taking their compliments at face value, she went on, 'It seems that my brush-work is extraordinary ... I myself believe that what the Chinese authorities tell me is true.'

She sent photos of her paintings to Ei-ling in New York to get the opinion of foreign experts. The appraisal was encouraging but not quite so ecstatic. Three experts agreed that the painter had 'real ability', but the paintings seemed to be 'copies of other paintings'; they recommended that 'the artist do more original work'.

Outside her peaceful studio and her prayer group, a 'white terror' enveloped the island. Chiang Kai-shek, his defeated army and administration, together with their families, totalling some 2 million people, had come to a destination that did not welcome them. There had been a massacre two years before, when the Nationalists took over the island after the Japanese were gone. Much of the population had initially welcomed the return to Chinese rule. But enthusiasm quickly turned to outrage. The same 'calamity of victory' that had turned people on the mainland against the Chiang regime similarly repelled the Taiwanese, who had lived on the island for generations. Rampant corruption, incompetent administration (particularly compared to the highly efficient Japanese), and the newcomers' unconcealed contempt for the local people – these and many other ills that accompanied the Nationalist takeover led to a riot starting on 28 February 1947. Brutal military suppression caused the deaths of thousands.

Chiang's problems were not limited to the locals. He had reason to believe that large numbers of Red agents had infiltrated the exodus, and would in time act as a Trojan horse. To secure his haven, he imposed martial law that lasted for the rest of his life, with his son, Ching-kuo, heading his security apparatus. This secret police had a blank cheque to arrest and execute real or imagined Red spies. People lived in fear.

The island was guarded like a fortress. The entire coastline over 1,500 kilometres was off limits to the average islander. It was impossible to have a swim in the sea. Hiking in the mountains was equally out of the question: they were sealed off as well, to deprive any would-be guerrillas of hiding places.

Chiang made sure there was now less corruption. Unlike on the mainland, he quickly endorsed land reforms, including the reduction of land rent (which was much easier to introduce here as the owners of the land were local Taiwanese and the enforcers had no vested interest). Still, the Generalissimo showed scant interest in economic development on the island, and there was little improvement in people's lives during his rule.

Chiang promoted his own personality cult, on a scale he had not quite managed on the mainland. His statues were erected everywhere, along with the statues of Sun Yat-sen, still called the Father of China. The Generalissimo was trumpeted as the model of the nation. So schoolteachers who wanted the children to shave their heads (probably to prevent lice) told them that the shaven – or bald – head had a desirable name: the 'Chiang-style head' (zhong-zheng-tou). The Generalissimo had little hair and was thought of as being bald. When he learned this from his grandson, he was not pleased.

★

Once Taiwan was safe, May-ling itched to leave. In summer 1952 she was in New York again. The earlier pattern was repeated: her husband implored her to come home; she pleaded health problems. She was away for eight months and would have stayed on had there not been a crisis in Taiwan. The civilian governor, Dr K.C. Wu, found himself unable to work with the Generalissimo and was determined to resign. Wu, a liberal, was favoured by the Americans and his resignation would damage Chiang in the eyes of Washington. A key issue was that Dr Wu was appalled by the summary arrests and executions. He tendered his resignation in 1953. Chiang refused to let him go.

May-ling was anxious to keep Wu on in his job and returned to Taiwan to persuade him to stay. When Wu came to see her to explain his decision, she took his arm and walked him to the end of the verandah, telling him that there were surveillance bugs everywhere else, as Chiang wanted to know what visitors were talking about. Wu told her about his aversion to the secret police under Ching-kuo, and named one particular case which involved a businessman who had been arrested and sentenced to death on the charge of being a Communist spy. Wu felt that the charge was unfounded, and May-ling was upset. Wu and his wife had been invited to lunch. When Chiang entered the dining room, May-ling said to him furiously, 'Look! Look at what your son is doing!' Then, taking the Wus by the hand, she said, 'Let's go!' and the three of them walked out of the lunch.

Chiang did not give in to his wife. And Wu insisted on resigning. Things reached an impasse on Good Friday. On Easter Sunday, the Wus left for their country house in the hills. Just before they got into the hills, they stopped for lunch, deviating from their habit of having sandwiches for lunch in the car. During the break, the driver checked the car because he felt it had been behaving oddly. He found that the wheel nuts for both the front wheels were missing. If this had not been discovered, the wheels could well have come off on the bumpy roads, causing a fatal accident. The car had been serviced the night before, so the chance that this was the result of negligence was minuscule. Wu was certain that the car had been tampered with. He suspected Chiang, and tried several ways to find out whether Chiang was involved. Everything he learned convinced him that Chiang at least knew about the plot beforehand.

Wu did not breathe a word of his suspicions, as he knew he might never be able to leave Taiwan if the murder attempt leaked out. But he was even more determined to decamp. By coincidence, his alma mater, Grinnell College in America, was awarding him an honorary doctorate and had invited him to the ceremony. There were various other standing invitations to speak in the States. Citing these invitations, he applied for passports for himself and his family. There was no reply. Eventually, Wu wrote to May-ling that if he was refused passports, he would let people who had invited him know the reason. He got the passports – except the one for his thirteen-year-old son. The Generalissimo was keeping the boy as a hostage.

From America, Wu repeatedly wrote to request the passport for his son. In order to get the child out, he kept silent about his dispute with Chiang – and about the 'car accident'.

Wu wrote three letters to May-ling asking for help. She replied, but said that there was nothing she could do. During this period, she immersed herself in 'painting, painting', as she told Emma, after saying, 'you know how much I dislike politics'.

To pre-empt Wu, Chiang started a smear campaign, accusing him of fleeing with stolen public funds. This backfired: Wu went public with allegations against Chiang – although still saying nothing about the 'accident'. His revelations made the front page of the *New York Times*. With the media in hot pursuit for more stories, Wu wrote to Chiang with an ultimatum: let my son have his passport within thirty days, or there would be more unpalatable details. The 'blackmail' worked. Exactly thirty days later, an official appeared at the home of Mrs Wu's sister with whom the boy was staying, and handed him his passport.

By now, the child had been kept as a hostage for a year. He had been repeatedly taken to the Nationalist Youth League, and told to condemn his father in public. This was the same treatment to which Ching-kuo himself had been subject when he had been a teenage hostage in Russia some twenty years before. Now the method was passed on to his underlings.

Chiang freed Wu's son and secured Wu's silence. The whole episode was hushed up with the help of the powerful US China Lobby, who were vociferous backers of the Nationalists. When Wu began to expose the Generalissimo, key figures in the Lobby leapt into action and told Wu to shut up and issue a statement supporting Chiang. Wu declined to issue the statement, but said no more. Eventually he took a teaching job in Georgia and faded out of the public eye. Only years later did he tell his story.

May-ling, who had played her role in getting Ching-kuo home, did her best for Wu's son. As soon as the son was free, she left Taiwan for America, disregarding the imminent inauguration of her husband as the 'elected' president on 20 May 1954. Before the 'election' she had told Emma wryly: 'Undoubtedly my husband will be re-elected; he has designated Chen Cheng as his Vice. Yesterday at the opening meeting [of the National Assembly], I had to be present with him, and the effort has made me very tired.'

On 3 September that year, Mao, following his own, rather unexpected agenda, opened artillery fire on the Nationalist-held island of Quemoy (Jinmen), a few kilometres off the mainland coast.* As this small island was considered the most likely jumping-off point for any move on Taiwan, it appeared that Mao might try and seize the last Nationalist base. May-ling flew back in October to be at her husband's side.

Washington responded to Mao's sabre-rattling by signing a Mutual Defense Treaty with Taiwan. It formalised America's recognition of Chiang's regime as the legitimate and sole government of the whole of China, and Taiwan was able to retain the 'China' seat at the UN. To sustain this position, Chiang made retaking mainland China his basic state policy. 'Fight back to the mainland!'

---

* For Mao's objectives in the shelling of Quemoy now and in 1958, see Jung Chang and Jon Halliday, *Mao, the Unknown Story*, Chapters 37 and 38.

was the core slogan of his regime. This was both his dream and a stance he must maintain if he wanted to keep the seat in the UN. It also gave hope to the millions of army men and civilians who had fled their homes with him, and who yearned to be reunited with their loved ones.

The shelling of Quemoy brought May-ling a strong sense of 'the menace of Communist aggression'. News from the mainland about the deaths and suffering of former Nationalist members and their families had already horrified and appalled her. One night she sobbed loudly in her dreams and, when her husband asked her what the matter was, replied that she had seen Ching-ling bidding her farewell. She was afraid Red Sister had been killed.

She came to regard her husband as a defender of Taiwan and began to sympathise with his use of an iron, if bloody, fist. The couple were now kindred spirits once again. When Chiang wrote an important book, *Soviet Russia in China*, she was his dedicated collaborator and editor. Their renewed intimacy and camaraderie showed in the Author's Note, in which Chiang wrote, 'On this very day, December 1, 1956, my wife and I are quietly celebrating our [twenty-ninth] wedding anniversary.' In the quintessentially Chiang Kai-shek style of mother-worship, he dedicated the book 'to the sacred memory of our dearly beloved mothers, the late Madame Chiang, née Wang, and the late Madame Soong, née Nie. By this token my wife and I dedicate ourselves once more, as it were, to the supreme task to which we are called and thus strive to be not unworthy of our upbringing.'

May-ling exerted a softening influence on Chiang's harsh repression. She employed a Baptist minister, Rev. Chow Lien-hwa, who had obtained a PhD at Southern Baptist Theological Seminary in the US, to be the chaplain to the Chiangs, and sent him to preach in prison. Rev. Chow turned out to be a big hit with the political prisoners. One who was serving ten years recalled the minister's impact. The world he and his fellow inmates inhabited was bleak and brutal, consisting of hard labour, physical and mental abuse, as well as daily gatherings to chant 'Generalissimo Chiang is our nation's great saviour!', 'Kill Zhu [De, Communist army chief] and

Mao!' Rev. Chow brought in an air of humanity and moments of relief and relaxation. With his presence and his messages, the prisoners felt dignified and human again. The intelligence apparatus did not like the Reverend; but May-ling made sure he was untouchable.

In 1958, May-ling went back to America. This time, she travelled the country warning the Americans about the Communist threat. As if to illustrate her point, Mao, again seemingly inexplicably, lobbed tens of thousands of shells onto the same small island of Quemoy in August. The Americans responded to May-ling's speeches emotionally. And their very public support for Taiwan boosted the morale of the Nationalists. Mao's bellicosity had made Chiang's rule only more secure.

Ching-kuo cabled May-ling about his father's delight – and his. This year marked a watershed in the relationship of the stepmother and stepson. Up to now it had been polite and formal. Ching-kuo had been addressing her as 'Madame Chiang', or not using any form of address. Now he started to call her 'my respected mother'. And in her communications with him she now simply referred to herself as 'Mother'. May-ling was happy. One evening at Christmastime, she was watching the musical *42nd Street* with old friends. Emma noted in her diary that 'two or three times Mayling picked up her long Chinese gown and danced gaily around the room, imitating the steps, improvising a few wriggles & kicks of her own ... It was wonderful to see her in such good spirits.'

May-ling returned to Taiwan in June 1959 without her husband having to plead with her. Chiang came as always to the airport, but this time the couple's beaming smiles in the brilliant sunshine were exceptional. Wearing sunglasses, a topee and a Sun Yat-sen suit, Chiang held up his wife's arm as she stretched out her gloved hand to shake hands with the welcome crowd. It was a picture of joy and affection. When Chiang was again 'unanimously elected' president in 1960, May-ling acted quite differently from six years before, when she had been absent from his inauguration. This time, she busied herself in the 'innumerable activities connected with the President's inauguration', she told Emma. 'There have been so many functions and so many guests.' In her letters to friends she referred to her husband as 'the President'. The harmony lasted, and Little Sister wrote to her brother T.V. in 1962 that they had just 'spent a very happy 35th wedding anniversary'.

May-ling really settled down in Taiwan to life with her husband. There were a lot of children around them: Ching-kuo's children, and T.A.'s two sons, who came from San Francisco for holidays. Their aunt engaged a tutor to teach them Mandarin. The boys 'are perfect darlings, so well behaved, obedient and oh, so cute', she enthused. She cooked for them and danced with them. Everyone laughed a lot, even the Generalissimo.

Taiwan's first lady performed her official duties and charmed visiting VIPs. On discovering that polio was widespread on the island, she started a hospital for child sufferers. She went to see children of deceased soldiers often, and her knack of making the children feel loved and the teachers appreciated won her many fans. Twice she visited a hospital for lepers. Her photographer saw her going up to the patients, taking off her gloves without hesitation and shaking hands with them warmly and naturally. He was touched.

Much of the time, the Chiangs' life was one of leisure. Little Sister was rarely out of bed before eleven. She painted and played chess, saw a few women friends, and was followed round by a large pack of dogs (one was unpopular with the staff as it bit several of them). She took an interest in creating a rose garden in the presidential mansion. The Generalissimo's days consisted of reading newspapers and a few documents – or listening to other people reading them to him. He made a few inspection tours. In the early years, he had liked holding weekly meetings at which the main agenda was him delivering lengthy moralising lectures, which caused many a participant to doze off. Now, as years went by he dropped the lecturing and was content just to be glancing at the papers, napping, strolling, watching old movies and sightseeing. For someone who was apparently dedicated to retaking mainland China, he was doing remarkably little, no more than making one or two fantastical 'plans'. Chiang was a realist and knew that the entire dream depended on the US attacking China militarily, the hope of which was slim.

The Generalissimo no longer wore uniform or struck a fighting pose. He appeared relaxed in a long flowing traditional gown, a walking stick in hand. He had a stoop, and his eyes narrowed and the corners of his mouth drooped. He grew into an old man in Taiwan.

He and May-ling travelled all round the gorgeous island. Since the coastline and mountains were sealed off to prevent a Communist invasion, the Chiangs had virtual monopoly of the beauty spots. Up to thirty villas dotted around were for their exclusive use, from old and elegant Japanese houses to new imitation imperial palaces. The last addition was a large nondescript complex euphemistically named the Revival Guest House. It was set deep in the hills only an hour's drive from the capital – and so suited Chiang in old age. The Generalissimo supervised the building work personally, visiting the site five days a week, and telephoning constantly when an idea struck him ('change the colour of the walls', 'plant more plum trees', etc.). May-ling added her touch, from the quality of the upholstery to the colour of her bathroom (it must be pink). Husband and wife had a row over where a particular window should be facing. They were united, though, in installing a chapel there, as they did in other resorts they frequented.

All the Chiang villas boasted magnificent views – those of the mountains or the ocean were for their eyes only. The lakes were slightly different. They could not be deemed off limits on the grounds of preventing a Red invasion, and the locals were not denied access. Still, if the Generalissimo liked a lake – such as Taiwan's pride, the Sun Moon Lake – a sizeable part was cordoned off. Regarding all land as his own, Chiang had a pagoda built on the islet in the middle of the lake to commemorate his mother.

Contrary to the popular impression that Chiang led a spartan life, the Generalissimo cared very much about comfort. He had anticipated that many mountains and forests on the island could not be reached by cars, and had brought two sedan chairs with him from the mainland, complete with chair-bearers.

Transport acquired while he was in Taiwan included fancy planes. When the Boeing 720 was produced, Chiang immediately bought one. His former personal pilot, General I Fu-en, argued strongly against it, pointing out that the plane was too big to be useful on the island; and far too expensive for this poor place that was facing the threat of war. The advice fell on deaf ears. Huge sums were spent; the plane was little used. Chiang also bought a seaplane, just so the couple could land on the lakes. During the trial flight, it crashed on landing, the pilots barely escaping drowning. This idea had to be abandoned.

Thanks to America, and Mao's war-posturing, the Chiangs lived a fine life in peace and style for two decades. Although he lost mainland China, Chiang was actually having a much grander time in Taiwan. Here he was more of an absolute ruler and able to impose much tighter control, and his Taiwan days were the most prolonged time of pleasure in his life and in their marriage. Even the heat was no problem: there were many cool retreats in the hills, where it was unnecessary even to use electric fans. The Generalissimo preferred to have staff fan him from behind. May-ling refrained from this type of indulgence.

When the Chiangs' lifestyle was made public later, it did not seem to enrage the locals. Chiang kept Taiwan from Mao's tyranny, for which people remain grateful. As for May-ling, with her counterpart on the mainland, Mme Mao, for comparison, nobody could deny that Taiwan was lucky to have her as its first lady. It is generally recognised that she did her duty conscientiously, that she exercised benign influence on the Generalissimo – and that she was a decent and kind person.

In 1971, when Chiang was eighty-four and May-ling seventy-three, their pleasant life was shattered. US President Richard Nixon sought a rapprochement with mainland China, and announced that he would visit Beijing early the following year. While his National Security Adviser Henry Kissinger was in Beijing to prepare the trip, in October, the UN passed a resolution giving the 'China' seat to Beijing, forcing Taiwan to leave the UN. As Western politicians began beating a path to Mao's door, May-ling, in anguish, fell back on her faith. Again and again, she recited this passage from the Bible: 'We are afflicted in every way, but not crushed; perplexed, but not driven to despair; persecuted, but not forsaken; struck down, but not destroyed.'

To Emma she wrote, 'I am hopeful that the pendulum of good sense and decency will sooner or later swing back ... What is of import is not what happens, but how we react to it.'

Her husband hated Nixon violently, calling him 'Ni[xon] the Clown' (ni-chou). He asserted that Nixon took this step purely to settle a personal score, viz. that Chiang had declined to contribute to his campaign fund. In his diary, Chiang wrote: 'Before Ni the Clown was elected, he visited Taipei. He was full of hope that we would supply him with funds for his election campaign.' 'I regarded him as a loathsome politician and treated him as a man of no substance. And I did not agree to help his campaign.' 'Ni the Clown holds a grudge against me and so tries to do damage to me.'

Besides Nixon, Chiang's wrath was directed towards Ei-ling's son David – and even May-ling: 'The change of policy to the worse by Ni the Clown must be blamed on [David]. Yet my wife believes in him.' 'All this is the result of my wife only listening to [David]. He is criminally responsible for landing our country in this catastrophe.'

The Generalissimo sometimes took out his fury on the staff, striking them with his walking stick when in a temper. How heavy the blows were became a measure of the old man's physical condition. One day an aide told a doctor (Chiang, sensibly, was always polite to doctors; and he did not hit women), 'The president is well now – his knocks are quite powerful today!'

Chiang's health was deteriorating. He had a stroke, which left him with a speech impediment. One day, while taking a stroll, his legs suddenly gave way and he had to be carried back into the house. His health problems were kept strictly secret, but Chiang began preparing to hand over power to his son Ching-kuo. At the end of 1971, he made Ching-kuo the prime minister and commander-in-chief of the armed forces (Chiang himself remaining the president). These appointments would be confirmed the following spring when the rubber-stamp national congress convened.

Her husband's health crises and Ching-kuo's impending succession gave May-ling a new, and purely personal, cause for anxiety: her presidential lifestyle might be in jeopardy. She had been living in considerable grandeur, with dozens of staff at her beck and call. While in the US, when she desired, the magnificent C-54, *China–America*, was dispatched for her use. Once her husband was gone, would Ching-kuo keep her in the same style? If she were to live in New York, which she wished to do, who would pay for the large staff she was used to, including round-the-clock security men, on whom her peace of mind depended? And twenty-four-hour nursing in her old age? Who would cover the salaries, living expenses and medical bills of her old faithful servants from Taiwan, whom she wanted to continue to employ? Even the fortune of the Kungs might not be sufficient. The Taiwan government had to foot most of the bill. But she was not at all sure she could count on Ching-kuo to do so. The Generalissimo's son and his own family were famous for living simply, even frugally. He might well find her extravagance unacceptable, however friendly he was with her. Ching-kuo and his family were not Soongs, and to May-ling this was very important. Once, when Ching-kuo's children were staying, together with T.A.'s sons, she tucked some gifts into her nephews' hands and whispered to them, only half in jest, not to tell the Chiang children. 'You are my own flesh and blood,' she said.

May-ling decided that to protect her interest someone from her own family had to be in charge of Taiwan's money. She tried to persuade her husband to make nephew David the finance minister at the forthcoming congress, claiming that the fifty-six-year-old had made unrecognised contributions to the Nationalist cause.

Chiang was irritated. David, along with the Kung family, had been roundly condemned by many Nationalists for causing their party to lose the mainland. He had never worked in the Taiwan government – and had never even lived in Taiwan. On top of these obvious strikes against him, Chiang was already blaming him for Nixon's rapprochement with Beijing. As Nixon was about to go to Beijing, May-ling's demand could not have been made at a worse moment. It might seem that Little Sister had taken leave of her senses. But she was in a panic. There had never been a time under the Nationalist government when her family (which included Chiang the father, but not Chiang the son) did not hold the key to the country's coffers. The future scared her. She could not wait for a more opportune time to talk to her husband: his heart condition was such that he might die at any moment.

She kept badgering Chiang, which he found intolerable, and he shunned her company. He now only wanted to be with Ching-kuo, who would come every evening he could manage to have supper with his father. When Ching-kuo was delayed by work, Chiang would wait for him; he would not eat without his son. As soon as Ching-kuo appeared, Chiang would look happy and, after dinner, they would take a car ride together. (Chiang had no interest in his other, adopted, son Wei-go, and would send him away almost the minute he appeared.) When Ching-kuo was not with him, Chiang read his son's diary for comfort. Once Ching-kuo went to Quemoy for an inspection tour, and Chiang, having told him to take a break there for a few days, was restless until his son came back.

Eventually, Chiang relented and saw his wife. He was amicable at her seventy-fourth birthday party. May-ling grabbed the chance to promote her nephew again: the next government was about to be formed. At her instruction, David came to see his uncle to try to impress him. But his presence only got on the nerves of the Generalissimo, who became angry with his wife. In this period, Chiang described his wife implicitly as someone who if allowed to be close would behave 'with impertinence'. 'Never, ever let [that] woman get close,' he wrote in his diary on 12 June 1972. As for David, Chiang now regarded him as the source of all his misfortunes: 'Shame, humiliation, hatred and rage – not for a moment is my mind free of them. The cause of my illness is [David]. The cause of my country's shame is also him.'

These words were written on 11 July. On the 20th, a car ride with May-ling left him in a state of 'vexation and annoyance'. She may well have raised the matter of David's job again and he felt he was 'enduring suffering'. The next day, he endorsed the final line-up of the Ching-kuo government, emphatically signalling that David was not included. This was the last entry in Chiang's diary. On the following day, the 22nd, he was hit by a massive heart attack and sank into a coma, which lasted six months.

At the beginning of 1973, Chiang Kai-shek woke up. He lingered in this world as a very sick man for two more years and died in hospital on 5 April 1975, aged eighty-seven. He had selected his burial ground: a splendid spot next to Sun Yat-sen's grandiose mausoleum in Nanjing. As Nanjing was in Red China, Chiang gave orders for his coffin to be placed in his villa on the outstirts of Taipei, Cihu, waiting for the day when Communist rule collapsed on the mainland.

In his final years, his relationship with May-ling was tranquil. She resigned herself to reality, and showed tenderness towards the dying man. She would sit with him, chatting and keeping him company. Shortly before his death, she was diagnosed with breast cancer. About this most serious and life-threatening malady of her life, she breathed not a word to her husband – contrary to her past constant complaining about her relatively minor ailments. Before she went into hospital for surgery, she told the staff to say that she had flu and had to stay away in order not to infect him. May-ling cared about her husband. And she knew that her husband cared about her.

When Chiang died, May-ling burst into tears in private. In public, she was completely dry-eyed, making complicated arrangements with decisiveness and standing through the funeral with composure. She was a picture of dignity and restrained sorrow. In contrast, Ching-kuo wailed in public till he collapsed, and had to be supported to stand up. At one point, May-ling suggested that the doctors give him an injection to calm him down (it was not given.) This display of uncontrollable grief was most unusual. A heavy-built bear of a man, Ching-kuo was in his mid-sixties and the ruler of a dictatorial regime. He had also acquired superhuman strength to harness his feelings during his years as a hostage in Russia. And yet he seemed unable to handle his anguish this time. It was not only intense but also long-lasting. Long after his father's death, he continued to write his stepmother letters like these:

> I sat alone in silence at Shilin [Chiang's official residence], in Father's bedroom, thinking about him and missing him with all my heart. In the evening, my whole family dined at Cihu to keep Father's bier company. Sadness and sorrow penetrated every fiber inside me...

> Last night I went to sleep at Cihu, amidst autumn wind and autumn rain; already, a hint of chill was in the air...

> Returning to Shilin, I saw that the yellow autumnal chrysanthemums in the garden were in bloom. This brought back so many memories that I missed Father with acute pain...

> I just returned from Cihu where my wife and I had gone to pay respect to Father's bier. There I cut a branch of flowering osmanthus and placed it in front of the bier...

> Last night I slept at Cihu. In the mountains the moon was bright, shining on the blooming flowers of camellia. I was touched by the calm and serenity of the place surrounding Father's bier. My only regret is that he is here alone and may feel isolated and sad...

It fell on May-ling to comfort him and remind him that compared to her own experience (she had hardly spent any time with her father, having left home as a child and returning when he had only months to live), Ching-kuo was lucky: his father died at a ripe old age and they were together for many decades.

The most extraordinary way Ching-kuo mourned his father could only be the outcome of something really exceptional. It may be that during one of those long private conversations in his last years,

Chiang Kai-shek had divulged the secret of how he had managed to secure Ching-kuo's release from Stalin's clutches. That his father had got him out at such a high price – he lost mainland China – would have been a truly shattering thought.

Another emotional farewell was performed by a rather unlikely man – Mao, ruler of Red China, who had deposed Chiang and slaughtered millions to keep him deposed. Mao saw the Generalissimo as a worthy rival. One day bedridden at eighty-one, he sat up for hours in his enormous wooden bed. He did not eat, or speak. At his order, an eight-minute tape of stirring music was played over and over again to create a funereal atmosphere, while he beat time on his bed, wearing an emphatically solemn expression. The music had been set especially for Mao to a twelfth-century 'poem of farewell'. Mao was bidding farewell to Chiang. He even rewrote the last two lines of the poem to emphasise the sense of a valediction. The rewritten lines read: 'Go, let go, my honoured friend, / Do not look back.'

May-ling left Taiwan for New York five months after her husband's death. She kept a picture of Chiang in his younger days on her bedside table. Her family and staff sometimes saw her talking to the photo, calling him 'Honey'. Once when she was caught gazing at the photo by a nephew, she smiled to him and said, 'He is so good-looking, isn't he?'

A sizeable retinue followed her across the ocean, including chefs, drivers, guards and nurses. Later, when she was very old, the number of her staff would reach thirty-seven. Ching-kuo, now Taiwan's leader, saw to it that she was sumptuously provided for. He had made a tearful pledge to his father before Chiang died. When they were alone together, Chiang had several times asked him to look after May-ling: 'I can only rest in peace if you do this.' And once when they were together with May-ling, the Generalissimo had held both their hands and told Ching-kuo: 'My son, you must love your mother as you love me.' After Chiang's death, Ching-kuo and May-ling maintained a close relationship, thrown further together by the changing future of Taiwan. May-ling never had to worry about her lifestyle as long as Ching-kuo was alive.

22

The Hollywood Connection

While May-ling spent most time with her husband in Nationalist Taiwan after the Communist takeover of China, Ei-ling visited the couple frequently, but made New York her permanent home. Big Sister had a large house in Locust Valley on Long Island, surrounded by woods. Her life was private and quiet, her main social activity was playing bridge and cards with a few select and very discreet friends. She shunned all public occasions. As always, God was central to her routine, and Ei-ling would pray before making all important decisions, including investing.

Her mind, which May-ling considered the sharpest of the three sisters, was still very much active, and she watched the situation in Taiwan with acute attention. One October day in 1956, while visiting Little Sister, she gave Chiang Kai-shek a piece of advice that would benefit the island in the years to come. In Chiang's rigidly controlled regime, few young people were permitted to study abroad. No one dared to suggest that the ban should be lifted, and May-ling did not have the kind of political brain to propose such initiatives. On this day, the sisters and the Generalissimo were strolling in the garden of the presidential mansion, when Chiang, with a big smile, took Ei-ling's arm. She turned to him, 'Listen, Brother Chiang, we are lagging so far behind in science and technology ... and you still don't open up and allow students to study abroad. You really should let the students go and study in America!' Chiang accepted her advice, and so began what would become a tidal wave of Taiwanese young men and women crossing the ocean.

In America, Ei-ling helped the Chiangs deal with personal problems. In 1964, a letter arrived from a Lawrence Hill, literary agent for the Generalissimo's ex-wife, Jennie. She was hard up, and planned to publish her memoirs. Hill said he wanted to check some facts with Ei-ling. Once published, the book would be tremendously embarrassing for the Chiangs, and Big Sister, working behind the scenes, prevented the publication. Jennie accepted $250,000 and promised never to publish it. The money undoubtedly came out of Ei-ling's pocket.*

In things big and small, Ei-ling played the provider of the family – always handsomely. When a son of her youngest brother T.A. first visited her, she handed him a $100 bill as a present – a colossal sum for the boy, whose weekly pocket money from his parents was twenty-five cents. Key staff members for the Chiangs received expensive gifts such as Rolex watches. When Chiang's doctor was invited to stay with her for a week, she fed him shark's fin soup, the most costly food, every meal. The doctor was put off the delicacy for ever, but he was charmed by Ei-ling's hospitality.

By all accounts, she was the brains in her marriage to H.H. Kung, who had been prime minister of China for years. H.H.'s own judgement, it was widely observed, could be erratic. In his reminiscences, which offered much candid insight, he boasted that 'Roosevelt had one hundred per cent confidence in me. Whatever I told him, he accepted as the truth ... Roosevelt was really a good friend of mine.' Similarly, Mussolini had the highest opinion of him: 'Mussolini thought that China sent big, important men to all the European capitals [as ambassadors] ... I think Mussolini confidentially suggested that he would like to have me.'

During his official trip to Europe in 1937, he had a private meeting with Hitler. He suggested that he had great rapport with the Führer, who 'told me that the Communists tried to ruin Germany but the German people were alert enough to realize the danger. The

---

* Hill, the agent, was beaten up during this period – probably by Chiang's thugs. But it was the payout that ultimately did the trick. Jennie's memoir was not published until the 1990s, long after she and Chiang had both died (she in 1971).

Communists were driven out of Germany before they could go too far.' Hitler said to him 'I understand that you, Herr Doktor, realize the danger of Communist doctrines.' H.H. also believed that 'I was able to make Hitler think twice before getting too close with Japan.'

From Taiwan he received frequent messages begging him 'to go back', he claimed. 'They think that if I go back, I could help the Government recapture the mainland.'

Ei-ling was well aware that she did much of the thinking for her husband – and that she exerted unparalleled influence over Little Sister and the Generalissimo. Once she told the mother of Debra Paget, the Hollywood star who married her youngest son Louis, 'In many ways we are very much alike.' She meant that they each engineered the success of their kin (apart from the fact that they were both deeply religious).

Debra Paget, the lead lady in Elvis Presley's first film *Love Me Tender*, was pushed into Hollywood by her dominant mother, Maggie Griffin, described as 'a shrewd, talkative, charming ex-burlesque queen who is a well-loved local figure in her own right'. Maggie was determined that Debra and her siblings would make their careers in show business. Shortly after Debra was born in 1933 in Denver, Colorado, the family moved to Los Angeles to be close to the film industry. Debra had her first professional job at the age of eight. By the time she co-starred with Elvis in his movie debut in 1956, she had made nineteen films, and assumed the role of promoting Elvis. She told her fans: 'I will gladly take a chance on predicting that Elvis Presley will continue to retain his popularity ... Elvis Presley is here to stay.'

During the shooting of the movie, her mother sat on the set bantering with Elvis. Maggie had made it a rule to be wherever Debra was filming. She stood at the centre of the actress's relationship with the future rock 'King'. To the audience of the then influential *Milton Berle Show*, Debra said:

I looked forward to my first meeting with Elvis Presley with mixed emotions. I had heard and read a lot about this new young singing sensation from Tennessee – and most of it was not complimentary ... The first thing I recall was the way he greeted us. When Mr Berle introduced us, Elvis grabbed my hand firmly and said, 'I'm glad to meet you, Miss Paget.' Then he shook my mother's hand with equal vigor, excused himself, and a couple of minutes later came back with a chair for her ... From then on my family and I saw a lot of Elvis ... my folks considered Elvis a member of the Paget clan – a feeling which, I believe, he reciprocated.

Apparently, Elvis proposed to Debra. But Maggie vetoed the marriage. 'If it had not been for my parents,' Debra said in a television interview, 'I would have married him.'

As it happened Debra divorced her first husband (actor David Street) after ten weeks, and left her second (director Budd Boetticher) nineteen days after their wedding. In 1962, at the age of twenty-eight, she met and married Ei-ling's youngest son, Louis. The Sandhurst-trained former captain of the British Army had turned forty, remained a bachelor, and was now an extremely wealthy oilman in Houston, Texas. He owned a private plane and was protected by a team of security guards.

Ei-ling was instrumental in the union. She liked Debra, not least because the red-haired 'glamour girl' was as devout as she was. Describing Elvis, Debra would say, 'And he loves God – that's the best part.'

Ei-ling had a house in Beverly Hills, and Debra was invited to dinner to meet Louis. The invitation was delivered by a mutual friend. Maggie told the press: 'It was all so proper. He invited me, too. And introduced his mother to us. She is a lovely person. It was all so proper, so old-fashioned that Debra just had to fall in love with him. I know I did.'

When Louis and Debra were engaged, Maggie purred, 'He wooed my daughter in such a wonderful, old-fashioned way – I just could not ask for a nicer son-in-law ... I just love him and I know his mother loves my daughter, too.' Debra had been contracted to make films in Rome. But Louis flew her instead to Las Vegas, where the wedding took place in the First Methodist

Church, in the presence of both mothers. When the couple went on honeymoon, Maggie again gushed to reporters: 'I was as excited as Debra ... I think my baby has found real happiness this time.' Ei-ling was pleased, but as always, refrained from talking to the press.

The home to which Louis brought Debra was 'a fortress' outside Houston, in the middle of hundreds of acres of wooded pastureland. Here the headquarters of his oil company and family mansion were fitted with bulletproof windows. In the grounds there was a man-made pond, with Chinese pavilions of blue-tiled roofs, looking dainty and decorative on the Texas plain. On closer inspection, these ornaments turned out to have been made from reinforced concrete and equipped with gun ports for machine guns.

Underneath the pond, Louis had built one of the world's biggest private nuclear bunkers: the Westlin Bunker. He took the possibility of nuclear attacks by Red Russia or China very seriously. The bunker was reached through hidden stairwell entrances, including ones inside the pavilions. It was a massive subterranean compound, designed to withstand any known cataclysm, even a forty-megaton blast. This underground city in miniature had its own generators and a capacity to stockpile water, food and fuel for 1,500 people for ninety days. Bunk beds were stacked up neatly; one room housed 115 triple-decker bunks, each with its own reading light. There were canteens with tables and chairs, toilets and decontamination showers ready for use, a clinic – and even a jail, with four steel-encased cells. Louis had thought of everything, not least trouble.

In the event of a nuclear attack, a wall-mounted panel in the control room would send out flashing lights and other signals and the lock-down facility of the bunker would be activated. Geiger counters for measuring radioactivity would go into action, checking the water and ventilation systems.

On the website of Houston Architecture.com, which described the bunker, a reader, Todd Brandt, left a message: 'I supervised the construction of the elevator house and interior remodel of the Westlin Bunker. It was fascinating, you'd have to see it to believe it. This thing had a lake on top of it but no leaks. Coolest job I ever built.'

This fantasy cavern cost Louis $400–500 million (in today's terms). During Houston's oil bust in the 1980s, he lost title to the property (though he was far from bankrupt personally). This extraordinary Cold War folly remained unfinished and sat frozen in time until fairly recently, when it opened for leasing in 2005. After hurricanes Katrina and Rita, large companies came knocking on its door in their dozens. Some, like Continental Airlines, wanted to use it as a crisis-operations centre. Others found it an ideal internet data centre. Today, it is advertised as being able to provide 'some of the most secure hosting and data warehousing possible. Weatherproof. Watertight. And survivable in case of nuclear attack.' Louis' refuge in case of a deathly assault has taken on a new lease of life.

Louis loved Cold War gadgets fit for a James Bond film. Once he gave a young nephew a comb that was a knife in disguise. May-ling came for a visit, and was driven in a custom-made limousine whose boot would open to reveal two giant spotlights powerful enough to blind pursuers, while the exhaust pipes shot out flames. The down-to-earth Mme Chiang Kai-shek commented to her brother T.V. that 'Louis is not very stable.' T.V. replied that he 'has the capacity of dreaming'. Louis had many hobbies. He owned a handsome estate in Louisiana, where he went duck shooting. May-ling's entourage liked him as he gave them a good time.

Louis and Debra were divorced after eighteen years, but the couple stayed close. 'We're the best of friends,' Debra said. She maintained her friendship with the Kungs and Soongs after Louis' death in 1996. This 'wonderful relationship' was partly thanks to their son, Gregory, for whom Debra had given up her film career.

Gregory was born in 1964 in a house on Beverly Hills next door to Frank Sinatra. When H.H. Kung came to see his grandchild, he brought a jade *ru-yi*, a curved sceptre that was normally a ceremonial well-wishing gift and had to be carried in both hands. Ei-ling looked after the infant like a well-practised grandmother. When Gregory was a young boy and was brought to see May-ling in New

York, his august great-aunt told him off: he had not learned the etiquette of rising from a seat when an adult entered the room, or of sitting properly, not lounging. She later could not praise him enough as he grew into a courteous young man. She was also relieved that he was not on drugs.

Gregory was Ei-ling's only grandchild. Of her four offspring, David and Jeanette never married, and Rosamonde's two marriages produced no children. Gregory, single child of Louis and Debra, is the sole descendant of the Kungs. He was devoted to looking after Debra who, in her eighties at the time of writing, is still very good-looking – and keenly religious. Mother and son are extremely close.

Neither Ching-ling nor May-ling had children of their own, thanks to the life – and husbands – they had chosen. So Gregory, who does not have children either, is the solitary 'heir' of the three Soong sisters. He is not interested in spending his life being the keeper of their legacy and remains a fiercely private man.

23

New York, New York

The three Soong sisters were daughters of Shanghai. But for political reasons none of them died there. Ching-ling, a leader of Red China, spent her final years in Beijing, where she worked for the Communist government to her last breath. She did not like the capital and missed Shanghai; but she had no choice. Ei-ling and May-ling were exiled from their native land, and chose to live out their last years in New York, a city reminiscent of their birthplace. They loved New York and were virtually New Yorkers. In the hustle and bustle of this metropolis they found peace and tranquillity.

Also settled in New York were two Soong brothers. One, T.L., was a year younger than May-ling. A former banker, he lost most of his money fleeing the mainland and was unable to make a living in America. After his savings ran out, he had to rely on his siblings' support for a living. Financial dependency is never a recipe for an easy bond. In a city littered with such fraught relationships, T.L., like many others in his position, scarcely saw his relatives, living modestly and quietly with his wife and daughter. He was the only Soong who sent condolences for Red Sister's death in 1981; but Beijing did not make a big thing out of it – it almost seemed as if he was not a Soong. His death in 1987 at the age of eighty-eight received no attention.

Another Soong brother who was drawn to the magnet of New York after 1949 was T.V., the eldest and most prominent of the three brothers. He had an apartment on Fifth Avenue overlooking Central Park, but lived in a permanent state of alert fearing for his life. One evening, a grandson of his was watching television, when there was a sudden commotion on the programme. The grandson was shocked to see his grandfather rushing in with a gun in his hand. He always carried a gun and, when he left New York, he would not tell people where he was going and for how long. T.V. was on Mao's list of 'war criminals', but his real worry was Chiang Kai-shek's ill will towards him. During the civil war, he had dallied with his brother-in-law's Nationalist opponents who had been trying to oust the Generalissimo. This brief burst of 'disloyalty' antagonised Chiang profoundly. T.V. had to take precautions.

T.V. knew that Nationalist agents kept a close eye on him in New York and that the biggest taboo from the point of view of his brother-in-law was him being close to Washington (which could potentially back him as a replacement of Chiang). So, although he had many prominent American friends, T.V. saw almost none of them. He stayed away from visiting officials from Taiwan as well. His was an entirely private life: daily walks in Central Park, watching American football on television, playing cards or hide-and-seek with his grandchildren. This was hardly a satisfactory substitute for the limelight he had enjoyed since his youth. But he had a happy family: a loving (and beautiful) wife, three well-behaved daughters and nine grandchildren.

Of his sisters, he had no communication with Ching-ling, sealed off as she was in Maoist China. He rarely saw Ei-ling though they lived in the same city. Big Sister held it against him for replacing H.H. Kung as prime minister near the end of the Japan war. She saw it as back-stabbing and colluding with Chiang to make H.H. a scapegoat.

He remained close to May-ling – but thousands of miles separated them when she was in Taiwan. Over the years, they exchanged letters and gifts, and performed little services for one another whose real purpose was to show they each had the other in their thoughts. In one long intimate letter in 1962, May-ling told her brother, 'In a few days will be Sister's birthday ... I hope that you will telephone her to wish her a happy birthday, for the older I grow, the more convinced am I of the wisdom of the saying "Blood is thicker than water".'

T.V. contacted Big Sister as May-ling suggested, and Ei-ling responded by inviting him to stay in Los Angeles. While he was there, the Cuban missile crisis erupted. It ended, at least in the public eye, with a climbdown by the Russian leader Nikita Khrushchev. T.V. celebrated with Ei-ling, and they made up. Happy and excited, he wrote to May-ling at once, 'I stayed at sister E's elegant house in Los Angeles where I found her in fine shape and spirits. We were much cheered by the confrontation Kennedy put up to Khrushchev. This is the beginning of a new chapter in history, and affords renewed hope of returning to our homeland.'

Encouraged by her success at bringing her brother and sister back together, May-ling set out to engineer a reconciliation between T.V. and her husband. In February 1963, while in Manila visiting a married daughter, T.V. received an invitation to nearby Taiwan. The invitation was carried specially by T.A., who as the Little Brother often acted as the messenger between his politically divided elder siblings. T.V.'s immediate reaction was caution. He loved his sister, but could not trust her husband. He was worried that Chiang might rob him of his freedom, if not his life. Preparing himself for this scenario, T.V. wrote several letters to his wife, telling her that he was only going 'for a week or two' and that she 'should not worry in the slightest. I shall be back before the end of the month.'

Chiang Kai-shek let T.V. spend a dozen or so pleasant days in Taiwan, but he did not welcome him with open arms, as he did H.H. Kung. Nor did he ask T.V. to do anything for him in the US. Like his in-laws, Chiang was elated by President Kennedy's tough stance in the Cuban missile crisis, and was planning to send his son Ching-kuo over in September to try to persuade Kennedy to back him to attack Red China. He agreed to May-ling's plea to enlist T.V.'s help. W. Averell Harriman, undersecretary of state for political affairs in the Kennedy government, was an old friend of T.V.'s.

T.V. saw Harriman after his Taiwan trip, and wrote May-ling a long and detailed letter afterwards reporting the conversation, which May-ling translated into Chinese for her husband. The report carried no jolly news for Chiang. The American government had no wish to be engaged in any 'major conflict' with Beijing. The ice in Chiang's heart towards his brother-in-law remained frozen. Chiang took care not to involve T.V. in Ching-kuo's visit to Washington.

In October 1964, China detonated its first atomic bomb. Around this time, France recognised Beijing, obliging Taiwan to cut its diplomatic ties with Paris. The following year dealt Chiang a further blow. Li Tsung-jen, who had briefly supplanted him to be the acting president of China in 1949 and had been living in New York since, evaded secret Nationalist surveillance and made a dramatic appearance in Beijing. As he stepped out of the plane onto the red carpet, in the line-up of ex-Nationalist bigwigs to welcome him there were friends of T.V.'s, and friends of friends. Chiang's dark mood grew darker. T.V. was never invited to Taiwan again, even though he tried hard to be of service.

On 26 April 1971, T.V. died suddenly at the age of seventy-six, while dining with friends. He had 'choked on piece of meat', recorded the death certificate. It may well have been a stroke: there had been signs earlier that day, and a day or so before.

As soon as she heard the news, May-ling told her husband she was going to New York for her brother's funeral, which was scheduled for 1 May.

The night before her departure, Chiang had second thoughts. In his diary entry of 29 April, he wrote: 'This evening I suddenly heard that Soong Ching-ling may be going to New York for T.V.'s funeral with the intention of using the opportunity to talk peace [i.e. Taiwan's capitulation] with my wife. So I decided to order my wife not to go to New York tomorrow.'

There is no evidence that Red Sister was going to New York. This was a time when China was sealed off from the outside world. Beijing had no diplomatic relations with Washington. Kissinger had yet to go on his secret (July) mission to the Chinese capital. It was impossible that Ching-ling, the figurehead of Red China, could suddenly jump into a plane. T.V.'s family in New York had had no contact with her for decades and did not issue an invitation. Nor did they receive any approach from Beijing. There was no sign Ching-ling made any request to go. Even when a much less political Soong,

T.A., died in 1969, all she could do was send a cable of condolences. And this simple objective had been achieved only by Red Sister appealing to Prime Minister Zhou En-lai through Zhou's wife.

The idea that Beijing might send Ching-ling to T.V.'s funeral to try some stunt may have flickered across the Generalissimo's mind. A story that month would have raised his hackles: some American ping-pong players had been invited to China, in an unprecedented move by Beijing. Chiang was on the lookout for similar moves. But ultimately, the Generalissimo was loath to let his wife go all the way to mourn T.V. Resentful thoughts towards his brother-in-law had been churning in his head lately. Going over the loss of mainland China, he had 'many regrets', he wrote in his diary. Prominent among them was the employment of T.V., who he claimed had messed up the finances out of 'ignorance and unwillingness to obey orders or to take responsibilities'. It was in this frame of mind that Chiang told his wife that he forbade her to go to New York.

Absence from T.V.'s funeral was a sore point for May-ling. When her friend Emma wrote to express sympathy, she rather abruptly changed the subject: 'The family deeply feels the loss of him and of my younger brother T.A., who died just two years previously ... Madame Kung has been here for the summer having come in April for my birthday.'

Ei-ling, who was in Taiwan at the time, did not go to T.V.'s funeral either. As a result, the Soong family presence at the occasion was scant, compared to the funeral of T.A., which May-ling had gone to San Francisco to attend. So had T.V.; so had Ei-ling, who had struggled up from her sick bed in New York.

When H.H. Kung, Chiang's other brother-in-law, died aged eighty-five on 15 August 1967, May-ling had flown from Taiwan to New York for the funeral; in Taiwan, Chiang had held a large-scale memorial service for him. The Generalissimo had penned a fulsome eulogy. T.V. got none of these. Chiang sent only a piece of calligraphy, of the kind that emperors used to have framed and bestow on worthy subjects, like a filial son, a chaste widow, or a long-suffering mother who kept the family line going.

★

It was in New York that Ei-ling finally succumbed to cancer, aged eighty-four, on 18 October 1973. She had been besieged by illnesses in her old age. May-ling had made sure she had the best possible care in Taiwan whenever she was there, and stayed with her in the hospital for days on ends. When she was dying, May-ling flew over and kept vigil at her bedside, before rushing back to her husband, who was fading.

A year after Chiang's death in 1975, May-ling settled permanently in New York, living with David Kung at 10 Gracie Square on the Upper East Side, Manhattan. This was a large corner apartment on the ninth floor of an imposing 1930s building, overlooking the East River. In choosing the apartment Mme Chiang Kai-shek very much had her own safety in mind. The building had a covered driveway inside the security barrier, which ensured that she could get in and out of a car practically inside the building. A stone's throw away across a patch of green was the New York mayor's official residence, Gracie Mansion, which meant that the whole place was likely to be well guarded. Even so, her windows were bulletproof.

Surrounded by guards and staff, she sometimes went to stay in the Kung mansion on Long Island, which now belonged to Jeanette, who was like a daughter to her. Jeanette continued to manage her household, and kept the staff on their toes day and night (night-shift nurses must not doze off). As ever, her rough manners caused much resentment from the staff, but she was indispensable to May-ling. Her devotion to her aunt was singular. She would take any new medicine May-ling was prescribed, to see whether there were any side effects. Well into her seventies, she would kneel down to scoop up May-ling's feet and cut her toenails, not trusting any pedicurist.

Jeanette's death in 1994, after David's in 1992, was a particularly heavy blow to May-ling. She was in low spirits for months. Seeing how badly she was affected, an admirer decided to do something to cheer her up. At his suggestion, a number of US senators held a reception for her at Congress in 1995, on the fiftieth anniversary of the defeat of Japan. She went to Washington for the day. On the plane there, the ninety-seven-year-old was busy revising her speech. She talked energetically and impressively. Afterwards, at the residence of the Taiwan representative, she was mobbed by Chinese Americans at a buffet lunch, and reciprocated with her full charm, chatting and having photographs taken with them. Afterwards she flew back to New York, showing no sign of fatigue. Her adrenalin rush lasted for days, during which all around her could feel her elation.

Rosamonde, Ei-ling's eldest daughter, took over the job of looking after May-ling. But she herself was in her late seventies, and she did not get on with her aunt nearly as well as Jeanette. The former first lady's large staff was now practically her family, superbly managed by a devoted former air-force colonel named Sung. An able, courteous and tactful man, he made a tremendous difference to the last decade of May-ling's life. She was polite and kindly to the staff, and they did their jobs diligently. Once or twice a year, the war orphans, now also in old age, paid her a visit. When she received them, and other occasional visitors, mainly from Taiwan, she would change, make up, compose herself and appear with her queenly graciousness. Once she said to the gathered group: 'When you were small, I used to stroke your faces. Now come over and let me stroke you.' They laughed and adored her.

Apart from these visitors, she saw no one outside her household. She accepted few invitations, public or private, and met virtually no friends. Emma Mills, with whom she had maintained a correspondence for decades, saw her just a couple of times in over ten years since she settled in New York after her husband's death. (Emma died in 1987, aged ninety-two.) She talked to no neighbours – a fleeting smile when she bumped into them was all she would manage. And she rarely went out. She might as well have been living anywhere, Taiwan included, where all her staff came from anyway, at immense cost. But Little Sister had to live in New York. The *buzz* of the city was in the air: it floats through closed windows and locked doors and fills all space. Even in her seclusion, May-ling was nevertheless connected with the world.

In the Face of a Changed Time

May-ling's last years in New York coincided with the transformation of mainland China after the death of Mao in 1976. Deng Xiao-ping, the post-Mao supreme leader, opened the doors of the country and embraced capitalism. Beijing gained international appeal. When America established full diplomatic relations with Beijing in 1979, Taiwan seemed to be in trouble. May-ling, worried, was disappointed with her adopted country. During Taiwan's negotiations with Washington to define a future relationship, she told Ching-kuo that he must insist that America have no contact with the mainland. It was such an unachievable goal that Taiwan did not put it on the table. May-ling berated Ching-kuo. Feeling frustrated and helpless, she came up with the idea of donating large sums of money to anti-Communist lobbies in Washington and sent a secret messenger to Ching-kuo to deliver her plan. But nothing could reverse the tide.

To May-ling, post-Mao China was no different from what it had been in Mao's time. She referred to Deng Xiao-ping as 'Deng the Bandit', continuing the old-style language used by her late husband. She was in despair that the world seemed to be taken in by Communist China.

In 1981, when Ching-ling was dying, Beijing invited May-ling to pay her sister a final visit; she did not reply. After Red Sister died, she was again invited, to the funeral; again she ignored the invitation. May-ling felt sad that she could not have a last meeting with her sister. Once she sat up all night talking to an aide about Red Sister, reminiscing about the time when Ching-ling had brought her, a child, to America. But she was determined not to lend the Communists any propaganda ammunition.

At this time, a leading Chinese-language newspaper in America published a letter allegedly written by Ching-ling to the Central Committee of the CCP, sharply criticising it. The letter, which was in fact a fake, made May-ling ecstatic. She wrote to Ching-kuo that the pain inside her for thirty years over the fact that her sister had chosen to stay and collaborate with the Reds was now eased. Her sister had seen through them after all, and had spoken up! 'She became disillusioned with the Communists – I am so relieved.' She started to imagine that if she or Big Sister had been in Shanghai at the time of the Communist takeover, they might have been able to persuade Ching-ling to leave. For many days, she lived in exhilaration and urged her stepson to announce the news to the next Nationalist congress. Ching-kuo seems to have known that the letter was not genuine and refrained from making the announcement. Not wishing to disappoint his stepmother, he told her that he had to protect the identity of the source, a Nationalist agent working underground on the mainland.

The following year, Beijing made another overture to Taiwan by having the veteran official Liao Cheng-zhi, son of Zhong-kai, who knew the Generalissimo well, send a lengthy telegram to Ching-kuo. The leader of Taiwan refused to respond. He sent it on to May-ling – and she offered to reply, to his delight. May-ling wrote a fiery open letter, which was carried in all the newspapers in Taiwan. It was the kind of writing that Red Sister used to do against Chiang Kai-shek, when Little Sister had remained rather detached. Now, it seems that, in their old ages, Ching-ling's moral outrage had faded and May-ling's righteous passion had grown intense. Reminding Liao the junior that he had just 'barely escaped the mouth of the tiger' through surviving the horrendous Cultural Revolution, in which untold millions had suffered appallingly, May-ling asked him whether he was out of his mind to expect Taiwan to submit to such a regime.

It was in rage and frustration that May-ling lashed out at a book called *The Soong Dynasty* by the writer Sterling Seagrave, which was published in 1985 and became a bestseller in America. The book portrayed the Soong family in a highly unfavourable light. This was no new experience for May-ling: she had seen worse accusations. But at this point she resented more than ever the fact that her family was singled out for blame for the misfortune of China while the Communists seemed to get off scot-free. Claiming that the author was a 'tool of the Communist bandits', May-ling reacted in an unprecedented militant manner. She told Ching-kuo to send over his smart son Hsiao-yung to be given instructions on how to deal with the book. She presided over a 'strategy', which included taking out full-page advertisements in the *New York Times* and the *Washington Post* with the headline: 'A Solemn Statement Refuting Distortions of Modern Chinese History in THE SOONG DYNASTY'. Although written in the name of a host of historians in Taiwan, the advertisements were obviously the handiwork of the regime. They only excited public interest in the book and boosted its sales enormously. Much ridicule was brought onto Taiwan. But May-ling was adamant. She called what she was doing 'a general offensive against the bandits', and asserted that this would 'without doubt thwart the burgeoning sales of the book'. When Seagrave told a television interviewer that he was hiding on a boat for fear of being bumped off, she scoffed.

A few months before, a Taiwanese author and biographer of Ching-kuo, Henry Liu, had been gunned down in San Francisco by gangsters working for Nationalist intelligence. The American public had been appalled and had condemned Ching-kuo's government as a gangster-style outfit just like that of his father. Now they were further repelled. It seemed that US arms sales to Taiwan might be in jeopardy. But May-ling remained obsessed with her battle against Seagrave.

Still in this mood, she returned to Taiwan in 1986 for the upcoming centenary of her late husband's birth. The main event was held on the colossal Chiang Kai-shek Memorial Square dominated by a vast memorial hall with a gigantic statue of Chiang, befitting the tradition of the modern personality cult pioneered by the Nationalists' Father of China, Sun Yat-sen. Fifty thousand well-organised men and women gathered. Masses of colourful balloons were released, as were white doves. May-ling read out a speech in her somewhat stilted Mandarin. It was a hard Party piece, only softened by a charming smile on her face when she finished reading.

This occasion turned out to be the last vestige of the Chiang era. The Generalissimo's successor, Ching-kuo, was about to end his father's legacy of dictatorship.

During the twelve years when he was a hostage in Stalinist Russia, Ching-kuo had been exiled to factories, a village and the gulag. Struggling at the bottom of society, he had developed an affinity with the ordinary people, and had come to like them and admire them. He made many Russian friends. One was an orphan named Krav, who was a technician in one of the factories. 'He taught me many things ... We became friends in need, sharing our pleasures, our sorrows and our hardships.' The workers liked Ching-kuo, recognised his talent and recommended him to be an assistant director. When he worked as a peasant, the mostly illiterate villagers respected him and trusted him to manage the affairs of the village. In the gulag, he did hard labour alongside people from all walks of life who had fallen foul of the regime, and again he formed a profound 'attachment in my heart for these people' – so much so that when he was released, he was almost unwilling to leave. 'I was so sentimental that I could hardly bid my poor companions good-bye.'

Although in the early 1950s Ching-kuo took his father's orders and carried out the 'white terror' in order to secure the new base for the Nationalists, he nevertheless managed to gain the reputation of being 'a man of the people' after he came to power. In contrast with his father who had had virtually no contact with the locals, Ching-kuo went out of his way to approach them. On his non-stop inspection tours, he preferred to eat in small, roadside food stalls, chatting to other customers. In appearance, he ditched his father's posture of awesomeness, or willpower, and chose to look ordinary. In substance, he reversed much of his father's policy as soon as the Generalissimo died. Chiang the senior had taken scant interest in

Taiwan's economic development; Ching-kuo made it his top priority. He oversaw 'the Taiwan Miracle', during which the island enjoyed double-digit growth, and average income tripled in the six years from 1977. A considerable degree of liberalisation followed. For the first time, citizens were able to leave the island freely as tourists. Old Nationalist soldiers who had fled the mainland were allowed to go there and visit their families. The coastline and mountains that had been sealed off were opened to the public.

The Ching-kuo government was widely reputed to be incorrupt. He and his own family accumulated no wealth. Around him he gathered a group of public-spirited talents, who prided themselves on being in office for public service and not personal gain. This absence of corruption and the spirit of performing their duty with diligence underscored Taiwan's success. While his one-party rule refused to tolerate the Communists or activists for Taiwan independence, repression under him was restrained and he was largely popular.

And he would lead Taiwan onto the road to democracy.

In 1985, Ching-kuo publicly and definitively rejected passing over power to members of his family, by announcing that none of his three sons would inherit the presidency. His own succession had not been of his choosing. It had been thrust on him and he had felt more the weight of responsibility than pleasure. His staff noticed that he was always agitated on the night before the day scheduled for top-level meetings. A man of simple tastes, he was not attracted to the perks of a dictator.

Under Ching-kuo Taiwan was changing into a very different place. Economic prosperity created a society bubbling with aspirations. Calls for reforms rose from every corner, not least from those who had been abroad for tourism and studies, which numbered 300,000 every year. Publications defying the official line were mushrooming. With this tremendous groundswell for democratisation, in 1987, Ching-kuo lifted martial law, allowing opposition parties and a free press.

This historic step was taken while May-ling was in Taiwan: she had lingered there after attending her husband's centenary celebration – to watch where the reforms would lead. She had mixed feelings. She was not against democratisation, but she was anxious that her husband should remain sacred and her own interest must be protected. For now she was not too worried. Ching-kuo was only in his seventies, and could be in charge for many more years.

On 13 January 1988, Ching-kuo suddenly died, aged seventy-seven. Although he had been sick from diabetes and other ailments, his death was unexpected. That morning, his son Hsiao-yung had put his head round the door to say good morning and had then gone off to have lunch with May-ling. Shortly after the young man left, Ching-kuo passed away. None of his family was with him.

Lee Teng-hui, the vice president and a native Taiwanese, stepped into the presidency. This alarmed May-ling. Lee had no manifest loyalty to herself or her husband. She feared, once again, that her future comfort might be under threat. Within days, her niece Jeanette had flown in from New York and aggressively taken over the Grand Hotel of Taiwan. Situated on top of a hill and looking like a traditional Chinese palace, with sweeping golden roofs and colossal bright red pillars, this landmark building was constructed in the 1950s to serve as a luxury government guest house. May-ling had been closely involved in building it, and Jeanette had managed it, in reality if not in name, treating it as if it were her family property. When Ching-kuo came to power, new rules were introduced and Jeanette was marginalised. Now she descended on the hotel, tore up the regulations, literally, in front of the manager, fired the chief accountant, and forced the chairman of the board to resign. Backed by May-ling, a Chiang crony was made the chairman, and Jeanette was in charge of the lucrative cash cow again.

To protect her interests, the ex-first lady, now ninety, sought political power. She tried to keep the chairmanship of the Nationalist party from President Lee. (Both the Chiangs had been party chairmen as well as presidents.) As the new party chairman had to be formally nominated by its leadership, May-ling asked the Nationalist leaders to delay the nomination – so that she could buy time and install a man of her choice. Her proposal met with resistance across the board, including from old Chiang devotees. They wanted Lee to take over. One midnight she telephoned an official who had been her husband's protégé, but he declined to do what she asked. It was clear that no one wanted her to interfere and all longed to move on, into a new era. The newly liberated media turned against her. May-ling had to back down. She made one last attempt at trying to tell the Nationalist party not to deviate into novel and fundamental changes. The party listened politely, but paid no attention.

May-ling, still physically tough and mentally agile, offered no further resistance. She accepted defeat and returned to New York in 1991, disassociating herself from politics in Taiwan. The island raced forward towards democracy, and in 1996 President Lee became the first democratically elected president.

Democratic Taiwan actually treated May-ling generously. Although rules introduced under Lee stipulated the allowances for retired presidents and spouses – and Ching-kuo's widow and family followed those rules strictly – an exception was made for Little Sister. Her lifestyle was by and large guaranteed. The Grand Hotel continued to serve as her private kitchen, sending chefs and waiters to America. Security guards, nurses and servants were still coming year after year. But some extravagance had to be toned down. In 1994, when she made her last trip to Taiwan to visit Jeanette who was dying of cancer (Jeanette preferred to be treated in Taiwan and not in America because there she could indulge in such privileges as having her dog to stay with her in her hospital suite), the Taiwan government booked a whole first-class cabin for the former first lady rather than dispatching a special plane. It also asked the Kungs to contribute a portion of her upkeep, which they did, even though some relatives grumbled offstage.

For a while May-ling fretted about being short of money. But on the whole, she faced the changed time with quietude. Praying and reading the Bible, the major activities of her last years, gave her peace. Near the end of a long and dramatic life, and at the top of the world at times, she hardly ever reminisced about her past and never mentioned any glories. She declined all interview requests. When people suggested naming a street after her, she vetoed it, quoting a verse from Ecclesiastes: 'Vanity of vanities, says the Preacher, vanity of vanities! All is vanity.' She waited for God to take her away, often muttering, 'People of my generation and even the younger generation are gone one after another; I am still here.' 'God has forgotten me.'

God remembered her when she was 105 and had lived to see three centuries. On 23 October 2003, May-ling died peacefully in her sleep. She left no will, except saying that she wished to be interred with her sister Ei-ling's family. The Kungs had bought two private family rooms in Ferncliff Cemetery, forty kilometres north of midtown Manhattan. These rooms were constructed of fine pale-white marble and decorated with stained-glass windows and simple altars. May-ling's funeral was arranged by her relatives and staff, and was low-key. There was even a glitch during the placing of the casket: it could not be fitted into the slot. Some demolition work had to be done on the spot to enlarge the space. All this was a far cry from the elaborately planned and executed interment of her husband. But then, Chiang Kai-shek's remains, kept in style for public display, had to endure red paint splashed over it by protesters, and constant public dispute about whether it justified taxpayers' money. May-ling, buried like an ordinary New Yorker, was left in peace, next to her beloved sister and her family. The day after the burial, Taiwan's then president, Chen Shui-bian, came to her Manhattan home to pay respects, and honoured her by presenting a flag of Taiwan to her relatives. Chen was the first Opposition leader to have been elected president, in the year 2000. May-ling had truly moved with history into the twenty-first century.

Notes

Chapter 1: The Rise of the Father of China

4 **'Drive out the Manchus'**: Sun Yat-sen (Chen Xi-qi et al. eds.), vol. 1, pp. 4–5; **Cuiheng and family poverty**: Sun Yat-sen (Chen Xi-qi et al. eds.), vol. 1, p. 74; Sun, Victor, p. 24; Shang Ming-xuan et al. eds., p. 513

5 **against sister's foot-binding**: Linebarger, Paul, pp. 79–81; Sun Hui-fen, p. 18; **such a thing as 'thinking'**: Miyazaki, Tōten 1977, p. 7

6 **'a wonder-house'**: Linebarger, Paul, p. 116; **school life in Hawaii**: Sun, Victor, pp. 79, 89–92; Linebarger, Paul, pp. 122–31; Chung Kun Ai, p. 106; Wong, J. Y. 2012, pp. 193–224

7 **despoiling the North God**: Chan, Luke and Taylor, Betty Tebbetts, pp. 3, 12–13, 147–8

8–9 **1884: registered at the Central School, marriage to Mu-zhen, baptised**: Sun, Victor, pp. 86–7, 98–9; Hager, Charles R., pp. 382–3; **changed his name to Yat-sen**: Sun Yat-sen (Chen Xi-qi et al. eds.), vol. 1, p. 36; **did not believe in God**: Shanghai Managing Committee of the Historical Objects of Sun Yat-sen and Soong Ching-ling ed., vol. 1, p. 265; Epstein, Israel, pp. 42–3; **at Hong Kong College of Medicine for Chinese**: Sun Yat-sen (Chen Xi-qi et al. eds.), vol. 1, pp. 46–7; Chen Shao-bai, p. 5; **diploma not recognised**: Schiffrin, Harold Z., p. 30, Sheng Yong-hua et al. eds., p. 70

10 **'the Second Hong'**: Chen Shao-bai, pp. 6, 8

11 **Soong Charlie and Sun**: Sun Yat-sen, *Collected Works*, Chapter 8 of *The Sun Theory*, 1919/06, http://sunology.culture.tw/cgibin/gs32/sigsweb.cgi?o=dcorpusands=id=%22CS0000000030%22.andsearchmode=basic; Letter to Li Xiao-sheng, 1912/04/14, http://sunology.culture.tw/cgibin/gs32/sigsweb.cgi?o=dcorpus&s=id=%22TG0000001329%22.andsearchmode=basic

12 **many wary of Sun**: Tse Tsan Tai, p. 4; **'Let me deal with Yeung'**: Chen Shao-bai, p. 29

13 **Sun fleeing Canton**: Deng Mu-han; cf. Wong, J. Y. 2012, pp. 587–93; Chen Shao-bai, pp. 29–30; **newspapers blasted him**: Wong, J. Y. 2012, pp. 574, 578

14 **Dr James Cantlie**: Cantlie, Neil and Seaver, George, pp. xxv, xxviii; Cantlie, James and Sheridan, Charles Jones, p, 18; interview with his grandson Hugh Cantlie, 12 April 2016

15 **'like a poisonous snake'**: Sun Yat-sen (Chen Xi-qi et al. eds.), vol. 1, p. 110

15–22 **Slater's Detective Association reports**: Luo Jia-lun, pp. 100–76

16 **Cantlie's testimony**: The National Archives, London, UK, FO 17/1718, p. 122; **'Well, I suppose you are'**: The National Archives, London, UK, FO 17/1718,

p. 121; **Sun came to the conclusion**: Luo Jia-lun, pp. 45, 48–9; The National Archives, London, UK, FO 17/1718, pp. 119–21

17 **Dr Patrick Manson**: The National Archives, London, UK, FO 17/1718, p. 122

19–21 **Sun's detention and release**: Luo Jia-lun; The National Archives, FO 17/1718, pp. 9–498; Cantlie, Neil and Seaver, George, pp. 103–5; Cantlie, James and Sheridan, Charles Jones, pp. 43–4; cf. Sun Yat Sen, *Kidnapped in London*; Chen Shao-bai, pp. 34–5

21 note Luo Jia-lun, pp. 53, 61

22 **'accosted … and compelled to enter'**: *The West Australian*, 26 October 1896; **'it was done in a friendly manner'**: The National Archives, London, UK, FO 17/1718, p. 120; **'that troublesome friend of yours'**: Cantlie, Neil and Seaver, George, p. 107

23 **'I get what I want'**: Chan, Luke and Taylor, Betty Tebbetts, p. 171

23–24 **Triad revolt 1900**: Yang Tian-shi 2007, pp. 221–5, pp. 212–13; Sun Yat-sen (Chen Xi-qi et al. eds.), vol. 1, pp. 232, 244–9; Hsu Chieh-lin, pp. 21–4

24 **repeated setbacks**: Papers of 3rd Marquess of Salisbury, Hatfield House Archives/3M/B24; **Empress Dowager Cixi**: Chang, Jung 2013; **'a thousand li a day'**: Sun Yat-sen (Chen Xi-qi et al. eds.), vol. 1, p. 346; **Dr Charles Hager**: Hager, Charles R., pp. 385–6

25 **colleagues accused him**: Yang Tian-shi 2007, pp. 272–312; Sun Yat-sen (Chen Xi-qi et al. eds.), vol. 1, pp. 469–76; **New York Times observed**: *New York Times*, 2 October 1910

26 **he told the newspapers**: Sun Yat-sen (Chen Xi-qi et al. eds.), vol. 1, pp. 558–9, 568; **Sun cabled Huang**: Sun Yat-sen (Chen Xi-qi et al. eds.), vol. 1, p. 557; **He also claimed**: Sun Yat-sen (Chen Xi-qi et al. eds.), vol. 1, pp. 558–9, 590–9; Zhang Tai-yan, p. 18

Chapter 2: Soong Charlie: A Methodist Preacher and a Secret Revolutionary

28 **Charlie born in 1861**: Shanghai Managing Committee of the Historical Objects of Sun Yat-sen and Soong Ching-ling, and Shanghai Association for Soong Ching-ling Studies eds. 2013a, p. 1; **about fourteen years old**: Fifth Avenue United Methodist Church Archives

29 **comments about Charlie**: Burke, James, p. 13; Haag, E. A., pp. 30–1

30 **Charlie's letter to his father**: Shanghai Managing Committee of the Historical Objects of Sun Yat-sen and Soong Ching-ling ed., vol. 2, pp. 281–2; **Letters between Charlie and Dr Allen**: Shanghai Managing Committee of the Historical Objects of Sun Yat-sen and Soong Ching-ling ed., vol. 2, pp. 281–5, Shanghai Managing Committee of the Historical Objects of Sun Yat-sen and Soong Ching-ling, and Shanghai Association for Soong Ching-ling Studies eds. 2013a, p. 7

31 **John C. Orr recalled**: *World Outlook*, April 1938, p. 8; **'with the greatest respect'**: Haag, E. A., p. 79; **Jerome Dowd noticed**: Charlie Soong at Trinity College; **Bishop McTyeire to Dr Allen**: Burke, James, p. 17; **People remembered Charlie**: Haag, E. A., pp. 74–9; Charlie Soong at Trinity College; Hahn, Emily, 2014b, p. 8

32 **Charlie's letter in 1882**: Charlie Soong at Trinity College; **Ella Carr**: Haag, E. A., pp. 50–1; **To Miss Annie**: Shanghai Managing Committee of the Historical Objects of Sun Yat-sen and Soong Ching-ling ed., vol. 2, pp. 287–8

33 **May-ling remembered**: Soong May-ling 1955, p. 34; **Observations of Charlie**: Haag, E. A., pp. 48–9

34 **Allen to Bishop McTyeire**: Burke, James, pp. 31–2

35 **dealing with Allen**: Shanghai Managing Committee of the Historical Objects of Sun Yat-sen and Soong Ching-ling ed., vol. 2, pp. 288–9; **other problems confronting Charlie**: Shanghai Managing Committee of the Historical Objects

of Sun Yat-sen and Soong Ching-ling ed., vol. 2, p. 288–90; Haag, E. A., p. 91;
Burke, James, pp. 32–3

36 **'I knew my mother'**: Soong May-ling 1934, p. 131; **'there was a strength of
character'**: Charles Jones Soong Reference Collection; **jokey notice**: Haag, E. A.,
p. 118; **Bill Burke's memory**: Burke, James, pp. 43–4

37 **'a very congenial couple'**: Charles Jones Soong Reference Collection; **'My reason
for leaving'**: Haag, E. A., pp. 127–8; **'can never be Chinese enough'**: Burke, James,
p. 43; **did not like Chinese food**: Hahn, Emily 2014b, p. 24; Haag, E. A., p. 111;
Ei-ling's description: Hahn, Emily 2014b, p. 24

38 **'gained the impression'**: Charles Jones Soong Reference Collection

39 **sending Sun money over the years**: Charles Jones Soong Reference collection;
Sun Yat-sen, *Collected Works*, Chapter 8 of *The Sun Theory*, 1919/06, http://sunology.
culture.tw/cgi-bin/gs32/sigsweb.cgi?o=dcorpusands=id=%22CS0000000030%22.
andsearchmode=basic, Letter to Li Xiao-sheng, 1912/04/14, http://sunology.
culture.tw/cgi-bin/gs32/sigsweb.cgi?o=dcorpusands=id=%22TG0000001329%22.
andsearchmode=basic; **'vile criminal'**: Zhang Zhu-hong; **'I know no man'**:
Shanghai Managing Committee of the Historical Objects of Sun Yat-sen and
Soong Ching-ling ed., vol. 2, p. 295; **Charlie revealed his secret to Mrs Roberts**:
Charles Jones Soong Reference Collection

Chapter 3: Ei-ling: A 'Mighty Smart' Young Lady

43 **Ei-ling to McTyeire School**: Hahn, Emily 2014b, pp. 22–9

44 **'a dreamy and pretty child'**: Hahn, Emily 2014b, p. 22

45 **'As a child'**: Shanghai Managing Committee of the Historical Objects of Sun
Yat-sen and Soong Ching-ling ed., vol. 1, p. 265

45 **May-ling childhood**: Hahn, Emily 2014b, pp. 35–6

45–6 **Family life**: Hahn, Emily 2014b, pp. 22–6, 40; Burke, James, p. 161; Soong May-ling
1934, p. 131

46–48 **Ei-ling journey to America**: Burke, James, pp. 157–68; Clark, Elmer T., pp. 46–8;
Hahn, Emily 2014b, p. 42; http://www.wesleyancollege.edu/about/soongsisters.cfm

49–50 **Ei-ling at Wesleyan**: Burke, James, pp. 166–8; Wesleyan College Archives and
Special Collections: Soong Sisters, 'article – undated, 2/10', 'Sketches – Questionnaire
Replied – *Circa* 1943', 'Sketches – College – undated, 2/8', 'Publication by – Ei-ling
"My Country and Its Appeal" – undated, Box Folder 5'

51 **Ei-ling 'scolding' May-ling**: Wesleyan College Archives and Special Collections,
'Sketches – Questionnaire Replied – *Circa* 1943'; **'undoubtedly the most brilliant
mind'**: 13 September 1917, Papers of Emma DeLong Mills, MSS.2, Wellesley College
Archives; *The Japanese Girl*: Burke, James, p. 168

52 **'a coward'**: in Wong, J. Y. 2005, p. 318; **George Morrison reported**: Lo Hui-Min,
vol. 1, pp. 666, 721; **'A revolution does not depend on money'**: Sun Yat-sen,
Collected Works, interview with the *Dalu* newspaper in Shanghai, 1911/12/25,
http://sunology.culture.tw/cgi-bin/gs32/sigsweb.cgi?o=dcorpusands=id=%
22TL0000000138%22.andsearchmode=basic

53 **one from Fujian**: CPPCC 1981, vol. 6, p. 250; **Tao Cheng-zhang**: Yang Tian-shi
2007, pp. 298–9; Yang Tian-shi 2008, vol. 1, pp. 3–12; Chiang Kai-shek (The Second
Historical Archives of China ed.), pp. 17–18

54 **Huang Xing, and the assassin**: Huang Xing (Mao Zhu-qing ed.), pp. 181–5, 237–8;
Miyazaki, Tōten 1977, pp. 53–63

55 **Sun conceded to arrangement before voting**: Shang Ming-xuan et al. eds.,
pp. 779–80; CPPCC 1981, vol. 1, pp. 117–9; Huang Xing (Mao Zhu-qing ed.), p. 245;

Sun publicly pledged to step down: Sun Yat-sen (Chen Xi-qi et al. eds.), vol. 1, p. 615; 'Why do you not want peace talks?': CPPCC 1981, vol. 1, p. 118; cf. Sun Yat-sen (Chen Xi-qi et al. eds.), vol. 1, p. 633; 15 million yuan: Sun Yat-sen (Chen Xi-qi et al. eds.), vol. 1, pp. 647–8

56 failed to move capital to Nanjing: Gu Li-juan and Yuan Xiang-fu, vol. 1, pp. 188–92; CPPCC 1981, vol. 1, pp. 119–20

57 John Cline's description: Burke, James, p. 179; William Donald's account: Selle, Earl Albert, pp. vii, 134, 139; Tongues began to wag: Huang San-de, p. 8

58 Ei-ling deferential towards Mu-zhen: Huang San-de, p. 8; Luke Chan helped Sun family: Shang Ming-xuan et al. eds., pp. 518; Chan, Luke and Taylor, Betty Tebbetts, p. 22; cf. Wong, J. Y. 2012, pp. 552–4; Friends heard him say: Miyazaki, Tōten 1977, pp. 30, 130

59 Mu-zhen and Sun's mother miserable: Chan, Luke and Taylor, Betty Tebbetts, pp. 187–8; what comforted the women: Sun, Victor, pp. 360–6, 398

60 hung his head: Miyazaki, Tōten 1977, p. 141; 'behaved badly': Huang San-de, p. 8

60–1 Cui-fen: Sun, Victor, pp. 344, 407–21; Miyazaki, Tōten 1977, p. 130; Huang San-de, p. 8

62 Sun vetoed Ah Mi nomination: Sun, Victor, pp. 289–91

Chapter 4: China Embarks on Democracy

64 Lord William Gascoyne-Cecil: Gascoyne-Cecil, Lord William, p. 274

65 Cix committed to constitutional monarchy: Archives of Ming and Qing dynasties ed., vol. 1, pp. 43–4, 54–68; vol. 2, pp. 627–37, 667–84, 671–3, 683–4; Chang, Jung 2013, Chapter 29; 1909 provincial elections: Gu Li-juan and Yuan Xiang-fu, vol. 1, pp. 2–5; Archives of Ming and Qing dynasties ed., vol. 1, pp. 667ff; Zhang Peng-yuan 1979, pp. 364–8; Chang, David Cheng, p. 196; 'acting parliament': Gu Li-juan and Yuan Xiang-fu, vol. 1, pp. 88, 119–20, 156, 186–92

66 1913 general election: Gu Li-juan and Yuan Xiang-fu, vol. 1, pp. 2–16; Zhang Peng-yuan 2013, p. 76–110; Zhang Peng-yuan 1979, pp. 364–70; Chang, David Cheng, p. 215; French scholar concluded: Bergère, Marie-Claire, p. 226; members of first parliament: Gu Li-juan and Yuan Xiang-fu, vol. 1, p 523; Zhang Peng-yuan 1979, pp. 398–447; K'ung Hsiang-hsi, p. 39

67 assassination attempt on Yuan: Wu Chang-yi ed., pp. 18–19; 'would catch sight': Selle, Earl Albert, p. 134; core of this request: Sun Yat-sen (Chen Xi-qi et al. eds.), vol. 1, pp. 764, 773, 778, 782

68 Donald described: Selle, Earl Albert, pp. 135–6; Yuan countered: Sun Yat-sen (Chen Xi-qi et al. eds.), vol. 1, pp. 757–8, 782

69 Mu-zhen car accident: Chen Peng Jen, pp. 107–8; Sun Yat-sen (Chen Xi-qi et al. eds.), vol. 1, pp. 784–7

70 Song's last words to 'President Yuan': Song Jiao-ren (Chen Xu-lu ed.), p. 496; 'must have given the order': K'ung Hsiang-hsi, pp. 36–7; 'snake': Soong Ching-ling (China Welfare ed.), p. 189

Chapter 5: The Marriages of Ei-ling and Ching-ling

71 he saw Mrs Roberts: Charles Jones Soong Reference Collection; H.H. Kung met Ei-ling: K'ung Hsiang-hsi; Lo Hui-Min, vol. 2, pp. 478–9; Yu Xin-chun and Wang Zhen-suo eds., pp. 283, 299; Shou Chong-yi ed., pp. 42–3, 57, 77, 82

72 H.H. and Ei-ling steered away from Sun: K'ung Hsiang-hsi, pp. 36–43; Lo Hui-Min, vol. 2, pp. 478–80; Ei-ling wedding: Hahn, Emily 2014b, pp. 80–1

73 **Ching-ling's contemporaries remembered**: Wesleyan College Archives and Special Collections: 'Sketches – Questionnaire Replied – *Circa* 1943', 'Sketches – College – undated, 2/8', 'article – undated, 2/10'

74 **'I am taking a box'**: Hahn, Emily 2014b, p. 77; **'I ... went from dinners'**: Epstein, Israel, p. 7; **'He was made of stern stuff'**: Epstein, Israel, p. 36; **to Allie Sleep**: Rosholt, Malcolm, pp. 112–15

75 **about missionaries**: Epstein, Israel, pp. 7, 42–3; **'I just can't get Ching-ling'**: Soong Ching-ling (Shang Ming-xuan et al. eds.), vol. 1, p. 67; **Ching-ling teasing Sun**: Shanghai Managing Committee of the Historical Objects of Sun Yat-sen and Soong Ching-ling ed., vol. 2, pp. 293–5

76 **Parents against marriage**: Shanghai Managing Committee of the Historical Objects of Sun Yat-sen and Soong Ching-ling ed., vol. 2, p. 295; Epstein, Israel, pp. 38–9

77 **Japanese surveillance records**: Yu Xin-chun and Wang Zhen-suo eds., pp. 466–7

104 **Ching-ling wedding**: Shanghai Managing Committee of the Historical Objects of Sun Yat-sen and Soong Ching-ling ed., vol. 4, pp. 101–5; Yu Xin-chun and Wang Zhen-suo eds., pp. 78–80; Epstein, Israel, pp. 40–3; Yu Xin-chun and Wang Zhen-suo eds., p. 467; Rosholt, Malcolm, p. 116

78 **to Israel Epstein**: Epstein, Israel, p. 41; **Charlie never forgave Sun**: Lo Hui-Min, vol. 2, pp. 477–9; Shanghai Managing Committee of the Historical Objects of Sun Yat-sen and Soong Ching-ling ed., vol. 2, p. 295; Burke, James, p. 181

79 **'I am so absent-minded'**: Rosholt, Malcolm, p. 115; **carved dragon**: Lin Ke-guang et al., p. 16

80 **Sun eager to exploit Yuan's vulnerability**: Sun Yat-sen (Chen Xi-qi et al. eds.), vol. 1, pp. 976, 983–91; Sun Yat-sen, *Collected Works*, letter to Shanghai comrades, 1916/03/3, http://sunology.culture.tw/cgi-bin/gs32/sigsweb.cgi?o=dcorpus&s=id=%22TG0000001651%22.andsearchmode=basic

81 **The assassination of Chen**: Chen Qi-mei (Mo Yong-ming and Fan Ran eds.), pp. 426ff; Sun Yat-sen, *Collected Works*, letter to Huang Xing, 1916/05/20, http://sunology.culture.tw/cgi-bin/gs32/sigsweb.cgi?o=dcorpus&s=id=%22TG0000001707%22.&searchmode=basic

82 **After he was shot dead**: Chiang Kai-shek (Chin Hsiao-i ed.), vol. 1, pp. 22–3; Sun Yat-sen, *Collected Works*, cable of condolences to the family of Chen Qui-mei, 1916/05, http://sunology.culture.tw/cgi-bin/gs32/sigsweb.cgi?o=dcorpus&s=id=%22TG0000001718%22.&searchmode=basic; request for a state burial for Chen Qi-mei, 1916/05, http://sunology.culture.tw/cgi-bin/gs32/sigsweb.cgi?o=dcorpus&s=id=%22TG0000001794%22.&searchmode=basic; **Ching-ling jumped onto next ship**: Soong Ching-ling (Shang Ming-xuan et al. eds.), vol. 1, pp. 89–90

Chapter 6: To Become Mme Sun

83 **Li no burning ambition**: Sun Yat-sen, *Collected Works*, letter to Dai De-lu (James Deitrick), 1916/07/05, http://sunology.culture.tw/cgibin/gs32/sigsweb.cgi?o=dcorpusands=id=%22TG0000001744%22.andsearchmode=basic; Li Yuan-hong (Zhang Bei ed.), pp. 36–8, 53; **Li offer, Sun turned it down**: Sun Yat-sen (Chen Xi-qi et al. eds.), vol. 1, pp. 1004–5; **'You must be careful'**: p. 1010; **Documents from German archives**: Li Guo-qi, p. 323; cf. Wang Jian and Chen Xian-chun

84 **Germany money to Sun**: Li Guo-qi, pp. 325–6; Wilbur, C. Martin, pp. 93–4; Tang Rui-xiang, pp. 10–13

84 note Wilbur, C. Martin, pp. 93–4

85 'provisional president' – 'grand marshal': Sun Yat-sen (Chen Xi-qi et al. eds.), vol. 1, pp. 1051–3; Zhang Tai-yan, pp. 32–3; Tang Rui-xiang, pp. 26–8; **naval chief Cheng Bi-guang**: Luo Yi-qun, in CPPCC 1950s–, issue 4, pp. 9–10; issue 11, pp. 29–37; Sun Yat-sen (Chen Xi-qi et al. eds.), vol. 1, pp. 1089–92; Tang Rui-xiang, pp. 67, 90–1; Chen Jiong-ming (Chen Ding-yan ed.), pp. 475, 507; **People who saw him**: Chen Peng Jen, pp. 117–19

86 'completely and helplessly alone': Sun Yat-sen, *Collected Works*, reply to Hong Kong businessman Chen Gengru, 1918, http://sunology.culture.tw/cgibin/gs32/sigsweb.cgi?o=dcorpus&s=id=%22TG0000002243%22.&searchmode=basic; '**the handsomest**': Haag, E. A., p. 199; **George Sokolsky**: *New York Times Magazine*, 10 January 1932

87 *The Sun Theory*: Sun Yat-sen, *Collected Works*, Chapter 5 of *The Sun Theory*, 1919/06, http://sunology.culture.tw/cgibin/gs32/sigsweb.cgi?o=dcorpusands=id=%22CS0000000025%22 andsearchmode=basic; Sun Yat-sen (Chen Xi-qi et al. eds.), vol. 2, pp. 1175–6; '**Obey me**': Hu Shih, vol. 5, p. 596; **May-ling to Emma Mills**: 25 May 1919, Papers of Emma DeLong Mills, MSS.2, Wellesley College Archives; **Ching-ling to Allie**: Rosholt, Malcolm, p. 117

88 'I'll give you 500 guns': Soong Ching-ling (Shang Ming-xuan et al. eds.), vol. 1, p. 105; **envoys to Germany**: Li Guo-qi, pp. 327–9; Kriukov, Mikhail, pp. 69–87; **He implored Japan**: Sun Yat-sen (Chen Xi-qi et al. eds.), vol. 1, p. 1133

89 **Major Magruder observed**: 1 March 1921, microfilm publication M329, Records of the Department of State Relating to Internal Affairs of China, 1910–1929, Roll 26, file number: 893.00/3811–3975; **Major Philean**: 28 April 1922, microfilm publication M329, Records of the Department of State Relating to Internal Affairs of China, 1910–1929, Roll 29, file number: 893.00/4241–4440

90 **Hsu resignation**: *New York Times*, 2 June 1922; Sun Yat-sen (Chen Xi-qi et al. eds.), vol. 2, pp. 1456–7; Tang Jia-xuan ed., p. 108; Tung, William L., pp. 186–7; **Sun press conference**: Chen Jiong-ming (Chen Ding-yan ed.), vol. 1, pp. 507–9; **Sun fled 'presidential palace'**: Sun Yat-sen (Chen Xi-qi et al. eds.), vol. 2, pp. 1463–5; Shang Ming-xuan et al. eds., pp. 134–5; Tang Rui-xiang, p. 151

91 **only 'to reconnoitre'**: Sun Yat-sen (Chen Xi-qi et al. eds.), vol. 2, p. 1465

91–3 **Ching-ling's experience**: her article reproduced in Hahn, Emily 2014b, pp. 98–101; Soong Ching-ling (Shang Ming-xuan et al. eds.), vol. 1, pp. 122–4; Soong Ching-ling Memorial Committee ed., p. 25

93 'several minutes after': Tang Rui-xiang, p. 163; '**chatted and laughed**': Sun Yat-sen (Chen Xi-qi et al. eds.), vol. 2, pp. 1465–6; **Ching-ling suffered miscarriage**: Soong Ching-ling (Shang Ming-xuan et al. eds.), vol. 1, p. 122; Epstein, Israel, p. 97; **close friends noticed**: Hahn, Emily 2014b, p. 104

94 **Emma Mills wrote**: DeLong, Thomas A., pp. 52–3; **Snow recorded**: Snow, Edgar, p. 88

95 'look after' Ching-ling: Shang Ming-xuan et al. eds., p. 650; '**Will you do me a great favour?**': Rosholt, Malcolm, p. 118

Chapter 7: 'I wish to follow the example of my friend Lenin'

96 **messenger to Moscow's men**: *Far Eastern Affairs*, 1987, 2, p. 102; Sun Yat-sen (Chen Xi-qi et al. eds.), vol. 2, pp. 1472–3; **Sun messages to Moscow**: Huang Xiu-rong et al. eds., 1920–1925, pp. 110, 166, 149, 213

97 **2 million gold roubles annually**: Huang Xiu-rong et al. eds., 1920–1925, pp. 217, 226; Sun Yat-sen (Chen Xi-qi et al. eds.), vol. 2, pp. 1567, 1623; '**a leonine head**': Soong May-ling 1977, pp. 8–9

98 **Borodin wrote to Moscow**: Sun Yat-sen (Chen Xi-qi et al. eds.), vol. 2, pp. 1698–9; **CCP founded in 1920**: Chang, Jung and Halliday, Jon, Chapter 2; **'I do not care'**: Wilbur, C. Martin, p. 146

99 **Ching-ling government scholarship**: Zhang Hai-lin, pp. 354–5

100 **to Western observers**: Tuchman, Barbara W., p. 87; *Life* **magazine remarked**: *Life*, vol. 8, no. 10; **'China's honest warlord'**: *Time*, 8 September 1924

101 **'the language of the colonialists'**: Epstein, Israel, p. 116

102 **Ching-ling to Borodin**: *Far Eastern Affairs*, 30 June 2003 REA-No. 002, pp. 121–6; **'preside over the country'**: Sun Yat-sen (Chen Xi-qi et al. eds.), vol. 2, pp. 2042, 2048, 2052

103 **Borodin told the Kremlin**: Huang Xiu-rong et al. eds., *1920–1925*, pp. 567–8; **Japanese government rejected Sun**: Sun Yat-sen (Chen Xi-qi et al. eds.), vol. 2, pp. 2072–3

104 **Borodin noticed the gloom**: Huang Xiu-rong et al. eds., *1920–1925*, p. 568; **'a good man'**: K'ung Hsiang-hsi, p. 57; **Old Man Sun**: Huang Xiu-rong et al. eds., *1920–1925*, p. 572; **Zhang Zuo-lin**: McCormack, Gavan, pp. 87–8, 253; Shang Ming-xuan et al. eds., p. 413; Huang Xiu-rong et al. eds., *1920–1925*, p. 570

105 **Sun illness and pain**: Huang Xiu-rong et al. eds., *1920–1925*, p. 568; Sun Yat-sen (Chen Xi-qi et al. eds.), vol. 2, p. 2089; Shang Ming-xuan et al. eds., p. 649; **Ching-ling to Allie**: Rosholt, Malcolm, p. 120

106 **she was seen weeping**: Shang Ming-xuan et al. eds., p. 650; Sun Yat-sen (Chen Xu-lu and Hao Sheng-chao eds.), p. 325; **their last conversation**: Lee Yung, in Shang Ming-xuan et al. eds., p. 650

107 **Ei-ling and May-ling to Beijing**: May-ling to Liao Cheng-zhi, 1982–8–17, https://www.bannedbook.org/bnews/zh-tw/lishi/20120916/664998.html

108 **Wang Jing-wei at Sun's deathbed**: Sun Yat-sen (Chen Xu-lu and Hao Sheng-chao eds.), pp. 323–6; Soong Ching-ling (China Welfare ed.), p. 189; Huang Xiu-rong et al. eds., *1920–1925*, pp. 574, 578; Ishikawa, Yoshihiro; Sun Yat-sen (Chen Xi-qi et al. eds.), vol. 2, p. 2125; **'Deathbed Letter to Soviet Government'**: Ishikawa, Yoshihiro

109 **On 11 March**: Sun Yat-sen (Chen Xi-qi et al. eds.), vol. 2, pp. 2130–2; **'to prove that'**: Epstein, Israel, p. 135; Tang, Earnest, p. 100–2; **'I wish to follow'**: Sun Yat-sen (Chen Xi-qi et al. eds.), vol. 2, p. 2132

110 **'the Father of China'**: Li Gong-zhong, p. 234; Shanghai Managing Committee of the Historical Objects of Sun Yat-sen and Soong Ching-ling ed., vol. 3, p. 386; **Nationalist propagandists**: Li Gong-zhong, pp. 237–42; **'no one else'**: Li Gong-zhong, pp. 165–70; **locals petitioned**: Li Gong-zhong, pp. 128–9

Chapter 8: Shanghai Ladies

115 **May-ling school days**: Wesleyan College Archives and Special Collections: 'article – undated, 2/10', 'Sketches – Questionnaire Replied – *Circa* 1943'; Pakula, Hannah, p. 25

116 **'how I used to cook'**: 22 June 1941, *T.V. Soong Papers*, Hoover Institution Archives, Box 61, folder no. 31; **'Brother and I'**: 4 July 1917, Papers of Emma DeLong Mills, MSS.2, Wellesley College Archives; **first letter from Shanghai**: 7 Aug. 1917, Papers of Emma DeLong Mills, MSS.2, Wellesley College Archives

117–26 **all other quotes of May-ling to Emma**: 16 August 1917, 6 September 1917, 13 September 1917, 15 September 1917, 26 October 1917, 4 November 1917, 12 November 1917, 7 December 1917, 15 December 1917, 28 December 1917; 13 January 1918, 8 February 1918, 6 March 1918, 19 March 1918, 11 April 1918, 25 April 1918, 26 April 1918, 29 April 1918, 15 May 1918, 18 July 1918, 29 July 1918, 2 August 1918, 24 August

1918, 2 September 1918, 20 September 1918; 7 January 1919, 9 April 1919, 25 May 1919, 24 July 1919, 9 September 1919, 29 September 1919, 18 November 1919; 11 February 1920, 28 February 1920, 21 March 1920, 5 September 1920, 11 October 1920; 28 April 1921, 25 May 1921, 6 July 1921, 25 July 1921; Papers of Emma DeLong Mills, MSS.2, Wellesley College Archives

121 **lifelong regret for May-ling**: Chiang Ching-kuo (Zhou Mei-hua and Xiao Li-ju eds.), vol. 1, p. 366

122 **about five foot three**: interviews with Dr Jan Kung-ming, physician who treated May-ling in her last years; Chen Li-wen ed. 2014, p. 149

Chapter 9: May-ling Meets the Generalissimo

128 **favourable attention of Sun**: Chiang diary, 26 July 1943, in Yang Tian-shi 2008, vol. 1, p. 12; **Chiang kept distance from Sun**: Chiang Kai-shek (The Second Historical Archives of China ed.), pp. 24–5, 63ff; **'In my observation'**: 14 March 1924, Chiang Kai-shek (The Second Historical Archives of China ed.), p. 167; **Liao's reply**: Chiang Kai-shek (The Second Historical Archives of China ed.), pp. 168–9

130 **'Chiang is an ordinary soldier'**: Huang Xiu-rong et al. eds., *1920–1925*, pp. 383–5; **Liao told Borodin**: Huang Xiu-rong et al. eds., *1920–1925*, pp. 383–4; **Borodin was taken in**: Zhang Ke, in Shanghai Managing Committee of the Historical Objects of Sun Yat-sen and Soong Ching-ling, and Shanghai Association for Soong Ching-ling Studies eds. 2013b, p. 629; Epstein, Israel, p. 192; Huang Xiu-rong et al. eds., *1926–1927*, vol. 1, p. 141

131 **Chiang smokescreen**: Chiang Kai-shek (The Second Historical Archives of China ed.), pp. 538–9; Yang Tian-shi 2008, vol. 1, pp. 130–1; Yang Tian-shi 2010, p. 337; **Russians misreading Chiang**: Huang Xiu-rong et al. eds., *1926–1927*, vol. 1, pp. 169–88; Chiang Kai-shek (The Second Historical Archives of China ed.), pp. 528, 536–7, 540, 554

132 **'very much keener'**: 6 July 1921, Papers of Emma DeLong Mills, MSS.2, Wellesley College Archives; **Ei-ling anti-Communist**: K'ung Hsiang-hsi, p. 54

132–4 **Jennie's account of dinner party**: Ch'en Chieh-ju (Eastman, Lloyd E. ed.), pp. 186–93

133 **Ei-ling considered grande dame**: 6 July 1921, Papers of Emma DeLong Mills, MSS.2, Wellesley College Archives; **May-ling to Emma**: 12 Nov.1917, Papers of Emma DeLong Mills, MSS.2, Wellesley College Archives

134 **May-ling gave Chiang her address**: Yang Tian-shi 2010, p. 340; **Chiang wrote in his diary**: 2 July 1926, Chiang Kai-shek Diaries, Hoover Institution Archives; **Ei-ling and T.V. reaction**: Yang Tian-shi 2010, p. 341; Lu Fang-shang ed., p. 60

135 **'literally dragged me home'**: 21 April and 25 May 1921, Papers of Emma DeLong Mills, MSS.2, Wellesley College Archives; **H.H. attitude to Canton**: K'ung Hsiang-hsi, p. 45; **Of Marshal Wu Pei-fu**: K'ung Hsiang-hsi, p. 46; **with President Hsu Shih-chang**: May-ling to Emma, 14 Nov.1918, Papers of Emma DeLong Mills, MSS.2, Wellesley College Archives; K'ung Hsiang-hsi, p. 45; **Kungs' life in Beijing**: May-ling to Emma, 20 September 1918, 29 October 1918, 9 September 1926, Papers of Emma DeLong Mills, MSS.2, Wellesley College Archives; **Chiang rightly surmised**: Yang Tian-shi 2010, p. 341; **'New Strong Man'**: *New York Times*, 14 November 1926

136 **Vincent Sheean observed**: Sheean, Vincent, pp. 218–19

137 **May-ling appalled**: Soong May-ling (Madame Chiang Kai-shek) 1977, pp. 5, 69–75; **'May-ling, darling'**: Hahn, Emily 1955, p. 87; **conversations with Borodin**: Soong May-ling (Madame Chiang Kai-shek) 1977, pp. 7, 60

138 **'fashionably gowned'**: *New York Times*, 9 September 1927; Yang Tian-shi 2010, p. 346; **their engagement**: Yang Tian-shi 2010, p. 347; **Meeting Mrs Soong**: exhibit, The Chiang Kai-shek Memorial Hall, Taipei; **The wedding**: May-ling to Emma, 24 January 1928, Papers of Emma DeLong Mills, MSS.2, Wellesley College Archives; Hahn, Emily 2014b, pp. 123–4

139 **Chiang talks with Big Sister**: 11 and 21 December 1927, Chiang diaries, Hoover Institution Archives; **Chiang on Duan Qi-rui**: Chiang Kai-shek (Chin Hsiao-i ed.), vol. 3, p. 996; **Ei-ling told Chiang off**: 28 December 1927, Chiang diaries, Hoover Institution Archives; **people close to them testify**: e.g. Wu Kuo-Cheng, p. 15

Chapter 10: Married to a Beleaguered Dictator

140 **a flaming row**: 29 December 1927, Chiang Kai-shek Diaries, Hoover Institution Archives; **'rather agreed with her'**: 30 December 1927, Chiang Kai-shek Diaries, Hoover Institution Archives

141 **'Here was my opportunity'**: Soong May-ling (Madame Chiang Kai-shek) 1934, p. 133; **half of his victory**: Chiang Kai-shek: Family Correspondence, 1928; Lu Fang-shang ed., p. 61

142 **Marshal Wu Pei-fu**: Gu Li-juan and Yuan Xiang-fu, vol. 3, pp. 1708–15; Koo, V. K. Wellington 2013, vol. 1, p. 287; **'methods of struggle'**: Huang Xiu-rong et al. eds., *1920–1925*, p. 574; **'thunderous silence'**: Tuchman, Barbara W., p. 151

143 **he talked about how Sun's**: 13 April 1931, in Yang Tian-shi 2002, p. 32; **English newsreel**: YouTube: https://youtube.com/watch?v=Mej3UnDDjoQ

144 **'so we revolutionaries'**: Sun Yat-sen, *Collected Works*, speech on 'tutelage', 1920/11/09, http://sunology.culture.tw/cgi-bin/gs32/sigsweb.cgi?o=dcorpusands=id=%22SP0000000734%22.andsearchmode=basic; Li Gong-zhong, p. 300; **Hu Shih wrote**: Hu Shih, vol. 5, pp. 523, 579, 588; Yi Zhu-xian, pp. 292–322; Yang Tian-shi 2008, vol. 1, pp. 177–8

145 **'a reactionary'**: Hu Shih, vol. 5, p. 525; **Wellington Koo's mansion**: Koo, V.K. Wellington, Columbia University Archives, Vol. 3, Part 2, Sect. H, J, pp. 304–5; Koo, V.K. Wellington 2013, p. 391; Koo (Madame Wellington Koo), pp. 152–4 ; **the Farmers' Bank**: Chiang diary, 5 July 1934, in Lu Fang-shang ed., p. 64

145 note Koo, V.K. Wellington, Columbia University Archives, Vol. 3, Part 2, Sect. H, J, p. 305

146 **Assassination attempts and May-ling miscarriage**: 24 August–6 September 1929, Chiang Kai-shek Diaries, Hoover Institution Archives; Oursler, Fulton, pp. 350–3; *New York Times*, 7 September 1929; **yet another nightmare**: Chen Li-wen ed. 2014, pp. 24–5

147 **May-ling in Big War of Central China**: Chiang Kai-shek: Family Correspondence, 1930; Yang Tian-shi 2010, pp. 357–8; **payments to the Young Marshal**: May-ling to Chiang, 19 September 1930, Chiang Kai-shek: Family Correspondence; Koo, V.K. Wellington, Columbia University Archives, Vol. 3, Part 1, Sect. E – G, p. 141; Koo, V.K. Wellington 2013, pp. 299–300; Yang Tian-shi 2010, pp. 357–8

148 **Chiang to Ei-ling and Mrs Soong**: Chiang Kai-shek: Family Correspondence, 1930–1; **Sun's old associates**: K'ung Hsiang-hsi, pp. 74–7; **diaries are littered with**: Lu Fang-shang ed., pp. 30, 34

149 **In his own family**: Lu Fang-shang ed., pp. 28, 69; **Chen's two nephews**: Wu Kuo-Cheng, pp. 16–17, 134, 190; **Ei-ling had Chiang's ear**: Lu Fang-shang ed., p. 69; Chiang Kai-shek: Family Correspondence, *passim*; **'do the minimum'**: Hu Shih, vol. 5, p. 588

149 note Shou Chong-yi ed., p. 42; Snow, Edgar, p. 95

150 'have no shame': Huang Zi-jin and Pan Guang-zhe, vol. 1, pp. 602–7

151 **May-ling wrote in 1934**: Soong May-ling (Madame Chiang Kai-shek) 1934, pp. 131–3; **when Mrs Soong died**: Soong May-ling (Madame Chiang Kai-shek) 1955, pp. 10–11; cf. Chiang Kai-shek: Family Correspondence, 1931–2; Shanghai Managing Committee of the Historical Objects of Sun Yat-sen and Soong Ching-ling, and Shanghai Association for Soong Ching-ling Studies eds., 2013a, p. 127

152 **assassination attempt on T.V.**: Han Li-guan and Chen Li-ping, pp. 53–70; *North China Herald*, 23 July 1931

153 **other gunmen shot at Chiang**: *New York Times*, 30 July 1931; Chiang Kai-shek: Family Correspondence, 2 August 1931; **'the depths of despair'**: Soong May-ling (Madame Chiang Kai-shek) 1934, p. 133

Chapter 11: Ching-ling in Exile: Moscow, Berlin, Shanghai

154 **Vincent Sheean on T.V.**: Sheean, Vincent, pp. 194–5

155 **Sheean on Ching-ling**: Sheean, Vincent, p. 208; **'the contrast between her'**: Snow, Edgar, p. 82

156 **Borodin was also staying**: Zhang Ke, in Shanghai Managing Committee of the Historical Objects of Sun Yat-sen and Soong Ching-ling, and Shanghai Association for Soong Ching-ling Studies eds. 2013b, p. 629; Epstein, Israel, pp. 206, 219

157 **Ching-ling loved Moscow**: Epstein, Israel, pp. 213, 224; Soong Ching-ling (Soong Ching-ling Foundation and China Welfare eds.), vol. 1, p. 60; Snow, Edgar, p. 94; *New York Times* **report**: *New York Times*, 29 September 1927; Epstein, Israel, p. 207; Sheean, Vincent, p. 289

158 **'opportunism on both sides'**: Snow, Edgar, p. 85; **meeting with Stalin**: Zhang Ke, in Epstein, Israel, p. 218–19; **The Comintern**: Shanghai Managing Committee of the Historical Objects of Sun Yat-sen and Soong Ching-ling ed., vol. 1, p. 145; vol. 2, pp. 90–3; **Mrs Soong wrote**: Li Yun, in Soong Ching-ling Memorial Committee ed., p. 206

159 **Mao and others on Deng Yan-da**: Mei Ri-xin and Deng Yan-chao eds., pp. 1, 245, 248; Chinese Peasants' and Workers' Democratic Party Central Committee ed., p. 129; Deng Yan-da (Mei Ri-xin and Deng Yan-chao eds.), p. 127; **Yan-da meeting with Stalin**: Zhang Ke, in Epstein, Israel, p. 217–18; **Yan-da views**: Deng Yan-da (Mei Ri-xin and Deng Yan-chao eds.), pp. 261–2, 462; **Yan-da wrote Ching-ling**: Shanghai Managing Committee of the Historical Objects of Sun Yat-sen and Soong Ching-ling ed., vol. 1, pp. 140–5; vol. 2, pp. 87–9

160 **Ching-ling in Berlin**: Soong Ching-ling (Soong Ching-ling Foundation and China Welfare eds.), vol. 1, pp. 58–9; Epstein, Israel, pp. 219ff; Shanghai Managing Committee of the Historical Objects of Sun Yat-sen and Soong Ching-ling ed., vol. 1, pp. 136–50; Liu Jia-quan, pp. 56–62; Mei Ri-xin and Deng Yan-chao eds., pp. 301–4; **letter to mother**: Shanghai postmark 4 July 1928 (owner of this letter wishes to remain anonymous); **never felt so at home**: Soong Ching-ling (Soong Ching-ling Foundation and China Welfare eds.), vol. 1, p. 58

161 **Yan-da about wife**: Deng Yan-da (Mei Ri-xin and Deng Yan-chao eds.), pp. 452, 459, 472, 480

162 **Yan-da goodbye to Ching-ling**: Mei Ri-xin and Deng Yan-chao eds., p. 6; **'Falling in Love Again'**: Soong Ching-ling (Soong Ching-ling Foundation et al.

eds.), pp. 269–74; **'Mother-in-law of the Country'**: *North China Herald*, 28 July 1931; **French Concession police recorded**: Shanghai Managing Committee of the Historical Objects of Sun Yat-sen and Soong Ching-ling ed., vol. 4, pp. 198–200

163 **piece attacking Chiang**: Hahn, Emily 2014b, pp. 138–9; Shanghai Managing Committee of the Historical Objects of Sun Yat-sen and Soong Ching-ling ed., vol. 2, pp. 112–14; vol. 3, p. 199; **she wished to be in a country**: Soong Ching-ling (Soong Ching-ling Foundation and China Welfare eds.), vol. 1, p. 66; **with German Communists**: Liu Jia-quan, pp. 146–8, 156–9, 179; Soong Ching-ling (Soong Ching-ling Foundation and China Welfare eds.), vol. 1, pp. 68–9

164 **telegrams from her family**: Soong Ching-ling (Shanghai Soong Ching-ling Memorial Residence ed.), pp. 27–8

165 **'I've come to mediate'**: Epstein, Israel, p. 258; Chinese Peasants' and Workers' Democratic Party Central Committee ed., p. 143; **'downfall'**: Soong Ching-ling 1992, pp. 83–6; *New York Times, Magazine*, 10 January 1932; **Ching-ling joins the Comintern**: Yang Kui-song 2003

166 **I was smitten hard**: Isaacs, Harold, p. 64; **Liao Cheng-zhi**: article in *People's Daily*, 29 May 1982; Yang Kui-song 2003

167 **'car accident' vetoed**: Shen Zui, pp. 60–4; Ye Bang-zong, pp. 32–4; **sweet memories**: interview with a member of May-ling's household in New York, 21 October 2015; **'stood alone'**: Chiang Ching-kuo (Zhou Mei-hua and Xiao Li-ju eds.), vol. 2, p. 163; **May-ling also sympathised**: Chiang Ching-kuo (Zhou Mei-hua and Xiao Li-ju eds.), vol. 2, p. 564

Chapter 12: The Husband and Wife Team

169 **'considerably more tolerant'**: Yi Zhu-xian, pp. 349, 353; **Ching-ling helped push Hu**: Soong Ching-ling (Shang Ming-xuan et al. eds.), vol. 1, pp. 270–4; Yi Zhu-xian, pp. 348–55

170 **'May-ling Palace'**: http://baike.baidu.com/view/64757.htm?fromtitle=宋美龄别墅andfromid=5176397andtype=syn#reference-[5]-64757–wrap; https://baike.baidu.com/pic/美龄宫/1173649/0/29381f30e924b899e3e980d96806ed950b7bf67e?fr=lemmaandct=single#aid=0andpic=a50f4bfbfbedab648ab61d20f136afc37831e0

171 **'nothing but a little village'**: Hahn, Emily 2014b, p. 126; **Chiang would miss her**: Lu Fang-shang ed., pp. 22, 71–3, 80; **in vacated Red areas**: Soong May-ling (Madame Chiang Kai-shek) 1934, p. 134; Soong May-ling (Madame Chiang Kai-shek) 1935a, pp. 75–8

172 **Ei-ling stepped into mother's role**: Soong May-ling (Madame Chiang Kai-shek) 1955, pp. 11, 29; **'I was driven back'**: Soong May-ling (Madame Chiang Kai-shek) 1934, pp. 133–4

173 **launching New Life Movement**: Soong May-ling (Madame Chiang Kai-shek) 1935b, pp. 355–7; **'old, dirty, and repulsive'**: Leonard, Royal, p. 110; **'more disturbed'**: Soong May-ling (Madame Chiang Kai-shek) 1934, p. 131; **'if a man were sloppy'**: Soong May-ling (Madame Chiang Kai-shek) 1935b, p. 357

174 **Hu Shih wrote**: *Duli Pinglun*, Issue 95, 8 April 1934; Hu Shih, vol. 11, pp. 419–22; **May-ling reaction**: Soong May-ling (Madame Chiang Kai-shek) 1935b, p. 355; 1934, p. 134; Soong May-ling and Chiang Kai-shek, p. 44; **'like the president'**: Gunther, John, p. 234

175 **Christmas Day 1934**: Soong May-ling (Madame Chiang Kai-shek) 1935a, p. 75; cf. Soong May-ling (Madame Chiang Kai-shek) 1934, p. 131; **New Year's Eve**: Soong May-ling (Madame Chiang Kai-shek) 1935a, p. 76

Chapter 13: Getting Chiang's Son Back from Stalin's Clutches

176 **talk to Chiang about Ching-kuo release**: Chiang Kai-shek (Chin Hsiao-i ed.), vol. 2, pp. 334–5

177–8 **Ching-kuo in Russia**: Chiang Ching-kuo, in Cline, Ray S.; Qi Gao-ru, pp. 7–9, 13–14, 365

177 **Shao Li-tzu**: People's University ed., pp. 81–3; CPPCC 1985, p. 241; Chang, Jung and Halliday, Jon, Index: Shao Li-tzu

178 **Ei-ling suggestion and Chiang decision**: 1 November 1930, Chiang Kai-shek Diaries, Hoover Institution Archives; Chiang Kai-shek (Chin Hsiao-i ed.), vol. 2, p. 335

179 **Ching-ling to Chiang about hostage swap**: 16 December 1931, Chiang Kai-shek Diaries, Hoover Institution Archives; Shanghai Managing Committee of the Historical Objects of Sun Yat-sen and Soong Ching-ling ed., vol. 2, p. 56; **'In the past few days'**: Yang Tian-shi 2002, pp. 373–4

181 **'showing signs of willingness'**: Chiang Kai-shek (Chin Hsiao-i ed.), vol. 3, p. 994; **Chiang requests for Ching-kuo release**: Yang Tian-shi 2002, p. 375; Chiang Ching-kuo, in Cline, Ray S., pp. 178–9; Qi Gao-ru, pp. 365–70; **many documents in Russian Foreign Ministry files**: interview with Jon Halliday

182 **Kung–Bogomolov**: *DVP*, vol. 18 (1935), p. 438; **Chiang saw Bogomolov**: *DVP*, vol. 18 (1935), pp. 537–9; **Chen Li-fu**, interview, 15 February 1993; AVPRF, 0100/20/184/11, pp. 11, 14–15

Chapter 14: 'A woman protects a man'

184 **May-ling spoke to Chinese ambassador**: Jiang Ting-fu, p. 203; **descriptions of Young Marshal**: Leonard, Royal, p. 21; Tuchman, Barbara W., p. 196

185–6 **Young Marshal–CCP–Moscow**: Chang, Jung and Halliday, Jon, Chapters 16 and 17

186–7 **May-ling after Chiang detained**: Soong May-ling and Chiang Kai-shek; Selle, Earl Albert, pp. 260, 306, 319–20; Li Jin-zhou ed., pp. 72–3; Yang Tian-shi 1998, p. 466

187 **'I would have done'**: Snow, Edgar, p. 94; **H.H. message to Stalin**: Li Jin-zhou ed., p. 83

188 **'with good motives'**: Soong May-ling and Chiang Kai-shek, pp. 44–5

189 **May-ling to Xian**: Soong May-ling and Chiang Kai-shek, pp. 51–3; **Chiang–May-ling**: Soong May-ling (Madame Chiang Kai-shek) 1955, pp. 13–14, 23; Soong May-ling and Chiang Kai-shek, pp. 54–5; **Young Marshal to May-ling**: Soong May-ling and Chiang Kai-shek, pp. 56–7

190 **Zhou En-lai in Xian**: Chang, Jung and Halliday, Jon, Chapter 17; **message from Moscow to free Ching-kuo**: Wang Bing-nan was by the door and heard this, unpublished memoir, cited in Han Su-yin, p. 154

191 **Leonard recorded**: Leonard, Royal, pp. 107–8; **'I wanted to'**: Hahn, Emily 2014b, p. 207

192 **Leonard saw that**: Leonard, Royal, p. 108; **May-ling's account**: Soong May-ling and Chiang Kai-shek; **Chen Li-fu and Dai Ji-tao**: Yang Tian-shi 1998, pp. 464–9

193 **to kill Chiang**: Central Archives ed., p. 213; Zhang Xue-liang (Zhang You-kun and Qian Jin, eds.), p. 1124

Chapter 15: Bravery and Corruption

197 **Ei-ling setting up hospital**: Hahn, Emily 2014b, pp. 218–19; **'extraordinarily excited'**: Soong Ching-ling (Shang Ming-xuan et al. eds.), vol. 1, p. 345; **May-ling visiting hospital**: Selle, Earl Albert, pp. 339–40
198 **Central University**: Luo Jia-lun, pp. 141–53
200 **'avenge shame'**: Chiang Kai-shek Diaries, Hoover Institution Archives; **'What a life!'**: 26 September and 12 December 1938, Papers of Emma DeLong Mills, MSS.2, Wellesley College Archives
201 **'I am covered'**: Pakula, Hannah, p. 356; **'raging infernos'**: 10 May 1939, Papers of Emma DeLong Mills, MSS.2, Wellesley College Archives
202 **French-grammar book**: Soong May-ling (Madame Chiang Kai-shek) 1955, p. 16; **May-ling about 'our people'**: 10 May, 1 November and 10 November 1939, 10 April 1941, Papers of Emma DeLong Mills, MSS.2, Wellesley College Archives; Soong May-ling (Madame Chiang Kai-shek) 1955, p. 17; **'we shall fight on'**: 10 November 1939, Papers of Emma DeLong Mills, MSS.2, Wellesley College Archives
203 **Fort Bliss**: Chennault, Anna, pp. 93–4
203 **'My God, that face'**: Alsop, Joseph W., p.174; **Chennault on May-ling**: Chennault, Claire Lee, pp. 35, 54–5; **Sebie Biggs Smith**: Smith, Sebie Biggs, Columbia University Archives, OHRO/PRCQ, No. 1392
204 **a 'squeeze'**: Pakula, Hannah, p. 290; **May-ling – Chiang cables**: Chiang Kai-shek: Family Correspondence, p. 28
205 **Her argument**: Wu Kuo-Cheng, pp. 14–15, 183; Shou Chong-yi ed., pp. 79, 85
205–6 **Kung's corrupt practice**: K'ung Hsiang-hsi, pp. 128, 142–3; Shou Chong-yi ed., *passim*; I Fu-en, p. 130; Gunther, John, pp. 230–2
206 **'Mme Kung's voice shook'**: Hahn, Emily 2014b, p. 93; **$100 million**: Shou Chong-yi ed., pp. 79–80, 84–5
207 **Kung felt, he revealed**: K'ung Hsiang-hsi, pp. 128–34
208 **Donald–May-ling**: Selle, Earl Albert, pp. 348–9
208–9 **Jeanette's relationship with May-ling**: interviews with Dr Jan Kung-ming, Jeanette's physician, who also treated May-ling; Chen Li-wen ed., 2014, pp. 111, 197–202; Shong Wen, pp. 150–8; Shou Chong-yi ed., pp. 28–9, 86–90, 104–5, 260
209 **at a dinner party**: Tuchman, Barbara W., p. 234; **A favourite retort**: Hahn, Emily 2014b, p. 256; **Lauchlin Currie complained**: Shou Chong-yi ed., p. 32; **H.H. cabled**: K'ung Hsiang-hsi, p. 146; **Rosamonde**: Shou Chong-yi ed., p. 12; Soong Ching-ling (Shanghai Soong Ching-ling Memorial Residence ed.), p. 422; **Ei-ling's conviction**: Soong Ching-ling (Shanghai Soong Ching-ling Memorial Residence ed.), pp. 124–5

Chapter 16: Red Sister's Frustration

211 **'It is a matter'**: Soong Ching-ling 1952, p. 107
212 **Evans Carlson**: Epstein, Israel, pp. 344–6; **'With co-workers'**: Epstein, Israel, p. 368; **Sir Stafford Cripps**: Epstein, Israel, pp. 369–70
212–13 **Edgar Snow**: Snow, Edgar, pp. 85–90

213 **dinner-dance restaurant**: Hahn, Emily 2014b, pp. 273–4

214 **Wang blamed Chiang**: Wang Jing-wei (Cai De-jin and Wang Sheng eds.), pp. 248–269

215 **three sisters in Chongqing**: Soong Ching-ling (Shang Ming-xuan et al. eds.), vol. 1, pp. 405–9; May-ling to Emma, 7 and 9 May 1940, Papers of Emma DeLong Mills, MSS.2, Wellesley College Archives; Hahn, Emily 2014a, p. 170; 2014b, p. 284; **to Anna Wang**: Soong Ching-ling (Shang Ming-xuan et al. eds.), vol. 1, pp. 407–8; Epstein, Israel, pp. 334–5

216 **'stop suppressing'**: Soong Ching-ling (Soong Ching-ling Foundation and China Welfare eds.), vol. 1, p. 191; **on Yan-da**: Soong Ching-ling (Shang Ming-xuan et al. eds.), vol. 1, p. 434; Chinese Peasants' and Workers' Democratic Party Central Committee ed., p. 130; **to T.V.**: Wu Jing-ping and Kuo Tai-chun 2008a, p. 58

217 **He cabled May-ling**: Wu Jing-ping and Kuo Tai-chun 2008a, p. 58; **Ei-ling persuaded Ching-ling to leave**: Chiang Ching-kuo (Zhou Mei-hua and Xiao Li-ju eds.), vol. 2, pp. 162–3; Wu Jing-ping and Kuo Tai-chun 2008a, p. 58; **'the Ta Kung Pao'**: Wu Jing-ping and Kuo Tai-chun 2008a, p. 58

218 **The demonstrators shouted**: Yang Tian-shi 2010, pp. 257–64; **Zhou En-lai to Mao**: Soong Ching-ling (Shang Ming-xuan et al. eds.), vol. 1, pp. 437–8; **'The sisters are so kind'**: Wu Jing-ping and Kuo Tai-chun 2008a, p. 58; Hahn, Emily 2014a, p. 183; **'not care about'**: Wu Jing-ping and Kuo Tai-chun 2008a, p. 58; **Ching-ling life in Chongqing**: Soong Ching-ling (Soong Ching-ling Foundation and China Welfare eds.), vol. 1, pp. 205–16; Epstein, Israel, p. 414

219 **She told the Americans**: Ambassador Gauss to the Secretary of State, 16 February 1944, FRUS, vol. VI; **Stilwell sketch**: Tuchman, Barbara W., pp. 94–5; **Stilwell diary**: Epstein, Israel, pp. 396, 424

220 **John Melby**: Melby, John F., p. 121; **'so Fifth Avenue'**: Epstein, Israel, pp. 418–19; **'No stockings'**: Epstein, Israel, p. 415

221 **about her sisters to Brazil**: Epstein, Israel, pp. 401, 424; Ambassador Gauss to the Secretary of State, 16 February 1944, FRUS, vol. VI; **Anna Wang commented**: Epstein, Israel, p. 337

Chapter 17: Little Sister's Triumph and Misery

222 **Wendell Willkie**: Tuchman, Barbara W., p. 428; Soong Ching-ling (Soong Ching-ling Foundation et al. eds.), vol. 1, pp. 216–17 (Ching-ling on Willkie); **'I visualize'**: 14 January 1939, Papers of Emma DeLong Mills, MSS.2, Wellesley College Archives

223 **writing and rewriting speeches**: interview with a member of May-ling's household in New York, 21 October 2015; **he was worried**: Chiang Kai-shek: Family Correspondence, p. 30

224 **silk sheets change**: Tuchman, Barbara W., p. 448; Chiang Ching-kuo (Zhou Mei-hua and Xiao Li-ju eds.), vol. 2, p. 648; cf. Yang Tian-shi 2008, vol. 2, p. 533; **complaints about David and Jeanette**: DeLong, Thomas A., p. 184; Tuchman, Barbara W., p. 449; **David as her 'secretary'**: Koo, V.K. Wellington, Columbia University Archives, Vol. 5, Part E, pp. 748, 806; **Chiang repeated entreaties**: Chiang Kai-shek: Family Correspondence, pp. 29–30; Chiang diaries, in Yang Tian-shi 2008, vol. 2, p. 519

225 **The day May-ling returned**: 5 July 1943, Chiang Kai-shek Diaries, Hoover Institution Archives; **gloom marred reunion**: July 1943, Chiang Kai-shek Diaries, Hoover Institution Archives; Yang Tian-shi 2008, vol. 2, pp. 533–42; **On the plane to Cairo**: 20 and 21 November 1943, Chiang Kai-shek Diaries, Hoover Institution

Archives; 'had a particularly thin time': 6 April 1944, Papers of Emma DeLong Mills, MSS.2, Wellesley College Archives

226 **Sir Alan Brooke**: Alanbrooke, Viscount, pp. 471, 478; **Anthony Eden**: Eden, Anthony, p. 424

227 **'This morning my wife'**: 26 November 1943, Chiang Kai-shek Diaries, Hoover Institution Archives; **Winston Churchill**: 22 November 1943, Chiang Kai-shek Diaries, Hoover Institution Archives; **'Over my dead body'**: Koo, V.K. Wellington, Columbia University Archives, Vol. 5, Part E, p. 794

227 **'What joy'**: 31 December 1943, Chiang Kai-shek Diaries, Hoover Institution Archives; **Dr Moran**: Moran, Lord, p. 151

228 **'The Chinese soldier'**: Tuchman, Barbara W., p. 246; **Roosevelt wrote Chiang**: Tuchman, Barbara W., pp. 584–5, 600; **besieged by nightmares**: Yang Tian-shi 2008, vol. 2, p. 536

229 **'an attempt to get away'**: Lattimore, Owen, p. 186; **approached member of mission**: Lattimore, Owen, p. 186; **told her husband tearfully**: Yang Tian-shi 2008, vol. 2, p. 536; **farewell party**: Yang Tian-shi 2008, vol. 2, pp. 526–9; **Truman believed**: Miller, Merle, p. 310; **'her priceless sable'**: Pakula, Hannah, p. 504

230 **with Emma in New York**: DeLong, Thomas A., pp. 184–8; May-ling to Emma, 12 June 1946, Papers of Emma DeLong Mills, MSS.2, Wellesley College Archives; **Chiang wrote to her frequently**: Chiang Kai-shek: Family Correspondence, pp. 30–3

231 **corruption scandal**: Yang Tian-shi 2008, vol. 2, pp. 449–66; Koo, V.K. Wellington, Columbia University Archives, Vol. 5, Part F, p. 847; **Emma noticed the mood**: DeLong, Thomas A., pp. 184–90; **May-ling to Times Square**: DeLong, Thomas A., p. 191

Chapter 18: The Downfall of the Chiang Regime

232 **'what is the noise about'**: date missing, August 1945, Chiang Kai-shek Diaries, Hoover Institution Archives; **Mexican ambassador**: date missing, August 1945, Chiang Kai-shek Diaries, Hoover Institution Archives

233 **'come as summoned'**: 31 August 1945, Chiang Kai-shek Diaries, Hoover Institution Archives; **'I don't feel ready to go'**: DeLong, Thomas A., p. 191; **Mao in Chongqing**: Chang, Jung and Halliday, Jon, Chapter 27; Chiang Kai-shek (Chin Hsiao-i ed.), vol. 5, p. 2681; interview with Chen Li-fu, 15 February 1993

233–4 **Chiangs in Xichang**: I Fu-en, pp. 111–12

234 **Mao nervous breakdown**: Chang, Jung and Halliday, Jon, Chapter 27; **Chiang toured the country**: Wu Kuo-Cheng, pp. 1, 18–19; I Fu-en, p. 113; Huang Ke-wu et al., vol. 1, pp. 289–90; vol. 2, p. 55

235 **state-of-the-art C-54**: I Fu-en, pp. 107–9; Epstein, Israel, p. 424; **'slaves who have no country'**: Chang, Jung 1991, Chapter 4; Wu Kuo-Cheng, pp. 2–9, 38, 187

237 **Wellington Koo reception**: Koo, V.K. Wellington, Columbia University Archives, Vol. 5, Part F, pp. 861, 898; Tung, William L., p. 71; **T.V. lost faith in Chiang**: Beal, John Robinson, pp. 341–2; Wu Jing-ping and Kuo Tai-chun 2008a, pp. 97–104; *Hua Shang Daily*, 30 November 1947; Wu Kuo-Cheng, p. 189

238 **Ei-ling will-like letter**: Soong Ching-ling (Shanghai Soong Ching-ling Memorial Residence ed.), pp. 124–5

238 note Professor Wu Jing-ping, in *Sun zhongshan soong chingling yanjiu dongtai* (*News in the Studies of Sun Yat-sen and Soong Ching-ling*), 2006, issue 5, pp. 21–3; Shou Chong-yi ed., pp. 44, 61, 92–6, *passim*; Wu Jing-ping and Kuo Tai-chun 2008a, p. 150

238 **Her other messengers**: Soong Ching-ling (Shanghai Soong Ching-ling Memorial Residence ed.), p. 144

239 **'The last few months'**: 12 June 1946, Papers of Emma DeLong Mills, MSS.2, Wellesley College Archives; **John Beal recalled**: Beal, John Robinson, pp. 100–1; **hankered for New York**: 12 June, 31 August, 1 November 1946, 23 April 1947, 14 December 1948, Papers of Emma DeLong Mills, MSS.2, Wellesley College Archives

240 **outing to Hangzhou**: Epstein, Israel, p. 473; **sending delicacies**: Soong Ching-ling (Shanghai Soong Ching-ling Memorial Residence ed.), pp. 108, 144, 199

241 **Barr commented**: Topping, Seymour, p. 50; **Red moles**: Chang, Jung and Halliday, Jon, Chapter 29

241–2 **Big-Eared Du–David–May–ling**: Yang Tian-shi 2014, pp. 203–19; Chiang Ching-kuo 2011, pp. 258–67

242 **Chiang noted in his diary**: November 1948, Chiang Kai-shek Diaries, Hoover Institution Archives; Yang Tian-shi 2014, pp. 217

243 **May-ling bitterly upset**: 23 and 27 November 1948, Chiang Kai-shek Diaries, Hoover Institution Archives; Yang Tian-shi 2014, pp. 217–18; **President Truman**: Miller, Merle, p. 309; **'Time and God'**: Soong May-ling (Madame Chiang Kai-shek) 1955, p. 26; **'I wish I could fly back'**: Chiang Ching-kuo (Zhou Mei-hua and Xiao Li-ju eds.), vol. 1, p. 83; correspondence pp. 68–108; Chiang Kai-shek: Family Correspondence, pp. 34ff

244 **May-ling suggested rashly**: Chiang Ching-kuo (Zhou Mei-hua and Xiao Li-ju eds.), vol. 1, pp. 85–7; **Chiang–May-ling telegrams**: Chiang Ching-kuo (Zhou Mei-hua and Xiao Li-ju eds.), vol. 1, pp. 77ff; Chiang Kai-shek: Family Correspondence, pp. 34ff; **Ei-ling 'protest'**: Soong May-ling (Madame Chiang Kai-shek) 1955, p. 23

245 **1 December 1949**: Chiang Kai-shek: Family Correspondence, p. 38; **'I had accompanied'**: Soong May-ling (Madame Chiang Kai-shek) 1955, pp. 23, 26; **'I heard a Voice'**: Soong May-ling (Madame Chiang Kai-shek) 1955, pp. 23–4, cf. pp. 13–14

246 **'listened to [her] report'**: 13 January 1950, Chiang Kai-shek Diaries, Hoover Institution Archives; **legendary heroes**: Reflection of the week, 1950, Chiang Kai-shek Diaries, Hoover Institution Archives

Chapter 19: 'We must crush warm-feeling-ism': Being Mao's Vice Chairman

249 **May-ling to Red Sister**: Soong Ching-ling (Shanghai Soong Ching-ling Memorial Residence ed.), p. 199; **Red Sister did not reply**: Soong Ching-ling (Shanghai Soong Ching-ling Memorial Residence ed.), p. 421

250 **'The day ... at last come!'**: Zheng Peng-nian, p. 237; Soong Ching-ling (Shang Ming-xuan et al. eds.), vol. 2, p. 680; **Ching-ling declined to go to Beijing**: Soong Ching-ling (Shanghai Soong Ching-ling Memorial Residence ed.), vol. 2, pp. 175, 203, 206; Soong Ching-ling (Soong Ching-ling Foundation and China Welfare eds.), pp. 62, 188–9; Zhou En-lai, vol. 1, pp. 18, 47; **'for medical treatment'**: Zhou En-lai, vol. 1, pp. 47–54; **accepted the invitation**: Soong Ching-ling (Shang Ming-xuan et al. eds.), vol. 2, p. 684; Zhou En-lai, vol. 1, pp. 47–54

251 **'how our homeland'**: Epstein, Israel, p. 479; **'I am really getting'**: Epstein, Israel, p. 548

252 **donated family properties**: Soong Ching-ling (China Welfare ed.), p. 148; **'shameless falsification'**: Soong Ching-ling (Shanghai Soong Ching-ling Memorial

Residence ed.), vol. 2, p. 227; **East German reception**: Soong Ching-ling (Soong Ching-ling Foundation et al. eds.), p. 277; **Christmas party**: Soong Ching-ling (Soong Ching-ling Foundation et al. eds.), pp. 279, 335

253 **Edgar Snow**: Soong Ching-ling (Soong Ching-ling Foundation and China Welfare eds.), vol. 2, p. 292; **'"burn" or "destroy"'**: e.g. Soong Ching-ling (Soong Ching-ling Foundation et al. eds.), p. 288; **In 'the Three Antis'**: Soong Ching-ling (Soong Ching-ling Foundation et al. eds.), pp. 286, 289–90, 296–7; **'the right-wing way'**: Soong Ching-ling (Soong Ching-ling Foundation et al. eds.), p. 297

254 **deeply upset**: Shanghai Managing Committee of the Historical Objects of Sun Yat-sen and Soong Ching-ling ed., vol. 1, pp. 242, 269; cf. Soong Ching-ling (Shang Ming-xuan et al. eds.), vol. 2, p. 930; **Ching-ling articles about Sun**: Soong Ching-ling 1992, pp. 239–47; Shanghai Managing Committee of the Historical Objects of Sun Yat-sen and Soong Ching-ling ed., vol. 1, p. 274

255 **Ching-ling told what she should say and incensed**: Shanghai Managing Committee of the Historical Objects of Sun Yat-sen and Soong Ching-ling ed., vol. 1, pp. 269, 274; **cousin of hers wrote**: Shanghai Managing Committee of the Historical Objects of Sun Yat-sen and Soong Ching-ling ed., vol. 4, pp. 135–6; **she was not invited**: Shanghai Managing Committee of the Historical Objects of Sun Yat-sen and Soong Ching-ling ed., vol. 1, p. 242

255–6 **chief bodyguard and his deputy**: Tang Xiong 2006

257 **Liu Shao-qi visits**: Soong Ching-ling Memorial Committee ed., p. 187; **'Dear Elder Sister'**: Soong Ching-ling (Shang Ming-xuan et al. eds.), vol. 2, p. 917; **Sukarno of Indonesia**: Soong Ching-ling (Shanghai Soong Ching-ling Memorial Residence ed.), p. 409; Soong Ching-ling (Shang Ming-xuan et al. eds.), vol. 2, pp. 943–8; Soong Ching-ling (China Welfare ed.), p. 144; **Ching-ling–Ei-ling**: Soong Ching-ling (Shanghai Soong Ching-ling Memorial Residence ed.), pp. 421–2

258 **'the correct view'**: Soong Ching-ling 1992, vol. 2, p. 288

259 **'We must crush warm-feeling-ism'**: *People's Daily*, 10 September 1957; **Backyard furnace**: Soong Ching-ling (Shang Ming-xuan et al. eds.), vol. 2, p. 1012; Soong Ching-ling (China Welfare ed.), p. 103; **'I feel very tense'**: Li Yun; **to Anna Wang**: Soong Ching-ling (Soong Ching-ling Foundation et al. eds.), p. 346

260 **anxiety over her letters**: Soong Ching-ling (Soong Ching-ling Foundation et al. eds.), pp. 348–53; **some complaints**: Soong Ching-ling (Soong Ching-ling Foundation et al. eds.), pp. 358–9, 366–9; **Anna also sent her**: Soong Ching-ling (Soong Ching-ling Foundation et al. eds.), pp. 346, 348, 356–8, 362

261 **'Let her finish her pee'**: Yolanda Sui's interviews, http://history.sina.com.cn/bk/wgs/2015–004-13/1440118715.shtml; https://v.qq.com/x/page/t0163kzni44.html; Tang Xiong 2006, p. 207

Chapter 20: 'I have no regrets'

262 **Yolanda–Mama**: Yolanda interviews, http://history.sina.com.cn/bk/wgs/2015–04-13/1440118715.shtml; https://v.qq.com/x/page/t0163kzni44.html; https://tv.sohu.com/v/dXMvMzMiOTQxNjQwLzEyMTA0MzYiMC5zaHRtbA==.html; Tang, Earnest, p. 119; **Yong-jie**: Soong Ching-ling (Soong Ching-ling Foundation et al. eds.), p. 562; Tang Xiong 2006, pp. 163, 208

263 **Mrs Sui**: Tang Xiong 2006, pp. 168–9; Tang Xiong, in *Woodpecker* magazine, 2005, issue 7, http://www.360doc.com/content/15/0113/22/7915662_440550733.shtml; **'The news made'**: Shanghai Managing Committee of the Historical Objects of Sun Yat-sen and Soong Ching-ling ed., vol. 1, p. 259; **Yolanda later remarked**: yolanda

television interview with Lu Yu, https://tv.sohu.com/v/dXMvMzM4NDUw-MzYxLzExNzkwMTUzNS5zaHRtbA==.html

264 **new chief bodyguard**: Soong Ching-ling (Soong Ching-ling Foundation et al. eds.), p. 387; Tang Xiong 2006, pp. 194–5; Li Yun

265 **Fearing the Red Guards**: Soong Ching-ling (Soong Ching-ling Foundation et al. eds.), p. 648; Soong Ching-ling (Shang Ming-xuan et al. eds.), vol. 2, p. 1179; **Anna Louise Strong**: Epstein, Israel, p. 548; **Jin Zhong-hua**: Zheng Peng-nian, pp. 270–3; Hua-ping

266 **cousin Ni Ji-zhen**: He Da-zhang, pp. 189–94; **'partly responsible'**: Soong Ching-ling (Soong Ching-ling Foundation et al. eds.), pp. 401–2

267 **'The truth is that his clothes'**: Soong Ching-ling (Shang Ming-xuan et al. eds.), vol. 2, p. 1180; **saw adopted daughters**: Soong Ching-ling (Soong Ching-ling Foundation et al. eds.), pp. 395–6; Tang Xiong 2006, pp. 204–8

268 **China's 'holocaust'**: Soong Ching-ling (China Welfare ed.), p. 39; **'It was good'**: Ching-ling to Paul Lin, 11 June 1972, Paul T. K. Lin Papers, Hong Kong University of Science and Technology Archives; **Israel Epstein**: Soong Ching-ling (Soong Ching-ling Foundation et al. eds.), pp. 452–3; cf. Soong Ching-ling (China Welfare ed.), p. 74; **'This is no way'**: Soong Ching-ling (China Welfare ed.), p. 94; **'They said she came'**: Soong Ching-ling (Soong Ching-ling Foundation et al. eds.), p. 459; **Zhou smoothing her life**: Soong Ching-ling (Shang Ming-xuan et al. eds.), vol. 2, p. 1249

269 **Mao died**: Soong Ching-ling (Shang Ming-xuan et al. eds.), vol. 2, p. 1263; Soong Ching-ling (China Welfare ed.), p. 129; **'have no regrets'**: Yolanda interviews on television, https://www.youtube.com/watch?v=RRrPJo1gAyk; with *Huanqiu Renwu* (*Global Personalities*), http://history.sina.com.cn/bk/wgs/2015–04-13/1440118715.shtml; **Mao on Jiang Qing**: Chang, Jung and Halliday, Jon, beginning of Chapter 47, and last para of Chapter 56

269–70 **Ching-ling to friends**: Soong Ching-ling (China Welfare ed.), pp. 167, 145; Soong Ching-ling (Soong Ching-ling Foundation et al. eds.), p. 669

270 **'very relaxed'**: Yolanda interview with *Huanqiu Renwu* (*Global Personalities*), http://history.sina.com.cn/bk/wgs/2015–04-13/1440118715.shtml; **her health problems**: Soong Ching-ling (Soong Ching-ling Foundation et al. eds.), pp. 456–8; **doted on adopted daughters**: Soong Ching-ling (Soong Ching-ling Foundation et al. eds.), pp. 516, 555–6, 595, 562, 602, 616, 670, etc.; Epstein, Israel, p. 591; Tang, Earnest, pp. 120–3; Yolanda interview with Lu Yu, http://phtv.ifeng.com/a/20160624/41628425_0.shtml; Soong Ching-ling (China Welfare ed.), p. 115

272 **Fox Butterfield**: Butterfield, Fox, p. 130; **'You are too late'**: Yolanda interview with *Huanqiu Renwu* (*Global Personalities*), http://history.sina.com.cn/bk/wgs/2015–04-13/1440118715.shtml

273 **'I hope somebody eligible'**: Epstein, Israel, p. 592; Yolanda interview, https://v.qq.com/x/page/t0163kzni44.html; **Yolanda wedding and after**: Butterfield, Fox, p. 131; Soong Ching-ling (Soong Ching-ling Foundation et al. eds.), pp. 663–70; Isaacs, Harold, p. 69; Yolanda interviews; Tang, Earnest, pp. 126–7; **protective about Yong-jie**: Soong Ching-ling (Soong Ching-ling Foundation et al. eds.), pp. 533, 555, 608–9, 618; Soong Ching-ling (China Welfare ed.), p. 186; Tang, Earnest, pp. 114, 123–5

274 **Harold Isaacs wrote**: Isaacs, Harold, pp. 69–72; **'my Little Treasure'**: Yolanda interview with *Huanqiu Renwu* (*Global Personalities*), http://history.sina.com.cn/bk/wgs/2015–04-13/1440118715.shtml; Tang, Earnest, p. 127

275 **Mrs Liu said to her**: Soong Ching-ling (Shang Ming-xuan et al. eds.), vol. 2, p. 1430; **Little Sister refused to reply**: Chiang Ching-kuo (Zhou Mei-hua and Xiao

Li-ju eds.), p. 152; **'astonished to discover'**: Isaacs, Harold, p. 73; cf. Tang, Earnest, p. 134

276 **affection for natural family**: Yolanda interviews, https://tv.sohu.com/v/dXMvMzM4NDUwMzYxLzExNzkwMTUzNS5zaHRtbA==.html; https://v.qq.com/x/page/t0163kzni44.html; **accused Snow**: Tang, Earnest, p. 101

277 **'My Testament'**: Tang, Earnest, pp. 112–6, 140–1; **Yolanda and Yong-jie chief beneficiaries**: *Shiji* (*The Century*), February 2008; Tang, Earnest, p. 127

Chapter 21: Taiwan Days

278 **'Why had the communists'**: Soong May-ling (Madame Chiang Kai-shek) 1955, p. 27–31

279 **May-ling elated**: to Emma, 25 July 1950, 26 January 1951, Papers of Emma DeLong Mills, MSS.2, Wellesley College Archives; **May-ling learning to paint**: to Emma, 21 October 1951, Emma to May-ling, 11 February 1952, Papers of Emma DeLong Mills, MSS.2, Wellesley College Archives

280 **'Chiang-style head'**: Weng Yuan (with Wang Feng), p. 61

281 **The earlier pattern**: Chiang Kai-shek: Family Correspondence, pp. 39ff; **Dr K.C. Wu**: Wu Kuo-Cheng, *passim*; Chiang Kai-shek: Family Correspondence, p. 41

282 **'painting, painting'**: 19 December 1953, Papers of Emma DeLong Mills, MSS.2, Wellesley College Archives

283 **told Emma wryly**: 20 Feb. 1954, Papers of Emma DeLong Mills, MSS.2, Wellesley College Archives; cf. Chiang Kai-shek (Chin Hsiao-i ed.), vol. 8, pp. 3899–900; Chiang Kai-shek: Family Correspondence, p. 41

284 **sobbed loudly in her dreams**: 4 June 1951, Chiang Kai-shek Diaries, Hoover Institution Archives; *Soviet Russia in China*, Chiang Kai-shek 1957; **Rev. Chow Lien-hwa**: Hu Zi-dan

285 **Ching-kuo–May-ling**: Chiang Ching-kuo (Zhou Mei-hua and Xiao Li-ju eds.), vol. 1, pp. 198ff; vol. 2, p. 4; **Emma noted in her diary**: 28 December 1958, DeLong, Thomas A., p. 213; **'the President's inauguration'**: 30 May 1960, Papers of Emma DeLong Mills, MSS.2, Wellesley College Archives

286 **'a very happy'**: 10 December 1962, *T.V. Soong Papers*, Box 61, folder no. 31, Hoover Institution Archives; **'perfect darlings'**: 14 July 1956, to T.V., *T.V. Soong Papers*, Box 61, folder no. 31, Hoover Institution Archives; **Her photographer**: Huang Ke-wu et al., vol. 2, p. 485

287 **'change the colour'**: Huang Ke-wu et al., vol. 2, pp. 295, 432–4; Weng Yuan (with Wang Feng), pp. 112–13

288 **two sedan chairs**: Weng Yuan (with Wang Feng), p. 155; Huang Ke-wu et al., vol. 2, p. 490; **fancy planes**: I Fu-en, pp. 109–11; **have staff fan him**: Weng Yuan (with Wang Feng), p. 74

289 **'We are afflicted'**: Chen Li-wen ed. 2014, p. 92; **'I am hopeful'**: 8 June 1972, Papers of Emma DeLong Mills, MSS.2, Wellesley College Archives; **Chiang hated Nixon violently**: November 1971ff, Chiang Kai-shek Diaries, Hoover Institution Archives; Yang Tian-shi 2014, pp. 217–18; **wrath towards David**: 14 and 25 December 1971, Chiang Kai-shek Diaries, Hoover Institution Archives; Yang Tian-shi 2014, p. 217; **'The president is well'**: Huang Ke-wu et al., vol. 1, pp. 252–3; **had a stroke**: Shong Wen, pp. 118–19, 126; Weng Yuan (with Wang Feng), pp. 199–201, 233–8

290 **'You are my own flesh'**: interview with a relative who wishes to remain anonymous; **tried to make David finance minister**: Huang Ke-wu et al., vol. 1, pp. 304, 338; vol. 2, p. 165

291 **only wanted to be with Ching-kuo**: January 1972ff, Chiang Kai-shek Diaries, Hoover Institution Archives; Shong Wen, pp. 112, 120–1; Huang Ke-wu et al., vol. 1, p. 256; **against May-ling and David**: 17 and 26 March, 17 and 27 May, 12 June, 11 July 1972, Chiang Kai-shek Diaries, Hoover Institution Archives; Yang Tian-shi 2014, pp. 268–9

292 **'vexation and annoyance'**: 20 July 1972, Chiang Kai-shek Diaries, Hoover Institution Archives; **signalling David was not included**: 21 July 1972, Chiang Kai-shek Diaries, Hoover Institution Archives; **Chiang sank into a coma**: Weng Yuan (with Wang Feng), pp. 208–10, 223–8; **May-ling breast cancer**: Chen Li-wen ed. 2014, p. 195; Shong Wen, p. 121; Huang Ke-wu et al., vol. 1, p. 386; **When Chiang died, May-ling**: Huang Ke-wu et al., vol. 1, p. 615; vol. 2, p. 461; Chen Li-wen ed. 2014, pp. 45–6, 667; **In contrast, Ching-kuo**: Chen Li-wen ed. 2014, pp. 45–6; Huang Ke-wu et al., vol. 1, p. 666; Chiang Ching-kuo (Zhou Mei-hua and Xiao Li-ju eds.), vol. 2, p. 29

293 **letters like these**: Chiang Ching-kuo (Zhou Mei-hua and Xiao Li-ju eds.), vol. 1, pp. 326, 342–9; **It fell on May-ling**: Chiang Ching-kuo (Zhou Mei-hua and Xiao Li-ju eds.), vol. 1, p. 366

294 **Mao mourning Chiang**: Chang, Jung and Halliday, Jon, Chapter 58; **picture of Chiang on bedside table**: Chen Li-wen ed. 2014, pp. 18–19, 131; **number of staff thirty-seven**: interviews with Dr Jan Kung-ming, physician who treated May-ling in her last years; cf. Huang Ke-wu et al., vol. 2, pp. 295, 462–3; **Chiang asked son to look after May-ling**: Chiang Ching-kuo (Zhou Mei-hua and Xiao Li-ju eds.), vol. 1, pp. 325ff, 373, 586–8

Chapter 22: The Hollywood Connection

295 **'Listen, Brother Chiang'**: Huang Ke-wu et al., vol. 2, pp. 482–3

296 **$250,000 to Jennie**: Ch'en Chieh-ju, pp. 5–10; **provider of the family**: Shong Wen, p. 172; interview with a relative who wishes to remain anonymous; **H.H. boasted**: K'ung Hsiang-hsi, pp. 114, 121–3, 147

297 **Debra Paget, mother, Elvis**: interview with relatives who wish to remain anonymous; https://www.pinterest.com/pin/308848486919331646/; Milton Berle interview with Elvis, https://www.youtube.com/watch?v=8xouKy5GfMw; Shearer, Lloyd (15 July 1956), 'More glamor for Hollywood', *Albuquerque Journal*, pp. 68–9, *Newspapers.com*; https://en.wikipedia.org/wiki/Debra_Paget – cite_note-aj-2; 'When You Wish Upon a Star, or It's a Star-Spangled Life: Family Cast' at the Wayback Machine; http://www.elvis-history-blog.com/debra-paget.html; https://www.elvispresleyphotos.com/celebrities/debra-paget.html; https://www.newspapers.com/clip/2595360/the_san_bernardino_county_sun/

298 **'I looked forward to'**: https://www.elvis.com.au/presley/interview-milton-berle-elvis-presley.shtml; https://www.elvispresleyphotos.com/celebrities/debra-paget.html; **Maggie vetoed marriage to Elvis**: Debra Paget talks to Rick Stanley (Elvis Presley's step-brother), https://www.youtube.com/watch?v=EBZ5LPeRNJA; **Ei-ling–Debra–Louis**: https://www.newspapers.com/clip/2595390/independent/; https://www.newspapers.com/clip/2595390/

independent/; 'Debra Paget Weds Oilman, Nephew of Madame Chiang', http://www.glamourgirlsofthesilverscreen.com/show/214/Debra+Paget/index.html
299 **the Westlin Bunker**: https://www.google.co.uk/search?q=westlin+bunker
andtbm=ischandimgil=5axDGk-o2mwycM%3A%3BSYgUZJduRR2OnM%3
Bhttp%3A%2F%2Fwww.houstonarchitecture.com%2FBuilding%2F2124%2F
The-Westlin-Bunker.phpandsource=iuandpf=mandfir=5axDGk-o2
mwycM%3A%2CSYgUZJduRR2OnM%2C_andusg=__Oy5SF_7nb4TeMhfR9F
thaHc7n3I%3Dandbiw=1407andbih=892andved=oahUKEwjO_PSb9PnVAh
UoJ8AKHT8GD2oQyjcIXgandei=mQmkWY7MKajOgAa_jLzoBg#
imgrc=zP9BUecaM81YeM; http://www.houstonarchitecture.com/Building
/2124/The-Westlin-Bunker.php; *Wall Street Journal*, 2 October 2006, 'Continental
Airlines Finds a Safe Haven In a Texas Bunker'; Melanie Trottman, 'Cold War
Relic Gets New Use By Companies Worried About the Next Big Storm', https://
cryptome.org/eyeball/cal-bunker/cal-bunker.htm; interview with T.V.'s
grandson Michael Feng, 26 January 2016
300 **Louis–May-ling–T.V.**: T.V. to May-ling, 22 March 1969, *T.V. Soong Papers*, Box 61,
folder no. 31, Hoover Institution Archives; Huang Ke-wu et al., vol. 1, pp. 403–7;
interview with grandson Michael Feng, 19 October 2015; **'We're the best of friends'**:
http://www.glamourgirlsofthesilverscreen.com/show/214/Debra+Paget/index.
html
301 **May-ling on Gregory**: Chiang Ching-kuo (Zhou Mei-hua and Xiao Li-ju eds.),
vol. 2, p. 210

Chapter 23: New York, New York

302 **T.L.**: Soong Ching-ling (Soong Ching-ling Foundation and China Welfare eds.),
vol. 2, p. 823; Soong Ching-ling (Shang Ming-xuan et al. eds.), vol. 2, p. 1437;
T.V. in New York: Wu Jing-ping and Kuo Tai-chun 2008a, pp. 130–7; Wu Kuo-
Cheng, p. 161; interview with his daughter Laurette and grandson Michael Feng,
26 January 2016
303 **relationship with Kungs**: K'ung Hsiang-hsi, *passim*; T.V. letters, in *T.V. Soong
Papers*, Box 61, folder no. 32, Hoover Institution Archives; interview with grandson
Michael Feng, 19 October 2015; **May-ling told her brother**: 2 July 1962, *T.V. Soong
Papers*, Box 61, folder no. 31, Hoover Institution Archives
304 **he wrote to May-ling**: 31 October 1962, *T.V. Soong Papers*, Box 61, folder no. 31,
Hoover Institution Archives; **T.V. to Taiwan**: Wu Jing-ping and Kuo Tai-chun
2008a, p. 134; **T.V. saw Harriman**: T.V.–May-ling letters, 1 September and 7 October
1963, *T.V. Soong Papers*, Box 61, folder no. 31, Hoover Institution Archives
305 **T.V. death**: Wu Jing-ping and Kuo Tai-chun 2008a, p. 146; interview with his
daughter Laurette and grandson Michael Feng, 26 January 2016; **Chiang stopped
May-ling coming to T.V. funeral**: 22 [*sic*] and 29 April 1971, Chiang Kai-shek
Diaries, Hoover Institution Archives; **T.V. family re Ching-ling**: interview with
his daughter Laurette and grandson Michael Feng, 26 January 2016
306 **Ching-ling re T.A. death**: Epstein, Israel, p. 563; **Chiang resentful towards T.V.**:
15 April 1971, Chiang Kai-shek Diaries, Hoover Institution Archives; **'The family
deeply'**: 9 November 1971, Papers of Emma DeLong Mills, MSS.2, Wellesley
College Archives; **Ei-ling did not attend**: May-ling to Emma, 15 March and 9
November 1971, Papers of Emma DeLong Mills, MSS.2, Wellesley College Archives;
When H.H. Kung died: 24 August 1967, Papers of Emma DeLong Mills, MSS.2,

Wellesley College Archives; Chiang Ching-kuo (Zhou Mei-hua and Xiao Li-ju eds.), vol. 1, pp. 315–22; vol. 2, p. 624

307 **When Ei-ling was dying**: 12 May 1969, 7 December 1973, Papers of Emma DeLong Mills, MSS.2, Wellesley College Archives; Shong Wen, p. 172; **Jeanette devotion to her aunt**: interviews with Dr Jan Kung-ming, Jeanette's physician, who also treated May-ling; Shong Wen, pp. 149–58; Huang Ke-wu et al., vol. 1, pp. 246, 256, 391–2; vol. 2, pp. 164, 392–5, 406; **Congress reception for May-ling**: Chen Li-wen ed. 2014, pp. 112–13, 219–30, 264; interview with a member of May-ling's household in New York who wishes to remain anonymous, 21 October 2015

308 **'When you were small'**: Chen Li-wen ed. 2014, p. 55

Chapter 24: In the Face of a Changed Time

309 **she told Ching-kuo**: Chiang Ching-kuo (Zhou Mei-hua and Xiao Li-ju eds.), vol. 2, pp. 3–29, 92–9, 677–86; **'Deng the Bandit'**: Chiang Ching-kuo (Zhou Mei-hua and Xiao Li-ju eds.), vol. 2, pp. 601, 607, 675; **sat up all night**: interview with a member of May-ling's household in New York who wishes to remain anonymous, 21 October 2015; Chiang Ching-kuo (Zhou Mei-hua and Xiao Li-ju eds.), vol. 2, pp. 152–3

310 **letter allegedly written by Ching-ling**: Chiang Ching-kuo (Zhou Mei-hua and Xiao Li-ju eds.), vol. 2, pp. 163–9; **offered to reply**: Chiang Ching-kuo (Zhou Mei-hua and Xiao Li-ju eds.), vol. 2, pp. 278–88; **against Sterling Seagrave**: Chiang Ching-kuo (Zhou Mei-hua and Xiao Li-ju eds.), vol. 2, pp. 512ff; DeLong, Thomas A., p. 244

311 **Chiang centenary**: https://www.youtube.com/watch?v=les3zpWSPXs

312 **Ching-kuo hostage years**: Chiang Ching-kuo, in Cline, Ray S.

313 **His staff noticed**: Weng Yuan (with Wang Feng), pp. 428–9

314 **She had mixed feelings**: her speech 7 July 1988, http://blog.sciencenet.cn/blog-51807-883264.html; **son Hsiao-yung**: Weng Yuan (with Wang Feng), pp. 432–5; **Lee alarmed May-ling**: Chiang Ching-kuo (Zhou Mei-hua and Xiao Li-ju eds.), vol. 2, p. 399; **Jeanette took over Grand Hotel**: Zhou Hong-tao (with Wang Shi-chun), pp. 485–90; **May-ling tried to keep party chairmanship**: Shaw Yu-ming, p. 260; speech 7 July 1988, http://blog.sciencenet.cn/blog-51807-883264.html

315 **lifestyle guaranteed**: Chen Li-wen ed. 2014, pp. 32–3, 326–7, *passim*; **Kungs contribute a portion**: Chen Li-wen ed. 2014, pp. 19–20; **fretted about money**: Chen Li-wen ed. 2014, pp. 137–8; **Praying and reading the Bible**: Chen Li-wen ed. 2014, pp. 120, 341, 348, *passim*; **hardly ever reminisced**: Chen Li-wen ed. 2014, pp. 18, 265

316 **often muttering**: Chen Li-wen ed. 2014, pp. 113, 219; **interred with Ei-ling**: Chen Li-wen ed. 2014, p. 270; **funeral low-key**: Chen Li-wen ed. 2014, pp. 16–17, 270–1, 306–7; **Chen Shui-bian to pay respects**: Chen Li-wen ed. 2014, pp. 307–8

Archives Consulted

Academia Historica, Taipei, Taiwan

AVPRF (Archives of Foreign Policy of the Ministry of Foreign Affairs of the Russian Federation), Moscow, Russia

Columbia University Archives, New York, USA

Duke University Libraries, Durham, NC, USA

Fifth Avenue United Methodist Church Archives, Wilmington, NC, USA

Hatfield House Archives, Hertfordshire, UK

Hong Kong University of Science and Technology Archives, Hong Kong

Hoover Institution Archives, Stanford, CA, USA

National Archives, London, UK

National Archives, Washington DC, USA

Nationalist Party History Archive, Taipei, Taiwan

Royal Archives, Windsor, UK

Wellesley College Archives, Wellesley, MA, USA

Wesleyan College Archives, Macon, GA, USA

Bibliography

Alanbrooke, Viscount (Alan Brooke), *War Diaries 1939–1945*, Weidenfeld & Nicolson, London, 2002

Alsop, Joseph W., *I've Seen the Best of It: Memoirs*, W. W. Norton & Company, New York, 1992

Ao Guang-xu, 'Lun sun zhongshan zai 1924 nian xiabannian de shishifeifei' ('On the Rights and Wrongs of Sun Yat-sen in the Second Half of 1924'), in *Modern History Studies*, Beijing, 1995

Archives of Ming and Qing dynasties ed., *Qingmo choubei lixian dangan shiliao* (*Archive Documents on the Preparations to Establish a Constitutional Monarchy*), Zhonghua shuju, Beijing, 1979

Association of Chinese Historians ed., *Xinhai geming* (*The 1911 Revolution*), Shanghai renmin chubanshe and Shanghai shudian chubanshe, Shanghai, 1956

AVPRF (Archives of Foreign Policy of the Ministry of Foreign Affairs of the Russian Federation), Moscow

Beal, John Robinson, *Marshall in China*, Doubleday, Toronto and New York, 1970

Bergère, Marie-Claire, *Sun Yat-sen*, Stanford University Press, Stanford, CA, 1994

Bickers, R. and Jackson, I. eds., *Treaty Ports in Modern China: Law, Land and Power*, Routledge, London, 2016

Boulger, Demetrius C., *The Life of Sir Halliday Macartney, KCMG*, Cambridge University Press, online publication, 2011

Burke, James, *My Father in China*, Michael Joseph Ltd, London, 1945

Butterfield, Fox, *China: Alive in the Bitter Sea*, Hodder & Stoughton, London, 1982

Cantlie, James and Sheridan, Charles Jones, *Sun Yat-sen and the Awakening of China*, Fleming H. Revell, New York, 1912

Cantlie, Neil and Seaver, George, *Sir James Cantlie: A Romance in Medicine*, John Murray, London, 1939

Central Archives ed., *Zhongguo gongchandang guanyu xian shibian dangan shiliao xuanbian* (*A Selection of CCP Archives Documents on the Xian Incident*), Zhongguo dangan chubanshe, Beijing, 1997

Chan, Luke and Taylor, Betty Tebbetts, *Sun Yat-sen – As I Knew Him*, publisher and place of publication unknown, 1955

Chang, David Cheng, 'Democracy Is in Its Details: The 1909 Provincial Assembly Elections and the Print Media', in Sherman Cochran and Paul Pickowicz eds., *China on the Margins*, Cornell East Asia Program, Ithaca, NY, 2010

Chang, Jung, *Empress Dowager Cixi: The Concubine Who Launched Modern China*, Random House, London and New York, 2013

Chang, Jung, *Wild Swans: Three Daughters of China*, Simon & Schuster; HarperCollins; London and New York, 1991

Chang, Jung and Halliday, Jon, *Mao: The Unknown Story*, Random House, London and New York, 2005

Charles Jones Soong Reference Collection, Duke University Libraries, Durham, NC

Charlie Soong at Trinity College, Duke University Libraries, http://blogs.library.duke.edu/rubenstein/2014/05/22/charlie-soong-at-trinity-college/

Ch'en Chieh-ju, *Chen jieru huiyilu* (*The Memoirs of Ch'en Chieh-ju*), Zhongguo youyi chubabgongsi, Beijing, 1993

Ch'en Chieh-ju (Eastman, Lloyd E. ed.), *Chiang Kai-shek's Secret Past: The Memoir of His Second Wife, Ch'en Chieh-ju*, Westview Press, Boulder, CO, 1993

Chen Jiong-ming (Chen Ding-yan ed.), *Chen jingcun (jiongming) xiansheng nianpu* (*Chen Jiong-ming Chronology*), Li Ao chubanshe, Taipei, 1995

Chen Li-fu, *The Reminiscences of Chen Li-fu*, Columbia University Archives, New York

Chen Li-fu, *The Storm Clouds Clear Over China: The Memoir of Ch'en Li-Fu*, Hoover Institution Press, Stanford, CA, 1994

Chen Li-wen ed., *Jiang zhongzhen de xinyang jiqing* (*Chiang Kai-shek's Faith*), Zhongzheng jiniantang, Taipei, 2005

Chen Li-wen ed., *Jiangfuren soong meiling nushi xingyi koushu fangtanlu* (*Interviews of the Staff of Soong May-ling, Madame Chiang Kai-shek*), Academia Historica and National Sun Yat-sen Memorial, Taipei, 2014

Chen Peng Jen, *Sun zhongshan xiansheng yu riben youren* (*Mr Sun Yat-sen and Japanese Friends*), Shuiniu tushu chuban shiye youxian gongsi, Taipei, 1990

Chen Qi-mei (Mo Yong-ming and Fan Ran eds.), *Chen yingshi jinian* (*A Chronology of Chen Qi-mei*), Nanjing daxue chubanshe, Nanjing, 1991

Chen Shao-bai, *Chen shaobai zishu* (*The Reminiscences of Chen Shao-bai*), Renmin ribao chubanshe, Beijing, 2011

Chen, Percy, *China Called Me*, Little, Brown, Boston, MA, 1979

Chennault, Anna, *The Education of Anna*, Times Books, New York, 1980

Chennault, Claire Lee, *Way of a Fighter*, G. P. Putnam's Sons, New York, 1949

Chiang Ching-kuo, 'My Days in Soviet Russia' (1937), in Cline, Ray S., *Chiang Ching-kuo Remembered*, US Global Strategy Council, Washington DC, 1989

Chiang Ching-kuo, *Jiang jingguo huiyilu* (*Chiang Ching-kuo Memoirs*), Dongfang chubanshe, Beijing, 2011

Chiang Ching-kuo (Zhou Mei-hua and Xiao Li-ju eds.), *Jiang jingguo shuxinji: yu song meiling wanglai handian* (*Chiang Ching-kuo's Correspondence with Madame Chiang Kai-shek*), Academia Historica, Taipei, 2009

Chiang Kai-shek Diaries, Hoover Institution Archives, Stanford University

Chiang Kai-shek: Family Correspondence, Academia Historica, Taipei, Taiwan

Chiang Kai-shek, *Soviet Russia in China: A Summing-up at Seventy*, Farrar, Straus & Cudahy, New York, 1957

Chiang Kai-shek (Chin Hsiao-i ed.), *Zongtong jianggong dashi changbian chugao* (*Draft of a Long Chronological Record of President Chiang Kai-shek*), Taipei, 1978, courtesy of the editor

Chiang Kai-shek (The Second Historical Archives of China ed.), *Jiang jieshi nianpu chugao* (*A Draft Chronology of Chiang Kai-shek*), Dangan chubanshe, Beijing, 1992

Chinese Peasants' and Workers' Democratic Party Central Committee ed., *Deng yanda* (*Deng Yan-da*), Wenshi ziliao chubanshe, Beijing, 1985

Chow Lien-hwa, *Zhou lianhua mushi fangtanlu* (*Interviews with Pastor Chow Lien-hwa*), Academia Historica, Taipei, 2012

Chung Kun Ai, *My Seventy-Nine Years in Hawaii, 1879–1958*, Cosmorama Pictorial Publisher, Hong Kong, 1960

Clark, Elmer T., *The Chiangs of China*, Abingdon-Cokesbury Press, New York and Nashville, TN, 1943

Cline, Ray S., *Chiang Ching-kuo Remembered*, US Global Strategy Council, Washington DC, 1989

CPPCC (Chinese People's Political Consultative Conference) Canton Committee, Historical Documents Studies Committee ed., *Guangzhou wenshi ziliao* (*Canton Historical Documents*) Guangzhou, 1950s

CPPCC (Chinese People's Political Consultative Conference) National Committee, Historical Documents Studies Committee ed., *Bansheng fengyulu: jia yibin huiyilu* (*Memoir of Jia Yi-bin*), Zhongguo wenshi chubanshe, Beijing, 2011

CPPCC (Chinese People's Political Consultative Conference) National Committee, Historical Documents Studies Committee ed., *Xinhai geming huiyilu* (*Memories of the 1911 Revolution*), Wenshi ziliao chubanshe, Beijing, 1981

CPPCC (Chinese People's Political Consultative Conference) National Committee, Historical Documents Studies Committee ed., *Heping laoren shao lizi* (*Man of Peace Shao Li-zi*), Wenshi ziliao chubanshe, Beijing, 1985

CPPCC (Chinese People's Political Consultative Conference) National Committee, Historical Documents and Studies Office and the Museum of the Chinese Revolution eds., *Sun zhongshan xiansheng huace* (*Dr Sun Yat-sen: A Photo Album*), Zhongguo wenshi chubanshe, Beijing, 1986a

CPPCC (Chinese People's Political Consultative Conference) Shanghai Committee, Historical Documents Studies Committee ed., *Jiu shanghai de bang hui* (*Secret Societies of Old Shanghai*), Shanghai renmin chubanshe, Shanghai, 1986b

CPPCC (Chinese People's Political Consultative Conference) Zhejiang Committee, Historical Documents Studies Committee ed., *Jiang jieshi jiashi* (*Chiang Kai-shek's Family History*), Zhejiang renmin chubanshe, Hangzhou, 1994

CPPCC (Chinese People's Political Consultative Conference) Zhejiang Committee, Historical Documents Studies Committee ed., *Chen Yingshi* (*Chen Qi-mei*), Zhejiang renmin chubanshe, Hangzhou, 1987

Daily News, Perth

DeLong, Thomas A., *Madame Chiang Kai-shek and Miss Emma Mills*, McFarland & Company, Inc., Jefferson, NC and London, 2007

Deng Mu-han, 'Yiwei Guangzhou geming shimoji (The Full Story of the 1895 Canton Revolution)', in *Xinhai geming shiliao xuanji* (*Selected Historical Documents on the 1911 Revolution*), vol. 1, Hunan renmin chubanshe, 1981

Deng Yan-da (Mei Ri-xin and Deng Yan-chao eds.), *Deng yanda wenji xinbian* (*A New Edition of the Works of Deng Yan-da*), Guangdong renmin chubanshe, Guangzhou, 2000

Dikötter, Frank, *The Age of Openness: China before Mao*, University of California Press, Berkeley and Los Angeles, 2008

Ding Zhong-jiang, *Beiyang junfa shihua* (*A History of the Beiyang Warlords*), Zhongguo youyi chuban gongsi, Beijing, 1992

Duan Qi-rui (Liu Chun-zi and Yin Xiang-fei eds.), *Minguo zongtong zixu: Duan Qi-rui* (*Presidents of the Republic of China on Themselves: Duan Qi-rui*), Jiangsu fenghuang wenyi chubanshe, Nanjing, 2014

Duli Pinglun (*Independent Commentary*), Beijing

DVP (*Foreign Policy Documents*), Russian Ministry of Foreign Affairs, Moscow

Eden, Anthony, *The Eden Memoirs: The Reckoning*, Cassell, London, 1965

Epstein, Israel, *Woman in World History: Life and Times of Soong Ching Ling*, New World Press, Beijing, 1993

Far Eastern Affairs (Journal of the Institute for Far Eastern Studies), Russian Academy of Sciences, Moscow

Fenby, Jonathan, *Generalissimo: Chiang Kai-shek and the China He Lost*, The Free Press, London, 2003

Feng Yu-xiang, *Wode shenghuo* (*My Life*), Zhongguo qingnian chubanshe, Beijing, 2015

Feng Zi-you, *Feng ziyou huiyilu* (*Memoirs of Feng Zi-you*), Dongfang chubanshe, Beijing, 2011

Fifth Avenue United Methodist Church Archives: Charles Jones Soong, Wilmington, NC

FRUS (*Foreign Relations of the United States*), 1944, vol. VI, *China*, Washington DC, 1967

Gascoyne-Cecil, Lord William, *Changing China*, James Nisbet & Co. Ltd, London, 1910

George W. and Clara Sargent Shepherd papers, Bentley Historical Library, University of Michigan, http://quod.lib.umich.edu/b/bhlead/umich-bhl-2014151?view=text

Gu Li-juan and Yuan Xiang-fu, *Zhonghua minguo guohuishi* (*A History of the Parliament of Republic of China*), Zhonghua shuju, Beijing, 2012

Gunther, John, *Inside Asia*, Hamish Hamilton, London, 1939

Guo Song-tao, *Lundun yu bali riji* (*Diaries of London and Paris*), Yuelu shushe, Changsha, 1984

Haag, E. A., *Charlie Soong: North Carolina's Link to the Fall of the Last Emperor of China*, Jaan Publishing, Greensboro, NC, 2015

Hager, Charles R., 'Doctor Sun Yat-sen: Some Personal Reminiscences', in Sharman, Lyon, *Sun Yat-sen: His Life and Its Meaning*, Stanford University Press, Stanford, CA, 1934

Hahn, Emily, *Chiang Kai-shek*, Doubleday & Company, Inc., New York, 1955

Hahn, Emily, *China to Me*, Open Road Integrated Media, Inc., New York, 2014a

Hahn, Emily, *The Soong Sisters*, Open Road Integrated Media, Inc., New York, 2014b

Han Li-guan and Chen Li-ping, *Qinding yaofan hua kezhi chuanqi (The Extraordinary Story of Hua Ke-zhi)*, Jiangsu renmin chubanshe, Nanjing, 1998

Han Su-yin, *Eldest Son: Zhou Enlai and the Making of Modern China, 1898–1976*, Jonathan Cape, London, 1994

Hawaii's Queen, Liliuokalani, *Hawaii's Story*, Mutual Publishing, Honolulu, 1990

He Da-zhang, *Song qingling wangshi (Soong Ching-ling's Past Life)*, Renmin wenxue chubanshe, Beijing, 2011

Heinzig, Dieter, 'The Soviet Union and Communist China, 1945–1950', *Far Eastern Affairs*, 4, 1996

Hemingway, Ernest, *By-Line: Selected Articles and Dispatches of Four Decades*, Grafton Books, London, 1989

Hsu Chieh-lin, *Sun wen: zuihou baituo ribenren de kongzhi (Sun Yat-sen and Japan: the Real History)*, Wenyingtang chubanshe, Taipei, 2011

Hsu Shih-chang (Jin Hong-kui ed.), *Minguo zongtong zixu: xu shichang (Presidents of the Republic of China on Themselves: Hsu Shih Chang)*, Jiangsu fenghuang wenyi chubanshe, Nanjing, 2014

Hu Han-min, *Hu Hanmin Huiyilu (The Memoirs of Hu Han-min)*, Dongfang chubanshe, Beijing, 2013

Hu Han-min, *Hu hanmin zizhuan (The Autobiography of Hu Han-min)*, Zhuanji wenxue chubanshe, Taipei, 1987

Hu Lan-xi, *Hu lanxi huiyilu (The Memoir of Hu Lan-xin)*, Sichuan renmin chubanshe, Chengdu, 1995

Hu Shih, *Hu shi wenji (The Works of Hu Shih)*, Beijing daxue chubanshe, Beijing, 1998

Hu Zi-dan, 'He zhou lianhua mushi de wuci jianmian' ('Five Meetings with Pastor Chow Lien-hwa'), https://2011greenisland.wordpress.com/2012/11/20/

Hua Ping, 'Cong song qingling gei jin zhonghua de xin shuoqi' ('Starting from Soong Ching-ling's letters to Jin Zhong-hua'), https://big5.termitespest.com/article/eoe4effc-4b40-4e22-aaa0-bb7402cded08_2.htm

Hua Shang Daily, Hong Kong

Huanqiu Renwu (Global Personalities), Beijing

Huang Ke-wu et al., *Jiang zhongzheng zongtong shicong renyuan fangwen jilu (Records of Interviews with President Chiang Kai-shek's Staff)*, Zhongyang yanjiuyuan jindaishi yanjiusuo, Taipei, 2013

Huang San-de, *Hongmen genmingshi (A Revolutionary History of Hangmen)*, publisher unknown, 1936

Huang Xing (Mao Zhu-qing ed.), *Huang xing nianpu changbian (A Full Chronology of Huang Xing)*, Zhonghua shuju, Beijing, 1991

Huang Xiu-rong et al. eds., *Gongchan guoji, liangong (bu) yu zhongguo guomin geming yundong: 1920–1925*, Beijing tushuguan chubanshe, Beijing, 1997

Huang Xiu-rong et al. eds., *Gongchan guoji, liangong (bu) yu zhongguo geming wenxian ziliao xuanji: 1917–1925*, Beijing tushuguan chubanshe, Beijing, 1997

Huang Xiu-rong et al. eds., *Gongchan guoji, liangong (bu) yu zhongguo guomin geming yundong: 1926–1927*, vol. 1, Beijing tushuguan chubanshe, Beijing, 1998

Huang Zi-jin and Pan Guang-zhe, *Jiang jieshi yu xiandai zhongguo de xingsuo* (*Chiang Kai-shek and the Formation of Modern China*), Zhongyang yanjiuyuan jindaishi yanjiusuo, Taipei, 2013

I Fu-en, *Wode huiyi* (*My Memories*), Liqing wenjiao jijinhui, Taipei, 2000

International Security, the Belfer Center for Science and International Affairs at Harvard University ed., MIT Press, Cambridge, MA, 1976

Isaacs, Harold, *Re-Encounters in China*, M.E. Sharpe, Armonk, NY and London, 1985

Ishikawa, Yoshihiro, 'Guanyu sun zhongshan zhi suliande yishu' ('On Sun Yat-sen's Deathbed Letter to the Soviet Union'), http://jds.cssn.cn/webpic/web/jdsww/UploadFiles/upload/201011041311408553.pdf

Jiang Ting-fu, *Jiang tingfu huiyilu* (*The Memoirs of Jiang Ting-fu*), Zhuanji wenxue chubanshe, Taipei, 1984

Koo, Juliana Young (Mrs V.K. Wellington), with Genevieve Young, *My Story*, courtesy of the authors

Koo (Madame Wellington Koo), *No Feast Lasts Forever*, Quadrangle/The New York Times Book Co., New York, 1975

Koo, V.K. Wellington, *Gu weijun huiyilu* (*The Memoirs of Wellington Koo*), Zhonghua shuju, Beijing, 2013

Koo, V.K. Wellington, *The Reminiscences of Wellington Koo*, Columbia University Archives, New York

Koo, V.K. Wellington, Wellington Koo Papers, Columbia University Archives, New York

Kriukov, Mikhail, 'Once again about Sun Yatsen's North-west Plan', *Far Eastern Affairs*, 5, 9 January 2000

K'ung Hsiang-hsi, *The Reminiscences of K'ung Hsiang-hsi*, Columbia University Archives, New York

Kuo Tai-chun and Lin Hsiao-ting, *T.V. Soong in Modern Chinese History*, Hoover Institution Press, Stanford, CA, 2006

Lattimore, Owen, *China Memoirs*, University of Tokyo Press, Toronto, 1991

Leonard, Royal, *I Flew for China: Chiang Kai-shek's Personal Pilot*, Doubleday, Doran, Garden City, 1942

Li Gong-zhong, *Zhongshanling: yige xiandai zhengzhi fuhaode dansheng* (*Sun Yat-sen's Mausoleum: the Making of a Political Symbol in Modern China*), Shehui kexue wenxian chubanshe, Beijing, 2009

Li Guo-qi, 'Deguo danganzhong youguan zhongguo canjia diyici shijie dazhande jixiang jizai' ('A Few Documents about China's Participation of the First World War in the German Archives'), in *Zhongguo xiandaishi zhuanti yanjiu baogao* (*Reports on Special Subjects in the Studies of Modern Chinese History*), vol. 4

Li Jin-zhou ed., *Xian shibian qinliji* (*Personal Experiences of the Xian Incident*), Zhuanji wenxue chubanshe, Taipei, 1982

Li, Laura Tyson, *Madame Chiang Kai-shek: China's Eternal First Lady*, Grove Press, New York, 2006

Li Tsung-jen and Tong Te-Kong, *Li zongren huiyilu (The Memoirs of Li Tsung-jen)*, Li Ao chubanshe, Taipei, 1995

Li Yuan-hong (Zhang Bei ed.), *Minguo zongtong zixu: Li yuanhong (Presidents of the Republic of China on Themselves: Li Yuan-hong)*, Jiangsu fenghuang wenyi chubanshe, Nanjing, 2014

Li Yun, 'Sui song qingling zouguo sanshinian' ('Thirty Years with Soong Ching-ling')' in *Yanhuang chunqiu (Annals of the Chinese People)*, 2002, issue 3

Life magazine

Lin Hsiao-ting, *Taihai lengzhan jiemi dangan (The Cold War between Taiwan and China: The Declassified Documents)*, Sanlian shudian, Hong Kong, 2015

Lin Hsiao-ting and Wu Jing-ping eds., *Song ziwen yu waiguo renshi wanglai handiangao (T.V. Soong: Important Wartime Correspondences, 1940–1942)*, Fudan University Press, Shanghai, 2009

Lin Ke-guang et al., *Jindai jinghua shiji (Historical Sites and Stories in Beijing)*, Zhongguo renmin daxue chubanshe, Beijing, 1985

Linebarger, Paul, *Sun Yat-sen and the Chinese Republic*, The Century Co., New York and London, 1925

Liu Ban-nong et al., *Sai jinhua benshi (The Extraordinary Story of Sai Jinhua)*, Yuelu shushe, Changsha, 1985

Liu Jia-quan, *Song qingling liuwang haiwai suiyue (Soong Ching-ling's Exile Years)*, Zhongyang wenxian chubanshe, Beijing, 1994

Lo Hui-Min, *The Correspondence of G. E. Morrison 1895–1912*, Cambridge University Press, Cambridge, 1976

Lo Hui-Min, *The Correspondence of G. E. Morrison 1912–1920*, Cambridge University Press, Cambridge, 1978

Lou Wen-yuan, *Wenyuan wenji (Collected Writings of Lou Wen-yuan)*, Hanya zixun, Taipei, 2008

Lu Fang-shang ed., *Jiang jieshide qinqing, aiqing yu youqing (The Family Relationship, Love and Friendship of Chiang Kai-shek)*, Shibao wenhua chubanshe, Taipei, 2011

Luo Jia-lun, *Zhongshan xiansheng lundun beinan shiliao kaoding (A Study of Sun Yat-sen's Misfortune in London)*, Shangwu yinshuguan, Shanghai, 1930

Luo Jiu-fang and Luo Jiu-rong eds., *Luo jialun xiansheng wencun buyi (Supplementary Writings of Luo Jia-lun*, Zhongyang yanjiuyuan jindaishi yanjiusuo, Taipei, 2009

Manson-Bahr, Philip, *Patrick Manson*, Thomas Nelson & Sons Ltd, London, 1962

Manson-Bahr, Philip H. and Alcock, A., *The Life and Works of Sir Patrick Manson*, Cassell & Company, London, 1927

McCormack, Gavan, *Chang Tso-lin in North-east China 1911–1928*, Stanford University Press, Stanford, CA, 1977

Mei Ri-xin and Deng Yan-chao eds., *Huiyi deng yanda (Remembering Deng Yan-da)*, Guangdong renmin chubanshe, Guangzhou, 1999

Melby, John F., *The Mandate of Heaven*, Chatto & Windus, London, 1969

Microfilm publication M329, Records of the Department of State Relating to Internal Affairs of China, 1910–1929, National Archives, Washington DC

Miller, Merle, *Plain Speaking: an Oral Biography of Harry S. Truman*, Berkley Publishing Corporation, New York, 1974

Mitter, Rana, *A Bitter Revolution: China's Struggle with the Modern World*, Oxford University Press, Oxford, 2005

Miyazaki, Tōten, *Gongqi taotian lun sun zhongshan yu huang xing (Tōten Miyazaki on Sun Yat-sen and Huang Xing)*, Chen Peng Jen, tr., Zhengzhong shuju, Taipei, 1977

Miyazaki, Tōten, *Sanshisan nian zhimeng (My Thirty-Three Year's Dream)*, Chen Peng Jen tr., Shuiniu chubanshe, Taipei, 1989

Moran, Lord, *Winston Churchill: The Struggle for Survival 1940–1965*, Sphere Books Ltd, London, 1968

Munholland, J. Kim, 'The French Connection that Failed: France and Sun Yat-sen, 1900–1908', *Journal of Asian Studies*, vol. 32, issue 1, November 1972

Nanjing Archives and Sun Yat-sen Mausoleum Administration eds., *Zhongshanling dangan shiliao xuanbian (Selected Archive Documents of the Sun Yat-sen Mausoleum)*, Jiangsu guji chubanshe, Nanjing, 1986

New York Times

Newspapers.com

North China Herald, Shanghai

Oursler, Fulton, *Behold This Dreamer!*, Little, Brown & Company, Boston, MA, 1964

Pakula, Hannah, *The Last Empress*, Simon & Schuster Paperbacks, New York, 2009

Papers of Emma DeLong Mills, MSS.2, Wellesley College Archives, Wellesley, MA

Papers of 3rd Marquess of Salisbury, Hatfield House Archives/3M/B24

Paul T. K., Lin Papers, Hong Kong University of Science and Technology Archives, Hong Kong

People's Daily, Beijing

People's University ed., 'Gongchan zhuyi xiaozu he dangde yida ziliao huibian' ('A Collection of Documents and Interviews on the Early Communist Groups and the Party's First Congress'), unpublished, Beijing, 1979

Public Security Ministry Archives ed., *Zai jiang jieshi shenbian banian (Eight Years by the Side of Chiang Kai-shek)*, Qunzhong chubanshe, Beijing, 1997

Qi Gao-ru, *Jiang jinguode yisheng (The Life of Chiang Ching-kuo)*, Zhuanji wenxue chubanshe, Taipei, 1991

Qian Gang and Geng Qing-guo eds., *Ershi shiji zhongguo zhongzai bailu (Mammoth Disasters of Twentieth-Century China)*, Shanghai renmin chubanshe, Shanghai, 1999

Qian Yong-he, *Qian yonghe huiyilu (The Memoir of Qian Yong-he)*, Dongfang chubanshe, Beijing, 2011

Qiu Jie, 'Guangzhou shangtuan yu shangtuan shibian', in *Lishi yanjiu (History Studies)*, 2, 2002, Beijing

Qiu Zheng-quan and Du Chun-he eds., *Xinhai gemming shiliao xuanji (Selected Historical Documents of the 1911 Revolution)*, Hunan renmin chubanshe, Changsha, 1981

Rosholt, Malcolm, 'The Shoe Box Letters from China, 1913–1967', *Wisconsin Magazine of History*, vol. 73, no. 2, 1989–90

Schell, Orville and Delury, John, *Wealth and Power: China's Long March to the Twenty-First Century*, Random House Trade Paperbacks, New York, 2014

Schiffrin, Harold Z., *Sun Yat-sen and the Origins of the Chinese Revolution*, University of California Press, Berkeley, Los Angeles and London, 1970

Seagrave, Sterling, *The Soong Dynasty*, Corgi Books, London, 1996

Selle, Earl Albert, *Donald of China*, Harper, New York and London, 1948

Shang Ming-xuan and Tang Bao-lin, *Song qingling zhuan* (*A Biography of Soong Ching-ling*), Xiyuan chubanshe, Beijing, 2013

Shang Ming-xuan et al. eds., *Sun Zhongshan shengping shiye zhuiyilu* (*Memories of Sun Yat-sen's Life and Career*), Renmin chubanshe, Beijing, 1986

Shanghai Managing Committee of the Historical Objects of Sun Yat-sen and Soong Ching-ling ed., *Sun zhongshan song chingling wenxian yu yanjiu* (*Sun Yat-sen and Soong Ching-ling: Archives and Research*), Shanghai shudian chubanshe, Shanghai, 2009

Shanghai Managing Committee of the Historical Objects of Sun Yat-sen and Soong Ching-ling, and Shanghai Association for Soong Ching-ling Studies eds., *Song Yaoru shengping dangan wenxian huibian* (*A Collection of Archives Documents on the Life of Soong Charlie*), Dongfang chuban zhongxin, Shanghai, 2013a

Shanghai Managing Committee of the Historical Objects of Sun Yat-sen and Soong Ching-ling, and Shanghai Association for Soong Ching-ling Studies eds., *Huiyi song qingling* (*Memories of Soong Ching-ling*), Dongfang chuban zhongxin, Shanghai, 2013b

Sharman, Lyon, *Sun Yat-sen: His Life and Its Meaning*, Stanford University Press, Stanford, CA, 1934

Shaw Yu-ming, *Cisheng buyu: wode taiwan, meiguo, dalu suiyue* (*My Years in Taiwan, America and the Mainland*), Lianjing chuba, Taipei, 2013

Sheean, Vincent, *Personal History*, Citadel Press, NJ, 1986

Shen, Inyeening, *Jinling yiwang* (*My Years in Nanjing*), Shenyupei pub., Taipei, 2016

Shen Yun-long et al., *Fu bingchang xiansheng fangwen jilu* (*Records of Interviews with Fu Bing-chang*), Zhongyang yanjiuyuan jindaishi yanjiusuo, Taipei, 1993

Shen Zui, *Wo zhe sanshinian* (*These Thirty Years of My Life*), Beijing shiyue wenyi chubanshe, Beijing, 1991

Sheng Yong-hua et al. eds., *Sun zhongshan yu aomen* (*Sun Yat-sen and Macau*), Wenwu chubanshe, Beijing, 1991

Shiji (*The Century*), Beijing

Shong Wen, *Xiong wan xiangsheng fangwen jilu* (*The Reminiscences of Dr Shong Wen*), with Chen San-jing and Li Yu-qing, zhongyang yanjiuyuan jindaishi yanjiusuo, Taipei, 1998

Shou Chong-yi ed., *Kong xiangxi qiren qishi* (*Reminiscences about H. H. Kung*), Zhongguo wenshi chubanshe, Beijing, 1987

Smith, Sebie Biggs, *The Reminiscences of Sebie Biggs Smith*, Columbia University Archives, New York

Snow, Edgar, *Journey to the Beginning*, Vintage, New York, 1972

Song Jiao-ren (Chen Xu-lu ed.), *Song Jiaoren ji* (*Collected Writings of Song Jiao-ren*), Zhonghua shuju, Beijing, 2011

Song Jiao-ren (Liu Yang-yang ed.), *Song jiaoren riji* (*The Diary of Song Jiao-ren*), Zhonghua shuju, Beijing, 2014

Song Yong-yi, 'Did Soong Ching-ling Oppose Mao's Anti-rightist Campaign?', https://www.aboluowang.com/2017/0904/988392.html

Soong Ching-ling, *Song qingling xuanji* (*Selected Works of Soong Ching-ling*), Renmin chubanshe, Beijing, 1992

Soong Ching-ling, *The Struggle for New China*, Foreign Language Press, Beijing, 1952

Soong Ching-ling (China Welfare ed.), *Song qingling zhi chen hansheng shuxin* (*Letters from Soong Ching-ling to Chen Han-sheng*), Dongfang chuban zhongxin, Shanghai, 2013

Soong Ching-ling (Shang Ming-xuan et al. eds.), *Song qingling nianpu changbian* (*A Full Chronology of Soong Ching Ling*), Shehui kexue chubanshe, Beijing, 2003, 2009

Soong Ching-ling (Shanghai Soong Ching-ling Memorial Residence ed.), *Song qingling laiwang shuxin xuanji* (*A Selection of Correspondences of Soong Ching-ling*), Shanghai renmin chubanshe, Shanghai, 1995

Soong Ching-ling (Soong Ching-ling Foundation and China Welfare eds.), *Song qingling shuxinji* (*Collected Correspondences of Soong Ching-ling*), Renmin chubanshe, Beijing, 1999

Soong Ching-ling (Soong Ching-ling Foundation et al. eds.), *Song qingling shuxinji* (*xubian*) (*A Sequel to the Collected Correspondences of Soong Ching-ling*), Renmin chubanshe, Beijing, 2004

Soong Ching-ling Memorial Committee ed., *Song qingling jinianji* (*Commemorating Soong Ching-ling*), Renmin chubanshe, Beijing, 1982

Soong May-ling (Madame Chiang Kai-shek), 'What Religion Means to Me', *The Forum*, March 1934

Soong May-ling (Madame Chiang Kai-shek), 'Fighting Communists in China', *The Forum*, February 1935a

Soong May-ling (Madame Chiang Kai-shek), 'New Life in China', *The Forum*, June 1935b

Soong May-ling (Madame Chiang Kai-shek), *China in Peace and War*, Hurst & Blackett, London, 1940

Soong May-ling (Madame Chiang Kai-shek), *Conversations with Borodin*, Free Chinese Centre, place of publication unknown, 1977

Soong May-ling (Madame Chiang Kai-shek), *The Sure Victory*, Fleming H. Revell Company, Westwood, NJ, 1955

Soong May-ling and Chiang Kai-shek, *A Fortnight in Sian: A Coup d'état*, China Pub. Co., Shanghai, 1937

Spooner, Paul B., 'Song Ailing and China's Revolutionary Elite', Academia.edu

Sui Yong-qing and Zhang Lu-ya, 'Song qingling de xingfu he yihan' ('Soong Ching-ling's Happiness and Regrets'), in *Wenshi cankao* (*History Reference*), 4, 2011

Suleski, Ronald, *Civil Government in Warlord China: Tradition, Modernization and Manchuria*, Peter Lang Publishing, New York, 2002

Sun Hui-fen, *Wode zufu sun zhongshan (My Grandfather Sun Yat-sen)*, Nanjing daxue chubanshe, Nanjing, 2011

Sun Yat-sen, *Collected Works of Sun Yat-sen*, Full Text Retrieval System, National Dr Sun Yat-sen Memorial Hall & Sun Yat-sen Studies Database eds., http://sunology. culture.tw/cgi-bin/gs32/sigsweb.cgi/ccd=oYAcvF/search

Sun Yat-sen, *Kidnapped in London*, The China Society, London, 1969

Sun Yat-sen (Chen Xu-lu and Hao Sheng-chao eds.), *Sun zhongshan jiwaiji (A Supplement to the Collected Works of Sun Yat-sen)*, Shanghai renmin chubanshe, Shanghai, 1990

Sun Yat-sen (Chen Xi-qi et al. eds.), *Sun zhongshan nianpu changbian (A Full Chronology of Sun Yat-sen)*, Zhonghua shuju, Beijing, 2003

Sun, Victor, *Sun Mei, My Great-Grandfather*, Guangdong renmin chubanshe, Guangzhou, 2011

Sun zhongshan soong chingling yanjiu dongtai (News in the Studies of Sun Yat-sen and Soong Ching-ling), periodical, Shanghai

Sydney Morning Herald

Tang, Earnest, *Yongbu piaoshide jiyi (Everlasting Memories: The Friendship Between My Family and Soong Ching-ling)*, Dongfang chubanshe, Shanghai, 2013

Tang Qi-hua, *Bali hehui yu zhongguo waijiao (Paris Peace Conference and China Diplomacy)*, Shehui kexue wenxian chubanshe, Beijing, 2014

Tang Qi-hua, *Beiyang xiuyue shi (Treaty Revision Campaign of the Beijing Government, 1912–1928)*, Shehui kexue wenxian chubanshe, Beijing, 2010

Tang Jia-xuan ed., *Zhongguo waijiao cidian (Dictionary of Chinese Diplomacy)*, Shijie zhishi chubanshe, Beijing, 2000

Tang Rui-xiang, *Sun zongshan yu haijun hufa yanjiu (Research on Sun Yat-sen and the Navy in Defending the Constitution 1917–1923)*, Xueyuan chubanshe, Beijing, 2006

Tang Xiong, *Song qingling he tade baojian yisheng (Soong Ching-ling and Her Physicians)*, Hualing chubanshe, Beijing, 2014

Tang Xiong, *Song qingling yu tade weishizhang (Soong Ching-ling and Her Chief Bodyguard)*, Qunzhong chubanshe, Beijing, 2006

Taylor, Jay, *The Generalissimo: Chiang Kai-shek and the Struggle for Modern China*, Harvard University Press, Cambridge, MA, 2011

Taylor, Jay, *The Generalissimo's Son: Chiang Ching-kuo and the Revolutions in China and Taiwan*, Harvard University Press, Cambridge, MA, 2000

Time magazine

Topping, Seymour, *Journey Between Two Chinas*, Harper & Row, New York, Evanston, San Francisco, London, 1972

Tse, Tsan Tai, *The Chinese Republic: Secret History of the Revolution*, South China Morning Post, Hong Kong, 1924

Tuchman, Barbara W., *Stilwell and the American Experience in China*, The Macmillan Company, New York, 1971

Tung, William L., *Gu weijun yu zhongguo zhanshi waijiao (Wellington Koo and China's Diplomacy during the War)*, Zhuanji wenxue chubanshe, Taipei, 1978

T.V. Soong Papers, Hoover Institution Archives, Stanford University

Waldron, Arthur, *From War to Nationalism: China's Turning Point, 1924–1925*, Cambridge University Press, Cambridge, New York and Melbourne, 1995

Wall Street Journal

Wang Da-lu and Liu Qing-yun, *Huang qixiang zhuan* (*A Biography of Huang Qi-xiang*), Zhongguo wenshi chubanshe, Beijing, 1994

Wang Jian and Chen Xian-chun, 'An Analysis of the Changes of Sino-German Relationship during WWI', in *Silin* (*History*), 1993

Wang Jing-wei (Cai De-jin and Wang Sheng eds.), *Wang jingwei shengping jishi* (*A Record of the Life of Wang Jing-wei*), Zhongguo wenshi chubanshe, Beijing, 1993

Wen Fei ed., *Wo suo zhidaode wu peifu* (*The Wu Pei-fu I Know*), Zhongguo wenshi chubanshe, Beijing, 2004

Wen Fei ed., *Wo suo zhidaode zhang zuolin* (*The Zhang Zuo-lin I Know*), Zhongguo wenshi chubanshe, Beijing, 2004

Wen Xiao-hong, '1924nian guangdong "shangtuan shibian" zaitan' ('A Further Study of the Canton Merchants' Corps Incident in 1924'), in *Zhejiang Social Science*, 3, 2001

Weng Yuan (with Wang Feng), *Wozai jiang jieshi fuzi shenbian sishisan nian* (*I was with Chiang Kai-shek and His Son for Forty-Three Years*), Huawen chubanshe, Beijing, 2003

Wesleyan College Archives and Special Collections: Soong Sisters, Macon, GA

West Australian

Wilbur, C. Martin, *Sun Yat-sen: Frustrated Patriot*, Columbia University Press, New York, 1976

Wong, J. Y., *Sanshisui qian de sun zhongshan* (*Sun Yat-sen Before Thirty*), Zhonghua shuju, Hong Kong, 2012

Wong, J. Y., *Sun yixian lundun mengnan zhenxiang* (*The Real Story of Sun Yat-sen's Misfortune in London*), Lianjing chuban shiye gongsi, Taipei, 1998

Wong, J. Y., *Sun yixian zai lundun: 1896–1897* (*Sun Yat-sen in London: 1896–1897*), Lianjing chuban shiye gongsi, Taipei, 2006

Wong, J. Y., *Zhongshan xiansheng yu yingguo* (*Sun Yat-sen and Great Britain*), Xuesheng shuju, Taipei, 2005

World Outlook Journal

Wu Chang-yi ed., *Bashisantian huangdi meng* (*An Emperor Dream that Lasted Eighty-three Days*), Wenshi ziliao chubanshe, Beijing, 1985

Wu Jing-ping and Kuo Tai-chun, *Song ziwen yu tade shidai* (*T.V. Soong: His Life and Times*), Fudan University Press, Shanghai, 2008a

Wu Jing-ping and Kuo Tai-chun, *Song ziwen zhumei shiqi dianbao xuan* (*Selected Telegrams between Chiang Kai-shek and T.V. Soong, 1940–1943*), Fudan University Press, Shanghai, 2008b

Wu Xiang-xiang, *Chen guofu de yisheng* (*A Life of Chen Guo-fu*), Zhuanji wenxue chubanshe, Taipei, 1980

Wu Xiang-xiang, *Song jiaoren zhuan* (*A Biography of Song Jiao-ren*), Zhongguo dabaike quanshu chubanshe, Beijing, 2009

Wu Xiang-xiang, *Sun yixian zhuan* (*A Biography of Sun Yat-sen*), Zhuanji wenxue chubanshe, Taipei, 1969

Wu Kuo-Cheng, *Cong shanghai shizhang dao 'taiwan shengzhuxi': wu guozhen koushu huiyi* (*The Reminiscences of Wu Kuo-cheng*), Shanghai renmin chubanshe, Shanghai, 2015

Xiao Jian-dong, '"Yizhan" shiqi zhongguo duide xuanzhande lishi zhenxiang' ('The Historical Truth about China's Declaration of War against Germany during WWI'), *Journal of Wuhan University of Technology: Social Science Edition*, Vol. 21, 1, 2008

Xu Feng-hua, 'The Party Member outside the Party – A New Discussion about the Relationship between Soong Ching-ling and Both the Nationalists and the Communists', History at China Welfare, http://www.cwi.org.cn/zh/zgflhhsg/content.aspx?id=8487

Xu Xue-er et al. eds., *Song jiaoren xuean* (*The Murder of Song Jiao-ren*), Yuelu shushe, Changsha, 1986

Yan Hui-qing, *Yan huiqing zizhuan* (*The Autobiography of Yan Hui-ching*), Zhuanji wenxue chubanshe, Taipei, 1989

Yang Kui-song, 'Song qingling heshi jiaru gongchandang' ('When Did Soong Ching-ling Join the Communist Party'), *Sun zhongshan soong chingling yanjiu dongtai* (*News in the Studies of Sun Yat-sen and Soong Ching-ling*), 4, 2003

Yang Kui-song, *Yang kuisong zhuzuoji: geming* (*Collected Works of Yang Kui-song: Revolution*), Guangxi shifan daxue chubanshe, Guilin, 2012

Yang Tian-shi, *Jiangshi midang yu jiang jieshi zhenxiang* (*The Secret Archives of Chiang Kai-shek and the Truth about Him*), Shehui kexue wenxian chubanshe, Beijing, 2002

Yang Tian-shi, *Jindai zhongguo shishi gouchen: haiwai fangshilu* (*Discoveries Overseas about Modern Chinese Historical Events*), Shehui kexue wenxian chubanshe, Beijing, 1998

Yang Tian-shi, *Wanqing shishi* (*Miscellaneous Historical Events of Late Qing*), Zhongguo renmin daxue chubanshe, Beijing, 2007

Yang Tian-shi, *Zhaoxun zhenzhengde jiang jieshi* (*In Search of the Real Chiang Kai-shek*), vol. 1, Shanxi renmin chubanshe, Taiyuan; vol. 2, Huawen chubanshe, Beijing, 2008

Yang Tian-shi, *Zhaoxun zhenzhengde jiang jieshi* (*In Search of the Real Chiang Kai-shek*), II, Huawen chubanshe, Beijing, 2010

Yang Tian-shi, *Zhaoxun zhenzhengde jiang jieshi: huanyuan 13ge lishi zhenxiang* (*In Search of the Real Chiang Kai-shek: The Truth of 13 Historical Events*), Jiuzhou chubanshe, Beijing, 2014

Yanhuang chunqiu (*Annals of the Chinese People*), Beijing

Ye Bang-zong, *Jiang jieshi shiweizhang huiyilu* (*Memoirs of Chiang Kai-shek's Chief Bodyguard*), Tuanjie chubanshe, Beijing, 2012

Yi Zhu-xian, *Hu shi zhuan* (*A Biography of Hu Shih*), Hubei renmin chubanshe, Wuhan, 1987

Yu Xin-chun and Wang Zhen-suo eds., *Sun zhongshan zairi huodong milu: riben waiwusheng dangan* (*The Secret Records of Sun Yat-sen in Japan: Archives from the Japanese Foreign Ministry*), Nankai daxue chubanshe, Tianjin, 1990

Yuan Wei-shi, *Zuotiande zhongguo*, Zhejiang daxue chubanshe, Hangzhou, 2012

Zhang Bo-feng and Li Zong-yi eds., *Beiyang junfa* (*The Northern Warlords*), Wuhan chubanshe, Wuhan, 1991

Zhang Hai-lin, *Duanfang yu qingmo xinzheng* (*Duanfang and the New System in the Late Qing*), Nanjing daxue chubanshe, Nanjing, 2007

Zhang Kai-yuan et al. eds., *Xinhai gemingshi congkan* (*Periodical of the History of the 1911 Revolution*), Zhonghua shuju, Beijing

Zhang Peng-yuan, 'Cong minchu guohui xuanju kan zhengzhi canyu' ('Political Participation Seen through Parliamentary Elections in the First Years of the Republic of China'), *Bulletin of Historical Research*, Taiwan Normal University, Taipei, 1979

Zhang Peng-yuan, *Cong minquan dao weiquan* (*From People's Power to Autocrat's Power*), Zhongyang yanjiuyuan jindaishi yanjiusuo, Taipei, 2016

Zhang Peng-yuan, *Zhongguo minzhu zhengzhi de kunjing: 1909–1949 wanqing yilai lijie yihui xuanju shulun* (*Democratic Politics in China: A Study of Parliamentary Elections since the Late Qing, 1909–1949*), Shanghai Sanlian shudian, Shanghai, 2013

Zhang Tai-yan, *Zhang taiyan xiansheng ziding nianpu* (*Mr Zhang Tai-yan's Self-written Chronology*), Shanghai shudian, Shanghai, 1986

Zhang Xue-liang (Zhang You-kun and Qian Jin eds.), *Zhang xueliang nianpu* (*A Chronological Record of Zhang Xue-liang*), Shehui kexue wenxian chubanshe, Beijing, 1996

Zhang Yao-jie, *Shui moushale song jiaoren* (*Who Murdered Song Jiao-ren*), Tuanjie chubanshe, Beijing, 2012

Zhang Zhu-hong, 'Meiguo guanyu Sun zhongshan he xinhai geming de yanjiu' ('Studies on Sun Yat-sen and the 1911 Revolution in the United States'), http://jds.cssn.cn/ztyj/wqzzs/201605/t20160506_3323423.shtml

Zheng Hui-xin, *Dudang yueshi: minguo zhengshi yu jiazu liyi* (*From the Archives and Studies: The Politics of the Republic of China and Family Interests*), Zhonghua shuju, Beijing, 2014

Zheng Peng-nian, *Song qingling he tade zhushou jin zhonghua* (*Soong Ching-ling and her Assistant Jin Zhong-hua*), Xinhua chubanshe, Beijing, 2001

Zhong Bo-yi and Deng Jia-yan, *Zhong boyi deng jiayan koushu zizhuan* (*The Reminiscences of Zhong Bo-yi and Deng Jia-yan*), Zhongguo dabaike quanshu chubanshe, Beijing, 2009

Zhou En-lai (CCP Central Documents Studies and Central Archives eds.), *Jianguo yilai zhou enlai wengao,* (*Writings of Zhou En-lai since the Founding of Communist China*), Zhongyang wenxian chubanshe, Beijing, 2008

Zhou Hong-tao (with Wang Shi-chun), *Jianggong yu wo: jianzheng zhonghua minguo guanjian bianju* (*Mr Chiang Kai-shek and Me: Witnessing Key Moments of Change in the Republic of China*), Tianxia yuanjian, Taipei, 2003

Zhou Zhi-ping, 'Zhangchi zai ziyou yu weiquan zhijian: hu shi, lin yutang yu jiang jieshi (Between Liberty and Authoritarian Rule: Hu Shih, Lin Yu-tang and Chiang Kai-shek)', http://www.cuhk.edu.hk/ics/21c/media/articles/c146-201406005.pdf

Zhu Zong-zhen and Yang Guang-hui eds., *Minchu zhengzheng yu erci geming* (*Political Struggles at the Beginning of the Republic and the Second Revolution*), Shanghai renmin chubanshe, Shanghai, 1983

Zou Lu, *Zou lu huiyilu* (*Memoirs of Zou Lu*), Dongfang chubanshe, Beijing, 2010

Acknowledgements

I am fortunate to have had the support of many people when researching this biography. Helpful librarians and archivists in the following archives and museums made my work much easier as I went about obtaining the documents (and photographs) that form the basis of the book. In the USA: Columbia University Archives; Duke University Libraries; Fifth Avenue United Methodist Church Archives (Wilmington); Hoover Institution Archives; Library of Congress; National Archives, US Senate Historical Office; Wellesley College Archives; and Wesleyan College Archives. In the UK: Hatfield House Archives (I am grateful to the Marquess and Marchioness of Salisbury for special permission to use their private archives); Historical Photographs of China at University of Bristol; National Archives; and Royal Archives. In Taiwan: Academia Historica; National Chiang Kai-shek Memorial Hall; National Dr Sun Yat-sen Memorial Hall; National Human Rights Museum; and Nationalist Party History Archive. In Hong Kong: Hong Kong University of Science and Technology Archives. I thank all who assisted me and am only sorry not to be able to name them all here.

One person I would like to mention is Sue Hammonds of the Fifth Avenue United Methodist Church Archives, who collected documents for me even when she was extremely ill. Most sadly she died when she was still putting the file together. (Her colleague Barbara Gallagher sent me the package Sue had assembled.) I shall always remember her with deep gratitude.

Descendants of the Soong and Chiang families, members of their households and family friends kindly shared their recollections and insights. I wish particularly to thank Mme Laurette Soong Feng, Mr Michael Feng, Mr Chiang Wan-an, Mr Victor Sun, Dr Kung-ming Jan, Mme Juliana Young Koo, Mme Gene Young and those key witnesses who prefer to remain anonymous. I owe a special thank you to Gene Young, who introduced me to the Soong family in New York.

The Lung Yingtai Cultural Foundation invited me to Taiwan and made arrangements for my research there; I am deeply indebted to it. The Foundation's conscientious and efficient staff were a joy to work with. Lung Ying-tai herself, an influential writer who contributed to the democratisation of Taiwan, enabled me to gain a better understanding of that historical moment, and democratic Taiwan in general.

I benefited greatly from interviews with the following eye witnesses and scholars, to all of whom I am thankful: Dr Hugh Cantlie, Mr Chin Him-san, Mr Lou Wen-yuan, Dr P.G. Manson-Bahr, Mr Howard Shiang, Mr Su You, Mme Tu Kui-mei, Professor Chang Cheng, Professor Chang Peng-yuan, Professor Chao Chien-min, Professor Chen Li-wen, Professor Chen Peng-jen, Mr Hsieh Ying-chung, Professor Huang Ko-wu, Professor Kuo Tai-chun, Professor Li Chun-shan, Dr Lin Hsiao-ting, Dr Lin Kuo-chang, Professor Lin Tung-fa, Professor Liu Wei-kai, Professor Lu Fang-shang, Professor Pang Chien-kuo, Professor Shaw Yu-ming, Professor Tang Chi-hua, Mr Jay Taylor, Mr Wang Shinn-huey, Professor Wang Wen-lung and Professor Wu Mi-cha.

In the past decades when I was writing my previous biographies, especially *Mao: the Unknown Story* (with Jon Halliday), I conducted hundreds of interviews, and many of those remain highly relevant to this book. Indeed some historical figures, now deceased, were close to the Soong sisters. Going over the records of our interviews again, I felt blessed that they had allowed me to preserve their unique and invaluable experiences. They include: Zhang Xue-liang (the Young Marshal), Chen Li-fu, General Chiang Wei-go, General I Fu-en, General Hau Pei-tsun, Emily Hahn, Israel Epstein, Rewi

Alley, George Hatem, Percy Chen, Jin Shan-wang, and Li Yun. My two good, late, friends, Maggie Keswick (who knew Ching-ling) and Emma Tennant, were the first to urge me to write about the Soong sisters.

The following people kindly effected introductions, answered queries, sent material, made suggestions and generally facilitated my research: Jeffrey Bergner, Marie Brenner, Marco Caboara, Eddy Chancellor, John Chow, Anhua Gao, Jane Hitchcock, Jong Fang-ling, Kan Shio-yun, Yung Li, Tim Owens, Shen Lyu-shun, Jane Shen-Miller, William Taubman, Carola Vecchio, Stanley Weiss, Grace Wu, Wu Shu-feng, Xue Yi-wei, Shirley Young, Jeanette Zee and Pu Zhang. My apologies for any omissions, which will be corrected in future editions.

My agents, Gillon Aitken and Clare Alexander, took great care of the book and gave me excellent advice. My publishers and editors at Cape and Knopf – Bea Hemming, Sonny Mehta, Dan Frank and their teams, including my copy-editor David Milner – did a superb job editing and publishing the book. I am indebted to them all.

As with my previous books, Jon Halliday's constantly sought counsel has been indispensable. It is impossible to exaggerate the importance of having him in my life.

Index

A Note About the Author

Jung Chang is the internationally best-selling author of *Wild Swans: Three Daughters of China; Mao: The Unknown Story* (with Jon Halliday); and *Empress Dowager Cixi: The Concubine Who Launched Modern China.* Her books have been translated into more than forty languages and have sold more than 15 million copies outside Mainland China, where they are banned. She was born in China in 1952 and moved to Britain in 1978. She lives in London.